POWERSHARING

SUNY Series on the Presidency:
Contemporary Issues
John Kenneth White, Editor

POWERSHARING

WHITE HOUSE-CABINET RELATIONS IN THE MODERN PRESIDENCY

Shirley Anne Warshaw

FOREWORD BY STEPHEN HESS

State University of New York Press

Published by
State University of New York Press, Albany

© 1996 State University of New York

For information, address State University of New York
Press, State University Plaza, Albany, N.Y., 12246

Production by E. Moore
Marketing by Dana E. Yanulavich

Library of Congress Cataloging-in-Publication Data

Warshaw, Shirley Anne, 1950-
Powersharing : White House-Cabinet relations in the modern
presidency / Shirley Anne Warshaw.
p. cm. -- (SUNY series on the presidency)
Includes bibliographical references (p.) and index.
ISBN 0-7914-2869-9 (hc : alk. paper). -- ISBN 0-7914-2870-2 (pbk.
: alk. paper)
1. Presidents--United States. 2. Presidents--United States-
-Staff. 3. Cabinet officers--United States. 4. Executive
departments--United States. 5. United States--Politics and
government--1945-1989. 6. United States--Politics and
government--1989- I. Title. II. Series
JK611.W37 1996
353.04--dc20
                                                      95-16871
                                                        CIP

10 9 8 7 6 5 4 3 2 1

For Allen,
Chris, Andy, and Bobby

CONTENTS

FIGURES

TABLES

FOREWORD

George Washington's cabinet could have sat around a bridge table. The four persons—representing State, Treasury, War, and the Attorney General—reflected the new nation. Today there are fourteen Cabinet departments and a federal work force of over three million.

For most of the nation's history, the federal government's management process fell to the Cabinet officers. Presidents worked closely with their Cabinets in defining the objectives of the administration and ensuring that those objectives were met. However, this process began to change during the administration of Franklin Roosevelt. When besieged by the problems of rebuilding a broken economy and a looming international war, Roosevelt sought Congressional approval for an enlarged White House staff.

In response to Roosevelt's appeal for staff, Congress passed the Reorganization Act of 1939, the first major change in the White House–Cabinet relationship since the Jacksonian era when the spoils system replaced the merit system in Cabinet selection.

The new law was vague. The responsibilities of the White House staff and even their titles would be left totally to the president. Roosevelt's decision to use the added staff for policy development rather than departmental oversight or any other function, set in motion an in-house advisory system often at odds with the Cabinet. The president now had staff in the White House to analyze issues in administrationwide terms rather than simply narrow departmental terms.

In spite of his desire to enhance his own advisory system, Roosevelt's White House staff remained fairly modest. Truman's remained similarly modest. The first significant increase began under Dwight Eisenhower, as he sought to increase organizational efficiency of the White House. Eisenhower, ever the general, felt that Roosevelt and Truman staffs were far too chaotic. In a move to bring greater order to the expanding White House staff, Eisenhower added a chief of staff and a congressional liaison office.

The White House staff continued to slowly expand during the Kennedy and Johnson years. One of the more significant additions to the staff came

during the Johnson administration when Joseph Califano began to focus solely on domestic legislation and the unfolding Great Society programs. Richard
Nixon, faced with massive changes in federal programs brought on by the
Great Society legislation, created a formal position in the White House known
as the Assistant to the President for Domestic Policy. This began the transformation of the White House staff into a minibureaucracy, capable of providing the president major policy analysis and counsel.

The relationship of the president to his cabinet has changed significantly since the Roosevelt era, when cabinet secretaries provided the essence of
policy advice to the president. By the Nixon era, presidents had an in-house
advisory structure that rivaled the departmental advisory structure. Since
Nixon, every successive president has strengthened the domestic policy staff
and broadened its responsiblities. The Clinton administration has gone so far
as to split the domestic policy office into two sections, one responsible for
domestic policy and the other for economic policy.

The question that *Powersharing: White House–Cabinet Relations in
the Modern Presidency* seeks to answer is whether this change in the president's advisory structure is for the better. Have presidents sacrificed the professional judgment of the departments with their strong institutional memory
for short-sighted political gain conceived by White House staff? Or have presidents created a structure that ensures broad-based policy analysis, meets
administrationwide goals, and ensures political consistency?

Shirley Anne Warshaw examines the role of the White House staff in
policy development from the Nixon through the Clinton years, of each administration's cabinet and White House staff selection process, appointees' past
relationship with the incoming president, and the structure that was instituted
for policy development.

Her conclusion is that the increasing role of the White House staff in
policy development and management is essential to presidential control of the
executive branch. Without clear policy guidance from the White House,
departments easily move in their own directions to satisfy constituent and
Congressional demands. The White House sets the agenda for the administration and ensures that each of the Cabinet-level departments understands
and supports that agenda.

Throughout the book, Professor Warshaw examines various methods
used by recent presidents to utilize their cabinet officers in an advisory capacity. She illustrates how Cabinet Government, used in administration after
administration, has proven to be poorly conceived and always quickly
rescinded. Every president from Nixon through Clinton has chosen to expand
the role of the White House staff after Cabinet Government has failed to produce policies that meet the president's goals and objectives.

Powersharing is a major study of Cabinet–White House relations in the modern presidency. Professor Warshaw argues forcefully that presidents need a strong White House staff to manage the often conflicting goals of the departments and ensure a clear focus to the adminstration's agenda. Without that focus, departments will move in their own directions to satisfy the numerous demands on their own agendas.

STEPHEN HESS
BROOKINGS INSTITUTION

ACKNOWLEDGMENTS

This book was the product of several years research and writing. Grant support was provided by the National Endowment of the Humanities, the Gerald R. Ford Library, and Gettysburg College. I am grateful for each and every one of these generous grants. In addition, I am endebted to many students who worked on the research. These included Nicole Huckerby, John Zimmerman, Jason Smith, Jack Blackford, Merril Springer, Lyanne Lawson, Amy Powell, April Kelly, Michael Strazzella, Kevin MacMillan, and Jen Cable. Their work included not only basic research on the presidencies, but interviewing White House staff and Cabinet members. In addition, I am endebted to Matt Diaz who worked tirelessly on the index, and to Suzanne Welsh who masterfully designed all the graphics and handled numerous other details of this manuscript. Many people have also reviewed the manuscript, including nearly everyone who was quoted in the text. Without their help, I would not have been able to achieve the level of accuracy and detail that is in the text.

ONE

INTRODUCTION

The president's Cabinet has never become quite the advisory system for the president that Alexander Hamilton envisioned. Hamilton foresaw the Cabinet as "deputy presidents," serving as the president's primary advisors and departmental managers. Since the role of the president's Cabinet was never mentioned in the Constitution, George Washington followed Hamilton's advice and relied heavily on his four Cabinet officers for both policy and political advice in the course of his government.

Washington's relationship with his Cabinet was followed for nearly forty years, until Andrew Jackson introduced the spoils system, using Cabinet positions as a reward to his supporters, particularly from the newly admitted states. The presidential-Cabinet relationship changed under Jackson, as Jackson turned to other sources for policy and political advice. Cabinet officers continued to manage their departments and provide broad-based programmatic advice.

The Jacksonian model of White House–Cabinet relations remained operative throughout the nineteenth and early part of the twentieth centuries. This model dramatically changed in the Roosevelt administration, following passage of the Reorganization Act of 1939, which gave the president a White House staff capable of providing a new source of policy and political advice. Although presidents since Roosevelt have maintained personal advisory networks, the White House staff has now become the president's primary advisory source. Cabinet officers, who maintain administrative responsibilities for their departments, respond to White House policy initiatives by providing detailed programmatic analyses and implementation strategies. The departments have moved to a reactive rather than proactive position in developing the administration's major policy proposals. White House staff now develop the administration's policy agenda and guide departmental proposals to meet that agenda.

The White House staff, which has grown in size throughout every administration since Franklin Delano Roosevelt, has suffered its setbacks during its growth process. Richard Nixon, in particular, sought to reduce both the size and the power of the White House staff. During the 1968 election, Nixon popularized the phrase *cabinet government* and promised to restore the Cabinet to its conciliar role as *deputy presidents*. Nixon promised a return to a Cabinet-based rather than a White House–based policy development system.

Once elected, Nixon aggressively moved to reduce the role of the White House staff and to increase the role of the Cabinet. However, within nine months of taking office, Nixon abandoned his efforts at Cabinet Government and moved policy-making power back to the White House staff. Most of Nixon's successors followed similar paths, starting office with a commitment to a strong cabinet and within a year restructuring the policy process to restore power to the White House staff.

What is it about the modern presidency that seems to preclude the Cabinet from dominating the policy process? Are there fundamental political and institutional barriers to a policy-making system centered in the Cabinet? The answer is quite clearly yes, as Richard Fenno noted in his seminal study of the Cabinet in 1959:

> Cabinet members themselves are inextricably involved in the activities of the legislature, the bureaucracy, the political parties and the political interest groups. The Cabinet, and especially its individual members, participates in a great multiplicity of external relationships which are not in the first instance matters of its internal characteristics nor of its presidential tie. [1]

Cabinet members establish strong relationships with players outside the executive branch in order to fulfill their statutory mission, relationships that presidents have not always supported. [-]

The debate on the role of the White House staff in policy formulation and management has moved to the forefront of scholarly literature on presidential management style. As the Cabinet has become increasingly captured by its own clientele,[2] the White House staff has emerged as the central player in the policy process.[3]

The focus of more recent literature on White House–Cabinet relations centers on the degree to which White House staff should become involved in policy matters and how the White House–Cabinet relationship should be structured. That debate has sharpened in recent years. Some have argued that presidents should reduce the size of the White House staff and allow the departments greater independence in policy development.[4] Louis Koenig, for example, argues that "power has gravitated excessively from the departments and the cabinet to the presidential staff."[5]

A larger group, however, supports a strong White House staff in policy development. Harold Barger, for example, urged "an expanded presidential establishment [as] essential to the President's staying on top of the action forcing processes that confront him."[6] Hugh Heclo similarly supports "continual presidential involvement" in guiding departmental policy initiatives.[7] Lester Salaman argues that "presidents incur great costs when they rely totally on the agencies and departments to formulate policies."[8]

While the debate continues on the degree to which the White House should control the policy development process, there is far more consensus on how the White House staff should be structured for policy-making. Research consistently indicates that White House staffs need to have a clear view of presidential goals and objectives, and need to have these goals constantly reinforced personally by the president.[9] Staff also need to have a high level of issue agreement and goal compatibility not only among themselves but with the president.[10]

Literature on the structure of the White House staff has been sparser, with current literature focusing on a strong role for the chief of staff rather than the structure of the internal policy operation.[11] Most current studies on White House staff structures have focused on the Reagan White House and its use of cabinet councils to manage domestic policy.[12] The broader issue concerning structural options for White House–Cabinet interaction in policy development and internal White House policy structures has not been the subject of general concern in the literature.

The research in *Powersharing* is aimed at expanding the literature on the Cabinet's role in policy development and on structural organizations within the White House to manage policy development. All the material included in this research involves domestic policy and the expanding role of the White House staff in managing the administration's domestic policy initiatives. National security policy and foreign policy were excluded from the research for a number of reasons.

The most important reason for this exclusion concerns the narrow framework of foreign policy development, focused within the province of only two departments, State and Defense, both of which have a limited clientele. The president remains the primary client of the departments, although the defense industry certainly influences the decision process. In contrast, the outer Cabinet, composed of the domestic policy agencies, is in the less tenable position of serving several clients in addition to the president, notably

Congressional committees, staff, departmental clientele, and bureaucratic interests. As a result of these centrifugal forces, Cabinet officers often are pulled away from the president's policy objectives. This tug of war for departmental policy control has led recent presidents to exert greater White House control over the entire domestic policy process.

A second basis for focusing this research on domestic policy was the sheer size of dealing with two policy mechanisms in the White House. The domestic policy process itself was a major undertaking. It is also worth noting that numerous documents regarding White House action in national security policy remain classified. Other files on national security have been placed out of the reach of scholars due to law suits. Henry Kissinger, for example, has tied up nearly all the key files on Vietnam, détente with Russia, and the China initiative. Similarly, Caspar Weinberger, Oliver North, and others have tied up many of the Iran-Contra files. More recent files, such as those on the Persian Gulf War, are not open for scholars yet.

The final decision to focus this research on domestic policy centered on the availability of primary sources. Both White House staff and Cabinet officers were accessible for interviews. Since so many departments were involved, as opposed to only two in foreign policy matters, far more material was available.

The White House–Cabinet relationship remains a fragile one. The most appropriate role for either the Cabinet or the White House staff as the President's domestic-policy advisor is defined in each administration and shaped by the president's personal management style. Powersharing between the White House staff and the Cabinet is inevitable in today's complex bureaucratic policy process.

Six presidencies are examined in depth: those of Richard Nixon, Gerald Ford, Jimmy Carter, Ronald Reagan, George Bush, and Bill Clinton. These six presidencies are reviewed to see how they structured White House–Cabinet relations for domestic policy development. How large were the White House staffs in each administration and what was their role in policy coordination and policy development? Did Cabinet officers have to be screened by White House staff before they saw the president on policy issues? How was the White House–Cabinet relationship structured in each administration and why did it flourish or fail? Is there a White House–Cabinet relationship that is workable within the constraints of the existing institutional and political framework from which the president must deal? Have the White House staff permanently surplanted the Cabinet as the president's chief policy advisors?

It is the central thesis of this book that the White House staff have indeed surplanted the Cabinet as the president's chief policy advisors. The primary function of the White House staff in the modern presidency has emerged as one that designs a narrow, achievable agenda within the parameters of campaign objectives. That agenda has incorporated the central themes of the campaign within its current political and fiscal constraints.

The White House staff has also emerged as the focal point of the administration, guiding departmental policy-making within the framework of the presidential agenda. Interdepartmental clashes and competition for limited revenue sources have been minimized as a result of White House oversight of departmental policy-making. Department heads, who are constantly nurtured by White House staff and ensured of their role in the presidential circle, have remained loyal to the administration agenda. Cooption within the Cabinet by bureaucratic and constitutent interests has been mitigated by strong alliances forged between the White House and the Cabinet.

It is, therefore, a difficult task that the White House staff faces. They must frame administration policy goals and simultaneously build bases of support within the Cabinet for those goals. Most administrations have been successful at one or the other of these tasks, but few have been successful at both. The test of future administrations will be to ensure success at both endeavors.

T W O

THE CABINET EMERGES IN A POLICY ROLE

As we examine the American White House–Cabinet relationship, a comparison with the British system is valuable. The American structure of policy-making is deeply rooted in the British system. Our debates on what the most appropriate role for the White House staff should be bears a striking similarity to the debates on the role of the king's advisors in the British system. How much power should those advisors have? What are the parameters of power-sharing?

BRITISH HERITAGE OF THE CABINET

The first evidence of the Cabinet as we know it today was seen in early England when kings surrounded themselves with a small group of aristocratic advisors whose role was to provide advice on matters of state. These advisors had neither formal title nor formal duties until the fourteenth century when they became known as the King's Council.

At some point during the course of the next one hundred years, the term King's Council was replaced by the term Privy Council, considered to be a more appropriate title for the advisory group who were *privy* to the decision-making processes of government. In the sixteenth century, the responsibilities of the Privy Council, as it was now commonly called, were expanded from a purely advisory role to a management role, which included the administration of government offices. These changes were the first step toward an institutionalized advisory and management role for the British Cabinet.

As the role of the Privy Council changed during this period, so also did the role of Parliament. The seeds of parliamentary government were sewn during the seventeenth century when the House of Commons sought a voice in the composition of the Privy Council. They wanted to be part of the selection process for the membership of the Privy Council. In 1641 the House of Commons formally petitioned Charles I "to employ such persons in your great and public affairs, and to take such to be near you in places of trust, as your Parliament may have cause to confide in."[1] This was a major divergence from the traditional system in Great Britain in which the king had sole control over selection of the members of the Privy Council.

The king, not unexpectedly, refused to accede to Parliament's demands and as a result a bloody civil war ensued. Charles I subsequently lost the throne. The end of civil war brought the coronation of Charles II in 1660 and the restoration of the Privy Council. As a condition of armistice, Charles II agreed to the demands of the House of Commons. He enlarged the Privy Council to forty members and included members of Parliament in the council. The enlarged Privy Council, however, proved to be an unworkable size for the king, who complained that "the great number of the council . . . make it unfit for the secrecy and dispatch that are necessary in many great affairs" of state.[2] In order to solve the problems caused by convening a large group, Charles II relied on a small group within the Privy Council to serve as his principal advisors. The smaller group, or Cabinet, consisted of the major officers of the Privy Council (Treasury, State, top military officers) and personal supporters of the king. Charles II eventually purged the Privy Council and relied on a small "Cabinet Council" to rule. During the reign of Charles II the Cabinet Council became the king's principal source of advice and political management.

When the throne passed to the House of Hanover with the crowning of George I in 1714, Parliament moved a step closer to controlling executive policy-making through the Cabinet. Unlike his predecessors, the German-born George I was not interested in ruling and relied on the Cabinet to establish the nation's policies. This period is particularly important to the evolution of the Cabinet because George I's lack of participation in governmental decision-making allowed the Cabinet to gain a preeminent position in political and administrative duties.

Until the House of Hanover took over the British Crown, the Cabinet Council had been a tool of the king rather than of Parliament.[3] The king guided the government and was the central figure in the deliberations on national policy. Yet when George I relinquished the traditional role of the king in 1714 as the nation's policy leader, a void in leadership resulted. The king was no longer primary in national policy decisions, as he had been for centuries. The void was filled in 1721 when Sir Robert Walpole, First Lord of the Treasury, became the principal (prime) minister at the encouragement of George I. Walpole held the

position for twenty-one years (1721–1742), becoming the first (though not officially so named) <u>Prime Minister</u>. Walpole also gained considerable power within the Cabinet through his post as First Lord of the Treasury, a position that
required working with Parliament to gain passage of appropriation bills.

Throughout the eighteenth century monarchs continued to be completely
disinterested in the administrative details of governing. The Cabinet Council
continued as the center of the decision-making process of the executive branch,
with the king appointing a Cabinet and its senior minister. Under George III, the
title Prime Minister became an accepted part of the political vocabulary, as evidenced by the official designation of William Pitt the Younger as Prime Minister
of the Cabinet Council (1783–1801).

During the nineteenth century the Cabinet Council emerged as the center
of executive policy-making with a membership that included members of
Parliament, reminiscent of the Privy Council during the reign of Charles II. The
Cabinet was chosen by the Prime Minister and the king together, rather than by
the king alone from an elite group of his friends. Subsequently, Prime Ministers
began during the latter half of the eighteenth century to build coalitions of key
members of Parliament by inviting them into the Cabinet. This assured that
Cabinet-sponsored legislation (although technically sponsored by the Crown)
received adequate support in Parliament.

This phase in the evolution of the British Cabinet system marked the shift
from a Cabinet with advisory status to one with independent authority. The
Cabinet had emerged as the heart of the decision-making process. The Crown
gradually receded to a ceremonial rather than policy-making role. Political theo-
rist Walter Bagehot concluded in the mid-1800s that the Crown was not an effective partner in the political process.[4] Bagehot refers to the monarchy as the "dig-
nified" part of government, but a part that had no effective role in the political
process. In effect, the expansion of political and administrative power by the
Cabinet was an effort to curb the abusive powers of the Crown. It was not a
planned development, but rather an evolution of political power over four centuries.

The result of this evolutionary process has been to produce a Cabinet in
Great Britain whose members have individual responsibility for departmental
management and collective responsibilities for national policy issues. While the
American Cabinet does not share a collective policy-making role with its British
counterpart, the advisory and administrative responsibilities of the American
Cabinet are deeply rooted in the British system.

AMERICAN HERITAGE OF THE CABINET

The American Cabinet had much less of an evolutionary beginning than
did the British Cabinet, for it was incorporated into our earliest governmental

structures. The first appearance of the Cabinet in the United States came in 1781 following the adoption of the Articles of Confederation and Perpetual Union by the states.

The Cabinet under the Articles of Confederation

In practical terms, the Articles of Confederation provided for only minimal changes in the manner in which Congress had governed the nation since 1775. The Articles of Confederation were designed to provide for a loose confederation of states rather than a powerful central government. The states were adamant about protecting their sovereignty. The final document called for each state to be guaranteed "its sovereignty, freedom and independence, and every power, jurisdiction, and right not expressly delegated to the United States, in Congress assembled."[5]

As a result of this mandate for state sovereignty, the new Congress was faced with the dilemma of maintaining the states' independence while establishing a strong national government. Priority went to state sovereignty, which left Congress without the authority to tax or regulate trade either between the states or with other nations. These powers were reserved for the individual states. But the national government was determined to deal with certain issues on behalf of all the states. At this point the nation's first Cabinet became operational.

Under the Articles of Confederation, the Congress was given responsibility for managing the new national government. Neither an executive nor legislative branch was created, only a unicameral Congress, which was given complete control over the affairs of state, both for international and domestic policy. The Congress had both its traditional legislative authority and all the executive authority. In order to deal with the executive part of its responsibilities, the Congress decided to create an administrative structure of executive departments. The department staff would handle the implementation of the laws for the Congress. By 1780, even prior to the official adoption of the Articles of Confederation (in 1781), members of Congress debated ways to structure the executive departments. The debates included the internal structure of these executive departments and particularly who would be responsible for reporting to Congress. The Journals of Congress on November 24, 1780, quotes a discussion dealing with the specific structure of the departments, and the establishment of "a single officer responsible to Congress."[6] This is the earliest official discussion of the Cabinet officer as we now know it.

These discussions on the Cabinet in 1780 were based on the systems already being used by the Congress to manage government. During the Second Continental Congress, prior to ratifying the Articles of Confederation, the management of the nation's affairs had been handled by committees composed of delegates. The creation of the executive departments was the natural evolution of the committee system.

As early as November 29, 1775, the Committee of Secret Correspondence had been created by Congress for its members to deal with foreign affairs. Following the declaration of independence from Great Britain, the Committee on Foreign Affairs was established on April 17, 1777, to succeed the Committee on Secret Correspondence. Presumably the new title of the committee was more appropriate to a national government in which secrecy was no longer paramount in international negotiations. Although the name was changed, the function of the committee remained essentially the same.

Once the Articles of Confederation had taken effect, the delegates chose to give responsibility for managing the government to executive departments rather than continue the system of managing the administrative responsibilities through committees, such as the Committee on Foreign Affairs. Members of Congress sought to change the committee system to a department system in order to free their time for the wide-ranging legislative issues that were beginning to consume their time. The roles and responsibilities of these departments, however, continued to be modeled after those of the Congressional committees. The Department of Foreign Affairs was formally established on August 10, 1781 to replace the Committee on Foreign Affairs. On September 23, 1781, with his selection as Secretary of Foreign Affairs, Robert R. Livingston gained the distinction of becoming the nation's first Cabinet officer.

The Cabinet under the Constitution

When the Constitution was ratified, in 1789, the first Congress continued the Department of Foreign Affairs as an executive department. On July 27, 1789, Congress passed "An Act for establishing an Executive Department, to be denominated the Department of Foreign Affairs." On September 15, 1789, following in the tradition of the legislation that guided the Department of Foreign Affairs under the Articles of Confederation, further legislation was approved that designated the principal officer of the department the Secretary of Foreign Affairs, a title that soon became the Secretary of State. The title Secretary was thus firmly established within the legislative framework as early as 1781.

The period 1775 to 1789 had been watershed years for the development of the Cabinet. In this brief period the concept of separate executive departments to manage governmental affairs was established, as was the concept of a single department head, called a Secretary, who would report to Congress. While the term Cabinet had not been applied to department heads during this period, the foundation was laid for the president's Cabinet.

Although the first Congress under the Constitution established executive departments as one of its earliest acts, the role of the department head was the subject of great debate during the Constitutional Convention in the summer of 1787. The debate focused on the role of the department heads, who were informally referred to as part of the president's Cabinet. Would the Cabinet officer become part of a collective decision-making process, as it was in Great Britain? Or would the Cabinet officer be merely an administrative officer carrying out presidential orders? Or would the Cabinet officer become part of a close circle of presidential advisors as in early England?

Constitutional Debates on the Cabinet

Of all the issues to be debated during the Constitutional Convention, the role of the president and his advisors proved to be the most volatile. There was overwhelming sentiment within the convention for a chief executive with limited powers. The delegates wanted to limit the power of the presidency in order to mitigate, if not preclude, any possibility of a monarchy arising in the new government.

Given this abiding concern for the office of the president, the issue of the powers of the presidency arose early in the debates. In fact, even prior to the official opening of the convention (in Philadelphia) in May, several delegates began examining the office of the president in some detail. One delegate, Charles Pinckney of South Carolina, began exploring the power of the presidency in December 1787, a full five months before the convening of the convention in Philadelphia. Pinckney proposed a cabinet council as part of the presidential advisory system in which the president would be required to seek the advice of a group of official counselors and of the heads of the administrative departments. Pinckney wrote:

> He will have a right to consider the principals of these departments as his Council, and to require their advice and assistance whenever the duties of his office shall render it necessary. By this means our government will possess what we have always wanted butnever yet had, a Cabinet Council.[7]

Pinckney's proposal was brought up in the early discussions of the Constitutional Convention. However, it was soon lost to the more intense debate on a totally new structure of government offered by the Virginia delegates. On June 1, two weeks after the opening of the convention, the committee of the whole began debate on the executive branch as part of its deliberations on the plan proposed by Governor Edmund Randolph of Virginia. As had Charles Pinckney, Edmund Randolph and the Virginia delegation had spent the months prior to the convention preparing organizational solutions to the inadequacies of the Articles of Confederation.

Randolph's proposal, known as the Virginia Plan, called for the separation of governmental functions into three branches—an executive, legislative, and judicial branch. This was a major change from the structure of government operating under the Articles of Confederation in which the unicameral legislature performed all three governmental functions.

The proposal stated that "a national executive be instituted," which was to be elected by the national legislature and would serve for a fixed term (which was not established by the proposal), and who was to be ineligible for "a second time" in office. James Wilson of Pennsylvania immediately moved that the executive be composed of one person only, a notion that Charles Pinckney quickly seconded. Benjamin Franklin, the senior member of the convention at age 81, concurred with Wilson and Pinckney that the national executive be focused in the hands of one person, not several. The Virginia Plan called for the executive power to be vested in a singular executive. This concept foreclosed the idea of a mandatory advisory system focused in the Cabinet. In essence the Virginia Plan repudiated the plural executive system that had evolved in England with Cabinet Government.

John Rutledge, one of South Carolina's four delegates, began the discussion on the Virginia Plan by urging adoption of a singular executive since the "Executive magistrate" was to be simply an "agent" of the congress, and was not to be feared as a powerful branch of government. Rutledge's view of a preeminent Congress within the new governmental structure was the view held by the majority of delegates. In order to mitigate the power of the chief executive, the majority of power, they felt, had to be concentrated within the two legislative chambers. Taxing powers, raising armies, and declaring war, all traditional powers of the chief executive, were overwhelmingly considered to be the province of the legislature by the convention delegates. Since Rutledge believed that the chief executive would not threaten the power of Congress, the logical organization of the executive was to simply have one person at the helm rather than a group of persons.

The debate continued briefly, but was not concluded. The only agreement reached approved a national executive to be instituted, but no concurrence was reached by the delegates on either a single or a plural executive. Discussion on the national executive turned to the powers of the national executive rather than continue with the issue of the number of executive officers or how power was to be shared by a Cabinet Council.

The next day, June 2, the committee of the whole returned to the question of a singular versus a plural executive. John Rutledge of South Carolina moved, with Charles Pinckney seconding, that the office of the chief executive be charged to one person. Surprisingly, Governor Randolph immediately opposed the proposition, listing a host of problems with the single executive concept. He urged "(1) that the permanent temper of the people was adverse to the very semblance of monarchy, (2) that a unity was unnecessary, a plurality being equally competent to all the object of the department, (3) that the necessary confidence would never be reposed in a single Magistrate, (4) that the appointment would generally be in favor of some inhabitant near the center of the Community, and consequently the remote parts would not be on an equal footing." Randolph urged that the chief executive be composed of three persons, "drawn from different portions of the Country." The country would be divided into three sections with an executive elected from each section. For the first time during the convention, the debate over a singular executive became intense.

Roger Sherman of Connecticut urged a single executive and a council of revision while John Rutledge and James Wilson continued to support a single executive without a council or split representation. Randolph again argued that the single executive was too closely allied to a monarchy, but Wilson retorted that everyone knew that a single executive was not a king. Wilson strenuously opposed the plural executive by noting that in such a triumvirate as Randolph proposed, there would be constant fighting and bickering among the three.

The delegates, as was their regular custom, did not meet on Sundays (June 3). They returned to the debate on the chief executive on Monday, June 4. James Wilson of Pennsylvania answered the objections of Governor Randolph. Wilson argued that the people were not adverse to a single executive simply because it bore a resemblance to the single executive within the British system. A single executive does not by its very nature imply either monarchy or tyranny.

Wilson continued his defense of a single executive by noting that the thirteen states had a single executive as governors. Wilson argued that none of the states had a plural executive. When the vote was taken later that day, three states, New York, Delaware, and Maryland, voted against a single executive. Despite the New York delegation vote, one member of the delegation, Alexander Hamilton, was solidly in favor of it and later became its most ardent supporter. The remaining states voted in favor, with the motion being carried.

Following adoption of the Constitution on September 17, 1787, the document was sent to the states for ratification. The ratification process again stirred many of the same debates that had been raised during the Constitutional Convention, among which was the debate over the use of the Cabinet as part of the plural executive.

Opponents of the Constitution opposed ratification partly on the grounds that the single executive would centralize power within a single individual and could easily deteriorate into a tyrannical office. The Cabinet Council system would preclude this, opponents argued. Alexander Hamilton became the principal defender of a strong single executive during the ratification process, and argued his position in a series of articles written for the *New York Packet*, later known as the *Federalist Papers.*

Writing in the *Packet,* in what came to be known as *Federalist* Number 70, Hamilton defended the Constitution's existing language. He cited a variety of examples in which the chief executive, who was officially designated the president in the signed version of the Constitution, would be unable to function adequately were the Cabinet to be considered an equal partner in decision-making. He described the problems of a collective decision-making process in which the president is "over-ruled by my Council," in spite of being the only elected official among the group.[8] Hamilton found that this violated the very essence of a democratic structure.

He also noted in *Federalist* Number 70 that a plural executive composed of the president and his Cabinet Council could lead to a situation in which the "council were so divided in their opinions that it was impossible to obtain any better resolution on the point," another plea against collective decision-making. The thrust of Hamilton's argument was fundamentally different from that of Edmund Randolph. While Randolph had argued for a plural executive in order to reduce any possibility of monarchy or tyranny, Hamilton argued that a plural executive is administratively unworkable and is democratically unsound.

Due to their joint efforts, however, the president was incorporated into the Constitution as a single individual with no mandate to consult a Cabinet in decision-making. <u>The term Cabinet was purposely omitted from the Constitution to ensure that the president remained singular in nature</u>.

THE PRESIDENT'S CABINET—WASHINGTON TO ROOSEVELT

Although the Constitutional Convention had numerous debates on the role of the president's Cabinet, it still failed to provide any specific guidance to the president in dealing with department heads. The Constitution alluded to the existence of executive departments in Article II, Section I, but never specified their role or responsibilities. This wording ensured that department heads were not considered part of a constitutionally mandated Cabinet. The architects of the Constitution endeavored to ensure that the president was not subject to collective decision-making.

George Washington: Setting Precedents for the Cabinet

George Washington, as the nation's first president, was faced with the sizable responsibility of establishing the duties of his department heads and their role as presidential counselors. Among the questions to be resolved was whether the department heads should serve as both departmental managers and presidential counselors or should serve only as departmental managers. If the department heads were not also counselors, who would become the president's Cabinet Council? Would members of Congress advise the president in a manner fashioned after the British parliamentary system? Would the president rely on a close circle of friends to advise him, as the king had done three hundred years earlier? Washington had little guidance on how to structure his relationship with the department heads. Writing to a friend, he vividly described the problems he faced in setting up not only his Cabinet but the entire structure of the executive branch:

> I walk on untrodden ground. There is scarcely an action the motive of which may not be subjected to a double interpretation. There is scarcely any part of my conduct which may not hereafter be drawn into precedent.[9]

The last sentence of his letter was especially pertinent to the issue of the Cabinet, for his actions would be taken, as he said, as "precedent."

By September 1789 Congress had authorized the creation of an Attorney General and three executive departments: Treasury, War, State. For the Treasury Department, Washington named Alexander Hamilton, President of the Bank of New York. Hamilton had proven to be a loyal soldier, having served under Washington during the Revolutionary War and an able statesman during the Constitutional Convention. For Secretary of War he chose General Henry Knox, with whom he had also served during the Revolutionary War and who had served as Secretary of War under the Articles of Confederation. For Secretary of State, Thomas Jefferson, the nation's ambassador to France since 1784, was chosen. For Attorney General, Washington selected Edmund Randolph, the first Attorney General of Virginia and the architect of the Virginia Plan during the Constitutional Convention.

Washington's primary goal in Cabinet selection was to bring about a conciliation between the Federalists and the Republicans by choosing Alexander Hamilton, a Federalist, and Thomas Jefferson, a Republican, for the two major positions within the Cabinet. Washington sought to heal the wounds of the nation caused by the bitter war of words between the Federalists and the Republicans following the Constitutional Convention.

In addition to Washington's goal of forming a bipartisan Cabinet, he wanted representation from all regions of the young nation. Washington agreed with Edmund Randolph's proposal for an executive representing the three major regions of the nation, but sought to satisfy that goal not through a plural executive but through geographic balance within the Cabinet. Thomas Jefferson and Edmund Randolph of Virginia were chosen as representatives of the southern states, Alexander Hamilton of New York represented the middle Atlantic states, and Henry Knox of Massachusetts represented the northern states. Washington wanted to avoid any section of the country concerned that the government "was being unduly influenced by men from another area, for the bonds of loyalty were slim enough to be strained by such consideration."[10] The relationship between the states and the federal government was fragile enough after the ratification of the Constitution, that a concentration of Cabinet officers from one state or section of the country could jeopardize the acceptance of the national government.

Having constituted his Cabinet, Washington was then faced with the question of whether to bring the department heads together to discuss issues jointly or to deal with them separately as the Constitution seemed to suggest. Article II, Section II of the Constitution stated that the president "may require the Opinion, in writing, of the principal Officer in each of the executive Departments." The implication of this section was that the president would not meet collectively with his department heads but would deal with each individually. Again, this stemmed from the debate on the Cabinet emerging as a plural executive.

Although Washington did seek the opinions of his department heads in writing, and in individual consultations, he also convened the Cabinet as a group to discuss both departmental issues and general matters of state. He considered the department heads to be his primary assistants in the determination of administration policy, in part due to the recommendation of Alexander Hamilton. Hamilton had strongly urged that the Cabinet serve as both presidential assistants and as departmental managers, stating that "The persons, therefore, to whom immediate management these different matters are committed ought to be considered as the assistants or deputies of the Chief Magistrate ."[11]

During the first two years of the administration, Washington traveled extensively around the country in order to secure the support of those Republicans still leery of the national government. Washington believed that only he could convince the nation that the new federal system was fully cognizant of the sovereignty of states in most issues.

While Washington was gone, the Cabinet officers essentially ran the government. Washington kept in as close touch as possible by mail with each of the department heads, but he was often difficult to reach and mail correspondence often took weeks. Once he completed his travels, nearly two years after his inauguration, Cabinet meetings became a common occurrence.

When Washington returned, most policy issues were brought before the entire Cabinet for debate, with Washington balancing the merits of each argument before making a final decision. The Cabinet was never considered to have collective responsibility for policy-making, but rather was a forum for educated discussions on national policy issues. Washington brought to his Cabinet meetings discussions on such topics as the constitutionality of the Bank of the United States (which Hamilton favored and Jefferson opposed), the location of the new capital, and the need for neutrality during the war between France and England. The strength of the Cabinet as a presidential advisor was recorded within Congress, when it described the Cabinet as "the great council of the Nation" in 1798.[12]

During the early part of Washington's presidency, the term Cabinet was frequently interchanged with the terms council and conclave. Henry Barrett Learned, one of the leading scholars on the history of the president's Cabinet, endeavored to pinpoint when the phrase "President's Cabinet" was first used. He found that the term was not generally used until 1793, nearly four years after the appointment of the department heads. He quotes Thomas Jefferson's reference to "cabinet officers" and James Madison's remark concerning a paper "read in Cabinet for the first time."[13] Thus, by 1793 the department heads, who were functioning as the president's principal advisors, were commonly referred to as the President's Cabinet.

In summary, the concept of a Cabinet that administers the executive departments and serves as the president's counselors is clearly drawn from the British use of the Cabinet during the seventeenth and early eighteenth centuries. However, the American Cabinet did not follow the British pattern of a plural executive, which emerged during the eighteenth and nineteenth centuries. The architects of the Constitution carefully avoided any mention of the Cabinet in the Constitution as a means of preserving the unquestioned supremacy of the president within the executive branch.

Although the Cabinet's administrative duties were to a large degree established in departmental enabling legislation, George Washington, as the nation's first president, faced the task of establishing the degree to which the Cabinet would participate in policy decisions, both individually and collectively. The Cabinet's advisory role in policy-making became firmly established in the structure of the executive branch when George Washington set the precedent for the dual role of the Cabinet as both departmental manager and policy advisor.

Changes in the Presidential-Cabinet Relationship

During the one hundred sixty years between the presidencies of George Washington and Herbert Hoover, the presidential-Cabinet relationship underwent a series of changes. Principal among these changes was the increased use of the Cabinet as a source of political strength with political parties, Congress, and special interest groups.

One of the earliest changes in the presidential-Cabinet relationship involved a reexamination of the value of a politically diverse Cabinet. During his first term, Washington had brought together leaders of the nation's two political parties, the Federalists and the Republicans, into the Cabinet to maximize political support for the administration's policies. By having the leaders of the two major political parties within his Cabinet, Washington hoped to ensure bipartisan legislative support and to create the appearance of harmony within the national government. Divisiveness, Washington felt, would be disastrous to the fledgling national government.

However, Alexander Hamilton and Thomas Jefferson constantly disagreed on policy direction and lobbied members of Congress on opposing policy goals. Jefferson publicly opposed a number of major policy proposals initiated by Hamilton and supported by Washington, such as federal subsidies to the states and the establishment of a national bank. Angered by Jefferson's actions, Washington concluded that the Cabinet had to reflect only one political philosophy to perform its advisory role effectively. Following Jefferson's resignation from the Cabinet in 1794, Washington chose a Federalist, Edmund Randolph, to replace Jefferson. Washington later wrote on the conflicts of party within the Cabinet:

> I shall not, whilst I have the honor to Administer the government, bring a man into my office, of consequence, knowingly whose political tenets are adverse to the measures which the general government are pursuing; for this, in my opinion, would be a sort of political Suicide; that it would embarrass its movements is most certain.[14]

During his term as president, Thomas Jefferson was also acutely conscious of the Cabinet conflicts that had been prominent during Washington's administration. Accordingly, he nominated only Republicans to his Cabinet.

Politicization of the Cabinet

The next significant change in the presidential-Cabinet relationship during the nineteenth century involved the increased politicization of the Cabinet. Throughout the terms of Washington, Adams, and Jefferson, Cabinet members were chosen primarily on the basis of merit and on their personal relationship with the president. However, as the voting population began to increase dramatically both in size and diversity with the admission of new states to the union, the political pressures on presidential candidates grew.[15] Candidates were willing to trade political support for Cabinet appointments, using the Cabinet to gain regional advantage, to conciliate dissident factions within their own party, and to broaden ideological support.

The consequence of politicization was the selection of some Cabinet officers whom presidents neither knew nor trusted. Not surprisingly, presidents at times turned to a small group of close friends rather than their Cabinets for political and policy advice. Andrew Jackson had his "kitchen cabinet," Grover Cleveland his "fishing cabinet," Herbert Hoover his "medicine ball cabinet," and Franklin Roosevelt his "brain trust."

The trend toward politicization of the Cabinet was accelerated by the reluctance of Congress during the 1800s to approve presidential appointees to the Cabinet. Washington, Adams, and Jefferson had each been able to select their Cabinet without interference from Congress. James Madison, however, was never able to command the political leadership of his predecessors in Congress.[16] The Senate refused to confirm his appointment for Secretary of State and instead demanded the appointment of the brother of an influential senator. Madison was forced to concur in order to preserve harmony within his own party.

The nearly total politicization of the Cabinet during the administration of Andrew Jackson resulted in a Cabinet that was primarily administrative rather than advisory. Jackson was particularly adroit at using his Cabinet to gain political advantage, trading Cabinet appointments for political favors. Cabinet appointments became a prominent part of the spoils system, resulting in a Cabinet to which Jackson rarely turned for policy advice and which had little influence in policy determination. Jackson and his "kitchen cabinet" dominated the policy process, while the Cabinet officers served primarily as departmental managers.

Jackson's dominance over the policy process fueled attempts by the opposition party, the Whigs, to weaken his executive powers. After several unsuccessful attempts to win the presidency, the Whigs, who were committed to legislative supremacy, elected their first president, William Henry Harrison, in 1840. Harrison and the Whigs, under the leadership of Henry Clay and Daniel Webster, sought to limit presidential authority, in part, by imposing a system of collective responsibility within the Cabinet for policy decisions.[17] Since Harrison had appointed prominent Whig members of Congress to his Cabinet, Congress would have become an integral part of the policy process. However, Harrison died one month into his term and was succeeded by John Tyler, his vice president.

Tyler had never been an advocate of collective decision-making and battled the Cabinet, which Harrison had brought into office. As a result, all but one member of the Cabinet resigned during Tyler's first year in office, and there was a constant turnover in Cabinet officials throughout the remainder of Tyler's term. Twenty-one Cabinet officers revolved through the departments during Tyler's four years in office.

This scenario was repeated when Zachary Taylor, a Whig, was elected in 1848. Taylor supported the Whig philosophy of legislative supremacy and collective decision-making. But he died only sixteen months after taking office. His successor, Millard Fillmore, was less supportive of the collective decision-making process between the president and the Cabinet, and, like Tyler, had a high turnover in the Cabinet. James Polk, a Democrat elected between the Whig administrations of Harrison/Tyler and Taylor/Fillmore, sought to reestablish the advisory role of the Cabinet. During his four-year term, Polk sought the advice of the Cabinet in over three hundred fifty Cabinet meetings.

Lincoln: A New Relationship with the Cabinet

The advisory role of the Cabinet fluctuated in the mid-1800s, from a low under Andrew Jackson to a high under James Polk. Abraham Lincoln became the first president during this era to draw both political and advisory benefits from the Cabinet. Not since George Washington had a president sought a marriage of politics and merit to the degree that Lincoln did in 1861. The Lincoln Cabinet of 1861 was an attempt to forge a coalition of not only Republicans but dissident Whigs and Democrats. Both the Democratic and Whig parties had split over the slavery issue, with southern party members tending to remain within the party and northern party members joining the fledgling Republican Party.

In 1860 the issue of slavery and states' rights had so divided the Democratic Party that they held two presidential nominating conventions, one in Baltimore for northern delegates and one in Charleston for southern delegates. Similarly, southern Whigs met in Baltimore and northern Whigs attended the Republican convention in Chicago. Lincoln, the first Republican president, used his Cabinet as a tool to build national political support for the newly divided party. He particularly sought to bring southerners into his Cabinet to forestall the movement toward secession by the southern states.

In spite of the strictly political reasons for which he chose many members of his Cabinet, he sought to use the Cabinet as a forum for policy discussions in a manner similar to the Washington presidency. Nearly all major policy matters were discussed by the full Cabinet, with Lincoln present, before he made a final decision.

However, Lincoln never deferred to his Cabinet on issues on which there was disagreement, as evidenced by the celebrated statement he made during one Cabinet meeting in June 1862. After presenting each member of the Cabinet with a copy of the Emancipation Proclamation, Lincoln asked for his opinion as to whether he should deliver the proclamation. Secretary of State William Seward suggested that it be held off until some of the union forces gained a sizable advantage in the field, since he believed the proclamation might be considered empty words given recent Union losses. Lincoln accepted the suggestion. After the Battle of Antietam (September 17–19) Lincoln again asked his Cabinet whether he should issue the proclamation given the decisive Union victory. Every member of the Cabinet opposed the idea. After counting the seven no votes of his Cabinet against his one yes vote, Lincoln declared that his one yes vote carried the issue. The Emancipation Proclamation was preliminarily issued on September 22, 1862, with the official copy signed on January 1, 1863.[18]

Lincoln's relations with his Cabinet were antagonized by his difficulties with Congress. His term was characterized by constant battles with Congress over the range of presidential authority, particularly over issues connected with reconstruction. A confrontation developed in 1863 when both Congress and the president sought supremacy in determining the provisions under which secessionist states could return to the Union. Through a statute known as the Wade-Davis Bill, Congress endeavored to control reconstruction by establishing the criteria for states to reenter the Union. Lincoln was also attempting to control the process through executive order. In a statement issued to the newspapers describing why the Wade-Davis Bill was passed, members of Congress stated that only they had the authority to determine the criteria for reconstruction. That statement read, "the authority of Congress is paramount and must be respected."[19]

Cabinet-in-Congress Proposals

As a result of the deterioration in executive-legislative relations over the reconstruction issue, a bill was introduced in 1864 that endeavored to use members of the Cabinet as a bridge between the president and Congress. Representative George Hurt Pendleton (D-Ohio) introduced legislation that allowed for "the Secretaries of the Executive Departments may occupy seats on the floor of the House of Representatives."[20] The bill provided that Cabinet members would not be elected members of Congress nor have voting rights, but would be allowed to debate on the floor of the House. Pendleton, the House minority leader, saw the bill as a means of using the Cabinet to force Lincoln to share policy deliberations with members of Congress, and thereby minimize clashes on policies not jointly agreed upon. The bill died without a vote due to the pressure of the Civil War.

Congress renewed its interest in the Cabinet's influence in presidential policy-making in 1881 when George Hurt Pendleton, who had since been elected to the Senate, introduced legislation similar to his House bill of 1864. Pendleton again attempted to seat members of the Cabinet in Congress, but again the bill died without a vote. Pendleton subsequently turned his attentions to ending the spoils system, and sponsored the first federal civil service legislation, the Pendleton Act of 1883.

The latter half of the nineteenth century saw a continuance of the Cabinet's strong advisory role. With the exception of Ulysses S. Grant, presidents relied on their Cabinets for policy advice. Grant, however, was reluctant to turn to his Cabinet for advice, a fact that may account for the exceptionally high turnover within the Grant Cabinet. Within his first term, Grant had three Attorneys General, three Secretaries of War, and three Secretaries of the Treasury, the highest rate of turnover since John Tyler's Cabinet. During Grant's eight years in the White House, the six Cabinet offices turned over a total of twenty-one times.

The nineteenth century brought new pressures on the federal government as the nation expanded across the continent and moved from an agricultural to an industrial society. Three new Cabinet-level departments were added to manage the government's increasing responsibilities: Postmaster General (1829), Interior (1849), and Agriculture (1862). This brought the Cabinet to a total of eight at the turn of the century, with Commerce and Labor added in 1903. Ten years later, the Department of Commerce and Labor was divided by Congress into separate departments.

THE CABINET IN THE TWENTIETH CENTURY

Although the Cabinet had doubled in size, the emergence of the twentieth century had not altered the presidential reliance on the Cabinet for policy-making advice. During Theodore Roosevelt's term an official Cabinet Room was included in the construction of the west wing of the White House. Roosevelt continued the tradition of a strong relationship with his Cabinet, particularly with his Secretary of State, Elihu Root. Root was instrumental in developing Roosevelt's foreign policy initiatives, including the original proposal for the Panama Canal in 1902 and the establishment of diplomatic relations with the new Republic of Cuba.

The term of William Howard Taft saw a reintroduction of the Cabinet-in-Congress concept, which George Pendleton had first advocated during the Civil War. In a message to Congress in 1912, President Taft proposed that his Cabinet meet regularly with members of Congress as a means of improving executive-legislative relations. Faced with a Democratic Senate, a Republican House of Representatives, and a recent history of poor communication between the oval office and Congress, Taft proposed to use his Cabinet to enhance the administration's legislative initiatives. On February 18, 1913, Representative Henry S. DeForest introduced H. R. 846 in support of Taft's message. However, less than one month later, Woodrow Wilson was inaugurated. The bill died without a vote due to the lack of support from the Wilson administration.

In spite of Wilson's lack of support for the Cabinet-in-Congress concept, he had not altered his longstanding advocacy of a strong Cabinet.[21] He built a Cabinet to serve both his political and policy needs, drawing heavily on members of the Democratic Party and Congress. Wilson used several of his Cabinet appointments as a tool to mend political fences within the Democratic Party, most notably William Jennings Bryan as his Secretary of State, but he remained committed to Alexander Hamilton's philosophy that Cabinet members serve as the president's primary assistants in matters of policy.

Arthur Link, in his biography of Wilson, noted that Wilson gave substantial authority to members of his Cabinet to develop departmental policies. Wilson, Link said, "gave full rein to his subordinates (Cabinet) and stood loyally by them ... Moreover, he frequently took advice, and not a few of the administration's important policies were originated by Bryan, Lansing, McAdoo and others."[22]

Both Warren Harding and Calvin Coolidge continued to seek the counsel of their Cabinet in the determination of policy initiatives, as Wilson had. Coolidge was so determined to focus public attention on the Cabinet as his primary advisory source that he stated, "(My) counsellors have been those provided by the Constitution and the law."[23] Herbert Hoover, however, faced with a nearly total collapse of the nation's economy in 1929, relied on the counsel of a small cadre of personal friends for economic policy advice. Other matters of policy remained the province of the Cabinet in the Hoover administration.

The Cabinet: Franklin Delano Roosevelt to Bill Clinton

Although the Cabinet's advisory role fluctuated during the eighteenth and nineteenth centuries, in general the Cabinet remained the president's primary source of policy advice. Alexander Hamilton's recommendation that the Cabinet be considered the president's "assistants or deputies"[24] was followed by most presidents, principally due to an absence of viable alternatives for policy development. While several presidents relied on "kitchen cabinets" for policy advice, their members did not have the range of technical expertise to match that of the executive departments.

This began to change, however, with the creation of the Executive Office of the President in 1939 which gave presidents an advisory system within the White House capable of preparing major policy options. By 1969 the Executive Office of the President had grown to a staff of nearly three thousand, providing Richard Nixon an advisory system paralleling that of the Cabinet. The Executive Office of the President afforded presidents a viable alternative to the Cabinet for policy development. The creation of the Executive Office of the President and the White House staff under Franklin

Delano Roosevelt began to change the traditional role of the Cabinet as the president's primary counselors.

Creation of the Executive Office of the President

The groundwork for a White House policy-making system was laid by Franklin Delano Roosevelt in 1936 with the appointment of the President's Committee on Administrative Management chaired by Louis Brownlow. Roosevelt convened the Brownlow Committee to explore administrative systems that would provide the president the management tools for control of a rapidly expanding executive branch. The burgeoning responsibilities of the federal government had so overloaded Roosevelt with information and policy-making decisions that he simply could not make what he considered informed decisions on all the issues he was forced to decide.

As Roosevelt noted, the president was "overwhelmed with minor details and needless contacts."[25]   In January 1937 the Brownlow Committee completed its work and presented to Roosevelt a set of recommendations to provide both personal and institutional help to the president. A personal staff of six executive assistants would coordinate the flow of information to the president and provide general political advice. An institutional staff would provide the president an impartial analysis of budgeting and legislative submissions prepared by the departments and would provide a mechanism to coordinate these submissions. James MacGregor Burns provided a succinct description of the presidential assistants in his classic study of the presidency, *Presidential Government:*

> The [Brownlow] committee knew that presidential aides could not be anonymous; the voracious Washington press corps would prevent that. What the committee wanted was a personal presidential staff that would be given a privileged sanctuary under the President's wing against the kinds of political and organizational pressures that played on the more conspicuous men around the President . . . their responsibility and loyalty would be wholly and only to the President.[26]

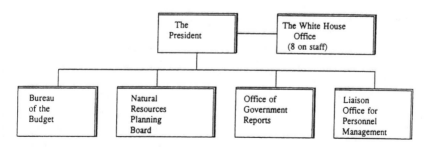

FIGURE 1. Executive Office of the President (1939)

Roosevelt accepted the committee's recommendations and later that year sought approval from Congress to establish the new White House staff. The original Reorganization Bill was defeated, but after two years of negotiations with Congress, Roosevelt finally won approval for his request.

Reorganization Plan I was enacted into law on April 25, 1939, establishing the Executive Office of the President (EOP) and transferring to it the Bureau of the Budget from the Treasury Department and the Natural Resources Planning Board from the Interior Department. The Office of Government Reports and the Liaison Office for Personnel Management were also added. One of the key facets of the EOP was the creation of an official staff within the White House for the president.

Roosevelt praised the legislation as providing "the tools of management and the authority to distribute the work so that the President can effectively discharge those powers which the Constitution now places upon him."[27]

The intent of the reorganization plan was not to alter the Cabinet's advisory role but rather to improve presidential management of the executive branch. The Brownlow Committee specified that the president's personal staff "would have no power to make decisions or issue instructions in (their) own right . . . and would not be interposed between the President and the heads of his Departments."[28] The White House staff was not intended to be a policy-making unit.

In ensuing years Congress enlarged the Executive Office of the President through creation of the Council of Economic Advisors (1946), National Security Council (1947), and the Council of Environmental Quality (1969). The president contributed to the enlargement of the EOP by creating, through executive order, advisory committees such as the Economic Policy Board, Council on International Economic Policy, Office of Telecommunications Policy, and the Economic Opportunity Council. The White House staff itself grew through the years as did all parts of the EOP.

The Expanding White House Staff

The emergence of an institutionalized White House staff followed a general decline in the advisory function of the Cabinet that began in Franklin Delano Roosevelt's first administration. Rather than rely on his Cabinet for overall policy advice, Roosevelt turned to a small informal group of friends and supporters known as the brain trust to supplement the Cabinet's policy recommendations.

As Edward Corwin notes of the brain trust, "Even when Mr. Roosevelt had free recourse to his official family for counsel he turned to individual members of it quite as frequently as to the Cabinet as a body, and this on large questions of policy."[29] The brain trust, which provided Roosevelt another sounding board for policy issues, tended to be less concerned with constituent demands and more concerned with pragmatic solutions and political realities than those of the Cabinet.

The Cabinet was also undergoing another transformation during the Roosevelt era in which fewer and fewer decisions were brought to the Cabinet for collective discussion. Roosevelt began to reduce the number of issues brought before the collective cabinet. He favored a system in which individual cabinet members met alone with him in the oval office or, alternatively, with him in small groups.

The transformation of the advisory role of the Cabinet in the Roosevelt administration was furthered by the creation of the White House staff as a result of the Reorganization Act of 1939. The Reorganization Act provided little guidance to the president on a structure for the new White House staff or a delineation of their roles. Roosevelt chose not to build a White House staff of policy experts, but rather of loyalists who were, according to Stephen Hess, "noted primarily for the duration of their dedication to Roosevelt."[30] The White House staff that emerged included eight staff—six professionals and two clerical. This structure reflected the Brownlow Committee's recommendation that the White House Office should be served by six administrative assistants, "possessed of high competence, great physical vigor, and a passion for anonymity.[31]

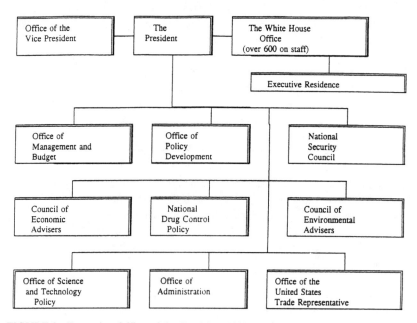

FIGURE 2. Executive Office of the President (1995)

TABLE 1. White House Office, 1939

Secretary to the President	Stephen Early
Secretary to the President	Brigadier General Edwin M. Watson
Secretary to the President	Marvin H. McIntyre
Administrative Assistant	William H. McReynolds
Administrative Assistant	James H. Rowe, Jr.
Administrative Assistant	Lauchlin Currie
Personal Secretary	Marguerite LeHand
Executive Clerk	Rudolph Forster

Source: United States Government Manual, 1939 (Washington, D.C.: U.S. Government Printing Office, 1939).

The six professional members of the White House staff had few specific functions. Most worked on presidential speeches, bill-drafting, and general coordination activities with the departments. There were no formal staff meetings, and each member of the staff had direct access to the president. Roosevelt was the first president to employ the "spokes of the wheel" process of staffing, in which the president served as the hub of the wheel with each of the staff serving as spokes. Each staff member was equal in importance and in relationship to the president. The White House staff structure had little definition and bore no similarity to the well-defined staff structures of later administrations. Roosevelt met frequently with each member of the staff and often encouraged competing advice and analysis from the staff.[32] This structure was later altered under Eisenhower with the centralization of White House staff under a chief of staff and the establishment of a hierarchial staffing structure.

The transformation of the informal staff structure into a more formal staff structure actually began during the later years of the Roosevelt administration. As the president's health began to fail and the war dominated his attention, White House staff played a greater role in policy development. Roosevelt added three additional advisers: Harry Hopkins, who often met with representatives of foreign governments and relayed their discussions to the State Department; Admiral William Leahy, who briefed Roosevelt on military affairs; and Samuel Rosenmann, who managed domestic matters. Rosenmann played an increasing role in domestic affairs as Roosevelt's attentions were dominated by the war in 1943 and 1944, requiring additional aides assigned to Rosenmann.

The foundation for White House control of the domestic policy process was essentially established by Rosenmann, who built the first in-house domestic policy advisory system.   This structure provided the foundation of the institutional bureaucracy that today not only rivals the Cabinet as a policy advisor but often controls the Cabinet.

Once the structure had been established, Roosevelt's successors continued to enlarge on it. Harry Truman publicly supported the importance of the Cabinet as an advisory mechanism, but continued to expand the White House staff. Truman believed that the Cabinet was "the principal medium through which the President controls his administration"[33] and that "government was simply too large" to be run by the White House.[34] For Truman, the White House staff was primarily a process manager and organizer, and less a policy initiator.

Truman's initial White House staff focused on assistants for press relations, correspondence, and appointments in addition to several general assistants. He did not continue the more specific roles that Hopkins, Leahy, and Rosenmann had played during the Roosevelt years. However, within a year after taking office, Truman reversed himself and expanded the White House staff to include functional, policy-oriented roles. Added to the initial list of staff were John Steelman as Assistant to the President, responsible primarily for labor-management issues: Clark Clifford as Special Counsel, responsible for broad domestic policy formulation; Charles Murphy as Administrative Assistant responsible for Congressional relations; Donald Dawson as Administrative Assistant responsible for personnel and patronage; and David Niles as Administrative Assistant responsible for liaison with minority groups.[35]

The Truman White House, far more than the Roosevelt White House, saw an emergence of functional responsibilities by White House staff. The institutional White House was changing not only in its functions, but also in its structure and its size. In particular, the role of domestic policy advisor, which Rosenmann had initiated under Roosevelt, was further expanded under Truman. Truman had formalized both a role for broad domestic policy advice in Clifford and a role for specialized domestic policy advice in Steelman.

The institutionalization of the White House staff continued under Dwight Eisenhower, with further specialization of assignment, centralization of authority, and expansion of sublevels of White House staff. The White House staff had grown to such proportions that by the end of the Eisenhower administration the Brookings Institution recommended to the newly elected President Kennedy that one option to be considered was to reduce the White House staff because it duplicated some of the "machinery" of the departments.[36]

By the time Eisenhower took office, the immediate White House staff had grown to thirty-two professionals, twenty-six more than on Roosevelt's original White House staff. Eisenhower continued the trend toward functional assignments of White House staff, and added to those assignments by increasing the size of the staff.

As had both Roosevelt and Truman, Eisenhower left his mark on the White House staff structure. Eisenhower's contribution was to establish a tradition of expertise by the staff. Where Roosevelt and Truman had used personal loyalty as the primary test for White House service, Eisenhower focused on professional expertise. Not a single member of the Cabinet or White House staff had close ties to the president. The only top member of the administration with long, personal ties to Eisenhower was Walter B. (Beetle) Smith, who was named Undersecretary of State. Bradley Patterson, who managed the White House Cabinet Secretariat, was a career staff member in the State Department who had built the department's secretariat; press secretary James Hagerty had been a journalist and press secretary; Congressional Liaison Wilton (Jerry) Persons had been a professional lobbyist.

Eisenhower's contribution to the White House staff structure also included the addition of a chief of staff to reduce the often chaotic nature of the "spokes of the wheel" structure. Sherman Adams, former governor of New Hampshire, was named chief of staff in 1953.[37] Adams viewed the role as the president's gatekeeper, ensuring an orderly flow of information from the ever-growing members of the presidential office. Adam's role was to provide a hierarchial decision structure to satisfy Eisenhower's plan for a military-style structure, with clear lines of command and authority.[38]

To fill out the other top staff positions, Eisenhower named Tom Stephens as Appointments Secretary; Bernard Shanley as Counsel; Gabriel Hauge as economics advisor; and D.D. Jackson and Emmet Hughes as the principal speech writers. The selection of Hauge as economics advisor continued the trend toward managing domestic policy from the White House. Hauge's role was broader than that of either Rosenmann or Steelman, for essentially any area that Hauge wanted to become involved in could be justified under the rubric of economic policy. Eisenhower also sought to enhance his coordination of national security and foreign policy issues by upgrading the National Security Council (NSC). Created in 1947 but rarely used by Truman, Eisenhower used the NSC as a working group that provided regular briefings to the president on national security and foreign policy issues.

Although the role of the White House staff was growing, the Cabinet continued to play a key role in the Eisenhower administration, as it had in both the Roosevelt and Truman administrations. Eisenhower relied heavily on his Cabinet and created the Cabinet Secretariat in the White House to serve as a formal mechanism to coordinate the Cabinet's preparation of policy recommendations.[39] The expansion of the White House staff was not intended by Eisenhower to rival the advisory role of the Cabinet, but rather to provide consistent direction to the Cabinet and a more orderly discussion of Cabinet-originated policy recommendations. Although Eisenhower expanded his White House staff with these objectives, the end result was somewhat different. As functional assignments grew and staff were regularly added to manage these assignments, the White House began to internally develop their own recommendations.

One of the further innovations of the Eisenhower White House staff was the Cabinet Secretariat, which was the first formal mechanism employed by presidents to develop a White House–Cabinet relationship. The Cabinet Secretariat was conceived primarily as a tracking system, in which White House staff followed up with Cabinet officers to ensure that presidential directives were carried out.

Another, perhaps more important, function of the Cabinet Secretariat was to prepare a Cabinet Action Status Report, listing all presidential actions during the period at hand.[40] This was circulated to all Cabinet officers and kept them abreast of major administration issues and presidential decisions on those issues. The White House staff used this technique to ensure that all members of the Cabinet understood the president's objectives and the decisions being made. This technique enabled Eisenhower to have a constant communication with his Cabinet officers, which reinforced their sense of inclusion in the president's team and served as a constant point of connection between the White House and the Cabinet.

The Eisenhower Cabinet Secretariat, built on Eisenhower's sense of order in his administration, laid the framework for later White House–Cabinet structures of communication. In particular, the Nixon Urban Affairs Council committees, the Carter cabinet clusters, and the Reagan cabinet councils, each of which was built on the concept of clear communication of White House goals and objectives that the Eisenhower administration developed with the Secretariat.

The evolution of White House–Cabinet relations continued as the role of the White House staff took yet another turn in the Kennedy years. John F. Kennedy chose not to follow the Brookings Institution recommendations in 1960 to reduce the White House staff, and instead he moved to enlarge the White House staff. Their role was to provide general policy and management advice to the president. According to Kennedy, the enlarged White House staff was to ensure that "important matters are brought here in a way which permits a clear decision after alternatives have been presented."[41] Arthur Schlesinger, Jr., commented that the role of the special assistant was not "to get between the President and operating chiefs of the departments and agencies, but . . . to make sure that the departmental and agency recommendations took full account of the presidential and national interests."[42] Contrary to Schlesinger's concept of the staff role, the special assistants under Kennedy did become a layer between the president and the Cabinet, reviewing all policy recommendations before they were given to the president. Although the members of the Kennedy staff were not responsible for policy development, they were a critical link in the policy advisory process.

The move by Kennedy toward greater centralization of policy-making authority in the White House was part of his plan to exercise greater control over the bureaucracy. As Patrick Anderson noted, "not since Roosevelt had there been a President so distrustful of the bureaucracy and so willing to let his personal aides prod, double-check, and bypass it."[43]

Kennedy initiated a system of White House supervision of agency policy, personnel, and legislative decisions to gain greater control over the executive branch. Part one of Kennedy's plan involved using White House staff to review departmental recommendations and advise him on the merits of those recommendations. The Eisenhower method of relying on the Cabinet Secretariat to review and coordinate departmental proposals was unacceptable to Kennedy. Kennedy subsequently divided responsibilities among his staff, with McGeorge Bundy supervising foreign policy and Theodore Sorensen supervising domestic policy. Indicative of the influence that White House aides had in policy-making was Kennedy's decision to support the Alliance for Progress against the advice of the State Department. Bundy's assistant, Richard Goodwin, convinced Kennedy to support the Alliance for Progress in spite of the State Department's contention that the alliance membership was too right-wing for the United States to deal with.[44]

Part two of Kennedy's plan involved the control of departmental personnel selection by using the White House staff rather than Cabinet officers to select key sub-Cabinet appointments. Among those appointed directly from the White House were Undersecretary of State Chester Bowles and Assistant Secretary of State G. Mennen Williams. Both were appointed before Dean Rusk was offered the position of Secretary of State. In addition, as part of his efforts to place blacks in senior federal positions, Kennedy appointed George Weaver as Assistant Secretary of Labor, Carl Rowan as Deputy Assistant Secretary of State, and Robert C. Weaver as Housing Administrator.[45]

Part three of Kennedy's plan involved increasing the role of the White House in managing the administration's legislative agenda to Congress. Kennedy wanted the White House liaison office rather than the departmental liaison staff to become the focal point of legislative pressure. Although Bryce Harlow had run a large Congressional Liaison office during the Eisenhower administration, each department had maintained separate responsibility for legislative action. Kennedy endeavored to coordinate all major legislative proposals through the White House to ensure that they met presidential objectives and received the necessary presidential support.

Kennedy further expanded his in-house advisory system through the creation of numerous advisory committees within the White House, such as the Office of Science and Technology and the President's Science Advisory Committee. Kennedy expanded the White House policy advisory structure far beyond that of Eisenhower, Truman, or Roosevelt.

The Johnson Era: Changes in the White House Staff

The pendulum moved even further toward the White House staff as a policy-maker during the Johnson administration. Johnson expanded the size of the White House staff and encouraged its active participation in preparing the administration's policies. White House staff emerged as major participants in both policy review and policy development. Prior to the Johnson administration, the role of the White House staff had generally been limited to advising the president on the merits of departmental recommendations.

Johnson viewed the bureaucracy with the same suspicion that Kennedy had. Doris Kearns described Johnson's predisposition toward his White House staff:

> Lyndon Johnson moved effectively to exploit his advantage. He used every tool at his disposal, most prominently his budget and his White House staff, to concentrate information, publicity, and decisions in the Oval Office. . . . He decreed that all major pronouncements on policy and programs would be issued directly from the White House. . . . He assumed personal control over decisions on the budget, forcing his Cabinet to plead with him directly for money and staff.[46]

Johnson followed Kennedy's plan for controlling the permanent government through White House supervision of agency policy, personnel, and legislative actions. However, Johnson enlarged his staff to accommodate staff specialization. For example, Johnson had one staff member, Lee White, specifically assigned to civil rights. Another staff member, Charles A. Horsky, was given responsibility for problems in the District of Columbia.[47] Kennedy had used a smaller White House staff than Johnson, most of whom were generalists rather than specialists. In addition, Johnson reduced his dependence on the Cabinet for policy advice by drawing on the advice of task forces, whose membership he controlled.[48]

Johnson's distrust of the federal bureaucracy was based on its expanding size and growing independence from the White House. Federal expenditures during the 1960s had resulted in dramatic increases in departmental responsibilities. The federal budget grew from $9 billion in 1940 to nearly $200 billion by 1968, as Congress steadily appropriated more funds for the growing role of the national government.

Departmental budgets grew in nearly direct proportion to the federal budget. Every department was increasing its personnel to meet its expanding programmatic responsibilities.

But during the mid-1960s, Lyndon Johnson became concerned that policy decisions from the Cabinet were frequently not in line with his policy objectives. As their budgets grew, Cabinet officers often made policy decisions without consulting the White House. Johnson considered many of these decisions to be out of line with the administration's overall goals and began to view his Cabinet officers as "captured" by their departments. Not surprisingly, Johnson began to seek ways to bypass the Cabinet for major policy initiatives. He found his solution by increasingly relying on White House and other EOP staff for policy advice and for policy development. The departments were increasingly told what to do, rather than incorporated into the decision-making process.

The Johnson era marked the emergence of the White House policy-making system, one which challenged the traditional participation of the Cabinet in policy development. Cabinet officers were often replaced by White House staff as the president's prime source of advice on policy issues.

Creation of a White House Policy-Making System

There are a number of explanations for Johnson's decision to move toward greater reliance on the White House staff in the policy process and the creation of a White House based policy-making system. None of the explanations alone account for this greater reliance on White House staff, but together provide a picture of the frustration that Lyndon Johnson felt with his Cabinet.

Perhaps the greatest influence on Johnson's decision to turn inward for policy advice was the growing role of the bureaucracy in departmental policy decisions. New demands on the departments to expand their programs and provide more services to the public had resulted in major expansions of all executive departments during the 1960s. Johnson often became frustrated at the growing power of the departments as both their budgets and their staff burgeoned. Even though the executive departments were under the president's jurisdiction, they frequently pushed for policies that served not the president's interest but the interests of members of Congress. After all, Congress provided the funds to keep the departments alive, and to alienate a key member of Congress could be disastrous for any department. Departments needed to protect their appropriations by meeting the policy demands of Congress. This expanded allegiance to Congress by the departments was unacceptable to Johnson, who saw it as a continuing erosion of presidential control over executive functions.

Johnson's frustrations with the behavior of the departments was aggravated by the numerous layers of staff within the departments that became involved in policy-making and the lengthy period of time that departments required to move a policy initiative through the process. Staff members, division chiefs, bureau directors, deputy assistant secretaries, assistant secretaries, and under-secretaries all had to review and approve the material before it proceeded to the level of the Cabinet officer. The process took weeks, generally months, after the basic research had been worked on.

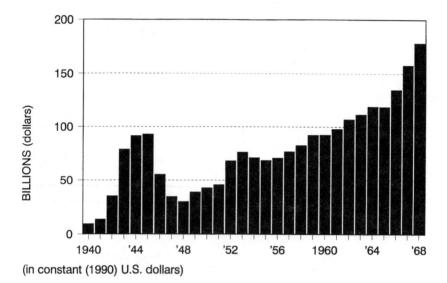

FIGURE 3. Federal Budget: 1940 - 1968

This lengthy time frame for the development of new policies by the departments set the Johnson White House staff into motion. With fewer demands on their time and fewer layers of internal staff to deal with, White House staff were easily able to prepare material for Johnson in substantially less time than their departmental counterparts.

Johnson's reliance on his White House staff for policy-making was furthered by the failure of the departments to fully understand Johnson's expanded social agenda and the emerging programs that he foresaw through Great Society legislation. The Johnson White House staff, many of whom, such as George Reedy, had worked under Johnson during his years in the Senate, were keenly aware of where Johnson wanted to move the administration. They were better positioned than departmental staff to forge the programs that Johnson envisioned.

There are no simple explanations for why Johnson and his successors turned inward to their White House staffs for policy advice. There is only a series of small problems that became one large problem. Another one of these small problems that Johnson faced was the Cabinet's own dissatisfaction with their treatment by the president. As Johnson began to rely more heavily on his White House staff and to reduce his communication with Cabinet members, a backlash emerged. That backlash was a movement by Cabinet officers away from the president to the security of their own departments. Unlike the president, the departmental staff showed great reverence for their secretary. Cabinet officers stayed away from the White House, where they were relegated to dealing with White House staff rather than the president, and chose to work within their own power centers.

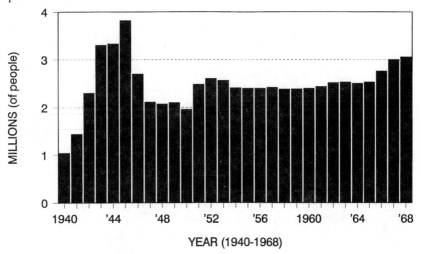

FIGURE 4. Civilian Federal Government Employees, 1940 - 1968

Still another factor that hurt White House–Cabinet relations during the Johnson era was the lack of direction that Johnson gave his Cabinet officers during and following the 1964 election. He did not establish a clear agenda for each of the departments, but rather established a broad agenda for the administration as a whole. This was due to the nature of the presidential election system, which requires candidates to skirt most issues for fear of alienating any segment of the electorate. The 1964 Goldwater-Johnson election was a one-issue campaign focusing on the Vietnam war and communism in general. As a result, Cabinet officers filled the vacuum in policy direction from the campaign and moved in their own direction on policy matters. These directions often proved at odds with where Johnson wanted to go.

This trend has continued. Presidential elections tend to skirt most issues of importance for fear of alienating any major sector of the electorate. As one Nixon aide commented on the 1968 Humphrey-Nixon campaign, "Beyond the Vietnam War and unemployment, what was the 1968 campaign about?" Most members of the electorate would be hard pressed to name any of the issues that the 1984 Mondale-Reagan or 1988 Dukakis-Bush campaigns involved. Even the 1992 Bush-Clinton election focused around the broad issues of change and economic recovery. Unemployment and defense spending tend to be the dominant issues in any campaign, leaving newly appointed cabinet officers the difficult task of preparing an agenda for their departments with little or no knowledge of what the president's position is. The classic election call for change has usually left cabinet officers broad discretion in their approach to policy development.

Creation of Cabinet Government:
The Cabinet Returns as the President's Chief Policy Advisors

Although Lyndon Johnson had used the White House staff as a major part of his policy-making structure, Richard Nixon saw Johnson's structure as riddled with disadvantages. <u>Nixon sought to reduce the role of the White House staff in policy-making and return to a system in which Cabinet officers were the president's chief policy advisors.</u>

One of the most serious problems that Nixon saw with Johnson's structure was the inability of the enlarged White House staff to build the support necessary for their policy initiatives. The policies developed in the White House had generally not taken into consideration the problems of legislative support or how the policy could be implemented in the field. White House staff often had the technical skills to put the program together, but lacked the expertise to mold a sellable program to Congress and to constituents.

Ironically, one of the major reasons Johnson had turned to his White House staff was his concern that departmental policy proposals did not address presidential needs. Yet, once the White House staff became responsible for policy matters, they failed to address the needs of Congress and the departments.

Nixon also realized, perhaps from his eight years in the Eisenhower administration, that Cabinet officers have to be constantly supported by the president. Unless Cabinet officers view themselves as part of the decision-making process, they will revert inward to their departments. In its study of presidential management of the executive branch, the National Academy of Public Administration cited the importance of agency heads remaining an integral part of the policy-making process. The study recommended:

> Agency heads. . . must be at the center of the flow of information and advice from the constituent units of their agency to the Executive Office. If any agency head is not in such as position, his authority and effectiveness will be quickly eroded and his or her ability to represent the President's program rapidly destroyed.[49]

The White House that Lyndon Johnson left in 1969 was completely restructured from the one he had taken over in 1963. In six years, Johnson had built a minibureaucracy in the White House. But as Jack Valenti of the Johnson White House noted, it was a bureaucracy "crusted with official barnacles," which had the same problems as the departmental bureaucracies.[50]

Nixon wanted to return to the streamlined White House staff, whose role was to advise him on departmental recommendations, not to develop those recommendations. During the 1968 campaign one of the central themes of the Nixon campaign was for a return to "Cabinet Government," as Nixon called it, and to reduce the power that the White House staff had gained under Johnson.

The Roller Coaster Ride of the Cabinet

Although Nixon did reduce the power of the White House staff at the beginning of his administration, he very quickly reversed his decision and returned to the Johnson system of a White House centered policy-making system. The Cabinet lost power throughout the Nixon administration.

This was a trend that continued throughout successive administrations. Presidents entered office committed to reducing the power of the White House staff, yet once in office could not maintain that commitment. White House staffs have gained in size, stature, and responsibility in every administration since Johnson.

Each of the six presidents that followed Lyndon Johnson (Nixon, Ford, Carter, Reagan, Bush, and Clinton) had a different experience with their Cabinet–White House relationships. Nixon and Carter felt their Cabinet officers had been coopted by their departments; Ford saw his Cabinet officers as lacking any understanding of his priorities; Reagan saw his Cabinet officers as simply program managers. In each case, the president moved the primary responsibility for policy development into the White House after trying a Cabinet based policy structure. While their experiences are somewhat different, the result was the same. The White House controlled policy development and became the dominant player in the administration's policy process. This is a trend that is continuing in current administrations, with little chance that it will subside.

To quote from Clinton Rossiter in his classic study of the presidency, "The President needs advice."[51] The debate over White House–Cabinet relations centers on the course of that advice. Where does the president draw the line as to which policies are most appropriate to White House development and which to Cabinet development? What is the advisory role of the modern Cabinet? What is the advisory role of the modern White House staff? Can there be powersharing between the two?

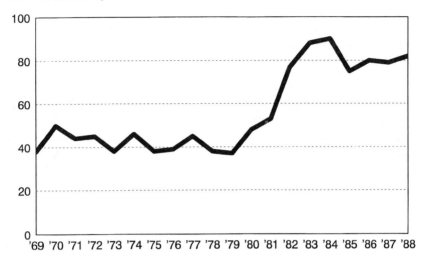

FIGURE 5. Total Senior White House Staff (1969 - 88)

THREE

THE NIXON YEARS

Richard Nixon, who had trained for the presidency during his eight years under Dwight Eisenhower, was finally elected president on his second try in 1968. After losing to John F. Kennedy in a bitter election in 1960, Nixon spent the following eight years expanding his knowledge of the presidency. He studied not only the issues, but the structure of the presidency itself.

When he finally took over the nation's highest office, Nixon had a clear sense of how he wanted to structure his advisory system. Throughout the 1968 presidential campaign and the postelection transition period, he had consistently pledged an expanded role for his Cabinet. The Cabinet would have far greater decision-making responsibilities than it had during either the Kennedy or Johnson administrations. He pledged that the Cabinet rather than the White House staff would be both coach and quarterback in the policy development system. His commitment was so ardent that he used the phrase Cabinet Government during the campaign to describe his return to a strong Cabinet.

THE CONCEPT OF CABINET GOVERNMENT

Nixon kept his promise for a strong Cabinet by directing his newly appointed White House staff to maintain a supporting not a policy-making role. Each member of the White House staff was repeatedly told that their role was simply to coordinate and facilitate departmental initiatives. A wonderful illustration of the enthusiasm that Nixon had for the new system was a press release issued soon after the inauguration.[1] The release promised that Nixon would not permit "empire building" within the White House, as there had been, by implication, in the Johnson White House. And the White House staff would not play a policy-making role.

At the heart of Nixon's plan for a strengthened Cabinet was his plan to free his time to concentrate on foreign affairs. Nixon saw a Cabinet-based policy system as the perfect means to delegate responsibility out of the White House for domestic affairs. He was fully convinced that his Cabinet officers could carry out his plans to phase out a multitude of Great Society programs. He did not view the process as creative, simply as administrative.

The primary role of the Nixon White House staff was not to make policy decisions but to ensure that administrative and policy decisions were handled at the departmental level. Firmly committed to decentralizing the policy process, Nixon noted:

> I felt that the matters brought before a President for decisions should be only those that cannot or should not be made at a lower level on the White House staff or by the Cabinet member directly responsible for them. This was a lesson that I had learned directly from Eisenhower, whose staff had too often cluttered his schedule with unimportant events and bothered him with minor problems that rained his time and energy.[2]

H.R. Haldeman mirrored Nixon's concern that policy decisions should be handled at the departmental level and not by White House staff. In a speech given to White House staff a few weeks before the inauguration, Haldeman said: "Our job is not to do the work of government but to get the work out there to where it belongs—out to the Departments. Don't let the work pile up on your desk—get rid of it, get it out to the Departments."[3] The White House staff was intentionally kept small and directed not to become involved in departmental policy-making.[4] The only sizable staff was maintained by the National Security Advisor, Henry Kissinger. Nixon presumed Cabinet officers could make the necessary policy decisions without oversight from the White House—a decision that later proved in error.

SELECTION OF THE CABINET

For Nixon to implement his plan for Cabinet Government, he needed, as he told Theodore H. White, a "competent Cabinet." Cabinet-building therefore became a major focus of the transition team after the 1968 election. But Nixon's cabinet-building strategy ultimately proved to be one of the major problems with Cabinet Government, for his Cabinet members were chosen for their political value rather than for their policy expertise or their loyalty to Richard Nixon.

Because he had captured only a bare majority of votes in the 1968 election (31,785,480 votes to Hubert Humphrey's 31,275,166 votes), Nixon sought to broaden the political base of his administration through his Cabinet. Bipartisan representation, geographic balance, and women and minorities were sought in the Cabinet in the effort to increase the political base.

Seeking Bipartisan Representation

Bipartisan representation was not a new concept, for it had been used in the last five administrations. Presidents Roosevelt, Truman, Eisenhower, Kennedy, and Johnson had each included members of the opposite party in their Cabinets. Franklin Roosevelt appointed two Republicans to his Cabinet, Secretary of War Henry L. Stimson and Secretary of the Navy Frank Knox; Dwight Eisenhower brought in Martin Durkin, a Democrat, as Secretary of Labor; John Kennedy named two Republicans, C. Douglas Dillon as Secretary of the Treasury and Robert McNamara as Secretary of Defense; and Lyndon Johnson appointed Republican John Gardner as Secretary of Health, Education and Welfare.

Nixon, however, was not as successful as his predecessors in achieving political balance. In his brief search for a bipartisan Cabinet, Nixon contacted two Democrats: Hubert Humphrey for Ambassador to the United Nations and Senator Henry Jackson for Secretary of Defense.[5]   Both declined. (Although he considered Daniel Patrick Moynihan as Secretary of Labor, Moynihan was never formally contacted because George Meany, President of the AFL-CIO, objected to Moynihan's lack of administrative experience.) Having been rebuffed by these two at the outset of the search, Nixon stopped seeking Democrats and directed his attentions to Republicans. His reappointment of Walter Washington as mayor of Washington, D.C., was as close as Nixon came to bringing a Democrat into the administration.

Team Players

Having failed to create a bipartisan Cabinet, Nixon focused his attentions on choosing his nominees from within the Republican Party. Wilson Blount, nominated Postmaster General, had raised funds for Nixon's 1960 and 1968 presidential campaigns, and had been a leader in the effort to rebuild the Republican Party in the south.[6] Walter Hickel, the nominee for Interior, was a Republican National Committeeman and strong supporter of Nixon in 1964 and 1968. John Volpe at Transportation had been active in Massachusetts Republican politics for twenty years and won national recognition in 1960 when he became the state's first Italian and first Catholic governor (in the same year that John Kennedy, the Democratic Massachusetts Senator, won the presidency). George Romney, Michigan's vocal governor, tapped to head

Housing and Urban Development, had long been active in both state and national Republican politics, including a 1968 run for the presidency against Nixon. Robert Finch, nominated for Health, Education, and Welfare, had worked for Nixon, first as a Congressman and then as vice president as his administrative assistant, and won election as California's lieutenant governor in 1966. Melvin Laird, the Wisconsin Congressman selected for Defense, had spent six years in the Wisconsin State Senate, sixteen years in Congress, and had held various positions in the Republican organization since 1960. John Mitchell and Maurice Stans[7] were part of the 1968 presidential campaign and William Rogers had been part of the 1960 presidential campaign. Only three members of the Cabinet, David Kennedy, George Shultz, and Clifford Hardin, were not active in party politics or in the 1968 campaign, but each was a Republican.

Seeking Women and Minority Representation

The strategy for Cabinet-building was also designed to enhance the public image of the Cabinet. If possible, Nixon wanted to include women and minorities in the Cabinet. The precedent for including minorities in the Cabinet had been set in 1966 by Lyndon Johnson, who had appointed Robert Weaver to head the newly created Department of Housing and Urban Development.[8] Weaver became the first black to serve as a member of a president's Cabinet. Accordingly, Nixon offered the United Nations' ambassadorship to Senator Edward Brooke, and the Housing and Urban Development stewardship to Whitney Young, Executive Director of the Urban League.[9] Both declined. Rather than further pursue the effort to include blacks in the Cabinet, Nixon attempted to fill sub-Cabinet positions with minorities. Five sub-Cabinet positions went to blacks, with the highest ranking position being that of assistant secretary. They were Samuel Jackson and Samuel Simmons at the Department of Housing and Urban Development; Arthur Fletcher at the Department of Labor; James Farmer at the Department of Health, Education, and Welfare; and Robert Lee as Deputy Postmaster General.[10]

As in the search for Democrats in the Cabinet, the search for minorities was short-lived and never given priority consideration. Clarence Mitchell of the National Association for the Advancement of Colored People (NAACP) commented that, "with few exceptions, the policy of the White House has been to think white first, and merit second."[11]

Women were never seriously considered for Cabinet positions, in spite of Nixon's public statements, but were given preference for other administration positions. Mrs. Ersa H. Poston, director of the New York State Civil Service Commission, was offered and declined the chairmanship of the U.S. Civil Service Commission, with the promise that it would be given Cabinet status.[12] The offer tendered to Ersa Poston was the highest position offered a woman in the Nixon administration.

Nixon's campaign had also included the promise to bring "thinkers" into the administration who "by the power of their intellect and the force of their ideals" would direct the nation's public policy.[13] As part of this promise, Nixon turned to two prominent academicians for his Cabinet, George Shultz and Clifford Hardin.

Nixon's frustration at not being able to bring Democrats, blacks, or women into the Cabinet (because everyone he offered the position to rejected it), led him to focus on achieving geographic balance and mending political fences within his own party.

Each of the four sections of the country was represented in the Nixon Cabinet. The south had one member (Wilton) Blount); the north had four members (William Rogers, John Mitchell, Maurice Stans, and John Volpe); the west had two members (Walter Hickel and Robert Finch); and the midwest had five members (Clifford Hardin, Melvin Laird, George Shultz, George Romney, and David Kennedy). Dominance by the midwest in the Cabinet was predictable, for Nixon had received electoral margins in all but three midwestern states (Minnesota, Michigan, and Missouri). Nixon's lack of support for southerners in the Cabinet reflected his poor showing in the south, where George Wallace had captured five states. Wallace won Arkansas, Louisiana, Mississippi, Alabama, and Georgia for a total of 45 electoral votes.

Nixon's choices for the Cabinet achieved not only general geographic balance, but also followed a pattern of geographic distribution set by recent presidents: the Secretary of Interior came from the west (Walter Hickel); the Secretary of Agriculture came from the midwest (Clifford Hardin); and the Secretaries of Labor and Commerce from the industrialized states (George Shultz and Maurice Stans).

Nixon added George Romney, John Volpe, and Walter Hickel to the Cabinet to placate the liberal wing of the Republican Party, from which he had long been alienated. Nixon's political strength had been in the conservative wing of the Republican Party. The result was a Cabinet chosen for political benefits rather than personal loyalty to Nixon. Nixon did not know many of his Cabinet officers, such as George Shultz, Clifford Hardin, and David Kennedy, and hardly knew many of the others. One nominee, George Romney, had been a political enemy for years.

The Cabinet officers he trusted the most, John Mitchell at the Justice Department, Melvin Laird at Defense, and William Rogers at State, were close political allies of many years whom Nixon trusted explicitly. Unfortunately for the success of Cabinet Government, Nixon simply did not know or trust the majority of his Cabinet officers, but he continued to believe that Cabinet Government could work.

SELECTION OF WHITE HOUSE STAFF

After focusing on the Cabinet selection process, Nixon turned to selecting his White House staff. His plan called for a small hierarchical staff with a few key advisors reporting directly to him and the remaining members of the staff reporting to a chief of staff. The structure of the White House staff lacked any precise, well-thought-out design.

Since Nixon believed in Cabinet Government and believed in a small, trim White House staff, the selection of the Cabinet, not the selection of the White House staff, dominated his attentions during the transition period. As a result of directing his public and private attentions to the Cabinet selections, Nixon spent relatively little time designing a White House staff structure or choosing the staff. H.R. Haldeman, as the chief of staff, was responsible for developing that design once in office. Nixon believed he needed only three people for major roles in the White House, since policy development would be focused in the departments. These three were a foreign affairs advisor, a domestic affairs advisor, and a chief of staff.

For the foreign affairs position he chose Henry Kissinger; domestic responsibilities were split between Daniel Patrick Moynihan and Arthur Burns; and H.R. Haldeman was assigned "operations and administration." Added to the senior staff were Bryce Harlow for Congressional relations, John Ehrlichman as Counsel to the President, and Herbert Klein to coordinate public information. The personnel choices, their titles, salaries, and responsibilities below the senior staff level were left to Haldeman. Of the seven senior staff, Haldeman was accorded the status of first among equals. All appointments to see Nixon had to be approved by Haldeman, and all material that Nixon was given during meetings had to be first shown to Haldeman.

Domestic policy responsibilities were split between Daniel Patrick Moynihan and Arthur Burns. Moynihan, a Democrat active in party affairs, had been a senior official in both the Kennedy and Johnson administrations. Although Nixon and Moynihan had not met prior to Moynihan's interview for the White House position, Nixon was familiar with Moynihan's articles on welfare reform. As director of the Harvard–Massachusetts Institute of Technology Joint Center for Urban Studies, Moynihan had written extensively on urban problems, particularly the national welfare system

Martin Anderson, Arthur Burns's White House assistant, later described Moynihan as follows, which in large part explained Moynihan's appeal to Nixon:

He had great persuasive resources. In the sea of dark gray and blue that surrounded Nixon, Moynihan, in his cream-colored suit and red bow tie, gleamed like a playful porpoise. He was a charming Irish rogue, a delightful dinner companion, a fascinating teller of tales. His presence lighted the gloom of national policy deliberations, and even his opponents liked to have him around.[14]

Equally important, however, to his personal appeal, Moynihan shared Nixon's approach to decentralization of federal programs and to a major reform of the welfare state. They were both passionately committed to restructuring the way government did business.

Sharing domestic responsibilities with Moynihan was Arthur Burns, chairman of the Council of Economic Advisers during the Eisenhower administration. Nixon viewed Burns's appointment as a "conservative counterweight" to Moynihan.[15]

Nixon's choice of Henry Kissinger for his foreign policy adviser resembled his choice of Daniel Patrick Moynihan on the domestic side. Nixon had read Kissinger's books, including *Nuclear Weapons and Foreign Policy,* and reviewed material covered in his course at Harvard on national security policy. Kissinger and Nixon had not been friends prior to the election nor had they been politically associated. Ironically, Kissinger was a supporter of Nelson Rockefeller, with whom he had been continuously associated since Rockefeller's 1955 appointment as Eisenhower's Special Assistant for National Security. Kissinger had worked for Rockefeller during the 1968 presidential campaign when Rockefeller challenged Nixon's candidacy.

In addition to the three major policy advisors on the staff, Nixon created four administrative positions within the White House. For each of these four positions he chose either a member of the campaign staff or a campaign advisor.

H.R. Haldeman, Nixon's 1968 campaign manager, was appointed chief of staff. Haldeman had worked with Nixon in every campaign since 1956, although had never resigned his position as vice president of the J. Walter Thompson advertising agency in Los Angeles. Haldeman in turn recruited John Ehrlichman, a college friend from the University of California at Los Angeles (UCLA), for the 1960 presidential campaign. Ehrlichman worked in every subsequent campaign, although he too maintained a separate career with his zoning law practice in Seattle. Once in the White House, Nixon appointed Ehrlichman to the position of Counsel to the President.

Another longtime political associate of Nixon was Herbert Klein, press secretary in each of Nixon's seven campaigns. Throughout this twenty-year span, Klein continued as a newspaper reporter. Not until Nixon won his presidential bid did Klein relinquish his newspaper position for the White House position of Director of Communications. The position of Congressional Liaison went to Bryce Harlow, a lobbyist for Procter and Gamble and former

Congressional Liaison during the Eisenhower administration.   Although
Harlow worked only briefly in the Nixon presidential campaign, he served as
Nixon's political confidante.[16]   Harlow had also secured Eisenhower's
endorsement of Nixon during the campaign.

CREATING AN ORGANIZATIONAL STRUCTURE FOR A STRENGTHENED CABINET

Once Nixon had selected his Cabinet and White House staff and had
moved into the White House, he set in motion the organizational structure for
a strengthened Cabinet.   Nixon wanted a system that gave the Cabinet broad
guidelines from the White House but did not seek to offer specific policy proposals: "I . . . plan a reorganized and strengthened Cabinet. . . . The President's
chief function is to lead, not to administer; it is not to oversee every detail but
to put the right people in charge."[17]

Foreign affairs was a different story, for Nixon sought to place primary
responsibility with the National Security Advisor and his staff rather than with
the departments.   Domestic policy, however, was to remain primarily Cabinet-
based.

Departmental Independence from the White House

When he introduced his Cabinet to the American public in a national
television presentation, he again firmly stated his support for a strong Cabinet:

> I don't want a Cabinet of "yes" men and I don't think you want a
> Cabinet of "yes" men.   Every man in the Cabinet will be urged to speak
> out in the Cabinet and within the administration on all the great issues
> so that decisions we will make will be the best decisions we can possi-
> bly reach.[18]

Two days after his inauguration Nixon held his first Cabinet meeting to
discuss his view of Cabinet Government.   In particular he discussed the
Cabinet's role in departmental management, including personnel decisions
and policy determination.[19]   He also reviewed his four-part strategy for the
implementation of Cabinet Government:

1.   The Cabinet would meet monthly to share advice and to "make certain we
     are doing the right thing for America and Americans know what we are
     doing."
2.   The Cabinet would function in subcommittees that would meet more fre-

quently than the full Cabinet, with each subcommittee having its own staff and each subcommittee acting on a problem-solving basis.

3. Cabinet members were to be deputy presidents in their own departments, and they would run their own shows and refer only key problems to the president.

4. Cabinet members could reach the president directly when needed.[20]

The strategy was clearly designed to give Cabinet officers a free hand in their own departments without White House staff overseeing every decision. Cabinet officers were free to hire staff without White House clearance and to make programmatic decisions without White House clearance. Most importantly, when a Cabinet member wanted to speak with the president, he could. There would be no chain of command in the White House that a Cabinet member would have to go through in order to talk to the president.

The system that Nixon developed to foster a strengthened Cabinet based policy development system included three key structures that brought the cabinet directly into the policy-making process: cabinet committees, executive directives, and a cabinet secretariat. The most important mechanism of the three was the Urban Affairs Council, which created a series of cabinet committees under the general guidance of the White House.

The Urban Affairs Council

As Nixon promised when he defined his strategy for Cabinet Government, Cabinet committees were created to manage policy development for domestic and economic issues. Created by executive order on January 23, 1969, the Urban Affairs Council was designed to develop a national urban policy and to work with the Cabinet on problems primarily related to the inner city, such as crime, housing, and welfare.[21] The Urban Affairs Council operated within the White House under the direction of Nixon's domestic policy advisor, Daniel Patrick Moynihan. Moynihan was given the title Assistant to the President for Urban Affairs.

Although Moynihan focused on urban issues, the problems of the rural poor were not lost in the White House. Many of the same problems, such as poverty and welfare, affected rural America to the same degree as urban America. The goals of the Urban Affairs Council included broad solutions to these problems, solutions that affected both rural and urban America.

Moynihan's concern for poverty and welfare across all sectors of America stemmed not only from his academic research, but from a national effort toward breaking the poverty cycle. As early as 1963, the Council of Economic Advisers issued a staff memorandum, "Program for a Concerted Assault on Poverty," which addressed the need for a coordinated attack to break the cycle of poverty.[22] This working paper was operationalized by a task force assigned to develop specific recommendations for the president in dealing with poverty. Moynihan was named to the task force and subsequently developed programs for job creation in all sectors, both rural and urban, of the economy. His participation in this task force heightened his concern for poverty and particularly rural poverty in the south and Appalachia.

Although the White House focused its efforts on managing urban issues, as a direct result of urban rioting in the mid and late-1960s, Moynihan never lost sight of the goal of the Urban Affairs Council, which was to break the poverty cycle throughout the nation without regard to geography.

Ten committees were subsequently formed within the Urban Affairs Council, each with several cabinet members assigned to them. These committees oversaw a broad spectrum of issues. They were officially referred to as the committee on:

1. The Future of the Poverty Program
2. The Future of the Model Cities Program
3. Minority Business Enterprise
4. Welfare
5. Crime
6. Voluntary Action
7. Internal Migration
8. Surplus Food and Nutrition
9. Mass Transit, and
10. The Transition to Peacetime Economy at the End of the Vietnam War

Membership on the committees was fixed, although most Cabinet members were part of several committees.

Nixon charged the committees with preparing policies as quickly as possible and pledged to meet with the committees regularly. Moynihan quotes Nixon as saying that "the magic time" for changing policies was the first few months of the administration.[23] Accordingly, Nixon wanted the committees to prepare a slate of policy initiatives to be rapidly submitted to Congress.

Although the committees were technically a function of the White House, their primary role was to serve as a coordinating mechanism to bring Cabinet officers together. Staffing for the committees was handled by the departments rather than the White House. Moynihan, who had a very small staff himself, served mainly as the facilitator for the group. On rare occasions, however, Moynihan took a lead role in policy development. The most significant example of Moynihan's direct participation was in the development of the Family Assistance Plan, which became the cornerstone of the administration's welfare reform package. The plan proposed a revised system in which welfare recipients were given minimum annual payments linked to job training or employment. Welfare reform was one of the three key components of the New Federalism, which became Nixon's term to describe the program changes he envisioned under his administration. The other two major changes he saw were manpower training, which would shift job training to the states, and revenue sharing, which would give state and local government a portion of federal tax revenues.

Moynihan limited his role, however, in policy development and gave the Cabinet officers enormous discretion on developing the programmatic goals within their committees. Neither Moynihan nor his staff attempted to lead the Cabinet committees.

Another cabinet committee created to give the Cabinet greater authority in policy-making was the Cabinet Committee on Economic Policy, created in January 1969 by Nixon.[24] Nixon used the Economic Policy Committee to increase the cabinet's participation in the economic policy process. The committee became the coordinating policy mechanism for such issues as tax reform and minimum wage increases. Its mandate was broader than that of any of the committees within the Urban Affairs Council, but its role as presidential counselor in a major policy area was the same.

Executive Directives

In addition to the Urban Affairs Council and the Cabinet Committee on Economic Policy, Nixon sought the advice of individual Cabinet officers on policy issues. In those areas of domestic policy not covered by the established committees, Arthur Burns, Nixon's economic policy advisor, sought policy proposals directly from individual Cabinet members. In general, these were proposals on specific issues that Nixon discussed during the 1968 campaign, but which did not fit into one of the areas covered by the Urban Affairs Council or the Economic Policy Committee. Burns used a mechanism for seeking Cabinet initiatives called executive directives. Executive directives were sent out by Burns to Cabinet officers on a wide range of issues. These were simply letters to Cabinet officers, sent under Nixon's name, which asked for general proposals on such topics as Medicare reform and agricultural reform.[25]

Through these three structures for building the Cabinet into the policy-making process, Nixon had minimized the influence of the White House staff in policy development. The departments remained at the center of the policy process.

Cabinet Meetings

Nixon's strategy for implementing Cabinet Government also included the frequent use of Cabinet meetings to maintain an open line of communication between the Cabinet officers themselves and between the Cabinet and the president.   These biweekly, two-hour meetings on Friday mornings were designed to ensure that each member of the Cabinet was adequately briefed on the major issues at hand. If Cabinet Government were to succeed, each Cabinet member had to be familiar with the wide range of issues facing the administration, not just narrow departmental issues.

The importance of Cabinet meetings was underscored by the creation of the Cabinet Secretariat on the White House staff. The Cabinet Secretary, John Whitaker, was responsible for developing the Cabinet meeting agenda and circulating background papers prepared by the Cabinet for the meeting. Whitaker was directly responsible to the president and did not report to the chief of staff. This was a position created in the Eisenhower administration but dormant in the Kennedy and Johnson administrations. Nixon wanted to use not only the policy system that Eisenhower had created but the policy structure as well.

National Security Council

A reliance on the Cabinet for policy development, though, broke down in the foreign affairs arena. In contrast to the plan for building a strong Cabinet to manage domestic policy, Nixon sought to centralize foreign policy development in the White House. When William Rogers was offered the job as Secretary of State, he did so with the clear understanding that foreign affairs would be managed by the White House. According to Rogers:

> I was prepared to play a subordinate role. I recognized that he [Nixon] wanted to be his own foreign policy leader and did not want others to share that role. After all, the man who ran for office and won deserves to make his own decisions. I knew that Nixon would be the principal actor and when Kissinger came along, I recognized that he would be a very valuable asset to the presidency.[26]

To build a strong White House foreign policy staff, Nixon consolidated the positions of Special Assistant for National Security Affairs and Director of the National Security Council. Henry Kissinger was given both assignments with the title of Assistant to the President for National Security. Nixon gave Kissinger the authority to develop and coordinate the administration's major foreign policy decisions from the White House. Kissinger's authority dramatically reduced the power of the Secretary of State and the Secretary of Defense, who had traditionally held the two most powerful positions in the administration.

The structure that Nixon set in motion in January 1969 was one that gave the domestic Cabinet primary responsibility for policy development.

They were given nearly a free rein to develop legislative packages for the administration. The only parameters of these legislative initiatives were that they meet the general guidelines established by Moynihan and Burns. The White House staff did not try to influence the direction taken by individual Cabinet members or Cabinet committees.

POWER MOVES INTO THE WHITE HOUSE

Richard Nixon unquestionably believed that he had carefully planned the organizational structure of his policy-making system to ensure the success of Cabinet Government. But the structure failed. By November 1969, barely ten months into his term, Nixon began to dismantle the policy-making structure he had created and to shift policy-making authority from the Cabinet to the White House staff. The pendulum of power began to move from the Cabinet into the White House with the staff reorganization of November 4, 1969. Daniel Patrick Moynihan and Arthur Burns were replaced as the president's domestic policy advisors by John Ehrlichman, who was moved from Counsel to the President to the newly created position of Assistant for Domestic Affairs. Moynihan and Burns were given new titles and new responsibilities while Ehrlichman became the president's chief domestic advisor. The move was completed in March 1970 with the creation of the Domestic Council by executive order to formally replace the Urban Affairs Council. Moynihan and Burns resigned from the White House soon after their jobs were changed.

The Domestic Council

The Domestic Council was charged with ensuring that "as much responsibility for policy formation as possible rests with the Cabinet."[27] But the Domestic Council quickly moved away from that charge and began to centralize power in the White House. Responsibility for policy formation was centralized in the Domestic Council staff within the White House.

John Ehrlichman, a Seattle attorney and a key member of Nixon's campaign, revised the manner in which domestic policy was developed. Under Moynihan, the Cabinet met regularly through the Cabinet committees to discuss policy issues. But under Ehrlichman the system was significantly changed. Ehrlichman established a system in which the White House staff worked directly with departmental staff on policy development. With the elimination of the Urban Affairs Council, the Cabinet committee system of policy development was eliminated and Cabinet members were no longer brought together regularly to forge policy initiatives.

Rather than relying on Cabinet committees to develop policy proposals, Ehrlichman established a system composed of White House staff and departmental staff. Cabinet members, however, did not participate in the "project group system," as it was called. These new groups were chaired by members of Ehrlichman's staff rather than departmental staff. Six project groups were initially formed by Ehrlichman: Financial Affairs; Natural Resources; Civil Rights, Youth and Culture; Justice; Urban Affairs; and Welfare and Education.[28] These committees were designed to not only operate differently than had the Urban Affairs Committee, but to cover entirely different subject matter. The focus was much broader under Ehrlichman, an indication of the movement toward centralization of broad policy development in the White House.

Under the reorganization White House staff became the major participants in policy development. The Cabinet was essentially excluded from the policy development process by Ehrlichman's technique of seeking information from lower level departmental staff rather than from the Cabinet officer. Ehrlichman argued that this process allowed the White House staff to "meet with the people in the departments and agencies who actually did the work on the documents that come over."[29]

In addition to their exclusion from the policy development process under the reorganization, Cabinet members were systematically excluded from meeting with Nixon except for Cabinet meetings and rare individual meetings. The meetings that Nixon had with the Urban Affairs Council's subcommittees were ended, as were meetings between Cabinet officers and Nixon on policy matters. Cabinet officers met with Ehrlichman's staff on policy issues. The frequency of Cabinet meetings was also reduced, adding another nail to the coffin of Cabinet Government.

Centralization of domestic policy-making in the White House was finalized when, in a March 12, 1970, message to Congress, Nixon formally created the Domestic Council, charged with "advising the President on the total range of Domestic Policy. . . it will also be charged with integrating the various aspects of domestic policy into a consistent whole."[30] Cabinet members in the Domestic Council were Treasury, Interior, Agriculture, Commerce, Labor, HEW, HUD, Transportation, and the Attorney General. In essence, the Domestic Council was to take control of the domestic policy process and to move policy-making out of the control of the departments.

Staffing Increases for the Domestic Council

Nixon proposed to staff the Domestic Council with fifty professionals, whose director would have the same authority in domestic affairs as the national security advisor had in foreign affairs. This immediately signaled

Nixon's plan to centralize domestic policy as he had with foreign policy. Creation of the Domestic Council and the redesignation of the Budget Bureau as the Office of Management and Budget (OMB) (as the Ash Council recommended) culminated Nixon's 1970 plan to centralize policy-making and management authority within the Executive Office of the President. By 1972 Nixon had further centralized power in the White House by moving all coordination of state and local relations into the Domestic Council.[31] This brought another layer of control into the policy process by the White House.

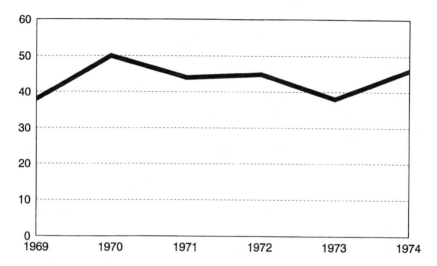

FIGURE 6. Total Senior White House Staff (Nixon)

With the increase in the Domestic Council and OMB staff, Nixon began a massive staffing increase in White House senior staff. The senior staff increased from thirty-nine when Nixon took office in 1969 to over fifty after the first year. That number dropped somewhat after the White House gained greater control over policy-making. The Watergate crisis caused the drop in 1973–74 after the public outcry at the power of the White House staff.

THE FAILURE OF CABINET GOVERNMENT

The rise and fall of Cabinet Government in less than a year was due to a number of problems that Nixon had failed to anticipate in his relations with the Cabinet. Not only did he fail to choose a Cabinet that had his full trust, but he failed to consider the basic political and institutional relationships between the Cabinet, Congress, and constituent groups.

Legislative Success Rate

Perhaps the most striking problem that Nixon faced during his first year in office was his inability to achieve a strong legislative success rate, for which he blamed the Cabinet. Of the 171 requests that the administration made for new legislation, only thirty-five requests, or a dismal 32 per cent, were enacted into law.[32] An even more dismal fact is that during the first quarter of the year, the administration sent only two significant requests to Congress for domestic legislation: reorganization of the Post Office Department and improving safety requirements in coal mines. The major legislative package for the first half of 1969 was not sent to Congress until April and, even then, lacked substantive legislative proposals. The package contained only general areas of policy interest to the administration rather than specific legislative initiatives.

During the second quarter of the year the administration increased the number of requests to Congress, but again they lacked major significance. Among the second-quarter submissions were a request for the Organized Crime Control Act to prosecute organized crime, a request for home rule for the District of Columbia, and a request for an extension of the 10 per cent surtax on income. Forty-one per cent of the administration's legislative submissions in 1969 were made between April and June.[33] None of the requests submitted to Congress were for major policy initiatives and few of the requests were passed during the quarter.

During this second quarter the administration won only one major legislative victory in domestic policy, which involved a six-month extension of the surtax. Nixon's delay in submitting a legislative package can be explained in a number of ways. One explanation is that he failed to develop specific policy goals during the campaign. Most of his speeches give only vague references to specific policies or to implementation strategies. Ronald Randall sums up the problem as follows:

> Richard Nixon had only vague notions of the specific directions that he wanted domestic policy to take. Despite his years in Congress and the vice-presidency and his acquaintance with Republican party workers around the nation, he knew surprisingly little about government in Washington. . . [He was] lacking a clear sense of purpose and specific policies.[34]

Nixon failed to articulate a clear agenda for the administration during the campaign, and provided little direction from which to orient the administration's policies.

The delay in submitting a legislative package to Congress can also be explained by the absence of a detailed party platform from which Nixon could draw. The Republican Party in its eight years out of power had failed to develop a detailed domestic agenda. In contrast, the Democratic Party had taken great pains during the 1950s to prepare a well-defined party platform on domestic initiatives. When John Kennedy won the White House in 1960 after eight years of Republican domination, he had a list of legislative priorities, which the Democratic Party had carefully prepared and refined in its years out of power.[35]

The lack of a well-defined party platform for domestic policy was exacerbated by Nixon's decision to bring Daniel Patrick Moynihan and Arthur Burns into the White House as his domestic policy advisors. Neither had been part of the 1968 presidential campaign nor had they been associated with Nixon prior to the campaign. Nixon had only known Moynihan from his writings on urban poverty and race issues. Burns had been part of the Eisenhower administration with Nixon, but they were not close friends nor did they have a continuing relationship.

As a result, Moynihan and Burns were not prepared during the transition period or in the period immediately following the inauguration to provide substantive guidelines to the Cabinet to develop detailed policy proposals. Neither Moynihan nor Burns had a strong enough relationship with Nixon to comfortably propose policy objectives during the early months of the administration. Both turned away from substantive issues early in the administration and concentrated on developing the organizational mechanisms, such as the Cabinet committees, for the implementation of Cabinet Government.

These problems during the first quarter of 1969 prevented the administration from profiting from the benefits of the traditional honeymoon period with Congress. Cabinet officers were unable to quickly move on policy details without clear guidance on the president's departmental goals. They allowed the policy ideas to emerge from their departments, which proved to be a slow and cumbersome process. It was this very process that had led Lyndon Johnson to centralize policy development in the White House.

However, Nixon's decision to support an unpopular antiballistic missile (ABM) system during the first quarter of the year also was a major stumbling block to a close working relationship with Congress. During March Nixon went on record as supporting an ABM system called the Sentinel, which had been proposed by the Johnson administration and constantly opposed in the Senate during the 1960's.[36] After a major lobbying effort by the administration, the Senate finally passed an authorization for the ABM system by a bare 50-50 vote in mid-1969. The vice president cast the tie-breaking vote.

Nixon's legislative success rate was further set back by his decision to concentrate on international affairs rather than domestic affairs. Within his first six months in office he made two major trips abroad. The first was an eight-day tour in February to meet with NATO allies. The second, five months later, was a wider-ranging tour to discuss the Nixon doctrine.[37]

During his first six months in office, Nixon's problems were compounded as he submerged himself in dealing with America's presence in Vietnam. As he had noted in his April 14 message to Congress, "Peace has been the first priority [of this administration]. It concerns the future of civilization."[38]

He became deeply involved in not only diplomatic decisions, but in military decisions in the war. In early February he ordered B-52 strikes against North Vietnamese troops stationed in Cambodia in order to deter their further moves into South Vietnam. These strikes were the first that the United States had made outside South Vietnam during the war, and thus signaled a major change in U.S. involvement in the war.

Nixon's relations with Congress, which had been strained in March over his decision to support the Sentinel system, further deteriorated when he decided to increase military assistance to South Vietnam. On June 25 the Senate passed the "national commitments resolution," Senate Resolution 85. Passed by an overwhelming 70–16 vote, the resolution expressed Congress's concern that it was being excluded from foreign policy decisions, specifically the commitment of U.S. forces for the defense of a foreign country.

Two days after the national commitments resolution was passed, Nixon again ran into trouble with Congress. Hugh Scott (R-Pa), the powerful Senate minority leader, publicly opposed the administration's policy on school desegregation. Neither the president nor the Secretary of Health, Education and Welfare—Robert Finch—had consulted Congress, including the Republican leadership, before publicly stating their new policy concerning federal funding for school districts.

The Department of Health, Education and Welfare took the position that federal funds should be cut off to any school district that failed to show progress in eliminating segregation. Scott argued that such action would jeopardize federal funding for numerous school districts, including those in his home state of Pennsylvania. According to the original guidelines, only dual-district school districts were included in the HEW policy, such as were prominent in many southern states. Scott objected to the change in policy that included all school districts, not just the originally targeted southern dual-districts. Scott's concern was that the de facto segregation, which existed in many urban school districts, such as Philadelphia and Pittsburgh, would be affected by the new HEW regulations. Scott, and many of his colleagues, argued that the policy change should be slowly phased into the funding formula, not suddenly dropped on the school districts in a complete change of position. The loss of Scott's support on the HEW issue barely six months into the administration had lasting consequences on executive-legislative relations.

Nixon's problems with Congress continued with the introduction of the Postal Reform Bill. The administration again failed to consult with members of Congress, particularly the Republican leadership, prior to the formal legislative request. The bill, which changed the post office department from an executive agency to a quasi-public corporation, removed the requirement that postmasters be subject to Senate confirmation. Congress thus lost a cherished source of patronage.

In spite of his years in Congress and the vice presidency, Nixon had not mastered the political nuances of the legislative process, nor had he coached his Cabinet officers in the etiquette of executive-legislative relations. To antagonize Republican Party leaders in Congress barely six months into the administration was a foolhardy move, and one that came back to haunt Nixon.

The Cabinet and Congress

The absence of a well-defined legislative agenda from the president and of a White House staff prepared to quickly develop such an agenda greatly hampered the Cabinet's ability to capitalize on the first-quarter honeymoon period between the Congress and the president.

But the Cabinet's relationship with Congress was further weakened by their own inability to mobilize constituencies on behalf of departmental programs. In an analysis of the Nixon administration's relations with Congress, Roger Davidson noted that the failure of the Nixon administration to build coalitions "was in a very real sense the measure of its shortcomings."[39]

The battle over mass transit funding in 1969 was a prime example of the administration's inability to mobilize the requisite political support for legislation. On August 7, 1969, Nixon sent to Congress a proposal for urban mass transit legislation providing for a twelve-year, $10 billion program for capital investments and research for mass transit systems. The bill was immediately opposed by cities, transit authorities, and a host of others who sought a revised bill that would allow funding from a trust fund rather than from annual appropriations. Trust funds, such as the highway trust fund, provided for a more stable source of funding than annual appropriations.

In spite of a major effort by John Volpe, Secretary of Transportation, to gain support for the administration's proposal, the administration was unable to garner a significant constituency on behalf of the matching grant program. The only major group to support the proposal was the National Governors' Conference, which believed that an extended battle over the trust fund would jeopardize the entire mass transit program and hold up funding indefinitely.

The bill provided for the Department of Transportation to spend $3.1 billion for the first year of the program, rather than for $3.1 billion to be spent for the entire five-year authorization period, as the administration had requested. This was a major blow to Nixon's efforts to reduce federal spending and to cut the rate of inflation. The administration was therefore given more funding than it had sought, and funding in a different time frame than it had sought. Although the Secretary of Transportation kept the mass transit fund legislation from being passed, he was unable to keep the administration's proposals from undergoing major amendments.

Another problem that weakened the Cabinet's relationship with Congress was a lack of sensitivity to the political needs of members of Congress, particularly the Republican members. This first became of major importance in March 1969 when the Secretary of Labor, George Shultz, announced that the Department of Labor intended to close fifty-nine Job Corps centers in order to save the federal government $100 million annually. This was part of Nixon's plan to systematically cut the federal budget, particularly social programs that had been created as part of the Great Society legislation.

Shultz, however, failed to consult with any members of Congress prior to the official announcement. Senator Jesse Helms (R-N.C.), a conservative who often supported administration policies, was particularly angered by the proposal to cut the Job Corps center near Brevard, North Carolina, in the heart of one of his state's most depressed areas. Helms blocked the closings.

Soon after the Job Corps decision, Nixon sent a revised message to Congress that cut domestic expenditures while, at the same time, increased defense expenditures. Again, the administration made little attempt to consult with Congress prior to the official release of the legislative request. Congress subsequently reacted by cutting $5.6 billion from defense, increasing social security benefits by 15 per cent, and adding $600 million to water control projects that the administration had not requested.

These are but a few examples of the problems that the Cabinet had with Congress, but they are indicative of the larger problem in executive-legislative relations. Many members of the Cabinet failed to privately work with members of Congress on administration proposals. This not only upset political egos in Congress, but closed the door on opportunities to work out conflicts between executive and legislative positions before critical votes were taken.

The Cabinet and the Bureaucracy

Nixon's decision to restructure his policy-making system was, in addition to these other points, due to his dissatisfaction with the Cabinet's relationship with the bureaucracy. Nixon was firmly convinced that the Cabinet had been captured by the bureaucracy, which he perceived to be basically Democratic and liberally oriented.[40] He fervently believed that the bureaucracy was ideologically opposed to the conservative goals of his administration.

Nixon was particularly critical of the career staff in the domestic agencies that were charged with implementing the Great Society programs passed during the Johnson administration. "The Great Society was created by liberal academics and bureaucrats," he said, "steeped in the myths of the New Deal."[41] He continued by stating that, "At the beginning of my second term, Congress, the bureaucracy, and the media were still working in concert to maintain the ideas and ideology of the traditional liberal establishment."[42]

Nixon's perception that the Cabinet had been captured by the bureaucracy was bolstered by the decision by most Cabinet officers to retain sub-Cabinet officials from the Johnson administration. Rather than recruit new personnel, many Cabinet officers appointed career staff to senior positions within their departments. Nixon had given the Cabinet officers complete control over their personnel decisions in the first Cabinet meeting as part of his plan for Cabinet Government, but assumed that Cabinet officers would bring into the administration their own colleagues rather than keep existing staff.

Nixon's distrust of the bureaucracy was the subject of several discussions by members of his staff after they had left office. Richard Nathan, assistant director of the Office of Management and Budget from 1969 to 1971, states that Nixon believed "the White House was surrounded" by bureaucratic interests opposed to the president's program.[43] H.R. Haldeman, Nixon's chief of staff, quotes Nixon as condemning the HEW staff, "HEW, the whole damn bunch," for their liberal orientation. Haldeman also quotes Nixon's statements expressing dissatisfaction with the Pentagon career staff, " . . . the people who ran the Pentagon before are still running the Goddamn Pentagon."[44]

Examples of career staff who were promoted to senior departmental positions were evident across the board. Alexis Johnson, for example, who was a career diplomat in both the Kennedy and Johnson administrations, was appointed by William Rogers to the position of Undersecretary of State for Political Affairs. Henry Petersen, who had been with the Department of Justice since 1951, was appointed by John Mitchell to head the Criminal Division. In the Department of Health, Education and Welfare, Robert Finch retained Mary Switzer, director of the Social and Rehabilitation Service, and Stephen Simonds, director of the Assistance Payment Administration, and recruited liberal (rather than conservative) Republicans to other senior positions.[45]

Although Nixon was unhappy with such appointments, he allowed his Cabinet officers the freedom to build their own staffs as part of his commitment to Cabinet Government. Within a few months, however, Nixon began to believe that the policies emanating from the departments were not in line with presidential goals. He blamed the sub-Cabinet officials and the career staff, whom he believed to be unsympathetic to conservative goals, for dominating the policy development process.[46] The departments tended to provide Nixon with policy advice that was more liberal than he sought.

Typical of this advice was a policy position which the Department of Health, Education and Welfare recommended to Nixon involving regulations that governed enforcement of the 1964 Civil Rights Act. Under the 1964 Civil

Rights Act, HEW was responsible for developing procedures for school districts that failed to move toward ending segregation. In 1966 HEW revised its guidelines and began vigorous enforcement of the law. By 1969 many school districts had complied with as much as they either could or wanted to, and were on the brink of shutting down. James Allen, Assistant Secretary of Education, favored adhering to the 1966 guidelines, a decision that Finch supported.

However, Finch was forced by Nixon to withdraw his support for the enforcement after Attorney General John Mitchell convinced Nixon that southerners would turn against the administration in the next election if the guidelines were strictly enforced. In August 1969 the Department of Health, Education and Welfare formally reversed its 1966 position and went to the Supreme Court to seek a stay on enforcement of departmental regulations.

To Nixon, cases such as this meant that the Cabinet officers had been captured by the bureaucracy. To the Cabinet, it meant that policies developed within their departments were cognizant of not only presidential goals but legislative intent and constituent pressures. This was particularly true in the Department of Health, Education and Welfare and the Department of Housing and Urban Development. Both displayed enormous dedication to their lead role in developing and implementing the Great Society legislation passed during the late 1960s.[47] These departments were reluctant to cut programs or redirect existing priorities just as they were beginning to implement the programs they had been charged with developing.

Policy Decisions by the Cabinet

During this first year, Nixon became increasingly disenchanted with the policy decisions of his Cabinet officers. Many of these decisions he blamed on the influence of the career bureaucracy, but many he blamed on the Cabinet officers themselves.

A prime example was the lobbying effort by Secretary of Housing and Urban Development George Romney for increased funding for the Model Cities Program. The Model Cities Program had been created in 1966 by Congress as a six-year demonstration project to eliminate housing blight in target cities. It had been one of the first major pieces of legislation within the Department of Housing and Urban Development, created by Congress the previous year.

The bill was described by President Johnson as the federal government's most comprehensive effort to attack poverty within the cities. Johnson sought to use the Model Cities Program as a major test of the federal government's ability to solve the problems of the poor within the inner cities. Romney, a former governor of Michigan, knew firsthand the problems of urban poverty and decaying housing. He described the program as "undeveloped and incomplete" soon after taking the helm of HUD, and sought to increase the administration's funding request for Model Cities.[48] Nixon, however, who called the program "an abomination" was adamantly opposed to any funding increase. Romney, who had discussed the program with Nixon and knew of his objections, still supported funding increases and lobbied Congress for their support. Over Romney's objections, Nixon announced a $215 million cut in the Model Cities program on October 1, 1969.[49]

Walter Hickel, Secretary of the Interior, similarly lost favor with Nixon because of departmental action during his first year in office. After an oil spill off the coast of Santa Barbara, California, by an off-shore drilling rig, Hickel tightened the restrictions for granting leases on federally owned properties. Nixon opposed the sanctions, and Hickel eventually eased them. However, several months later, Hickel again moved in a direction that Nixon opposed. In spite of Nixon's campaign pledge to increase the number of airports nationwide, Hickel fought construction of a major jetport in the Florida Everglades. A strong conservationist, Hickel feared the jetport would irreversibly damage the south Florida environment. In August 1969 the Department of Transportation introduced a major piece of legislation for airport development, which would be funded through a ten-year, $5 billion development program. Hickel succeeded in keeping the Everglades jetport from the development list because of its failure to meet environmental standards. Nixon could not block the decision by Transportation without the issue becoming a national nightmare, but Walter Hickel became persona non grata around the White House.[50]

The White House Domestic Policy Staff

The failure of Cabinet Government, however, cannot be totally blamed on the Cabinet's lack of direction from the president or from their own shortcomings. The White House staff failed to develop a general policy outline for the Cabinet to build on during the early months of the administration.

Throughout the first nine months of 1969 Nixon's two domestic policy advisors constantly disagreed on policy decision. Their most pronounced disagreement involved the development of the Family Assistance Plan (FAP) in the Urban Affairs Council. The FAP was an ambitious plan to overhaul the welfare system's basic cash assistance program. Moynihan had studied the problem of welfare at MIT and written extensively on the issue. Nixon, who had read Moynihan's works, agreed with his assessment of the welfare problem and gave Moynihan his full support in devising a new welfare program.

But Arthur Burns was unyielding in his opposition to Moynihan's Family Assistance Plan. Burns argued that the guaranteed income that the

FAP proposed would "have a detrimental effect on the productive capacity of the American people."[51] Burns lobbied HEW to oppose the plan, as he did members of Congress. This, of course, sent conflicting messages to the Cabinet officers on what the president actually wanted.

Burns opposed Moynihan on other issues as well, including legislation to extend funding for the Office of Economic Opportunity. Moynihan won the contest and the request was included in Nixon's August 8, 1969, address to the nation on his domestic priorities. Burns also had a series of conflicts with other members of the White House staff, including Paul McCracken, chairman of the Council of Economic Advisers. McCracken, who supported an economic program that dealt slowly with inflation, believed that in light of a simultaneously rising unemployment rate and inflation, the administration's economic policy should be a slow cut in spending. This, McCracken hoped, would minimize any jump in the unemployment rate. McCracken, in contrast to Burns, believed that inflation was the more serious of the two problems for the administration to address. Nixon supported McCracken's proposals over those of Burns, thus fueling internal problems of the White House staff.

The failure of Moynihan and Burns to gain control of the policy process resulted in a major overhaul of White House decision structures. By the second year of the administration, the Cabinet's role in policy-making had been minimized and John Ehrlichman's Domestic Council had gained control over the major policy initiatives that emerged within the administration. While Moynihan and Burns had centered their energies on giving broad direction to the Cabinet, Ehrlichman established very specific policy areas for departments to focus on. Ehrlichman used his staff to work directly with agency staff in the formulation of policy proposals to ensure consistency with White House objectives. The Cabinet Secretary, given great prominence in the first year of the administration and listed by the White House as a senior staff position, was completely dropped from future staffing lists. (See Appendix 1 for White House staffing lists.)

The Cabinet's decreasing role in policy development was matched by the increasing role of the entire Executive Office of the President (EOP) during the second year of the administration. The number of personnel within the EOP rose from 1,298 in 1969 to 1,788 in 1971, a 50 per cent increase. During the same period, Nixon increased the EOP budget from $31 million to $45 million.[52]

Nixon's drive to centralize policy-making in the White House and to gain greater control over the departmental management process included a brief effort to reorganize the cabinet along functional lines. In early 1973, shortly before his inauguration, Nixon sought reorganization authority from Congress to reorganize the existing seven departments into four superdepartments (Human Resources, Community Development, Natural Resources, and

Economic Affairs). This proposal stemmed from a series of proposals that the president's Advisory Council on Executive Organization, chaired by Roy Ash and better known as the Ash Council, made in late 1969. Among the Ash Council's recommendations were creation of the Domestic Council in the White House and the restructuring of the Bureau of the Budget to the Office of Management and Budget.[53] Both these changes were made in March 1970.

While Nixon moved quickly on the proposal to reorganize the Executive Office, he lingered for three more years on the proposal to reorganize the Cabinet. The proposal set forth by Nixon in 1973 called for a supercabinet, composed of new supercabinet secretaries (Weinberger, human resources; Lynn, community development; Butz, natural resources; and Shultz, economic affairs). They would have the dual responsibility of serving both as department heads and also as presidential counselors. Essentially, they would merge the role of presidential advisor with that of departmental secretary.

This proposal lacked support from the remaining department heads, the White House staff, and, most importantly, Congress. Congress had no interest in this proposal, for it would restructure long-standing committee jurisdictions and disrupt existing relations with both constituent and bureaucratic interests.[54] The Democratically controlled Congress was also in no hurry to support any proposal from the Nixon White House. As a result of the total lack of support, the proposal died. Watergate sealed its fate as all White House initiatives began to be spurned by Congress.

As a further means of minimizing the role of the departments in policy-making, Nixon increased the number of advisory committees within the White House and the size of budgets of existing White House advisory groups. For example, the Special Representative for Trade Negotiations on the EOP staff went from a budget of $481,000 and a staff of twenty-eight in 1969 to a budget of $757,000 and a staff of thirty- five in 1971. Nixon sought to centralize his advisory network and keep his Cabinet officers as far away as possible from policy development. Their role became one of implementation, and even that role Nixon eventually tried to mitigate with the movement toward the "administrative presidency." During Nixon's second term, H.R. Haldeman's chief lieutenant, Jeb Stuart Magruder, was placed in charge of a project to staff noncivil service policy positions within the departments using White House approved staff.

WATERGATE: THE WHITE HOUSE LOSES CONTROL

The White House centralized system that Nixon finally turned to as a means of managing his domestic policy process lasted for most of the administration. By 1973 Nixon was moving toward greater centralization of power in the White House and an even further reduced role for the Cabinet in policy development.

But when the Watergate scandal of the 1972 election began to unravel, the White House structure for policy development also unraveled. Both Ehrlichman and Haldeman resigned when charges of criminal conspiracy emerged as a result of the Watergate break-in of the Democratic National Committee. The House of Representatives began nationally televised hearings on Nixon's impeachment. Nixon became consumed with protecting himself from charges and ultimately resigned as an inevitable impeachment drew closer.

By mid-1974, when Nixon finally did resign, the White House had lost control over policy-making as it turned all its attentions on the impeachment hearings. The departments again controlled the policy process.

The Nixon administration had gone full circle, beginning with a strong Cabinet, moving to a strong White House staff, and ending with neither the Cabinet nor the White House staff fully in control. Ironically, the problems that Richard Nixon had seen with Johnson's centralized policy-making structure ultimately brought him down.

CONCLUSION: THE PARADOX OF THE NIXON YEARS

Throughout his presidency, Richard Nixon tried to be bold. He attempted major revolutions on the domestic front, from revenue-sharing to welfare reform to environmental policy. He had major plans for his second term for changes in federal-state relations by returning powers to state and local governments, for tax reductions, and a balanced budget. His foreign policy was even bolder, including détente with the Soviet Union, arms negotiations, the China initiative, and strong military action against North Vietnam.

His strategy for managing government was equally as bold, including reorganization of the Cabinet and a strengthened White House–Cabinet working relationship through the supercabinet. His management strategy did not neglect the White House staff itself, as he moved to broaden the authority of the White House to guide the administration's overall policy agenda.

Yet in spite of bold and imaginative plans for his administration, plans that had garnered enormous public support by the 1972 election, Richard Nixon lost control of his presidency. The events of Watergate began to dominate his attention throughout the election of 1972 and continued until his resignation in August 1974. Watergate destroyed the Nixon presidency and reduced many of his initiatives to the ashes of their press releases.

Nixon was in the end not the knight carrying forward the Republican agenda, but the criminal, who encouraged illegal wiretaps, covert operations on "White House enemies," and burglaries into the offices of political opponents. His fall from power reduced the Nixon presidency to the history books in which every chapter begins with "Richard Nixon, the only president to resign in disgrace. . . ."

The focus on Watergate and Nixon's resignation, however, should not ignore the influence of the Nixon administration in the structure of White House–Cabinet relations and the emerging power of the White House domestic policy office.

By formally creating the Urban Affairs Council within the White House, and later the Domestic Policy Council, Nixon institutionalized the role of the domestic policy advisor. Nixon's contribution to the evolution of the White House staff was as important as his predecessors, each of whom had expanded on the functional responsibilities of the White House staff.

Nixon's contribution went further than simply institutionalizing a role within the White House for a domestic policy advisor. Nixon created an entire office within the White House with broad policy-making and departmental oversight responsibilities. For the first time, the White House was becoming the centralizing mechanism for major domestic policy development and management. This followed a general thrust in the administration, as evidenced by the Ash Council recommendations, that sought to gain greater management control over departmental activities within the Executive Office. As the White House moved toward greater policy control, the newly established Office of Management and Budget moved toward greater fiscal control and programmatic oversight. These activities were designed to improve overall efficiency and coordination in government, an often reiterated goal of Nixon, and to enhance political coherence to departmental programs. John Ehrlichman, domestic policy advisor, described Nixon's view of the restructuring of White House responsibilities:

> [Nixon] looked on the Cabinet principally as managers of their respective bureaucracies. A good Secretary keeps things under control. Cabinet members were to be spokesmen, too. They should be out in the country making the case for the President and his policies. A good Secretary is a good P.R. man.[55]

In the final analysis, Richard Nixon changed the presidency. Watergate humbled the office and made future presidents more responsive to Congress and to the public at large. But the internal changes within the White House were equally important to the future of the presidency, for it reframed the manner in which presidents dealt with their own bureaucracies. The institutionalization and expansion of the domestic policy office provided Nixon and his successors an organizational structure to guide the administration's domestic agenda, forge key legislative initiatives, and ensure consistency throughout the departments in domestic policy. The paradox of the Nixon administration was that the White House gained control of the policy process but so isolated itself that it ultimately lost control of the presidency.

FOUR

THE FORD YEARS

Gerald R. Ford's experience with White House–Cabinet relations was quite different from that of Richard Nixon. Ford's problems with policy-making focused on a White House staff completely incapable of structuring a workable White House–Cabinet relationship. Constant fighting among White House staff and the lack of any clear agenda kept the White House staff from taking control of policy-making. Throughout the Ford administration, Cabinet officers controlled the policy agendas within their departments and ran their departments with little or no guidance from the White House.

FROM VICE PRESIDENT TO PRESIDENT

Unlike his predecessors, Gerald Ford was thrust into the job of president with little warning and no time to prepare a strategy for managing the responsibilities of the oval office. As the nation's first unelected president, Ford had not developed a strategy for managing the presidency.

His tenure as the nation's chief executive began almost as suddenly as did his tenure as vice president. Less than a year earlier, President Nixon had called Minority Leader Gerald Ford to offer him the job of vice president. Spiro Agnew, the elected vice president, had resigned in disgrace over allegations of kickbacks while an elected official in Maryland. On October 10, 1973, Richard Nixon announced his selection of Gerald Ford to replace Agnew.

The new nominee for vice president had first been elected to the House on November 2, 1948, representing Grand Rapids, Michigan. During his twenty-six years in the House, he had risen to the prestigious position of Minority Leader and was widely respected by his colleagues on both sides of the aisle — a quality that Richard Nixon needed to secure confirmation for his new vice president.

Transition Planning

Just over six months later, Gerald Ford would move into the presidency. What little planning that was done for the transition to a Ford presidency was accomplished by a small group of Ford's friends, spearheaded by Ford's former law partner, Philip Buchen. Buchen enlisted the aid of Clay T. Whitehead, director of the White House Office of Telecommunications Policy.[1] He also brought in three more members to the unofficial group: Lawrence Lynn, a former aide to Henry Kissinger at the National Security Council; Brian Lamb, Whitehead's assistant at the Office of Telecommunications Policy; and Jonathan Moore, a former aide to Nelson Rockefeller and later to Elliot Richardson. The group met five times in Whitehead's Georgetown home to develop a plan should Nixon suddenly resign.

As the inevitable grew closer, Buchen met with Ford and explained the deliberations of the small group. But he emphasized to Ford that they had only had generalized discussions and he felt the time was now appropriate for a detailed transition plan. Ford was still reluctant to approve any transition activities while Nixon was protesting his innocence and refusing to resign. The Buchen team remained the only transition group.

However, on August 5, 1974, White House tape recordings were made public, which included damaging conversations between Nixon and his chief of staff, H.R. Haldeman. The tapes involved Nixon's orders to Haldeman to use the Federal Bureau of Investigation to block the Watergate break-in investigation by Washington, D.C., police. Nixon was no longer the innocent victim that he had portrayed himself, but rather a participant in the cover-up. At that point, Ford realized the tide was turning on Nixon.

On August 6, after months of Congressional hearings on impeachment, Ford reluctantly agreed that Nixon might be unstable and suddenly resign. The Watergate break-in had caused a total breakdown in the Nixon presidency. Ford authorized transition planning and met with Buchen to assemble a more experienced group.[2] Ford wanted five persons brought into the new transition group: Senator Robert Griffin of Michigan; Eisenhower and Nixon advisor Bryce Harlow; former Congressman John Byrnes of Wisconsin; Secretary of the Interior Rogers Morton; and William Whyte, Vice President of U.S. Steel in charge of governmental relations. Buchen suggested that former Pennsylvania governor William Scranton be added to the group to placate the liberal wing of the Republican Party. All six agreed to work on the transition team. The group met for the first time the next evening, August 7, at the home of Whyte in suburban Washington, and for five hours developed a list of priorities for Ford.

The new transition group developed a narrow set of objectives for a Ford presidency focused primarily on the public image of the presidency:

- Restore the confidence and trust of the American people in their political leadership, institutions, and processes.
- Assume control which is firm and efficient.
- Create a national feeling of unification and reconciliation enabled by the character and style of the new President.[3]

Once the objectives of the impending Ford presidency had been established, the transition group felt their job was now complete and urged Ford to assemble a formal transition team. The new transition team could tackle the more complex issues regarding staffing and organizational structures.[4] Buchen subsequently provided Ford with a list of four names, which included Secretary of Interior Rogers Morton; former Congressman John Marsh of Virginia; Scranton; and former Nixon cabinet officer Frank Carlucci. Ford crossed out Carlucci's name and replaced it with Donald Rumsfeld, the current NATO ambassador. All four, each of whom had served in the House with Ford, were trusted by Ford to put his administration on the right track. Jerald ter Horst of the *Detroit News,* who was brought in as press secretary for the president, was also asked to participate in transition activities. Clay Whitehead was asked to keep the official records of the transition process for the team.

The role of the official transition team was to design an operating structure for the new administration. How was it to be organized? Who would be the key players? What policies were to be pursued? What role would the White House staff play? This was the first time that Ford and his advisors had tackled the problem of Cabinet–White House relations and staff functions.

Once in place, the official transition group broke itself into specific areas of responsibility. Rumsfeld, who had been Nixon's director of the Office of Economic Opportunity prior to becoming ambassador to NATO, was placed in charge of White House staffing.[5] Elected to the House in 1962, Rumsfeld had joined with his more senior colleague, Gerald Ford, and a group of moderate Republicans to oust Charles Halleck as Minority Leader in 1965. Ford and Rumsfeld never lost touch after Rumsfeld moved into the Nixon administration and then on to Brussels with NATO.

Each of the other four members of the transition team received very spe-

cific instructions on how to proceed. Morton was given the job of revitalizing the Cabinet relationship with the White House. Scranton, a classmate of
Ford's at Yale and Pennsylvania Congressman, was put in charge of personnel
changes. Marsh became the liaison with Congress.

Three days later, Nixon resigned. The transition team moved quickly
into operation. On the evening of August 9, 1974, just hours after the swearing in, they met with Ford. At 5:30 P.M. the group assembled in the cabinet
room to assess their new responsibilities.[6] Their immediate assignment was to
develop a plan for organizing the White House staff and to structure the White
House–Cabinet relationship. Ford, sensitive to the structure that Nixon had in
place, felt that the White House staff had dominated the Cabinet and had insulated Nixon. Ford made it clear to the transition staff that he wanted an open
administration in which both the Cabinet and White House staff had access to
him.

RECOMMENDATIONS FOR A STRONG CABINET SYSTEM

On August 10 Ford held his first Cabinet meeting and began the revitalization of a strong Cabinet. The transition team urged that he "reassure the
Cabinet of (his) respect for their abilities, (his) need for their help, and the
importance of an orderly continuation of the work of government," which he
did.[7] Just as importantly, he directed the Cabinet that "they are not to work
through the Domestic Council or Al Haig."[8] They were to work directly with
him as a signal of their preeminence in policy-making. This was a major
departure from the Nixon years, where Cabinet officers worked through White
House staff in policy issues.

But some members of the White House staff were uncomfortable with
Ford's directions to his Cabinet. While the transition team was urging Ford to
change his White House–Cabinet relationship and establish an open door to
his Cabinet, Al Haig, Nixon's chief of staff, was trying to continue in his role
as the president's doorkeeper. In addition to the transition team's briefing document prepared for Ford for the August 10 Cabinet meeting, Haig also prepared a briefing document, which stated that "You may want to reaffirm Al
Haig's role as Chief of Staff" and "Tell the Cabinet that you plan to have an
'open door' policy but the meetings should not waste the President's or the
Cabinet officer's time."[9] Clearly, the transition team had not taken Haig into
its confidence as it prepared Ford's remarks.

Ford followed the transition team's briefing document. Ignoring Haig's
suggestions, Ford urged the Cabinet "to come and see me with your problems.
I think we have a fine team here and I'm looking forward to working with each
and every one of you." In further support of his commitment to a strong

Cabinet, he said he wanted a Cabinet who were strong managers. "I would leave the details of administration to them and concentrate on determining national priorities and directions myself. I want men and women who would give me unvarnished truth, then lay out the options for decision that I would have to make."[10] Writing in his memoirs, Ford expanded on his support for his Cabinet:

> A Watergate was made possible by a strong chief of staff and ambitious White House aides who were more powerful than members of the Cabinet but who had little or no practical or political experience or judgment. I wanted to reverse the trend and restore authority to my Cabinet. . . I decided to give my Cabinet members a lot more control. [11]

Moving swiftly to build a strengthened Cabinet system, Rogers Morton began to meet with Cabinet officers to seek their advice on an improved White House–Cabinet working relationship. Each and every one that he met with complained that the Nixon White House dominated them and that they never knew in what form their proposals went to the president. Morton promised the Cabinet that Ford was approaching the policy process quite differently than Nixon had.

On Thursday, August 15, Morton and the other members of the transition team met for the second time with Ford to discuss their findings. Ford reiterated to the transition team his decision to build a strengthened system of White House–departmental cooperation. He made it clear to the group that the Cabinet was to serve as the central advisory system, with the White House staff and OMB less involved with programmatic details.

For the next four days, the transition team prepared a draft report. On Monday, August 19, the first full draft was given to the president, with the final report issued the following day. The 23-page document became the blueprint for the early months of the administration. Five areas were addressed in the final report: White House and Executive Office organization; specific ideas for the Ford presidency; review of policy proposals in process; interim measures; and action. But of these five areas, the bulk of the document, 15 pages, dealt solely with the organization of the White House and White House–Cabinet relations.

The report summarized the principles that were to govern the White House and the White House–Cabinet relationship. The recommendations were:

- For effective control, you should not have so many people reporting regularly to you that your span of control is exceeded. Nor should there be so few that power is overly concentrated in a few staff members.

- The organization must conform to your personal working methods.
- There must be someone in charge of administration, but there need not be a single control point for information, advice, access, or policy.
- Some decentralization is desirable. Some White House staff functions might be moved to Executive Office agencies, and some Executive Office functions might be moved back to the departments and agencies.
- White House staff traditionally do not testify before Congressional committees; Executive Office officials must be confirmed by the Senate and do testify regularly. The principal administration spokesmen should be the Cabinet and agency heads.[12]

The transition team had carefully woven Ford's charge for an open administration and a strengthened Cabinet system into their report. The organizational structure for White House–Cabinet relationship could be implemented. The organization structure, however, first needed a White House staff in place and operating.

Implementing the Transition Report: The White House Staff

As the transition team had noted, a redesigned White House staff had to be shaped. At the core of the new staff would be a system of nine equal staff members with direct access to Ford. Six of the staff would have direct responsibility for White House administration, press relations, speeches, Congressional liaison, personnel issues, and legal issues. In addition, three other staff would manage domestic policy, economic policy, and national security policy. There would no longer be a chief of staff who controlled access to the president, as Nixon had had.

The staff system was designed to be a spokes of the wheel system, with Ford at the center of a wheel with nine equal spokes. One member of the transition staff described what the spokes of the wheel staffing system meant for the White House:

> It meant that there would be no single individual in charge, no gatekeeper. There were going to be eight or nine senior aides, all of whom would report to the President. . . . There was this belief that the strong centralized chief of staff was wrong.[13]

Another member of the team described it in more colorful terms as "something analogous to the knights of the round-table where all are equal. The President doesn't want any Colonel House or Rasputin around here."[14]

Once the model for the White House staff had been developed, Ford prepared four principles to guide them in their daily work. These principles supported his goal for the White House of a small staff with equal access to the oval office and of a Cabinet-oriented policy system. He outlined each of these goals in a staff meeting:

- To ensure that key people always had ample access to the president.
- To guarantee that the organization reflected his personal style by assuring openness and the free movement of people and ideas.
- To reduce the overall size of the White House staff.
- To make the structure as flexible as possible.[15]

Each of the four principles nurtured a strong Cabinet–White House relationship. In a press release describing this relationship, Ford said that the White House staff function would be limited "to those that must necessarily be performed within the White House. The Cabinet and agency heads will be relied on to perform all appropriate functions best performed by their organizations."[16] Ford continued throughout the early months of the administration to support a lead role for the Cabinet in policy development.

INFIGHTING AMONG WHITE HOUSE STAFF

As he worked with the transition team throughout August, Ford thought that he had created a staff structure that guaranteed a greater role for the Cabinet in policy development. He had carefully framed the structure through which his White House staff would operate both within the White House and with the Cabinet, but he failed to take into account how conflicting personalities could upset that structure. From the first day of the administration, members of the White House staff were jockeying for power. Infighting became a way of life. Alexander Haig and Robert Hartmann became the chief antagonists, with each seeing his role as a surrogate chief of staff. But after Haig left, nothing changed. The infighting continued as Hartmann and Rumsfeld began to feud. When Nelson Rockefeller took over the Domestic Council, he joined the fray. The White House staff was in a constant turmoil as a result of in-house power struggles.

Most of these White House power struggles stemmed from the lack of cohesiveness among the staff. The nine senior staff were a hodgepodge of Ford and Nixon staff. The Nixon carry-overs included Henry Kissinger for national security, Kenneth Cole for domestic affairs, and Alexander Haig as the coordinator for White House administration. The Ford team included old friends, such as Jerald terHorst for press secretary, Philip Buchen as legal counsel, John Marsh as congressional liaison, and Bill Seidman for economic affairs. Robert Hartmann, Ford's chief of staff in the vice president's office, was named speech writer. The Ford staff did not trust the Nixon staff, and the various members of the Ford staff did not trust each other.

Haig vs. Hartmann

At the heart of the infighting were Al Haig and Robert Hartmann, who each felt they could manage the White House staff most efficiently for Ford. Haig continued to view his new job as essentially the same as he had held under Nixon. Hartmann contested that view.

Ford's failure to deal with the infighting from the start was more a factor of pressures on his time than concern with the problem. Although he knew of the unrest on the staff, he was in a whirlwind attempt to focus public attention on a revitalized presidency. During the first month of the administration, Ford went on a rapid series of public appearances to, as the transition team had urged, rebuild public confidence in the presidency. During August, all of Ford's energies went to traveling around the country giving speeches on the new openness of the administration. This left the White House in the hands of Ford's two senior advisors, Haig and Hartmann. But rather than organize a Ford team within the White House, they bickered over who controlled the president's schedule, who was hired, and who controlled White House administration.

By September Ford was spending more time in the White House. Haig saw that Hartmann had gained the upper hand and that he would soon be replaced. As was Haig's usual style, he tried to gain control of the situation by resigning before being fired. When he offered Ford his resignation, he put all his cards on the table and asked to be named chairman of the joint chiefs of staff. General Creighton Abrams had recently died and no replacement appointed.

Ford, initially agreeable to the scenario, was later convinced by his congressional liaison staff that there would be problems in the Senate confirmation process. The liaison staff felt strongly that Haig's testimony during Senate confirmation hearings would dredge up the specter of Watergate. Ford wanted to distance his administration from the Nixon years and did not want Haig talking about his role in the Nixon White House. As a result, Ford refused to support the Pentagon position but did offer Haig the position of Commander in Chief, U.S. European Command and Supreme Allied Commander in Europe. Haig accepted. Ironically, he was filling the job vacated by General Andrew Goodpaster, who had served as Eisenhower's chief of staff after the resignation of Sherman Adams.

Ford was now free to bring in his own coordinator for White House operations and he hoped to forge what had been a disparate group into one team. Rather than elevating Hartmann, Ford went outside the White House in an effort to minimize any divisiveness on the staff. His choice was Donald Rumsfeld, who only a month earlier had been a key player in the transition. Rumsfeld was contacted September 24 by Ford and immediately accepted. By September 30 he was in the White House.

RUMSFELD TAKES THE HELM AT THE WHITE HOUSE

On his first day on the job, Rumsfeld held a press conference to clarify his new role. Reporters wanted specific answers to how he would interact with the president and with other White House staff. He answered with the open-ended reply that "[the president] said that he has asked me to assume responsibility for overall coordination of the White House, and that he says my task in the period immediately ahead is to see that the White House operation is running smoothly and that the burden is on me and so on and so forth."[17] How he would ensure that the "operation is running smoothly" remained a mystery.

But the mystery was quickly solved as Rumsfeld's strategy became apparent. He would reduce the tension on the White House staff by hiring new staff. Rumsfeld's first appointment was Richard Cheney, who had worked for him at the Office of Economic Opportunity.[18] Other staff followed, all hired by Rumsfeld. He filled openings in the personnel office, appointments office, scheduling office, and the office of Cabinet Secretary.

With less infighting Rumsfeld hoped to develop a workable organization within the White House that would effectively implement Ford's spokes of the wheel concept and build a strong White House–Cabinet relationship, a relationship that was shaky at best. The Haig-Hartmann battles had allowed the Cabinet to continue to operate with little or no communication from the White House.

But even after the staff changes, the White House continued to be plagued with the same problems that it had faced throughout August and September. The infighting continued. Rumsfeld was unable to blend the factions within the White House into a team. Although Haig was gone, Rumsfeld and Hartmann were constantly battling, each seeking to outmaneuver the other as Ford's chief advisor.

Nixon Staff vs. Ford Staff

The wars continued not only between new staff such as Rumsfeld and vice presidential staff such as Hartmann, but between all the staff and the remaining Nixon staff. By October 1, 1974, nearly three months into the Ford presidency, most offices in the west wing of the White House continued to be occupied by Nixon staffers. The majority of Ford's vice presidential staff who were given White House appointments continued to operate out of the old executive office building. Nixon appointees such as Patrick Buchanan, Ray Price, Ken Clawson, John McLaughlin, and Jerry Jones continued to maintain their White House positions. The vice presidential staff bitterly complained to Ford that they not only were denied White House offices, but were often denied White House passes.

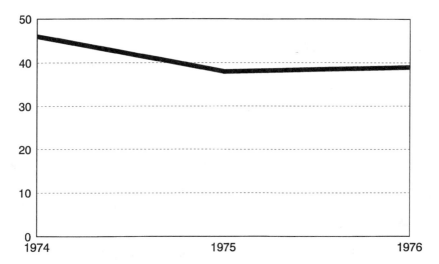

FIGURE 7. Total Senior White House Staff (Ford)

Ford finally decided in December to sweep out the Nixon holdovers and firmly establish a Ford White House to reduce some of the tensions on the staff. As the Nixon staff left, Rumsfeld brought in more of his own people to strengthen his position on the staff. Rumsfeld was quickly moving to gain control over the White House staff and all that it controlled.   Yet the battle for control of the White House was being waged on many fronts, and although Rumsfeld had seemingly gained control of the staff, other battles continued to be fought.

TABLE 2. October 1, 1974 White House Organization Chart

- *Counsellors John Marsh and Robert Hartmann*
- *Press Secretary Ron Nessen (who had replaced Jerald terHorst, who had resigned in protest over the presidential pardon of Richard Nixon)*
- *National Security Advisor Henry Kissinger*
- *Domestic Policy Advisor Kenneth Cole*

(Continued on next page)

Table 2. (*continued*)

_____

* *Economic Policy Advisor William Seidman*
* *OMB Director Roy Ash*
* *Counsel Philip Buchen*
* *Staff Coordinator Donald Rumsfeld*

_____

Prepared by Donald Rumsfeld

THE CABINET: SEEKING DIRECTION FROM THE WHITE HOUSE

As the jockeying for personal power was mounting in the White House, Cabinet officers were trying to determine exactly what their role would be in the new administration. What were the priorities of the new administration? How involved in policy development would the Cabinet be? Should the Cabinet be working with the White House staff on new program initiatives?

The Cabinet had received little direction from Ford or the White House staff on how the White House–Cabinet relationship would operate. Ford had stated during Cabinet meetings that he wanted to give the Cabinet officers primary responsibility for policy development, but had not provided the specific organizational structure for the process. His only discussion of the issue was that he wanted "to make better use of cabinet people. . .and to give (them) more authority . . . both in the planning and execution of policy than had been the case under the former administration."[19] Such broad statements were the only guidance the Cabinet had received on their role in managing the administration's policy objectives.

Among the unanswered questions were would the White House establish the parameters for administration objectives? Would there be a coordinating mechanism in the White House to resolve interjurisdictional disputes? The Cabinet was only told that the departments, not the White House staff, would be the locus of policy-making.

The Cabinet Secretary: An Ally for the Cabinet

One of the few steps that Ford set in motion to structure White House–Cabinet relations was to have the Cabinet, who were all Nixon holdovers, feel as if they were part of the Ford team. To do that, Ford tried to create a system that gave Cabinet officers regular access to the White House, a system promised at his first Cabinet meeting. Since Nixon had stopped having Cabinet meetings and had stopped seeing Cabinet officers in any kind of personal meetings, this step was welcomed by the Cabinet.

To ensure that Cabinet meetings went smoothly, and to rebuild Cabinet access to the oval office, Ford revitalized the Cabinet Secretariat, which had been briefly resurrected under Richard Nixon. Created by Dwight Eisenhower, the position had been used in varying degrees over the past decade and a half. Warren Rustand, a Nixon holdover who was handling scheduling, was moved into the Cabinet Secretariat. Rustand lasted only three months in the job, until January, when Rumsfeld hired James E. Connor for the job, who, like Dick Cheney, had worked for him at the Office of Economic Opportunity. Connor was responsible for the organization of Cabinet meetings, preparation of agendas, assembling background papers, accumulating meeting minutes, confirming attendance by Cabinet officers and White House staff, and coordinating follow-up activities. He was charged with assuring direct access to the president and mobilizing the Cabinet on behalf of key presidential initiatives, including Congressional votes.

Whether intentionally or not, this proved to be an important symbolic move by the White House. The Cabinet saw from the creation of the Secretariat that Cabinet meetings were being taken seriously and that Cabinet input into decision-making was critical to this administration. In addition, it put someone on the White House staff whose only job was to be an ally for Cabinet officers to ensure that they had access to the oval office. Cabinet officers had been ignored for nearly two years during the waning of the Nixon administration and were eager to again be in regular touch with the President.

Yet in spite of high hopes by Ford for an invigorated White House–Cabinet relationship, the buds of that relationship did not blossom. Cabinet officers quickly realized that the Economic Policy Board and the Domestic Council did not work in tandem, and that they were often vying for policy control. The White House did not have an effective policy mechanism to direct the departments. There were no clearly established policies coming out of the White House. Most importantly, Ford had offered no direction on priorities for the administration.

By October, Ford had still provided relatively little direction to the departments. Although he had established economic issues as the focus of his administration, he had not told his Cabinet how their existing programs fit into the economic strategy or what new programs should be considered. Cabinet officers continued to lack any understanding of what programmatic changes the president wanted to focus on and Cabinet meetings shed no additional light for them. The Cabinet Secretary was proving to be of little use to the Cabinet.

Growing Frustration in the White House: A Lack of Direction

The failure of the president to articulate a series of goals and objectives for the administration was visible not only to the Cabinet but to the White House staff itself. White House staff were as frustrated as the Cabinet in the lack of direction from the president. In particular, speech writers were unable to prepare the kinds of clear-cut speeches that Ford wanted, because they never quite understood what he wanted to say. One of the best examples of this was described by John Casserly, a senior member of the White House speech writing staff. Casserly was asked to meet with Bill Seidman, Paul McCracken (an economic adviser to Nixon), and Bill Simon to develop the basis for a speech that Ford was giving on December 10 in Detroit to business executives. This address was timed to follow up the December 8 address to the nation on economic policy.

When Casserly met with the three economists for input, he was unable to forge a consensus from them on the focus of the speech, leading to seven rewrites. In his book on the Ford administration, Casserly vividly describes this meeting by writing, "Why is it that a speech is forcing the President and his chief economic advisers to come to grips with our economic problems? Why isn't economic policy being made first and the speech written second?" Casserly continued his rather harsh assessment:

> With so many different shades of economic opinion around the President, I find it difficult to perceive how he will come to conclusions. Ford must formulate a clear economic policy in the midst of clashing opinion. Will he fight the recession first, or inflation, or both at the same time? Does a wage-price freeze have any chance? Should he increase or cut taxes? How many government jobs can he create without heating up inflation?[20]

Casserly's concern that Ford was unable to make decisions on the issues was echoed by other members of the White House staff. Jerry Jones, Staff Secretary, was just as frustrated as Casserly about the quagmire that the White House seemed to be mired in. At approximately the same time that Casserly was writing the Detroit speech, Jones was trying to identify some ways that the President could improve White House–Cabinet relations. Sitting at his desk in the White House in mid-December, he sketched out some of the problems and some possible solutions. As he identified the problems, he wrote to himself, "the President doesn't seem to be in complete control of government. . . the President doesn't seem to have a place he is trying to take the country." Seeking solutions, he wrote that the White House needed "policy offices in control of the departments" and "policy offices to develop programs to push themes." He also noted that the White House needed to "play off of the Cabinet better." [21]

Both Casserly and Jones, who had little to do with one another on the White House staff, saw the same problem: a lack of direction from the president and the failure of the White House staff to organize the Cabinet under one central theme. The result was a growing gap between the departments and the

White House with increasing power by the departments in policy development. The White House offered no mechanism for controlling the proliferation of departmental policy proposals or for the coordination of interjurisdictional proposals. In essence, the Cabinet was reliving the latter part of the Nixon years when they had nearly total autonomy in what their departments were doing.

THE DOMESTIC POLICY PROCESS: WHO'S IN CONTROL?

The absence of direction from the president on policy issues was at the heart of departmental autonomy in policy matters, but the power struggles within the White House significantly contributed to the lethargy in developing goals and objectives for the administration. The individual battles to gain positions of power in the White House were matched by a series of organizational battles of White House policy units. The Economic Policy Board and the Domestic Council were in a tug of war to gain control over domestic policy-making.

The Economic Policy Board

The Domestic Council had been the only White House unit involved in shaping domestic policy initiatives since the Nixon administration. Under Nixon, the Domestic Council managed both domestic and economic policy-making. But as part of his effort to gain public confidence in the administration, Ford moved to refocus domestic policy around the narrower issue of economic policy. With an annual inflation rate of almost 12 per cent and an unemployment rate of 6 per cent, Ford knew that bringing the inflation rate down was essential to the economy and to the health of his administration. Economic policy had to be the major policy issue that the administration tackled in its first year.

Ford examined a number of organizational structures that would meet his needs. On August 25 he called William Seidman to the oval office to explore organizational structures that would focus on economic issues. Seidman, a financial management consultant from Grand Rapids, Michigan, had long been a friend of the Fords and had recently moved to Washington as a member of Ford's vice presidential staff. Seidman urged Ford to develop a single organization in the White House to deal with economic policy to enable the White House to become the focal point for economic policy-making. This meant taking economic policy out of the Domestic Council.

The Seidman proposal, however, was not unanimously accepted by the White House staff. Many, including the transition staff, felt that economic policy-making should remain within the auspices of the Domestic Council, which would continue to work through the Cabinet. The transition team felt strongly that the Cabinet should have the primary responsibility for economic policies and that an economic policy-making office in the White House would reduce the administration's pledge for a strengthened Cabinet.[22] They argued that this structure would reduce the influence of the entire Cabinet in policy-making, particularly within the sphere of economic policy-making.

After weighing both sides, Ford decided to implement Seidman's plan and to create an office of economic policy within the White House, but one that continued to include the Cabinet in the policy process. William Simon, Secretary of the Treasury, would become the chairman of a newly formed Economic Policy Board to reinforce Ford's commitment that the Cabinet would be in charge of the policy process. Seidman would become Assistant to the President for Economic Affairs, charged with the day-to-day activities of the board. On September 30, five days after their initial discussions, Ford signed executive order #11808 creating the Economic Policy Board (EPB) within the White House. The EPB included all members of the Cabinet except the Attorney General and the Secretary of Defense, with an executive committee composed of the Secretary of the Treasury, the Chairman of the Council of Economic Advisers, the Director of the Office of Management and Budget, and Seidman.

Simon moved quickly to alleviate any fears of Cabinet members that the Economic Policy Board would be White House driven. He announced that he would hold monthly meetings of the full board. This, of course, gained the Cabinet's support and forged an immediate alliance between the Economic Policy Board and the Cabinet.

The Economic Policy Board went swiftly to business. Based on the recommendations of an economic summit that Ford convened in Washington on September 24, the EPB developed a program that sought voluntary wage controls, energy conservation, and a federal income tax surcharge. Ford went on national television on October 4 to urge everyone to undertake voluntary activities that would "Whip Inflation Now," soon referred to as the WIN Program. Because the departments were not asked to give up any of their programs, but only to support these voluntary activities, most eagerly supported the WIN package. By supporting the WIN package, they were also supporting the policy activities of the Economic Policy Board.

Less than a month after its creation, the EPB had become the focal point of not only economic policy but of domestic policy. Although the WIN Program affected a wide range of domestic programs, the Economic Policy Board, not the Domestic Council, was charged with overseeing its implementation.

The Domestic Council

As the Economic Policy Board was gaining in stature in both the White House and the departments, the Domestic Council was losing stature. Although it had been the driving force behind the Nixon domestic agenda for three years, it had lost its energy when its director, John Ehrlichman, resigned in 1973 as a result of his involvement in Watergate. His deputy, Kenneth Cole, subsequently became the Domestic Council's second director.

The power of the Domestic Council had been severely damaged by Watergate. As John Ehrlichman and H.R. Haldeman, Nixon's chief of staff, became increasingly drawn into the House of Representatives' impeachment hearings and into meetings with Nixon and his lawyers on legal strategies, the Cabinet became increasingly independent in their policy-making activities. During the waning months of the Nixon administration, Cabinet officers ignored the White House and moved in their own directions. There was no coordination from the Domestic Council on interjurisdictional issues or attempts to guide the departments on policy issues. The White House simply abdicated policy decisions to the departments.

When Gerald Ford took the reins of government, he took over a nonfunctioning Domestic Council and staff. It was relatively easy for the Economic Policy Board to gain the upper hand in the White House. It was also relatively easy for the Economic Policy Board to gain the support of the departments, which had had bitter relations with the Domestic Council under Ehrlichman.

Within a month after the Economic Policy Board had been created, Ken Cole realized that the Domestic Council had lost any vestiges of a policy-making body. In what proved to be a fruitless effort to revitalize the Domestic Council, Cole wrote Ford a memo on October 25, 1974, outlining what he saw as the best course for the council. He recommended that the council be strengthened, with "the capacity for development of a think tank to generate new ideas." As Cole described it, the council had been unable to tackle the long-term planning the Ash Commission had envisioned for it because of insufficient staff, "and because the domestic area is more fluid if only by virtue of the volume, variety, and number of people involved than is the economic or energy areas." But, according to Cole, that did not mean that long-range planning was impossible or undesirable for the Domestic Council.[23]

There is no record of an answer by Ford. However, no immediate changes were made in the role of the Domestic Council. The Economic Policy Board continued to dominate the administration's policy agenda and the Domestic Council continued to play a firefighting role, dealing with the day-to-day crises that arose in the White House. Frustrated at the continued decline of the Domestic Council's role in policy-making and the continued ascendancy of the

Economic Policy Board, Cole resigned. On December 13, he handed his letter of resignation into the president.[24]

On the same day that Cole handed in his letter of resignation, Nelson Rockefeller was being confirmed by Congress as the nation's second unelected vice president. Yet unlike other vice presidents who simply carve out whatever role they can once in office, Rockefeller told Ford that he would not be a show-case vice president. He wanted a clear area of responsibility that would utilize his talents and he wanted to establish that area before he accepted the job. Rockefeller saw those talents focusing on domestic policy, given his years in public life in the Eisenhower administration and later as Governor of New York. Ford agreed and asked Rockefeller to take control of the Domestic Council. This was exactly where Rockefeller wanted to be. Ford noted that "when I asked Nelson Rockefeller to be Vice President, I told him that he would be given major responsibility for the formulation of domestic policy, and I intended to keep that promise."[25]

While Rockefeller had been moving through a grueling confirmation process, he apparently was not aware of the organizational changes within the White House. There is no evidence that he knew of Cole's request to increase the role of the Domestic Council, which was turned down, or of the increasing responsibility of the Economic Policy Board. He seemed to move into the White House with little understanding of the emphasis on a Cabinet-based policy-making system or on the reduced role of the Domestic Council.

The Domestic Council under Rockefeller

Rockefeller's first move in taking control of the Domestic Council was to bring in his own staff: James Cannon as executive director and Richard L. Dunham as deputy director, both of whom had long working relationships with Rockefeller. Cannon had been an editor for *Newsweek* until 1969 when he resigned to join Rockefeller's staff. Dunham had been New York's state budget director during the Rockefeller administration.

But the road for Rockefeller to gain control of domestic policy was mud-died from the beginning of his travels. Rumsfeld in particular was a major stumbling block for Rockefeller at every turn of the bend. As Rockefeller noted, "Rummy, no matter how I set it up, was opposed to it."[26]

The appointment of Cannon and Dunham was strongly opposed by Rumsfeld and Buchen, who preferred Philip Areeda, a Harvard law professor who had served in the counsel's office of the Eisenhower White House over-seeing domestic planning. Rumsfeld foresaw a return to the early months of the administration when the Nixon-Ford staffs divided the White House and did not want Ford-Rockefeller staffs to be pursuing different paths. But

Rumsfeld and Buchen lost the staffing battle, and Cannon and Dunham moved into the White House.

Rockefeller quickly realized the lack of support he was being given within the White House and sought Ford's endorsement for a revitalized Domestic Council. On February 13, 1975, Ford gave him that support and sent a memo to the Cabinet secretaries and agency heads announcing a new role for the Domestic Council. In clear support for Rockefeller's view of the Domestic Council, Ford said:

> In order to help me carry out my responsibilities for domestic policy formulation within a broad conceptual framework which is responsive to our present national urgencies, I want to have the Domestic Council exert full efforts to carry out all policy functions contemplated for it when it established in 1970.

Ford listed those functions in the memo:

- Assessing national needs and identifying alternative ways of meeting them.
- Providing rapid response to presidential needs for policy advice.
- Coordinating the establishment of national priorities for the allocation of available resources.
- Maintaining a continuous policy review of ongoing programs.
- Proposing reforms as needed.[27]

Yet the revitalization of the Domestic Council led to more problems within the White House. Ford had set in motion both organizational conflicts between the Economic Policy Board and the Domestic Council, and staff conflicts between the Rumsfeld and Rockefeller loyalists. In addition, Ford's support for a strong policy-making role for the Domestic Council led to problems with his Cabinet. The new functions outlined for the Domestic Council were not in line with his earlier support for a strong Cabinet-based policy-making structure.

It was clear, however, that Rockefeller never understood the problems ahead of him. Rockefeller was moving to increase the role of the White House staff in policy-making, while Ford and the key members of the White House staff were moving to reduce that role. Rockefeller's failure to see the road the Ford White House was taking stemmed from his late arrival into the administration. He was not part of the discussions during the transition that focused on rebuilding confidence in the presidency through, in part, a less powerful White House staff and a strengthened Cabinet.

Since Rockefeller brought in his own staff, no one in his immediate circle knew of the focus on policy-making that had been established at the start of the administration. Everyone surrounding Rockefeller was therefore eager to establish a strong presence for the Domestic Council. Rockefeller himself, though, was the driving force for making the Domestic Council a powerful force on the White House staff. In describing his plans for the Domestic Council, Rockefeller said:

> It is my intention to make the Domestic Council a parallel operation to the National Security Council as a means of serving the President. . . . The two are closely related. When you come to the crossroads and look fifty miles down the road, a decision you make today may have effects five or ten miles in the future.[28]

The Rockefeller group formally moved into their new positions in the Domestic Council in February 1975. Rockefeller's first act was to suggest to Ford that the Domestic Council develop policy options that would help in the formulation of a comprehensive and cohesive administration program for 1976. Ford approved the idea and on February 27 Rockefeller sent a memo to all members of the Domestic Council asking them to develop a brief statement of the policy issues facing their departments, plus a summary of five major priority goals for their areas of responsibility.[29]

Rumsfeld, who had not been involved in the Rockefeller-Ford discussions on the Domestic Council, saw Rockefeller and his staff as veering out of the narrower role that White House units were taking. In direct response to Rockefeller's initiatives, Rumsfeld called a staff meeting on February 28—which included Jim Cannon—and directed all White House staff to reduce their interaction with the departments. White House staff were told to "reverse the trend" of White House management of the departments. Departments were to handle their own policy issues with minimal White House involvement. "We should involve more agency people in decisions and restore balance to the executive branch," Rumsfeld told the assembled staff.[30] He went on to say that the president's staff had been cut from 540 to 490 members, and was seeking further reductions. Rumsfeld pointed out to the staff that since more and more policy responsibility was returning to the departments, the White House would need fewer staff involved in policy oversight.

The departments quickly realized that the White House was in disarray and that the most powerful member of the White House staff, Donald Rumsfeld, preferred to keep the White House staff out of policy matters. Not surprisingly, the departments were slow to respond to Rockefeller's February 27 memo and did not actively move to rebuild their bridges with the White House after Rumsfeld's February 28 statement to the White House staff.

When the departments failed to cooperate in any significant way,

Rockefeller told the Domestic Council staff to proceed with their own plans and develop base-line policy initiatives. This would have been less of a problem had there been sufficient staff to undertake the planning, but the Domestic Council staff was overwhelmed with a host of other responsibilities. These responsibilities had emerged when John Ehrlichman resigned the Domestic Council and its function as a policy maker had essentially ended. Under Ken Cole, the Domestic Council had been used primarily to handle a series of daily but routine firefighting tasks for the president. Rockefeller was now asking the Domestic Council staff to undertake new responsibilities even though they were up to their ears, as the saying goes, with their current responsibilities.

Frustrations Develop: Lack of Staffing in the Domestic Council

Rockefeller's frustrations grew. Although seemingly empowered by the president to revamp the Domestic Council and undertake major policy planning, the Domestic Council staff was not relieved of any of its other tasks.

As could be expected, Rockefeller then wrote another memo to Ford in March and requested an oval office discussion on the problem of staffing. In particular, Rockefeller saw the Domestic Council staff as too involved in reviewing Congressional testimony, providing information to the departments on presidential positions for congressionally sponsored bills, dealing with the Congressional Liaison staff, and preparing position papers on short-term issues.[31] This, he noted, was not the mandate of the Domestic Council. Ford had no immediate solution to the problem except to say that Rumsfeld was working on a staff reorganization. Thus, nothing changed. The Domestic Council staff continued to handle all the routine work for the president in addition to the policy initiatives that Rockefeller was pursuing. Rumsfeld made no effort to shift the existing workload of the Domestic Council to another White House unit.

Jim Cannon tried to calm Rockefeller by explaining that although the Domestic Council staff was focusing on short-term issues, there were some benefits. Cannon wrote in a memo to Rockefeller on March 21, 1975, "The more I study the documents that flow through the Domestic Council staff, the more I realize the degree to which long term policy is being shaped by issues that require immediate decisions."[32] The memo continued by describing one particular case in which HEW Secretary Caspar Weinberger had requested the Domestic Council to compile an overview of the president's position on higher education scholarships. Since there was no position on this, Cannon felt that his staff had provided a policy position for the department and had raised the larger question of how much assistance should go to students from low-income families versus students from middle-income families.

The Domestic Council staff was also responsible for preparing the decision memoranda for the president on enrolled bills. Every bill passed by Congress came to the president for his signature, and it was the role of the Domestic Council to prepare a summary of the bill and present all the points of view from the departments on whether the bill should be signed. On many issues, however, there were no official positions from the departments, and the Domestic Council staff offered recommendations to the president. Cannon felt that this was another way for the council to influence policy.

Rockefeller was still uncomfortable with the continued role of the Domestic Council staff as primarily a firefighting unit. Working with Cannon, he developed a staffing strategy that would provide additional staff for more systematic planning activities. They went over Rumsfeld directly to the source of White House funding: Congress. On April 22, 1975, Cannon met with members of the Senate Appropriations Committee to seek increased funding for the Domestic Council. He noted that 80 per cent of the council's time was spent on crisis issues, and only 20 per cent on policy-planning. The appropriations committee rejected the request.

To make matters worse for Rockefeller and Cannon, in early June 1975 Cheney sent a memo to Rumsfeld recommending that any recommendations that emerge from the Domestic Council have no impact or a reduced impact on the budget process. According to Cheney, all policies emanating from the Domestic Council should "consider doing nothing as an option, and also the possibility of doing less as an option."[33] This was part of the strategy developed by the Economic Policy Board to cut federal spending as a way of controlling inflation and reducing the deficit, a strategy that Ford had endorsed. Cheney's memo reinforced for the Domestic Council Ford's mandate for fiscal restraint.

Undaunted by a lack of staff, a mandate to reduce federal spending, and an apparent lack of cooperation from the departments, Rockefeller continued to seek Ford's support for long-range planning activities, which he received. Ford continued to tell Rockefeller that the Domestic Council had a place in his administration and that it should continue long-range planning. Ford approved Rockefeller's goals for a national health care plan, a new Model Cities–type program, and new programs in education for the future.

Many of the proposals that Rockefeller proposed were not new but had already been sketched out by a nonpartisan commission, the National Commission on Critical Choices for America, which the Rockefeller family had supported. The commission had defined problems and offered broadly described solutions, which Rockefeller wanted the Domestic Council to refine.

Yet these solutions were costly and Ford had mandated that cutting federal spending was a priority of his administration in order to bring down the inflation rate. The Economic Policy Board had urged the administration to undertake deficit reduction programs and the President himself had urged citizens to conserve energy as a tool in combatting inflation. Rockefeller seemed to be moving in opposite directions from other members of the White House staff with his call for new programs.

New York City: The Federal Bailout

The opportunity for a more significant role for the Domestic Council came in May, 1975. The mayor of New York City, Abraham D. Beame, and the governor of New York, Hugh Carey, came to the White House to seek a federal guarantee of $1 billion for New York City notes. The city needed the federal guarantee since the municipal bond market refused to support any more city bond issues, fearing that the city would default. Ford looked to the Domestic Council for an analysis of the issues, and Jim Cannon provided Ford with a detailed briefing memorandum. Both Rockefeller and Cannon saw this as a perfect opportunity to use the Domestic Council for both firefighting (dealing with the bailout issue) and for the longer-range issue of urban insolvency. New York City, they felt, was only one of a long list of cities which were barely solvent. They hoped to prepare a long-range plan for the administration to deal with a similar crisis, and perhaps to avoid future crises.

For the immediate time, Cannon dove into the issue and prepared a detailed memo for Ford on what the administration's options were for the New York City crisis. Cannon framed three options for Ford:

- Agree to support the concept of federal assistance,
- Flatly deny the request, or
- Deny the request, but leave a slight loophole.[34]

Cannon recommended option two, but Ford chose option three, which was to deny the request. In his "Dear Abe" letter, Ford wrote:

> Every family which makes up a budget has to make painful choices. As we make these choices at home, so must we also make them in public office too. We must stop promising more and more services without knowing how we will cover their costs.[35]

But Beame and Carey continued to seek federal help and predicted dire consequences for the state of New York and the nation's financial system if the city collapsed in bankruptcy.

During the summer of 1975 Ford continued to support the Domestic Council's work with the New York City bailout and in other areas of long-range planning. In July 1975 Ford supported Cannon's request for more funding for the Domestic Council. Cannon wanted an additional 23 professional staff and 6 secretarial staff to broaden his long-range planning section without jeopardizing its firefighting units. Although Ford agreed with the staffing increase, the Senate again did not. Rockefeller, though, took Ford's support for more staff as a further sign of support for the long-range planning activities.

As the bailout issue continued to dominate the agenda, Ford was bombarded with conflicting advice on the economic consequences of a New York City bankruptcy. The issues became increasing technical and narrower in scope. While the Domestic Council had played the lead role in the first series of discussions, Ford now saw that the economic issues were out of Cannon's area of expertise. He turned to Federal Reserve Board Chairman Arthur Burns and Treasury Secretary Bill Simon for advice. Both told Ford that Beame and Carey were greatly exaggerating the consequences of a bankruptcy. At their urging, Ford wrote Beame a letter stating that the "proper place" for New York City to seek help would be the state of New York, not the federal government.[36]

During the summer and fall of 1975 the city of New York continued to be on the brink of bankruptcy. In late September, however, Rockefeller began to see the advantages of providing some support to the city. In their weekly meeting on October 2, Rockefeller told Ford that some sort of loan would be important to the city's continued fiscal health. Rockefeller recommended a joint Domestic Council–Economic Policy Board working group to work out the details of a bailout. Ford continued to view the bailout as unneeded. The Domestic Council lost even further ground in the White House decision- making process at that moment, as Ford saw the Rockefeller group moving at odds with both his thinking and that of the Economic Policy Board. Rockefeller and the Domestic Council were now nearly out of the presidential advisory loop on the New York City crisis. Ford looked to Burns and Simon and the Economic Policy Board for advice, and essentially ignored the Domestic Council.

By October, the New York City delegation had been successful at having at least eight different proposals before Congress. Support for the city was mounting in both the House and the Senate, and indications were growing that some sort of relief package would emerge. Yet Ford would not back down and threatened to veto any bill that offered New York City a bailout. "I can tell you, and tell you now," he said, "that I am prepared to veto any bill that has its purpose a bailout of New York City to prevent a default."[37]

On October 11 Rockefeller threw what proved to be the fatal blow for the future of the Domestic Council and its role as an advisory mechanism for the president. At a Columbus Day speech in New York City, Rockefeller urged Congress to provide help for the beleaguered city in spite of Ford's public opposition.

As the legislation moved closer to passage, Treasury Secretary Bill

Simon realized that it would be better to have a presidential sponsored package, which gave control to the executive branch for monitoring the city, rather than allowing New York City total control over the bailout. Simon was now Ford's principal advisor on the bailout, with Rockefeller and the Domestic Council merely observers to the decision-making. Rockefeller's Columbus Day speech echoed in the White House. By mid-November, just days before the Thanksgiving recess, the Congress passed a relief bill for New York City that met Simon's concerns and staved off a presidential veto.

Rockefeller Loses Control of the Domestic Council

As Rockefeller slowly lost control of the bailout issue and was being shut out of other areas of policy-making, he decided to try another tact in convincing Ford of the importance of long-range planning for the administration. Cannon and Rockefeller decided to develop a series of nationwide forums to draw attention to national priorities. The Domestic Council developed a series of six public forums on domestic policy that were to be held in six cities across the country. These would be one-day meetings beginning in Denver on October 21, moving to Kansas City, Austin, Philadelphia, and Nashville, and ending in Los Angeles on December 9, 1975. Their purpose would be to help the administration focus on key issues that federal programs might address. Ford tacitly endorsed the concept and issued the press release through the White House press office explaining the goals of the forums.

But before the public forums began, they were doomed. On October 6, 1975, Ford publicly announced his budget for the 1977 fiscal year calling for a cut in federal spending to $395 billion. He further announced that current spending programs would be revised and reduced. This meant that Ford would not support any new programs that the Domestic Council developed. Rockefeller was furious. Not only had the rug been pulled out from under him, he had never been consulted. Ford had not included him in the meetings that led to the budget decision. The decision-makers had been from the Economic Policy Board, not the Domestic Council.

With a reduced staff and a clear instruction not to create new programs, the Domestic Council was rapidly returning to its post-Watergate days as a technical assistance program for the president. On November 3, 1975, the council suffered another major blow. Nelson Rockefeller announced that he would not be Ford's running mate on the 1976 ticket. On December 16, barely one year after confirmed as vice president, Rockefeller resigned as vice chairman of the Domestic Council. In a stinging five-page memo to Ford, Rockefeller criticized the president for allowing the council to continue with a constant shortage of staff and no relief from the firefighting activities. He also criticized the way domestic policy was organized, with no White House unit having clear control over the process. He felt that the Economic Policy Board, the OMB, the Energy Resources Council, and the Council of Economic Advisers all advised the president separately on domestic policy without coordination or long-range planning. While this was the role of the Domestic Council, the president had not used it as such. In his final paragraphs, Rockefeller blasted Rumsfeld and Cheney for not supporting the council's activities.[38]

The Domestic Council Withdraws as a Policy-Maker

With Rockefeller's resignation, the Domestic Council slipped into oblivion as a policy-making body. Rumsfeld, Cheney, Simon, and Seidman closed ranks and shut out the Cannon group. Without Rockefeller on the front lines, Cannon was relegated to a back-seat position. Cannon viewed his staff as reactive, not proactive as Rockefeller had wanted.[39]

The Domestic Council was handed primarily short-term issues, often issues arising that day. Little long-range planning was undertaken. In early 1976 Cannon tried to regain a policy-making role for the Domestic Council. Ford agreed to support a role in long-range planning for the Domestic Council.[40] But staffing problems and the absence of a clear agenda prevented Cannon from moving too far in this direction.

Morale grew increasingly low at the Domestic Council. Domestic Council staff often felt as if they were outcasts from the White House, not even referring to themselves as White House staff. The meeting notes from a Domestic Council staff meeting on January 21, 1976, reflect a growing feeling of isolation in the White House. "There was much discussion of the lack of coordination between Domestic Council and Baroody's operations; Domestic Council and the Scheduling Operation; Domestic Council and the Press operation." The notes continue with a very dramatic summary of the problems the Domestic Council faced. "JMC [Cannon] asked Cavanaugh [deputy director of the Domestic Council] to work with the White House staff and try and get this untangled."[41]

In less than eighteen months, the Domestic Council had gone full circle: moving from a hapless unit back to a hapless unit. The failure of the Domestic Council to gain control of domestic policy-making was a series of one crushing event after another. But in large part Nelson Rockefeller can be blamed for failing to understand how Gerald Ford wanted his White House staff system to interact with the Cabinet, and how the personalities on the White House staff interacted. Rockefeller did not understand the egos or the relationships that surrounded the oval office.

Rockefeller most of all never understood Ford's commitment to give the Cabinet primary responsibility for policy development. This commitment was echoed throughout the administration. Ford not only told his Cabinet that they would be the administration's primary policy initiators, but he repeatedly told his staff the same thing.

Donald Rumsfeld provided strong support for Ford's concept of a limited White House role in policy-making. Rumsfeld issued memos to White House staff to ensure that they did not become too involved in departmental activities and blocked any reorganization of the Domestic Council that gave it significant power. Part of Rumsfeld's refusal to support the Domestic Council was simply public relations. He knew that the public saw that Henry Kissinger dominated foreign policy and that Bill Simon dominated economic policy. Rumsfeld wanted to ensure that the public saw Gerald Ford as firmly in charge of domestic policy-making. In Rumsfeld's view, if the public saw Nelson Rockefeller as dominating domestic policy, Ford would be seen as a caretaker president without any leadership qualities. Therefore Rumsfeld skillfully maneuvered Rockefeller and the Domestic Council into a back-seat position and encouraged the Economic Policy Board, with its relatively narrow focus, to become the dominant player in the limited role that the White House would play in domestic policy.

WITHOUT DIRECTION FROM THE WHITE HOUSE, THE CABINET TAKES ITS OWN INITIATIVES

Although Ford had given the Domestic Council perfunctory authority to move ahead with long-range planning in his February 1975 speech, the Cabinet never considered the Domestic Council a major player in policy issues. Cabinet officers and agency heads continued to develop their own goals and objectives, often without consulting anyone in the White House. Most cabinet officers continued to operate little fiefdoms with little or no interaction with the White House. For all practical purposes, the Cabinet officers were in control of all policy issues surrounding their departments. The Domestic Council never gained control of the domestic policy process.

One of the most visible cases of departmental control of policy-making came in the fall of 1974 as the administration was trying to forge a role for White House policy-making. Even as the Economic Policy Board and the Domestic Council were trying to work with the Cabinet, many members of the Cabinet were ignoring the White House staff.

The Energy Czar and the Gas Tax: The Cabinet Takes Control

One of the earliest examples of an agency moving along without ever touching base with the White House was the Federal Energy Administration

(FEA).[42] Had the FEA worked more closely with the White House on its policies for energy conservation, they would have known that Ford had certain
preconceived ideas of how he wanted to approach the issue. The Federal
Energy Administration, however, decided to continue to develop their policies
by themselves and to steer away from White House staff.

The FEA's view of itself as the nation's authority on energy grew substantially as the energy crisis heightened in the winter of 1972–73. As the crisis became more severe throughout the year and finally peaked with the
October 1973 Arab oil embargo, the FEA developed into the dominant player
in shaping the nation's response. By the time that Gerald Ford took office in
August 1974, the FEA was firmly in charge of developing energy policy. In
the summer and early fall of 1974, the White House made little effort to gain
control of the FEA and develop a "Ford" energy package.

The FEA director, John Sawhill, quickly saw that the FEA had the upper
hand and that no other agency nor the White House staff was moving to control its activities. The policy that evolved from the FEA was one of conservation, a policy that was in line with most members of the White House staff.
Sawhill saw conservation as the only tool available to reduce the energy shortage that had resulted in massive gasoline lines and severe cutbacks in home
heating oil. Sawhill was convinced that energy conservation was the only way
to reduce our dependence on foreign oil.

His decision to reduce dependency on foreign oil was not universally
supported in the administration, and was particularly opposed by Henry
Kissinger. Kissinger felt that it would destablize the world economy to cut
U.S. investment in foreign oil. He also felt, perhaps egotistically, that he per-
sonally could convince the oil producers to continue to supply the United
States at current levels at reasonable prices.

Rather than try to work with Kissinger or discuss the matter with key
members of the White House staff, Sawhill tried to go directly to Ford urging
a policy of fuel conservation. When Sawhill did not hear from Ford, he decided to go public. On October 1, Sawhill went on the NBC morning show,
Today, and urged a 20-cents per gallon tax on gasoline as one way to reduce
consumption.

Ford was furious, saying privately to staff that there would be a gas tax
"over my dead body."[43] Publicly, the White House press secretary, Ron
Nessen, issued a statement saying that cabinet officers were free to say what
they wanted since it was an open administration.

Sawhill did not last long. He was opposed by not only Kissinger, but
now by Simon and Ford. The inevitable was now only days away. On
October 17, Sawhill received a call from *Newsweek* saying they had a tip that
he was being replaced. *Newsweek* published its prediction in its October 21
issue. Without delaying any longer, Ford finally called Sawhill on October 25

to confirm the rumors: he was fired. As he had with the Nixon holdovers, though, Ford wanted to assure Sawhill that he had a job until he could find another one. Sawhill subsequently remained on the payroll as a consultant until the end of the year when a new director was confirmed. For his remaining days in office, though, Sawhill kept an extremely low profile and did not mention the energy tax. He finally left in the beginning of the new year to take over the presidency of New York University.

Sawhill's experience with the White House was indicative of the <u>total lack of control that White House staff exerted over the agency heads at the outset of the administration.</u> Sawhill was essentially given a free rein to design the administration's energy policy as part of Ford's support for a Cabinet-based policy system. Ford even backed his decision to reduce dependency on foreign oil, in spite of Kissinger's view. Had Sawhill not moved on a collision course with Ford on the taxation issue, he would have remained at the helm of energy policy-making. His replacement, Frank Zarb, continued the autonomy of the FEA in spite of Sawhill's setbacks and continued as the nation's "energy czar."

Throughout the next eighteen months of the administration, Ford kept his pledge of a Cabinet-based government. Major administration policies flowed from the departments, not from the White House. Only three significant issues emerged from the White House: the pardon of Richard Nixon, the rescue from Saigon, and the coyote problem. Other issues, such as regulatory relief, auto emissions, and welfare reform, all developed within the departments. Even the volatile issue of common situs picketing, which the White House eventually became involved in, was developed in the Labor Department with little White House involvement. Not until business leaders, members of Congress, members of the Governors' Conference, and numerous Republican leaders besieged Ford to stop Labor Secretary John Dunlop did Ford intervene.

The Nixon Pardon: A White House–Controlled Policy

Perhaps the most difficult decision that Gerald Ford made as president was the one to pardon Richard Nixon. This decision was one of the few that was totally controlled by White House staff. The Cabinet was not involved in the decision-making process. Ford relied on his old friend Philip Buchen to handle the process.

The issue began with some seriousness two weeks after Ford took office. At his first press conference on August 28, he found himself inundated with questions about a possible pardon for Nixon. Helen Thomas from United Press International asked the first question at the press conference: Should Nixon be given immunity from prosecution? Would he be pardoned before a trial?[44]

Ford realized that the issue would dominate the press coverage of his administration until Nixon was either pardoned or went to jail. The task of pursuing the issue of a pardon went not to the Justice Department, but to the White House legal counsel, Phil Buchen. When Buchen realized that the criminal indictments that the Special Prosecutor, Leon Jaworski, were pursuing were beyond his scope of legal expertise, Buchen still did not call in the Justice Department. He hired a private criminal attorney, Benton Becker, who had worked for the Justice Department in the 1960s in the case against Representative Adam Clayton Powell. Ford knew Becker from the Powell case and completely supported the appointment.

For the following two weeks Buchen and Becker examined every facet of the issue and determined that Ford should pardon Nixon in order to take public attention off the issue. In summarizing his view of the pardon, Ford said:

> I was very sure of what would happen if I let the charges against Nixon run their legal course. Months were sure to elapse between an indictment and trial. The entire process would no doubt require years: a minimum of two, a maximum of six. And Nixon would not spend time quietly in San Clemente. He would be fighting for his freedom, taking his cause to the people, and his constant struggle would have dominated the news. The story would overshadow everything else. . . . America needed recovery, no revenge. The hate had to be drained and the healing begun.[45]

After Buchen and Benton had made their recommendation, Ford called a small group of advisors together to gather their views on a possible pardon. Again, no one from the Cabinet was invited. It was strictly a White House policy decision. Those invited were Buchen, Haig, Kissinger (in his capacity as National Security Advisor), Hartmann, and Marsh. There were mixed feelings among the group, but the consensus was that Nixon should be pardoned for the sake of the Ford administration. Without the pardon, Ford had little chance of moving ahead. The nation would be stuck on Watergate even longer.

By September 3 the decision had been made to issue the pardon. Again the Justice Department was not contacted. Rather, Benton Becker spent the Labor Day weekend in law libraries researching the president's authority to grant a pardon before an indictment. Buchen assured Ford that he had the constitutional authority to issue the pardon at any time.

On September 4 Buchen and Becker met with Nixon's attorney and began to draw up a mutually acceptable wording for the pardon. A few days later, Becker flew to California to meet with Nixon personally to discuss the pardon. Becker told a somewhat disoriented Nixon that the acceptance of the pardon was an admission of guilt. Nixon agreed to the terms. On September 8 Ford issued the pardon. Not once during the process had the White House sought any advice from the Department of Justice or other Cabinet-level department. The pardon had been a White House orchestrated event with no input from the Cabinet.

The Coyote Issue: The White House Takes Control

The pardon case, however, was not typical of the policy-making process of the Ford administration. Rarely did the White House actively take control of the policy process. The argument could easily made, however, that the pardon case was not a policy-making issue and that the White House staff was handling an administrative rather than policy issue.

Generally the White House staff became involved with issues that the departments were handling only when political pressure was being placed on the president to reverse a departmental decision. These types of cases were what Nelson Rockefeller referred to as "firefighting." The White House staff was rarely involved in initiating policy proposals or even guiding the departments in policy proposals. Rather, the White House staff dealt with single-topic problems that were causing the president some political embarrassment.

In this particular case, members of the Congressional delegations from western states were lobbying Ford to permit the use of poison to kill coyotes. Because of the intensity of the issue to Ford's friends in Congress, the White House staff decided to become involved. While the coyote case certainly does not involve a major policy issue or initiative, it very clearly describes the type of minutia that the White House staff became involved in. The coyote issue became a central policy issue to the Ford White House and is a classic illustration of White House prioritization of domestic policy. The failure of the White House staff to focus on broader policy issues, rather than "firefighting" issues such as the coyote issues, is at the heart Ford's failure to gain control of the policy process. The Ford White House was not engaged in either broad agenda-setting or departmental management.

The case focused on the concerns of farmers that coyotes were ravaging their livestock, which were grazing on federal lands. The coyotes were causing a significant amount of financial damage by killing their cattle and sheep. The farmers and ranchers who used the federal lands wanted the federal government to spray the fields with toxicants that would kill, or at least deter, the coyotes. But President Nixon had approved an executive order that banned the use of toxicants on federal lands.

On the other side of the issue were environmental groups who wanted the ban on toxicants continued. The Environmental Protection Agency, which was responsible for the ban on toxins, refused to make any exceptions to the ban. The issue was then brought to the White House staff by members of Congress to resolve. So in the spring of 1975 the White House staff actively became involved in predator control, primarily because the issue had drawn so much support in Congress.

The issue of predator control began in 1972 when President Nixon signed Executive Order 11643 banning the use of chemical toxicants on federal lands as a way to kill predatory animals, particularly coyotes. The toxicants were used only in federal land areas that ranchers and farmers were allowed to graze their animals.

Charged with enforcing the action was the newly created Environmental Protection Agency. The EPA had taken over many of the responsibilities formerly held by the Department of Agriculture with regard to monitoring the use of toxic chemicals.

Prior to 1972 when the executive order was signed, ranchers and farmers had used a series of chemicals around their lands, to kill coyotes. But once those chemicals were banned, the options for protecting livestock were limited. Over the course of the next three years, the coyote population dramatically increased without the chemical controls, leading to numerous attacks by coyotes on various livestock. Farmers and ranchers in western states saw the coyotes destroy animal after animal of their cattle and sheep herds.

By the spring of 1975, after two full seasons of primarily young animals being attacked and killed, the ranchers and farmers sought political help from their Congressional delegation. Nearly every member of the Senate from the midwest and west supported the anticoyote movement. Led by Senator Mike Mansfield, members of the Senate delegation supporting the ranchers included Senators McClure, Garn, Moss, Domenici, Bentsen, Montoya, Fannin, Abourezk, Church, Tower, Bartlett, Laxalt, Curtis, McGovern, Hansen, Dole, Bellmon, and Hatfield.[46] They first went to EPA, but EPA refused to make any exceptions in their regulations. They next went to the White House, where the Domestic Council staff grappled with the issue.

After carefully reviewing the issue, Jim Cannon and his staff decided that the political pressures were severe enough to reconsider the use of toxicants for predator control. In July 1975, Cannon recommended to President Ford that he amend the Nixon executive order to allow the use of some chemical toxicants to control predatory animals on federal lands. This would keep EPA happy, since it did not have to succumb to political pressure, and would also keep the Congressional delegation satisfied. Ford signed a new executive order, #11870, on July 18, 1975, which allowed "the development of economically feasible and environmentally acceptable methods to protect livestock producers from coyote predation."[47] But the new executive order did not allow for sodium cyanide capsules to be used, which had previously been extremely successful.

The sheepranchers were not satisfied with the limited toxicants available to them and pressured their Congressional delegation again for the ability to use the sodium cyanide capsules. The administrator of the EPA, Russell Train, agreed that the sodium cyanide capsules could be used, but did not want to see further relaxation of the ban on toxicants. In a memo to Ford in the fall of 1975, Cannon argued that "the public lands must be protected by Executive action for the benefits offered to all Americans, not just the few who are allowed the use of these lands for sheep and cattle grazing." Cannon couched his argument, though, by saying that if the federal government allowed the use of the sodium cyanide capsules, they would not "remove the safeguard that the Executive Order offers against the relaxation of prohibitions on other, and more unacceptable, chemical toxicants."[48] Ford approved the limited use of toxicants—that is, the sodium cyanide capsules—on federal lands where sheep and cattle were allowed to graze as Cannon recommended.

The coyote issue, as it became known, demonstrated the type of issue that the Domestic Council and the White House staff became involved in. As Nelson Rockefeller often said, the White House staff did too much "firefighting" and not enough policy development.

The coyote issue was being managed by the Domestic Council staff at the same time that the New York City bailout was being debated within the White House. Both issues were in full swing during the summer of 1975. To some extent, Cannon was using the coyote issue as a means of staying close to Ford. Since Seidman and Simon were controlling the bailout, Cannon needed an issue to have constant access to the oval office and key members of the White House staff. There is no doubt that the coyote issue should never have reached the White House and certainly should never have reached the president. For the president to spend numerous meetings discussing a relatively small matter was a misuse of his time. Yet Cannon allowed the issue to remain in the White House as a means of gaining access to Ford. Cannon's misjudgment of the type of issue the Domestic Council should focus on was another contributing factor to the demise of White House control of policy-making.

CONCLUSION: AN ADMINISTRATION OF FIREFIGHTING

When Donald Rumsfeld moved over to the Defense Department in late 1975, Dick Cheney moved up to staff coordinator, or more precisely White House chief of staff. Little changed. The personalities in the White House continued to be diverse and lacking any sense of shared vision. The Domestic Council and the Economic Policy Board continued to vie for dominance in domestic affairs.

For two and one-half years Gerald Ford operated a White House with little control over the domestic policy-making apparatus of government. Policy-making was handled in the departments. The White House staff, beset with personal and organizational conflict, never gained control over any aspect of the policy process. Even when Ford shuffled his Cabinet officers, there was still no significant change in the Cabinet–White House relationship. The departments continued to pursue their own agendas with minimal guidance from the White House. Since Ford and Rumsfeld had decided that cutting the federal budget was their priority, and that no new programs would be accepted, they viewed the role of the White House staff in policy-making as almost nonexistent. Without a White House staff to guide and coordinate the departments, Cabinet officers remained in control of their own agendas as long as they kept their budgets to a minimum. Cabinet Government was operational during the Ford administration.

In 1979 Gerald Ford wrote his memoirs, entitled *A Time to Heal.* Ford's choice of a title for the book is in many ways his own description of a White House that never took control. He chose a title that reflected what he saw as the agenda for his administration. Go slowly. Build public confidence in the presidency. Do not create waves.

Ford did not create waves. The most memorable act of his administration was the pardon of Richard Nixon. He did not pursue an activist agenda and capped any creative thinking in the White House. Since the departments were given no authority to develop new programs, Cabinet Government was an ideal way to go slowly and rebuild the presidency.

During his term in office Ford did exactly what the transition team urged him to do. He rebuilt public confidence in the presidency and tried to heal the wounds of Watergate. Those were his priorities and he accomplished them. In essence there were no other priorities in the administration. The White House staff never gained control over the policy process because there were no policies that it wanted to pursue. It was an administration of "firefighting."

FIVE

THE CARTER YEARS

As the fallout from Watergate brought the Nixon presidency crashing down, Jimmy Carter began to pursue the presidency. Even before Gerald Ford had taken over the reins of government from Richard Nixon, Carter was gearing up a run for the presidency. For over a year after he left the Georgia Governor's office in 1975, Carter campaigned for the 1976 Democratic presidential nomination. After a hard fought primary, Carter won the nomination and moved on to fight Gerald Ford in the general election. Carter edged by Ford with nearly two million votes.[1]

The issue of White House–Cabinet relations, particularly the power of the White House staff, again became an issue during the 1976 presidential campaign as it had eight years earlier. President Nixon's reliance on the White House staff for policy advice during most of his term led to frequent criticism from Carter during the 1976 campaign of a White House policy-making system. Carter constantly reminded the public of Ford's tie to the beleaguered former president.

Nixon's reliance on his White House staff led Jimmy Carter to redesign the White House–Cabinet relationship. Throughout the 1976 campaign, Carter promised to bring the Cabinet to the forefront of policy-making and declared his belief in "a Cabinet administration of our government." He firmly stated that the White House staff would never be in a position superior to that of the Cabinet, a direct reference to the authority that H.R. Haldeman and John Ehrlichman had wielded in the Nixon administration.[2] Throughout the campaign he ignored the Ford White House, which had essentially allowed Cabinet Government to flourish.

DEFINING THE WHITE HOUSE–CABINET RELATIONSHIP

Once elected to the presidency, Carter fulfilled his campaign promise and established a structure that gave the Cabinet authority over a wide range of departmental policy and management decisions. White House staff were directed to stay out of departmental affairs, particularly personnel selection, and to limit themselves to special projects, general strategy, coordination, and mediation activities. Presidential aides were not to become oversecretaries of any department. In an interview prior to the election Carter left no doubt of his position:

> There would be a much heavier dependence on the Cabinet members to run their departments than we've had in the past. I would not establish a "palace guard" in the White House with the authority to run the departments in the federal government.[3]

In another interview Carter stated:

> A White House staff of almost five hundred people is far too large. I want a White House staff which is organizationally lean and which functions in a true staff capacity, not a command role. I shall not permit the departments to remain isolated from the president.[4]

But in spite of Carter's intention to have a lean White House staff and a strong Cabinet, he was unable to work with the structure. By mid-1979 he had dismantled Cabinet Government and established a White House-based policy-making system. The changes in organizational structure made in mid-1979 included the appointment of a chief of staff within the White House to clear all appointments, including those with the Cabinet members; expansion of the domestic policy staff to initiate domestic policy proposals; and a personnel staff to approve departmental personnel selection. Cabinet Government lasted less than two years in the Carter administration.

Selection of the Cabinet

The Cabinet selection process, which was at the heart of Carter's plan to establish a strong Cabinet, focused on a Cabinet with "executive management ability" to guide programs both through Congress and the bureaucracy.[5] In describing his goals for Cabinet building, he stated that:

> I would put a strong emphasis on executive management capacity and sen-

sitivity to people's needs. Obviously compatibility would be an important factor— not only with me but with the members of the Cabinet.[6]

Carter's strategy for Cabinet selection focused on candidates with strong managerial and technical skills rather than candidates committed either to Carter personally or to his domestic or foreign policy goals.[7] He wanted department heads who would direct procedural and organizational changes within their departments rather than initiate major policy changes. He did not seek to move a host of personal or political allies into the Cabinet.

For Carter, the primary responsibility of his administration was starting a "drastic and thorough revision of the federal bureaucracy." Achieving "maximum bureaucratic efficiency" and pursuing federal reorganization were the top two priorities of the administration.[8] Not surprisingly he placed management skills at the top of the list of Cabinet prerequisites.[9]

Domestic and foreign policy initiatives fell well below procedural initiatives in his list of administration priorities. His Cabinet selection process was tuned to bring managers, above all, into the administration. Carter was less concerned with the policy views of his Cabinet designees than their ability to manage bureaucratic change.

Broadening the Political Base of the Cabinet

In accordance with these priorities of procedural and organizational change in governmental structure, Carter sought technical experts and experienced administrators for his Cabinet. Yet he also sought to build a collective Cabinet that would strengthen the political base of the administration. In particular, this was directed at his ties to the Democratic Party, damaged by bitter primary fights, and at repaying political debts from the general election. Carter chose the majority of his Cabinet from among a pool of experienced government administrators with strong Democratic ties. Patricia Roberts Harris, Michael Blumenthal, Cyrus Vance, Harold Brown, and Joseph Califano had each held senior positions during previous administrations and had each been active within the party. Of the eleven Cabinet officers, however, only two, Bob Bergland and Cecil Andrus, had held elective office.

Trilateral Commission

While the majority of Cabinet appointments were chosen to meet the goal of rebuilding ties to the mainstream of the Democratic Party, several also had prior working relationships with Carter. Three members of the Cabinet (Vance, Blumenthal, and Brown) had worked with Carter on the Trilateral Commission. The Trilateral Commission was a private, international organization created in 1972 by David Rockefeller to promote business relations among the "trilateral" world of North America, Europe, and Japan. Carter had joined the Trilateral Commission in 1973, while governor of Georgia, as a representative of the industrializing "new south." Its membership consisted of approximately 180 businessmen, lawyers, government officials, and others, including sixty from the Unites States.[10] Carter drew heavily on his contacts in the Trilateral Commission for Cabinet and sub-Cabinet appointments. Another Cabinet designee, Joseph Califano, had been a member of the Council on Foreign Relations, which was closely aligned with the Trilateral Commission. Califano had also been an advisor on family matters for Carter's 1976 presidential campaign.

Carter drew on a variety of other personal relationships to build his Cabinet. Cecil Andrus had worked with Carter on a number of panels of the National Governors' Conference and also had used departmental reorganization and cost efficiency as the hallmarks of his gubernatorial campaign. Griffin Bell had been a partner in King and Spalding, the Atlanta law firm of Carter's closest advisor, Charles Kirbo. In addition, Bell had been a member of the same country club as Carter in Americus, Georgia, during the 1960s.

Carter, however, did not know nearly half of his Cabinet nominees, such as Brock Adams, Bob Bergland, Juanita Kreps, Patricia Roberts Harris, or Ray Marshall prior to the meetings to discuss their Cabinet appointments. Their nominations had been supported by influential members of the Democratic Party. Bob Bergland, for example, was recommended by Walter Mondale; Brock Adams by Tip O'Neill; and Patricia Roberts Harris by Irving S. Shapiro, chairman of the Business Roundtable. Ray Marshall, although not labor's first choice, was supported by organized labor.[11]

Diversity in the Cabinet

Carter's strategy for Cabinet-building focused on candidates with strong managerial skills and with strong ties to the Democratic Party, but he was not adverse to a selection process that included geographic, ethnic, religious, and gender balance. As he noted in his memoirs, he actually sought such diversity: "My final choices had both geographic diversity and breadth of experience." And "These men and women— black and white, Protestants, Jews, and Catholics from all regions of the country."[12]

Geographic diversity, a criterion in every Cabinet selection process since 1789, was continued in the Carter Cabinet. After the final choices were made, the south had three nominees (Bell, Kreps, and Marshall), the north had four nominees (Vance, Blumenthal, Califano, and Harris), the west had three nominees (Brown, Andrus, and Adams) and the midwest had one nominee (Bergland). In part, the choices reflected Carter's electoral balance in the 1976 election. The larger midwestern states of Illinois, Indiana, Michigan, and Wisconsin had given Ford popular majorities. The larger northern states, however, had supported Carter and they had subsequently received the majority of Cabinet appointments. With the exception of Georgia, which gave Carter a nearly two to one voter edge over Ford, Carter's largest popular majorities had been in New York and Massachusetts.

Religious diversity was another area considered in the Carter Cabinet selection process. Carter's deeply-held religious beliefs (as a Baptist and born-again Christian) had been a constant issue during the campaign. Not since the 1960 election of John F. Kennedy, the country's first Roman Catholic president, had religion been a factor in presidential politics. Arthur Schlesinger, Jr., described Kennedy's religion as having affected the 1960 elections so deeply that Democrats lost congressional races they had expected to win. He noted that "The Democrats had lost twenty seats in the 1960 Congressional election. . . nearly all defeated because of the religious issue."[13]

Carter used the Cabinet selection process to send a clear and unequivocal signal that religion would not be a test of loyalty in his administration. The Cabinet nominees subsequently included representation from not only the Jewish and Catholic faith, but a wide range of Protestant faiths. The issue was of such concern to Carter during the campaign that he had focused public attention on the diversity of religious backgrounds of his advisors. In advertisements run in several Jewish newspapers, he pointed out that three of his closest advisors were Jewish: Robert Lipshutz, Stuart Eizenstat, and Gerald Rafshoon.[14] Ethnic representation, particularly black representation, was also considered in the Cabinet selection process. Carter, who had courted the black vote during the campaign, endeavored to repay that support through his Cabinet appointments.[15]

Similarly, Carter saw women as a major voting bloc and courted that support by promising to work for the passage of the Equal Rights Amendment, to gain greater representation for women in the 1980 delegate selection process of the Democratic Party, to appoint women to senior positions within his administration. Unlike Richard Nixon eight years earlier, however, Jimmy Carter did not try to create a bipartisan Cabinet.

SELECTION OF THE WHITE HOUSE STAFF

The White House staff selection process was considerably less methodical than that of the Cabinet selection process, for Carter essentially transferred his senior campaign staff into the White House. There were few criteria for White House staff other than loyalty and an established working relationship with Carter.

This process was predictable, for Carter had outlined his intentions as early as July 1976 when he stated that the White House staff would be composed of "those with whom I've been associated during the campaign itself up through November."[16]

Immediately after the election, Carter had his senior campaign staff design an organizational structure for the White House staff. Their recommendation was to create a structure that included a political advisor, administrative assistant, counsel, congressional liaison, press secretary, personnel director, domestic advisor, national security advisor, and economic advisor.[17]

Nine Senior Staff Emerge

The structure that was finally developed parallelled the recommendations during the transition. Carter's choices for the senior White House staff were primarily, as he had indicated, campaign staff members, most of whom had been involved in the Georgia gubernatorial campaign of 1970 and the presidential campaign of 1976. Carter created a senior White House with nine positions:

1. Press Secretary: Jody Powell
2. Political Affairs: Hamilton Jordan
3. Cabinet Secretary and Intergovernmental Affairs: Jack Watson
4. Domestic Policy Advisor: Stuart Eizenstat
5. Counsel to the President: Robert Lipshutz
6. Congressional Liaison: Frank Moore
7. National Security Advisor: Zbigniew Brzezinski
8. Public Liaison: Margaret Costanza
9. Energy Advisor: James Schlesinger

Of these nine, the first six had worked full-time on the national campaign, had known Carter at least since his tenure as Governor of Georgia, and were from Atlanta. Brzezinski, with whom he had worked on the Trilateral Commission, had been the campaign foreign policy advisor. Costanza had been the Carter campaign director in New York. Only James Schlesinger, Secretary of Defense under both Richard Nixon and Gerald Ford, was a relative outsider.

Organizational Structure

Unlike Richard Nixon, who had paid virtually no attention to the organizational structure of the White House prior to the transition, Jimmy Carter considered the options available to him at some length during the campaign.

Carter rejected the competitive staff structure that Franklin Roosevelt had used, preferring an organizational structure along strictly functional lines without overlapping responsibilities. He similarly rejected the organizational structure of the Kennedy/Johnson years which lacked definitive staff responsibilities and the formal, hierarchical design that both Dwight Eisenhower and Richard Nixon had used.[18] Carter preferred the "knights of the round-table" approach of the Ford administration, which had a senior staff with specific assignments and with equal access to the president.

The general assignments of senior staff were the result of a study that the Carter campaign staff had prepared during the transition. Officially entitled "White House Study Project, December 17, 1976," the study listed twenty-two separate functions within the White House that required staff supervision. Of the twenty-two functions, most involved the administrative activities of the White House.

Essentially, each member of the campaign staff was transferred to a similar position on the White House staff. Zbigniew Brzezinski, who had been the campaign's foreign policy adviser, became Carter's National Security Advisor. Stuart Eizenstat, who had been the campaign's issues director, became director of the Domestic Policy Group. Members of the campaign staff who had worked for Carter during his administration in Georgia, such as Jody Powell and Frank Moore, were given positions similar to those they had held in Georgia.

STRUCTURING THE WHITE HOUSE–CABINET RELATIONSHIP

On January 20, 1977, Jimmy Carter met with his newly sworn in Cabinet and reiterated his commitment to a strong Cabinet, stating emphatically that:

> I believe in Cabinet administration of government. There will never be an instance while I am President when the members of the White House staff dominate or act in a superior position to the members of our Cabinet.[19]

Carter subsequently delineated the Cabinet's role in departmental management and policy-making more specifically, by stating that:

1. Cabinet officers will play a major role in policy-making.
2. Cabinet officers will be free to set their own priorities.
3. Cabinet officers will be free to choose their own staffs. The White House will have veto authority but will not dictate the selections.
4. Cabinet officers will be able to administer their departments without White House interference.[20]

His plan for a strong Cabinet focused on using the Cabinet, rather than the White House staff, as his "first circle of advisors" in both domestic and foreign policy.[21] Carter wanted his Cabinet to have more responsibility for policy-making and discretion in decision-making than Nixon had allowed his Cabinet.

Key to the independence of the Cabinet was their ability to hire their own staffs. Under Jack Watson's direction, the campaign had developed lists of people through the Talent Inventory Program who were interested in working for the new administration. These lists, which were computerized and put into a data base organized by area of interest, were available to department heads. The names were not necessarily supported by the White House and were considered only one source of names for the departments.[22] Cabinet members did not have to use the names and were free to recruit on their own.

Reorganization Authority

One of Carter's first moves to strengthen the power of the Cabinet in policy-making was to seek Congressional approval to reorganize the Executive Office of the President (EOP). On February 4, 1977, Carter requested Congressional approval for restoring presidential authority to reorganize the executive branch. Carter sought a four-year extension of the Reorganization Act of 1939, which had expired in April 1973. The bill, approved and signed into law April 6, 1977, was part of Carter's overall plan to increase government efficiency by reducing the number of federal agencies and agency complements.[23]

The reorganization of the EOP allowed Carter to dismantle many of the White House advisory groups that competed with the Cabinet for policy-making authority. Included in this group were the Domestic Policy Council, Economic Opportunity Council, Federal Property Council, Office of Drug Abuse, Office of Telecommunications Policy, Office on International Policy, and the Energy Resources Council. Except for the Domestic Policy Council, whose domestic policy responsibilities were absorbed by the Domestic Policy Group within the White House, the responsibilities of the advisory groups were either assigned to specific departments or absorbed by Cabinet-level policy groups following the reorganization. This process enhanced the Cabinet's authority in policy development and reduced the possibility of conflict between the Cabinet and White House staff.

Cabinet Clusters Emerge

Central to his program to redesign policy-making, Carter established a structure that gave the Cabinet prime responsibility for policy initiation and development. This was accomplished through the establishment of groups of

Cabinet officers, known as cabinet clusters, who worked together on policy proposals. This structure was described by columnist James Reston as a "presidential council," which worked together in the "formulation of national policy."[24]

The cabinet clusters functioned through the White House Cabinet Secretariat, an office that Gerald Ford had reestablished after its dormancy during the Nixon administration. Although Nixon used the Cabinet Secretariat during his first year in office, its functions and staff were absorbed into the Domestic Council in 1970. Ford reinstated the Secretariat as part of his efforts to bring the Cabinet back to the forefront of policy-making.

Jack Watson was the senior staff member given authority over Carter's Cabinet Secretariat. He created the cluster system to bring groups of Cabinet officers together to work on specific policy issues. However, unlike the committee system of the Urban Affairs Council during the Nixon administration, which had permanent assignments and membership, the policy assignments and membership of the clusters varied throughout the administration. The exception was the economic policy cluster, which supplanted Ford's Economic Policy Board, whose membership consisted of the Secretaries of State, Treasury, Commerce, Labor, the Chairman of the Council of Economic Advisors, and the Director of the Office of Management and Budget. Clusters generally focused on narrow issues such as national health insurance, welfare reform, and energy policy, and on specific issues such as what to do with the ten federal regional councils that had been established during the Nixon administration. The White House did not attempt to control the final product, only to target the issue in the cabinet clusters. Those issues not addressed by the cabinet clusters remained the province of the departments. The White House provided minimal oversight over issue positions developed within the departments not related to cluster discussions.

Reducing White House Staff

The White House–Cabinet relationship that Carter structured after the inauguration had reduced the need for a large White House staff to manage policy development. In a televised "fireside talk" on February 2, 1977, he told the nation that his administration was rapidly moving to "bring the growth of government under control."[25] By eliminating presidential advisory councils and reducing the size of the Domestic Policy and National Security Council staffs, Carter had been able to reduce the complement of the White House staff.[26] Among the largest reductions that took place was in the size of the Domestic Policy staff, which was reduced from a high of seventy in the Nixon administration to its current level of twenty-two. The entire White House staff also saw major reductions, moving from 485 to 351, although it should be noted that many of those jobs were moved to the Central Administrative Unit within the

Executive Office. The Executive Office, which was cut from 1,712 to 1,459, had about one-third of the nearly 250 cut staff absorbed by other agencies.[27] Carter's efforts toward reducing staff were part of his campaign pledge that the White House would not dominate the policy process. This process was also designed to bolster his efforts in creating cabinet government structure of governing.

Review and Comment on Cabinet Policies: The Triumvirate

Although Carter used the Cabinet for policy development, the White House staff remained involved in the process through a review and comment process on major proposals. Carter created what he called a *triumvirate* system of policy development, with the Cabinet responsible for the initiation and development of policy proposals, the White House staff responsible for policy review, and the Office of Management and Budget responsible for budget review and legislative evaluation. Each component of the triumvirate managed a different aspect of the overall policy process.

The Domestic Policy Group

The White House component of the triumvirate was the Domestic Policy Group (DPG), under the direction of Stuart Eizenstat, which analyzed and commented on cabinet cluster proposals before Carter received them.[28] Carter had renamed the Domestic Council created by Nixon and continued by Ford. Eizenstat had a staff of twenty-two professionals by April 1977, far below that of the Domestic Council at its height. The total staff included Eizenstat, two deputy directors, nine senior policy analysts, ten junior policy analysts, two administrative assistants, fourteen secretaries, one messenger, and two research staff.[29]

The Domestic Policy Group's role was to ensure that policy proposals met administration goals and had examined a range of policy options. Bert Carp, the deputy director of the Domestic Policy Group and former Mondale Congressional assistant, described the responsibilities of this group:

> What we try to do is see that the paper that goes to the president is in decent shape; that people develop the options that should be developed; and, as best we can, that arguments that the president ought not to have to resolve are resolved among the parties.[30]

In essence, the evaluation prepared by the Domestic Policy Group looked at consistency with the administration's long-range goals. The review by DPG did not try to change the cabinet cluster recommendation, only to comment to Carter on the apparent problems with the proposal.

In contrast to the Nixon administration's Domestic Council, the Domestic Policy Group did not develop policy proposals.[31] During the Carter administration's early months, the Domestic Policy Group managed the review and comment process and operated as a special projects and crisis center. It handled presidential messages, coordinated interdepartmental programs, mediated jurisdictional disputes, and developed long-range goals for the administration. Reviewing cabinet cluster recommendations was only a small part of their activities.

Eizenstat kept the Domestic Policy Group from becoming the focal point for policy-making. According to Eizenstat, "Policy development was done in the departments. . . . We don't have the staff capacity, the computer capacity, or the historical knowledge that the bureaucracies of different departments can bring to a problem."[32]

Once the Domestic Policy Group had completed this review, their comments were compiled by Jack Watson, who circulated the cluster proposals to other White House staff for comments. The final package sent to Carter consisted of the original policy recommendation from the cabinet cluster, an evaluation from the Domestic Policy Group, a budgetary review by the Office of Management and Budget, and general comments from other White House staff. Carter then made the decision whether or not to allow the cluster proposal to go forward.

Neither Watson's nor Eizenstat's office attempted to guide or control the proposals developed within the cabinet clusters. The role of the White House staff was limited to the review and comment process. Carter's decision, though, was predicated on the recommendations of his staff.

EROSION OF CABINET AUTHORITY IN POLICY DEVELOPMENT

Control of the policy-making process by the departments lasted less than a year. By mid-1977 Carter began to redesign the relationship between the Cabinet and the White House staff. Policy development was moved out of the cabinet clusters into the Domestic Policy Group in the White House.

White House Staff Reorganization

In a reorganization of White House staff on July 15, 1977, management of the cabinet clusters was reassigned within the White House from Jack Watson's Cabinet Secretariat to Stuart Eizenstat's Domestic Policy Group. At a press conference Carter gave Eizenstat responsibility for managing the way in which domestic and most economic policy issues were prepared for presidential decision. The *Washington Post* noted that "Eizenstat's new domestic policy process is aimed at increasing the President's ability to oversee and control every step in framing major domestic programs."[33]

By September 1977 the role of the Cabinet Secretariat had been dramatically reduced and was essentially limited to preparing the agenda for the regular Monday morning Cabinet meetings and ensuring that Presidential orders given during the meetings were followed. The role of the Cabinet Secretariat was reframed more in line with the Eisenhower Secretariat. The cluster groups continued to meet on minor policy issues and on coordination matters, but had little direct responsibility for major policy initiatives. The Domestic Policy Group was centralizing the policy-making process in the White House. To support its new responsibilities, staffing in the Domestic Policy Group grew from twenty to forty-three full-time positions.[34]

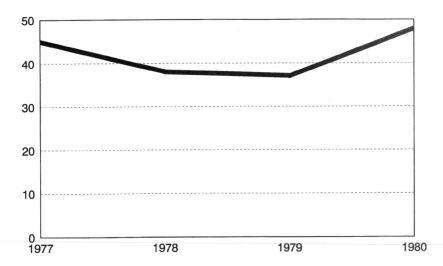

FIGURE 8. Total Senior White House Staff (Carter)

Eizenstat immediately moved to restructure how Cabinet officers participated in presidential policy-making. Cabinet clusters were convened less often and were convened only at Eizenstat's request. Policy discussions in the cabinet clusters focused on issues that the White House staff, rather than the Cabinet, developed. Prior to the Domestic Policy Group gaining control of the cluster process, Cabinet officers had set the agenda. They chose the issues that were to be discussed within the clusters.

Once the Domestic Policy Group gained control of the policy process, agenda setting moved into the White House. Eizenstat's staff prepared an issue definition memorandum for the cabinet clusters, which outlined the policy issue to be addressed, questions to be answered, the agencies to be involved, the timetable to be met, and the organization that would serve as a lead agency.[35] After reviewing the issue definition memorandum, Carter initialed his approval or disapproval. If approved, basic research was done by the lead agency under White House supervision with Eizenstat's staff synthesizing the departmental material into a Presidential Review Memorandum (PRM).[36] The PRM outlined the policy option for Carter, giving the pros and cons of each option. Cabinet officials had an opportunity to review the Presidential Review Memorandum and to recommend changes before it was sent to Carter.

The final memorandum, however, went from Eizenstat to Carter, not from a Cabinet member or cabinet cluster to Carter. This was a major blow to the independence of the Cabinet, for the White House staff controlled the final policy product submitted to the president. Even with the review and comment process in the early months of the administration, Carter was given the original proposal prepared by the cabinet clusters.

Camp David Meetings: The President and the Cabinet

The erosion of Cabinet authority, which began in July 1977 with the restructuring of the policy development process in the White House, took another dramatic turn in April 1978 when Carter gave the White House staff responsibility for approving departmental personnel selections and for clearing all statements of administration policy. On April 16–17, 1978, Carter called together his Cabinet at the presidential retreat in the Catoctin Mountains of Maryland and informed them of the new White House–Cabinet relationship.

The two-day retreat at Camp David, Maryland, was called for the purpose of improving the "weak spots" in the administration, according to the White House press release.[37] However, the purpose was actually to define new limits of Cabinet authority. Although Carter said the meeting was intended "to express criticism freely about the relationship between the White House and your own departments," in effect it was the death toll for the independence of the Cabinet.[38]

This particularly upset Griffin Bell, who felt Carter had not lived up to his promise for a strong and independent Cabinet. Bell said of the results of the Camp David meetings, "In the aftermath, the White House staff assumed more and more power, and the secretaries of most Cabinet departments were relegated to a lower level of authority."[39] In stark contrast, Robert Lipshutz, Counsel to the President, supported the need for greater centralization of policy in the White House, including that of the Justice Department. "I insisted," he said, "that the White House should play a major role in determining which side of those issues the Justice Department should be on because there were policy judgements. . . that should reflect the President's position."[40]

Responsibility for personnel decisions was one of the major changes that resulted from the Camp David meetings. Retreating from his earlier statements that Cabinet secretaries would have authority to choose their own personnel, Carter required that all noncivil personnel appointments within executive departments be cleared through the White House. Tim Kraft, who became the White House assistant for political affairs and personnel, had to approve all political appointments. Cabinet officers were no longer the final voice in departmental hirings.

Reassigning personnel responsibilities from the Cabinet to the White House staff was meant to enhance loyalty to Carter within the administration and provide an institutional mechanism for recruiting political appointees into the administration. Carter wanted to use patronage positions to build a campaign network for 1980 and to use as a bargaining tool with members of Congress.

Cabinet independence further deteriorated by the announcement at the Camp David meetings that Gerald Rafshoon, Carter's media advisor, was to clear major speeches, television appearances, and press interviews by Cabinet officers. Additionally Frank Moore, the Congressional liaison, was to approve any speeches that might affect Congressional relations.

CABINET FIRINGS

Carter's rearrangement of the relationship between the Cabinet and the White House staff at the April 1978 Camp David meetings was a significant retreat from the original plan for the Cabinet. The Cabinet was moving closer and closer to a position in which the White House dominated both policy-making and departmental management, a role Carter pledged would never happen.

Power Moves into the White House

The formal end to "Cabinet administration of our government" came in July 1979, when Carter reorganized his White House staff and fired nearly half of his Cabinet. All the trappings of Cabinet Government ceased as Carter centralized the decision-making and management processes in the White House. In a televised speech July 15, 1979, he referred to the "crisis of confidence" felt by the American people. In Carter's words, "the gap between our citizens and our government has never been so wide," implying, among other things, that the Cabinet secretaries were poorly managing their departments.

His solution to the "crisis in confidence" was to relieve the Cabinet of its decision-making authority and to transfer that authority to the White House. The next day Carter asked for the resignations of all twelve Cabinet officers, accepting those of Califano, Blumenthal, and Adams. Bell and Schlesinger resigned shortly afterwards, and Patricia Roberts Harris was moved from the Department of Housing and Urban Development to the Department of Health, Education and Welfare. Two days later, July 18, 1979, Hamilton Jordan was appointed chief of staff in the White House. Carter informed other White House staff of the change, stating, "they should no longer consider Mr. Jordan their peer, and they should act on his decisions as if they were" the president's own.[41]

Jordan Moves to Chief of Staff

Jordan's elevation to chief of staff meant the end of free access to the president by the Cabinet and an added level of clearance on material submitted to the president. Jordan was given complete authority to review all departmental correspondence to the president. Jody Powell, Carter's Press Secretary, issued a statement outlining Jordan's new duties:

> The President has told the White House senior staff and the Cabinet that Mr. Jordan will have the primary responsibility for insuring that the President's decisions are carried out. This decision was made to provide more coordination and efficiency in the White House and to ensure better coordination between the White House and the Cabinet and to relieve the President of the necessity of dealing with matters that can be decided at a lower level.[42]

The major impact on the Cabinet of Jordan's position as chief of staff was to add another layer of White House control to the policy process. Jordan rather than Carter became the final arbiter in interagency disputes, policy matters, and general departmental questions. It was his decision whether or not to involve Carter in the decision-making process. Cabinet secretaries were subject to Jordan's decisions as to what should be decided at a lower level. He, or members of the White House staff, were the lower level to which Carter referred.[43]

Jordan began his duties in a manner reminiscent of the Nixon presidency. As had Frederic Malek on Nixon's staff, Jordan sent out a thirty-question form for Cabinet members to evaluate their top staff. The questions dealt with work habits ("On the average what time does this person get to work?"), political skills, and personnel attributes ("How bright is this person?"). Most Cabinet members considered the questions insulting and ignored the form, which opened a permanent rift between Jordan and the Cabinet. Cabinet officers, who had taken their jobs with the understanding that they would have independence in personnel selection, were outraged at Jordan's actions.

By the fall of 1979, Cabinet changes had occurred in the Departments of Treasury; Justice; Commerce; Health, Education and Welfare; Housing and Urban Development; Transportation; and Energy. Seven of the thirteen Cabinet positions changed between July and November 1979. The Cabinet had not seen such a massive turnover since 1841, when all but one of President Tyler's Cabinet resigned.

THE FAILURE OF CABINET GOVERNMENT

Carter's decision to redesign the policy-making structure within the administration can be attributed to a combination of factors, including his dissatisfaction with the legislative success rate, interagency coordination, and the activities of some members of his Cabinet. Carter was convinced that the Cabinet's actions had contributed to his decline in the public opinion polls and were leading to public doubts about presidential leadership. His rating in the public opinion polls began slipping in the spring of 1977, reaching a low of 25 per cent in the summer of 1979. These ratings would be costly if not fatal, he believed, in the 1980 election.

The Cabinet and Congress

Although Carter did not anticipate the level of problems that he eventually faced with Congress, he was aware when he entered office of his own limitations in dealing with Congress. He had never served in an elected or appointed capacity in Washington and lacked a basic understanding of the dynamics of the federal legislative process. He tried to minimize that handicap by bringing Cabinet members into the administration who had a working knowledge of Congress and of the departmental-Congressional relationship. The strong working relationship between his Cabinet and members of Congress ultimately led to the downfall of the Cabinet as a major player on policy-making.

At the heart of Carter's dissatisfaction with his Cabinet's dealings with Congress were the efforts by Bob Bergland and Brock Adams to block Congressional support for presidential initiatives, and the effort by Joseph Califano to lobby for Congressional support for a program that the White House quietly opposed.

The most serious rift between Carter and a member of the Cabinet was with Bob Bergland, Secretary of Agriculture. Bergland strongly disagreed with Carter on the dollar amount of the administration's farm subsidies proposal and on the restructuring of the food stamps program.

The first issue, that of farm subsidies, involved revising the federal price supports for farmers that had been established in the Agriculture and Consumer Protection Act of 1973. Although Congress attempted to raise the supports in a 1975 emergency farm bill, President Ford vetoed it. Farmers' organizations again lobbied the Carter administration in 1977 for substantial increases in federal subsidies for wheat, corn, cotton, soybeans, and rice. Bergland, a wheat farmer himself, supported the increases and argued for price support levels in line with the farm organizations' requests. Carter opposed large increases for he felt they would be detrimental to his efforts to balance the federal budget by 1981. Bergland noted to Carter, though, that his refusal to meet farmers' demands was out of line with his promise at the Iowa State Fair on August 25, 1976, to "make sure that our support prices are at least equal to the cost of production."[44] Carter was ultimately successful in minimizing the increase in federal price support, but he strongly believed that Bergland had been ineffective in persuading farmers, farm organizations, and farm-state representatives in Congress to further reduce the target prices for federal subsidies.[45]

The second issue involving a conflict between Carter and Bergland concerned the food stamps program. Carter wanted to transfer the food stamps program from the Department of Agriculture to the Department of Health, Education and Welfare. As part of his welfare reform proposal, Carter wanted to consolidate all income subsidy programs into one department, HEW, and to eliminate the "stamp" concept by creating direct payments to welfare recipients.[46] The process was termed "cashing out" the food stamps program.

Bergland sought to block the transfer by lobbying members of the House of Representatives, particularly the House Ways and Means Committee, which had jurisdiction over the proposals. Bergland attempted to eliminate the food stamps program from the proposed consolidation within HEW of the Aid to Families with Dependent Children, Supplemental Security Income, food stamps, and general assistance programs. The issue was never directly addressed, however, for the welfare reform bill was never brought to the floor of the House for a vote.[47]

Another member of the administration who Carter believed was lobbying against presidential proposals in Congress was Brock Adams, Secretary of Transportation. Adams and Carter disagreed on a number of issues including deregulation of the airline industry, controls on the trucking industry, and mass transit funding. The mass transit issue was the most critical of their differences, for Adams adamantly opposed Carter's efforts to trim federal expenditures for mass transit. Although Adams' opposition was limited on Capitol Hill, Carter believed that Adams had not mobilized a strong enough coalition on behalf of administration policies.

Their major confrontation on mass transit erupted in February 1977 over Carter's emergency energy plan, which had been presented to Congress on January 31, 1977. In the plan, Carter proposed a tax on gas-guzzling cars, a tax that Adams wanted earmarked for mass transit. Carter objected to using the tax for mass transit, preferring to return it to the Treasury for general use.

In hearings before the House Ways and Means Committee over the tax, however, Adams supported its use for mass transit despite Carter's opposition. The bill subsequently died in committee and was resubmitted by the administration as a five cents per gallon increase in the federal gasoline tax. The bill was defeated. Although neither Adams nor Carter was successful in their original objective, Adams became an outsider in the Carter administration.

Adams and Carter clashed later in the year, again on mass transit, over Carter's refusal to request federal funds for mass transit in either the energy plan or the budget. In an effort to balance the budget by 1981, Carter proposed to eliminate new funding for mass transit in fiscal year 1979 but to include new funding in the 1980 budget request. Despite Carter's efforts to limit mass transit appropriations, Adams lobbied for a Senate bill that increased mass transit capital funding. Adams reminded Carter of his speech before the Democratic Platform Committee in 1976 in which he pledged that "arresting this deterioration [of mass transportation systems] and completing needed work on new urban transit systems must become the nation's first transportation priority."[48] In spite of Carter's objections, Congress passed an $8.65 million appropriations bill authorizing the funding of capital grants for mass transit.

Joseph Califano, Secretary of Health, Education and Welfare, was another Cabinet officer who Carter felt turned to Congress for support even though Carter opposed the departmental positions. Califano and Carter had worked well together on the welfare reform and health cost containment programs, but they disagreed on Califano's initiative for a national antismoking program. Califano sought regulatory changes that would prohibit smoking in public places, increase funding for HEW's research and educational budget on smoking, and, most controversial of all, reduce price supports to tobacco farmers. Although Carter never discussed the specific issue of smoking with him, Califano was urged to pursue all phases of preventive health care. Carter publicly urged broad preventive health care in an October 1976 address to the American Public Health Association: "I intend to provide the aggressive leadership that is needed to give our people a nationwide, comprehensive, effective preventive health care program, and you can depend on that."[49]

Califano interpreted a comprehensive health care program to include an antismoking campaign. In fact, Carter did not support such a program due to political concerns, but did not inform Califano of his position.

Among the first specific requests that Califano made of Congress for the antismoking campaign was for a hearing before the House Health Committee to require stronger warnings on cigarette packages. Califano wanted to replace "The Surgeon General has Determined that Cigarette Smoking is Dangerous to Your Health" with "Warning: Cigarette Smoking is Dangerous to Your Health and May Cause Death from Cancer, Coronary Heart Disease, Chronic

Bronchitis, Pulmonary Emphysema, and Other Diseases."[50] Califano briefed members of Congress on his proposals, explaining the reasons for the change.

He met with immediate objections from the North Carolina delegation, which represented the nation's largest tobacco industry. Carter, who had taken no public position on the antismoking campaign, at this very point privately urged Califano to withdraw his proposals due to the political fallout for the 1980 presidential election. But Califano continued his antismoking efforts, although no legislative action was taken. Carter never forgave Califano for the antismoking campaign, which became a major factor in the ultimate dismantling of Cabinet Government.

The Cabinet and Policy-Making

Carter's disillusionment with his Cabinet was broader than their dealings with Congress. Policy decisions often proved to be unacceptable to Carter and out of line with the presidential agenda. But Cabinet officers argued that they were not required under the rules established by Carter for Cabinet Government in 1977 to have White House clearance for every departmental policy.

Three members of the Cabinet in particular, Griffin Bell, Michael Blumenthal, and Joseph Califano, disagreed with Carter on the scope of their authority. Attorney General Griffin Bell, for example, was frequently cited by Carter for his failure to discuss the rulings of the Department of Justice with White House staff before they were issued. One of the most volatile issues that arose concerned the constitutionality of using federal funds under the Comprehensive Employment and Training Act (CETA) to fund staff in sectarian schools. Bell issued an opinion that CETA funds could not be used for sectarian schools because it violated the First Amendment requirement for the separation of church and state. Carter disagreed, overruling the department's decision, and allowed CETA funds to be used for church-related schools. Bell was told that the legal opinions of the Department of Justice were to be cleared by Stuart Eizenstat and Walter Mondale before being issued. Bell responded by stating to Carter that he had directed him at the outset of the administration:

> to establish an independent Department of Justice, a neutral zone in government where decisions will be made on the merits free of political interference or influence. I was asked for my opinion on a question of law. I was under an official obligation as your attorney general to state my frank and candid legal opinion on this question.[51]

Another conflict between Bell and Carter on the degree of independence that a Cabinet officer should be given arose with regard to judicial nominations in 1977, following passage of the Omnibus Judgeship Bill, which created 152 new federal judicial positions. Robert Lipshutz, Counsel to the President, and his staff endeavored to "assert White House staff control over the judicial nominations," as Bell notes, despite a tradition of noninterference by the president in recommending candidates for the nation's eleven judicial circuits.[52] Bell eventually won the battle, but lost the war of building collegial relations between the Department of Justice and the White House.

Michael Blumenthal, Secretary of the Treasury, was another Cabinet member who disagreed with Carter and members of the White House staff on major policy decisions. The most serious conflict between Carter and Blumenthal involved the tax reform bill, which Carter wanted to use as the foundation of an economic stimulus package. On the original proposal, prepared by the Treasury Department, the tax bill included tax investment credits directed at improving industrial productivity. Blumenthal directed his approach to economic recovery through a tax policy that stimulated industrial productivity. Stuart Eizenstat disagreed with the emphasis of the tax policy prepared by Blumenthal and sought to focus economic recovery on individual rather than business and industrial tax cuts. Eizenstat acknowledged, however, that the White House view was premised on a campaign pledge to lower individual tax rates, particularly to lower-income groups.

In a description of the conflict between the Treasury Department and the White House staff over the tax reform policy, the *New York Times* asserted that this was part of a growing gap between the departments and the White House. The *Times* stated that "Differences were as sharp between 'Eizenstat's kids' and other federal agencies as there were between the staff and Congress."[53]

The U.S. Chamber of Commerce was particularly critical of the White House intervention in the tax issue and criticized the White House staff, who were predominantly lawyers, for "a lack of economic skills."[54] Eizenstat eventually dominated the process and the final package sent to Congress included not only a reduction in the standard deduction for individual taxpayers but a $50 rebate.[55] Joseph Califano, Secretary of Health, Education and Welfare, was again another member of the Cabinet who came into conflict with Carter on the direction of departmental policy. Although both agreed that the federal government should not be a party to funding abortions, they disagreed on regulations that governed HEW's use of Medicaid funds for abortions. In 1977 the HEW appropriations bill prohibited the use of HEW funds for abortions "except where the life of the mother would be endangered if the fetus were carried to term."[56] Carter signed the bill and directed Califano to establish regulations for funding abortions that would endanger the life of the mother. Califano subsequently issued a ruling that allowed a sixty-day waiting period for victims to report rape or incest without jeopardizing their right to Medicaid funding for an abortion. Carter disagreed with the sixty-day waiting period as too lengthy, stating that the sixty-day period permitted "too much opportunity for fraud and would encourage women to lie."[57] In meetings with Carter on abortion funding, Califano convinced Carter not to change the waiting period, reminding him of the Congressional intent that it remain sixty-days. Carter ultimately accepted HEW's recommendations.

Interdepartmental Conflict

Carter's decision to reduce the power of the Cabinet reflected not only his dissatisfaction with his direct relations with the Cabinet but his dissatisfaction with interdepartmental conflicts. Carter's organizational structure for policy-making was intended to minimize departmental conflicts by bringing Cabinet officers together in the cabinet clusters to resolve differences. However, the system did not work as smoothly as Carter envisioned. Jurisdictional disputes and policy differences led to frequent interdepartmental conflicts in spite of the Cabinet cluster system.

Among the more publicized interdepartmental disputes were those between the Interior Department and the Department of Justice over the continuation of the Tellico Dam project in Tennessee. Cecil Andrus, Secretary of the Interior, sought to block the project in order to protect the snail darter, which, he argued, would be destroyed by the lake to be created by the Tellico Dam. The snail darter had been designated an endangered species in 1975 by the Interior Department. However, the Justice Department defended the project due to its importance in providing adequate electricity to a major part of Tennessee and North Carolina. The Justice Department supported the Tennessee Valley Authority's (TVA) position that the dam was critical. In 1978 the issue became so volatile that the Attorney General argued in the Supreme Court in behalf of the project representing the TVA, while the Interior Department argued against it.[58] The dam was eventually constructed. Carter, however, was furious at the disparity in administration goals.

The welfare reform proposal was another area in which the administration faced substantial conflict between departments. As part of the welfare reform package, Joseph Califano sought to consolidate the income subsidy programs into one department, Health, Education and Welfare. The consolidation proposal, which involved moving the food stamps program from the Department of Agriculture and the housing subsidy program from the Department of Housing and Urban Development into the Department of Health, Education and Welfare, was opposed by Secretaries Bergland (Agriculture) and Harris (HUD). Carter was forced to mediate the dispute, subsequently supporting Harris but not Bergland. Califano also faced interagency conflict in his efforts to merge the manpower training program of the Department of Labor into HEW as part of the same welfare reform package. Ray Marshall, Secretary of Labor, opposed the proposal and, as had Patricia

Harris, succeeded in keeping the program out of HEW after appealing to Carter.

The development of the energy plan, sent to Congress on April 21, was another example of interdepartmental conflict due to James Schlesinger's efforts to control the development of the legislation. Michael Blumenthal sought to become part of the policy process since an energy bill would dramatically affect of any future legislation on economic recovery. As Secretary of Treasury, Blumenthal wanted to participate in all economic issues. Other members of the Cabinet, particularly Brock Adams, similarly sought to participate in the development of the energy legislation due to its impact on their department. Carter believed that the lack of common ground by his Cabinet on such issues as the energy policy necessitated tighter control by the curbing of Cabinet autonomy in policy development.

Legislative Success Rate

Carter's problems with the Cabinet were not totally one-sided. Carter himself was guilty of not seeking their advice in executive-legislative relations. He had carefully sought Cabinet officers who were knowledgeable in Washington politics, yet turned to his White House staff to deal with Congress. The mistakes he made in dealing with Congress were unnecessary, especially given the amount of time he had spent in Cabinet-building to select savvy department heads. It was an early indication that the White House staff would quickly dominate the policy-making process.

With a sizable Democratic majority in both houses of Congress, Carter anticipated little opposition to his policy initiatives. The ninety-fifth Congress had sixty-two Democrats in the Senate and two hundred ninety-two Democrats in the House of Representatives. For the first time since Richard Nixon took office in 1969, the Democrats controlled both the White House and the Congress.

However, in spite of the Democratic majorities, Carter failed to achieve major victories in his legislative program during 1977. His victories were confined primarily to organizational changes within the executive branch. None of Carter's major foreign policy initiatives, such as the Panama Canal treaties and the Strategic Arms Limitations Talks agreements, were successful and Congress opposed his efforts to block development of the B-1 bomber and the Clinch River breeder-reactor.[59]

Most of Carter's failures in dealing with Congress stemmed from his failure to listen to his Cabinet and seek their advice. One of the first major setbacks to the presidential-Congressional relationship came when Carter announced on February 21, 1977, only one month after taking office, that he had identified nineteen water resource projects as "insupportable on econom-

ic environmental, and/or safety grounds."[60] The following day, in his budget
revision message to Congress, Carter announced that nineteen Army Corps of
Engineers water projects would be withdrawn from the administration's budget request because of "new priorities for water resources development."[61]
Any of his Cabinet officers could have warned him of the folly of this move,
yet he failed to discuss the issue with them.

The announcement stunned most members of Congress. Not only had
they been ignored prior to the announcement, but the projects had traditionally been a sacrosanct part of the budget. One Congressional staffer said that
"There is growing awareness on the Hill of the deep contempt for Congress on
the part of Carter's closest advisers."[62] By early March, Congress was there-
fore calling the White House staff, not the Cabinet, "his closest advisors."
After meeting with Carter following the February 22, 1977, budget message,
John Stennis (D-Mississippi) echoed the feeling of many members of
Congress when he stated "If you've done one thing by this, it's to unify
Congress."[63]

Among those particularly alienated by Carter's deletions of water projects from the budget was Russell Long (D-Louisiana), whose state lost five of
the projects. Long, chairman of the Senate Finance Committee, later became
a major stumbling block for the administration in its efforts to move key legislative programs through the committee. Long refused, for example, to support the economic stimulus plan, introduced January 31,1977, and the energy
bill, introduced April 20, 1977, both of which were under the jurisdiction of
the Finance Committee. Long was strongly opposed to the energy bill's proposal to limit production incentives for the natural gas industry, one of
Louisiana's largest employers and a major campaign supporter of Long. This
growing rift between Congress and the White House during the first year of
the administration was described by Joseph Califano in vivid terms:

> House Speaker Tip O'Neill had been insulted by the arrogance of the
> Georgians in the early days. Ineptness in handling appointments and
> making announcements, in introducing and pushing legislation had
> alienated many key Democrats. Congress was. . . angry about Carter's
> attempt to block Western water projects.[64]

Carter's initial and perhaps worst mistake in dealing with Congress was
his failure to personally seek the support of members of Congress for his legislative proposals as soon as he entered office. He assumed that the
Democratic majorities in Congress would support administration proposals
without question. However, Carter had based his campaign on an anti-
Washington, anti-Establishment theme, and had alienated many members of
Congress during that process.

Indicative of Carter's approach to Congress was the manner in which he structured the White House congressional liaison office. He used a small staff of approximately a dozen issue specialists to meet with individual members of Congress. This was not only smaller than the staffs employed by previous administrations, but also smaller then the liaison staffs of some executive agencies. The Department of Health, Education and Welfare, for example, employed fifty-four congressional liaison staff members.

The Carter liaison office was organized by jurisdictional rather than geographical lines. Carter's strategy was to have experts on his staff who would focus on the technical merits of the legislation in order to be able to explain adequately the administration's position on the proposal. They were not expected to bargain for Congressional support. However, as Charles O. Jones noted in his study of presidential-Congressional relations during the Carter administration, the system was a failure because it was "out of kilter with the multiple-issue demands on individual members of Congress."[65] It was, however, in keeping with Carter's focus on technical expertise in government. Carter, as noted earlier, was adverse to compromising what he believed were issues of principle. This philosophy guided his Congressional liaison operation, which was told to discuss technical merits but not to compromise, or politicize, the proposals.

Carter assumed that by appealing directly to the public through such mechanisms as televised "fireside chats," the requisite pressure would be applied to Congress for presidential initiatives. For example, Carter went on national television on April 18, 1977, two days before his submission to Congress of the energy plan, to mobilize public support for its passage. He had not met with the members of the Democratic leadership or House Ways and Means Committee, which controlled the legislation prior to the public announcement. Members were obviously stunned that they had not been informed earlier. The strategy backfired, for the public was not motivated to lobby for the passage of the bill and members of the Congress were furious over the unannounced energy plan.

Carter also damaged his relations with Congress by ignoring the traditional perquisites that presidents accorded members of Congress for their support. For example, one of his first executive acts was to sell the presidential yacht *Sequoia,* used by past presidents to reward members of Congress for their support and seek the help of others. Although Carter sold the yacht to cut costs and remove all vestiges of the imperial presidency, the *Sequoia* had been a bargaining chip unique to the presidency.

He was similarly oblivious to the value of small favors to members of Congress, such as pens from ceremonial bill signings. As one Congressional staff member noted:

When Jerry Ford would sign a bill, he'd use nice metal pens with his name on them, and then he'd pass them out to the members who had worked on the bill. But Carter signs bills with a felt tip pen, and then he puts the pen back into his pocket.[66]

Carter's legislative failures stemmed not only from such lack of attention to coalition-building within the Congress, but from his lack of understanding of the mechanics of the Congressional system. This was evidenced by his refusal to assign priority to major pieces of legislation, many of which went to the tax writing committees of Congress. During the same period of time, the House Ways and Means Committee had the welfare reform, income tax, hospital cost containment, and energy legislation prepared by the Carter administration. Not only was the committee overloaded with major administration proposals, but it was given no direction by the administration as to which were to be addressed first.

Carter's unfamiliarity with the Congressional system was further evidenced by his failure to court individual members of Congress. The breakdown of the seniority system in the early 1970s led to an erosion of party discipline and the necessity to broaden the administration's lobbying program. Party leaders could no longer be counted on to muster support from party members. This was particularly the case in the House of Representatives, due to a rule that House Democrats adopted in 1973 guaranteeing each Democrat a major committee assignment. The rule change ended the old system of having the leaders assign newly elected members to one or more minor committees

Carter's problems with Congress were aggravated by Congressional efforts to exert greater influence in national policy-making. The dominance of Lyndon Johnson's presidential government in the 1960s, the abuse of presidential power in the 1970s under Richard Nixon, and the governance by veto by Gerald Ford led to a move within Congress for greater involvement in policy-making and departmental programmatic oversight. Neither house of Congress was willing to give Carter blanket approval of policy initiatives. But Carter failed to understand this process of change in Congress and therefore failed to adequately deal with it.

CONCLUSION: TOO LATE TO GAIN CONTROL

As had Richard Nixon, Jimmy Carter tried to set in motion a strong Cabinet policy development system and to minimize the role of White House staff in policy issues. He gave Cabinet officers autonomy to develop their departments' major policy initiatives and to manage their offices without

White House intervention. White House staff were directed by Carter to give Cabinet officers complete discretion in the internal affairs of their departments, including personnel selection. Cabinet officers were free to hire sub-Cabinet personnel without the traditional White House clearance.

Carter further increased his reliance on the Cabinet for policy development by eliminating many alternative sources of policy advice within the Executive Office of the President. Carter reduced the size of the White House staff by nearly 20 per cent, primarily in the domestic policy staff, and eliminated many of the presidential advisory councils housed within the EOP. During his first year Carter abolished the Domestic Policy Council, Economic Opportunity Council, Federal Property Council, Office of Drug Abuse, Office of Telecommunications Policy, Office on International Economic Policy, and Energy Resources Council. The responsibilities of the advisory groups were either assigned to specific departments or absorbed by Cabinet-level policy groups.

Carter's first six months in office indicated a genuine commitment to a strong role for the Cabinet. He allowed his Cabinet to control the major legislative proposals such as welfare reform, energy, hospital cost containment, and tax reform.[67] White House staff focused on crisis issues such as the Emergency Natural Gas Plan and on special projects such as the reorganization request, the pardon of Vietnam war draft evaders, and the creation of a Department of Energy.

However, Carter quickly became dissatisfied with the independence he had given the Cabinet and within one year began to give White House staff greater control over policy matters. He redesigned his organizational structure from a Cabinet-based to a White House–based system of policy development and began to exercise greater control over departmental personnel decisions.

The end of the Cabinet's independence came in a series of three steps between 1977 and 1979 in which the authority of the Cabinet officers was systematically removed. The first step came in July 1977, when Carter transferred primary authority for domestic policy-making from the Cabinet clusters to the Domestic Policy Group within the White House. Under the direction of Stuart Eizenstat, the Domestic Policy Group began to control the development of every major domestic policy proposal.

The second step came in April 1978, during a two-day retreat for the Cabinet at Camp David, Maryland, when Carter gave the White House staff control over departmental personnel selection, clearance of departmental public statements, and Congressional testimony.

The third and final step came in July 1979, when Carter requested the resignations of every member of his Cabinet, five of which were accepted, and appointed a White House chief of staff. The appointment of Hamilton Jordan as chief of staff effectively closed the direct channel of communication between Carter and the Cabinet, and subjected every policy recommendation by the Cabinet to an additional layer of approval before reaching Carter.

The transformation of the policy-making process from a decentralized to a centralized system can be traced to several factors. The most important factor was the deteriorating relationship between the president and the Cabinet during the first months of the administration as a result of departmental policy positions, which were unacceptable to the White House. At the heart of these policy disagreements was Carter's promise to balance the federal budget. During the presidential campaign he had repeatedly stated his goal for containing federal spending and developing a balanced budget by fiscal year 1981.

Once in office Carter faced the conflicting goals of balancing the federal budget and supporting campaign promises that would result in increased federal spending. Carter's decision to support budgetary goals rather than campaign promises was a predictable trend of his administration, for throughout his term as governor he had consistently regarded cost reduction and government efficiency as his primary objectives. During the presidential campaign this theme was again constantly repeated. When budgetary restraint was at odds with campaign statements, Carter supported restraint but guaranteed that the project was only on hold.

However, members of the Cabinet viewed the decision to concentrate on fiscal retrenchment rather than policy implementation as a failure to honor campaign commitments. They had agreed to join the Cabinet based on the assurance that the administration would remain committed to the policy goals discussed during the campaign. Several members of the Cabinet felt that they had been misled by Carter when they agreed to take the Cabinet position, for fiscal restraint had not been prioritized over policy goals in their discussions. Ronald Reagan learned from this mistake and quite clearly prioritized fiscal restraint to his Cabinet officers.

But Cabinet members were not without blame, for they often failed to consider the political needs of the White House in their policy decisions. This became increasingly true during the second and third years of the administration when Carter became deeply concerned with building support for the 1980 presidential election. He did not want departmental decisions to adversely affect his support among major voting blocs, and wanted Cabinet officers to consider the political goals of the administration in every policy position taken by the department.

By mid-term Carter believed that the independence of the Cabinet encouraged jurisdictional disputes between departments. Prominent examples of such disputes were the Department of Health, Education and Welfare's attempt to incorporate programs in the Labor, Housing and Urban Development, and Agriculture Departments into its welfare reform program, and the clash between the Interior and Justice Departments over the Tellico Dam project. Carter saw decentralization as fostering such problems due to a lack of direction from the White House.

Finally in 1979 Carter realized the problems inherent in the system that he had put in place at the outset of his administration. Trying to salvage his administration, he fired half of the Cabinet and placed control over the policy-making process in the White House. In addition, he centralized the personnel selection process for political appointees in the White House as a further means of gaining control over departmental policy-making. Carter's attempts, however, were in vain, for he never gained control over the policy-making process.

The Cabinet had not provided the level of support for the administration that Carter had expected. Cabinet members had placed priority on their own programs and frequently ignored the political needs of the White House as the election grew closer. Carter, who had sought to minimize the political nature of the Cabinet in the Cabinet selection process, ultimately found the Cabinet to be an extremely political part of the presidency.

SIX

THE REAGAN YEARS

After two unsuccessful runs for the presidency in 1968 and 1976, Ronald Wilson Reagan finally captured the White House in 1980. His promise of dramatically cutting the role of government and, more importantly, cutting the expenditures of government, led to broad-based public support for the sixty-nine year old former actor and two term governor of California.

Throughout the arduous campaign, Reagan often discussed his view of a successful governing process and repeatedly promised that he would take control of the burgeoning federal bureaucracy. Government, he was convinced, was growing at an unprecedented rate, with the annual budget rapidly approaching $1 trillion. There was, he insisted, no reason that a competent and experienced manager could not control this mammoth government. His landslide election over Jimmy Carter was in large part due to the public perception that he could fulfill this promise and that, in spite of Carter's inability to govern successfully, it was not an impossible task.[1]

His promise for successful governing was, in his view, tied to a strong management team through the combination of a strong Cabinet and a strong White House staff. The role of the Cabinet was to control the bureaucracy, reduce departmental programs, and ensure that policies developed within the departments were in line with presidential objectives. The role of the White House staff was to ensure that the Cabinet officers understood presidential objectives and focused their programs around those objectives. Unlike Nixon, Ford, and Carter, Ronald Reagan entered office with the view that a strong White House staff was essential to managing government.

DEFINING THE WHITE HOUSE–CABINET RELATIONSHIP

Reagan's definition of a strong Cabinet was framed within his own view of government. After eight years of managing the largest state in the union, with a budget and bureaucracy greater than most nations, Ronald Reagan had developed a clear sense of how to govern. His view was that Cabinet officers should be central in policy-development and operations, but the White House staff should provide the overall direction for both policy and operational issues. While the role of White House staff was not to articulate specific policies for the departments, it was to set parameters from which departmental policies could be focused.

The team that was assembled for the Reagan Cabinet understood the parameters of their policy-making responsibility and the nature of Reagan's definition of a strong Cabinet. Most of all, the Cabinet officers understood that all the policies that emerged from their departments had to mesh with the objectives that the White House established.

There is also one other noteworthy factor that allowed the system to flourish. Cabinet officers willingly became lightning rods for Reagan, allowing the "teflon" president to remain detached from unpopular positions. Reagan's support for a strong Cabinet helped him to avoid identification with controversial issues. One White House staffer was quoted as saying, "The president feels that he ought not to be answering questions about the B-1 bomber or anything else that specific. Let Cap Weinberger take the heat on the B-1 and Ted Bell take the heat for cuts in school aid. We believe in the delegation of authority."[2] By constantly reiterating his support for a strong Cabinet, it was easy for Reagan to deflect criticism by letting Cabinet officers appear to have made the decisions. This, of course, did not diminish the power within the White House itself, but did provide Cabinet officers at least an aura of independence.

What allowed the Reagan system to work as well as it did? How did the Cabinet retain some degree of power within the policy development framework without the White House totally dominating the policy process?

One of the most important reasons for the success of the strong Cabinet–White House relationship was the relatively limited domestic agenda of the Reagan administration. Reagan and his staff allowed department heads to pursue policies that the career staff endorsed if they did not impede the administration's overall goals. Neither the president nor the White House staff endeavored to micromanage the departments. White House staff focused on the larger issues.

The key factor in the success of the Cabinet–White House relationship was the strong personal relationship between Ronald Reagan and his Cabinet. Reagan chose men who were remarkably similar to himself in age, background, wealth, and outlook. All were successful business executives who had been active in Republican politics throughout their careers. With the exception of Samuel Pierce, all were white. There were no women in the president's original Cabinet, except for Jeane Kirkpatrick, named as U.S. Representative to the United Nations. While given Cabinet status (a rank first accorded the position during the Eisenhower administration), she was in reality under the jurisdiction of the Secretary of State and not directly responsible to the president. Later in the administration, Reagan added two other women to the Cabinet, Elizabeth Dole at Transportation and Margaret Heckler at Health and Human Services.

The political philosophy of each of the Cabinet nominees was identical to that of Reagan: streamline the federal bureaucracy, cut the federal budget, and reduce the federal tax burden on individuals. Each Cabinet officer was a conservative Republican committed to reducing the federal government's regulatory and economic role. Reagan did not pursue a Cabinet-building strategy to broaden his political base, as had Nixon and Carter, since he had accomplished that goal through his policy agenda. From the day he took office, Ronald Reagan trusted his Cabinet to carry out his charge.

The theme of strong personal relationships was carried throughout the administration and became a critical part of the Cabinet–White House relationship. The White House staff, also remarkably similar to Reagan in background and political philosophy, worked closely with the Cabinet both individually and through groups called cabinet councils.

Cabinet councils built rapport among members of the Cabinet and between the White House staff and the Cabinet. Members of the Cabinet were able to work easily with one another and with the White House staff in developing interjurisdictional policies and focusing administration priorities. The bond that developed between the Cabinet and the White House staff kept the Cabinet within the presidential sphere and reduced the chances of cooption by the career staff. There was a clear sense of teamwork that emerged from the cabinet council system.

In addition, the success of the strong working relationship between the Cabinet and the White House staff can be traced to the presidential personnel management system. From the very beginning of his administration, Reagan insisted on centralizing control within the White House of all five thousand political appointments (2700 presidential and 2300 "Schedule C" and similar jobs named by Cabinet officers). Reagan's management strategy was to guarantee bureaucratic responsiveness to the Reagan agenda by filling top, middle, and even low-level posts with Reagan loyalists. The appointment strategy that Richard Nixon initiated,[3] but never fully developed during his years, was brought to fruition under Ronald Reagan.[4] During the first year of the Reagan administration, Pendleton James and Lyn Nofziger approved most of these five thousand political appointments. They had six criteria for prospective appointees to the Reagan administration:

1. Are you a Carter appointee? If so, you're rejected.
2. Are you a Democrat who didn't work for Ronald Reagan? If so, you're rejected.
3. Are you a Republican? Are you the best Republican for the job?
4. Are you a Ronald Reagan-George Bush supporter?
5. Did you work in the Reagan-Bush campaign? How early before the convention?
6. Are you the best qualified person for the job? But that's only number 6.[5]

Unquestionably, the White House moved politically active Reagan supporters into the second and third tier of department positions. Although this produced grumbling from some of the Cabinet, such as Terrel Bell, most acquiesced without a fight.[6]

The personnel strategy enabled the White House to limit the policy initiatives rising through the system that did not meet administration goals. Such policies were snuffed out early in the policy development process by the sub-Cabinet loyalists and never rose to the level of the department head. Cabinet officers were prevented through this process from having to reject a departmental policy and losing departmental support, or from having to support a departmental policy and losing presidential support. The personnel system insulated Cabinet officers by providing a buffer zone from bureaucratic policy initiatives. This was part of the strategy to keep the Cabinet officers from being coopted and to keep them within the presidential sphere. Martin Anderson, a senior campaign staff member who coordinated the organizational structure for White House–Cabinet relations, quipped in an interview that "if you don't set up the right structure in the first place, they [Cabinet officers] get coopted quickly."[7]

The issue of cooption by the senior staff was directly dealt with from the outset of the administration. All staff who held plum positions were invited annually to meet with the president in Constitution Hall for two to two-and-a-half hours. The Executive Forum, as it was called, was an opportunity for the senior staff to be with the president and to hear the president personally reaffirm the administration's agenda. This provided for a constant reinforcement of ideology for the senior staff.[8]

REAGAN'S PROMISE FOR A TEAM APPROACH TO MANAGEMENT

Reagan's promise to control the growth of government meant bringing a group of managers into the departments who could remain true to the fundamental objectives of the campaign and not be drawn into the narrow interests of the bureaucracy. Reagan insisted on a strong Cabinet as a key component of his management team. His reference to Cabinet Government throughout the 1980 campaign with statements such as "Cabinet Government can and will work" reinforced his belief that the Cabinet would be central to this new management team, and not be second-class citizens, as they often had become under past administrations.[9] Reagan saw himself as the chairman of the board with the Cabinet working closely with White House staff to form the management team.

This system paralleled that of Dwight Eisenhower nearly three decades earlier. Herbert Brownell, Eisenhower's first Attorney General, described the Eisenhower Cabinet as one where "loyalty to the president and the ability to function as part of a team are required." But Brownell, also acutely aware of the power of the White House staff, added to that statement that there were "many times . . . the president chooses personal advisers who become more powerful than Cabinet officers."[10]

There appear to be several explanations for Reagan's commitment to keeping the Cabinet a key part of the decision-making process. His commitment was not simply based on his managerial structure for government. It was to some extent due to the political stigma that a centralized policy development system continued to have. The public was still shivering from the imperial presidency of the Nixon years and the arrogance of the Carter years. Political logic dictated support for a trimmed down White House staff. Reagan was trying to distance himself from the domineering management style of the Nixon White House and from the incompetence of the Carter staff.

The management aspect of Reagan's structure for Cabinet–White House relations was a critical part of Reagan's support for the system. Reagan liked to delegate authority and was considered a "hands-off" manager. The Iran-Contra affair in 1985–86 was an example of Reagan's lack of interest in programmatic detail. However, lack of interest in programmatic detail should not be confused with lack of interest in policy direction. Reagan constantly sought to reinforce his policy direction for his Cabinet officers. Using individual meetings, Cabinet meetings, and cabinet council meetings, Reagan never failed to ensure that the Cabinet officers understood presidential objectives. This was essentially the system Reagan had used during his two terms as governor of California.

There were times, however, in which the Cabinet and the White House staff bitterly disagreed with each other over policy issues. Aid to the Nicaragua resistance was one such issue. As Lou Cannon described it, "While Reagan settled into his role as chief salesman for the freedom fighters, his principal subordinates battled one another with a ferocity rarely equaled by the contras in combat."[11] Members of the National Security Council (NSC) staff were at odds with chief of staff Jim Baker. Michael Deaver and Bill Clark argued continually. And Jeane Kirkpatrick often clashed with George Shultz, who himself clashed with Caspar Weinberger. The infighting led the NSC staff to develop a covert program to help the contras, eventually leading to the scandal that nearly destroyed the Reagan presidency.

While the Iran-Contra affair, as it became known, was not typical of the administration, it was indicative of the control that the White House staff felt it had over policy issues. Unquestionably, the White House staff, in both domestic and foreign policy matters, felt that they were the dominant player and controlled the ultimate decisions. But the Cabinet gained more and more power in the policy-making process in the second administration. This was in large part due to the paralysis within the White House caused by the Iran-Contra affair, which dragged on for nearly two years. But it was also due to bitter in-house battles that developed between Michael Deaver and Jim Baker, William Clark and Bill Casey, and Nancy Reagan and Don Regan, among others. These battles for turf tended to erode the strong Cabinet–White House relationship fostered early in the administration.[12]

SELECTION OF THE CABINET

Perhaps the key to Reagan's success in establishing a strong working relationship between the Cabinet and the White House staff during the first term was the selection of the Cabinet. Reagan learned from the Nixon and Carter experiences that using the Cabinet to broaden the political base of the administration was a tactical error. Reagan's Cabinet–selection strategy was quite different from that of his predecessors, for he selected Cabinet members who were politically and ideologically similar to himself. He made no attempt to broaden the political base of the administration through the Cabinet. His electoral margin of 9.7 per cent was significantly stronger than either Richard Nixon's .9 per cent electoral victory over Hubert Humphrey or Jimmy Carter's 2 per cent electoral victory over Gerald Ford. Reagan believed he had a clear electoral mandate and broad public support.[13]

Reagan's goal for Cabinet selection was to assemble a group, as the *Washington Post* noted, "steeped in the ways of the board rooms and corporate management, who live by the executive branch equivalent of Sam Rayburn's famous adage: 'To get along, go along'."[14] The Reagan Cabinet was primarily a Cabinet of businessmen, not politicians. Their only client was the President. Jimmy Carter, on the contrary, had brought into his Cabinet a large group of politicians who had won elections on their own and had independent political bases. The Carter Cabinet was composed of such experienced politicians as Edmund Muskie, Brock Adams, Cecil Andrus, Neil

Goldschmidt, and Moon Landrieu. Except for Drew Lewis, the Reagan Cabinet was conspicuously void of politicians.[15]

The Role of Meese and James

The Cabinet selection process began even before the Republican nomination in July. In the fall of 1979, Ed Meese approached Pendleton James to design a plan for choosing staff in a Reagan presidency. As a result, James joined the drive to bring Reagan to the White House serving as an unofficial personnel coordinator for future political appointees. He operated with no staff but regularly consulted with Meese on the names he was working on. Once Reagan was nominated, James was given a budget of $80,000 to move into full swing. He used the funds to rent an office in Alexandria, Virginia, and to hire several staff. When Reagan captured the election, Meese himself formally took over as personnel coordinator/transition director with James working side by side with him.

During his stint as the unofficial head-hunter, James developed a short list of names for each Cabinet office, a list that he shared with Meese. The list often included the same name for several Cabinet positions. For example, Caspar Weinberger's name was on the list for Defense, the Office of Management and Budget, and State. However, no one was ever contacted during this period. The list remained a closely guarded secret between James and Meese.

Not until the election had been secured did Reagan broaden his transition group. Meeting the day after the election at his Pacific Palisades home, Reagan moved his chief campaign advisors onto the transition staff. Joining James and Meese were Jim Baker, George Bush, Michael Deaver, Bill Casey, and Paul Laxalt.[16] At that meeting James shared his list of names for Cabinet nominees with the wider group and opened up the process for discussion.

At the same time that Pendleton James had been working on a short list of names, a small group of Reagan's personal friends had been developing a similar list.   The group consisted of Justin Dart, William French Smith, Holmes Tuttle, William A. Wilson, Hal Wallis, Alfred Bloomingdale, Walter Annenberg, Earle M. Jorgensen, Theodore E. Cummings, Charles Wick, Jack Wrather, Henry Salvatori, Joseph Coors, Caspar Weinberger, William Wilson, and Daniel Terra. The group was chaired by Smith, Reagan's personal attorney and business advisor.

Criterion for Cabinet Selection

The criteria that the working group used for Cabinet selection was described by Henry Salvatori as relatively narrow. Salvatori said, "The three criteria we followed were: One, was he a Reagan man? Two, a Republican?

And three, a conservative? Probably our most crucial concern was to ensure that conservative ideology was properly represented."[17]   In essence, these were the same criteria that James had used in his selection process. The names that the "kitchen cabinet" group produced were given to Reagan, who in turn gave them to James and the official transition group. Not surprisingly, many of the names that the kitchen cabinet had developed were also on the transition group's list. Thus, although the transition group made the final decisions on all nominees, the kitchen cabinet believed that Reagan had used many of the names from their list for his decisions.

There were three notable exceptions to the Cabinet selection process that was managed by Meese and James. The first exception involved the selection of the Secretary of the Interior; the second exception involved the Secretary of Energy; and the third exception was the Secretary of Agriculture. Each resulted from traditional political pressure from Republican activists who felt their interests were underrepresented in the new administration.

The Secretary of Interior had traditionally been a position into which western members of Congress had enormous input since a large percentage of western land was owned by the U.S. government. One of the senior members of the western delegation, Senator Paul Laxalt (R-Nevada), was given authority by Reagan to identify a likely Interior Secretary without dealing with the transition group. Laxalt had been an early supporter of Reagan during the presidential campaign (in both 1976 and 1980) and had built a base of western conservative support for the Reagan-Bush team. He quickly became a key member of the inner circle and was widely known to be a favorite of Nancy Reagan.[18] In addition, he had been part of what came to be known as the "sagebrush rebellion," whose mission was to excite western ire over the massive federal landholdings in the western states, especially the Forest Service and Bureau of Land Management lands. They aggressively sought to soften the federal regulations governing the private use of that land, such as grazing rules and limitations on off-road vehicles, and to fight against converting any of those lands into wilderness status. The parks themselves were generally not their targets, although landholders there had organized themselves and were fighting any moves by the parks to use eminent domain and buy them out. The sagebrush rebels were vitriolically antifederal government and proexploitation.

Laxalt queried Clifford Hansen, a former two-term governor of Wyoming, about joining the administration as Secretary of the Interior. Hansen, however, was not willing to provide the financial disclosure statements required by the White House and withdrew his own name. Laxalt was then instrumental in bringing Wyoming rancher James G. Watt into the administration in order to ensure that the post went to another conservative member of the sagebrush rebellion. Watt met all of the criteria established by the transition team, yet was not a personal friend of Reagan.[19]

The second exception in the carefully developed strategy came when southern senators stormed the Reagan camp in a fury. When Reagan's first choice for Secretary of Energy, Michael Halbouty, also declined to disclose his finances, the position was suddenly available. Led by Strom Thurmond of South Carolina, southern senators demanded representation for the south in the Cabinet. They succeeded in bringing in a relative outsider, a dentist and former governor of South Carolina named James Edwards, as Secretary of Energy. Reagan gave in to Thurmond without a fight, since he had promised to abolish the department once in office.

The third exception was Agriculture Secretary John Block, who was recommended by Senator Bob Dole (R-Kansas). Block, a pig farmer from Illinois, had been active in Republican politics and was widely known in Republican circles as an advocate for farm interests.[20] He had not been one of the prime candidates for the position until Dole pushed his nomination.

There is also evidence that George Bush directly influenced the choice of Malcolm Baldrige for Secretary of Commerce. Baldrige, a Connecticut businessman, provided Bush a voice in the Cabinet. One description of the selection process notes that "Baldrige appealed to Reagan largely because Baldrige's hobby was roping cattle at rodeos."[21]

Once the transition team made the selection from the short list, Reagan was asked to approve or disapprove of the choice. If he approved the name, a meeting was quickly scheduled to bring the nominee to meet the president-elect. For most nominees, the interviews took place in California, although some met with Reagan in Washington, D.C. Early nominees met Reagan in California; later nominees met him at Blair House in Washington, D.C. The primary topic in each of these interviews was the candidate's philosophy of government, not the departmental policies. Reagan instilled in each member of his administration the need to focus on the conservative agenda and that everyone in the administration was working for the "common good."[22]

By and large the Cabinet was composed of men whom Reagan did not personally know but who shared his conservative philosophy of government. Only two members of his personal advisory network moved into the Cabinet: William French Smith became Attorney General and Caspar Weinberger became Secretary of Defense. Two other members of that network moved into senior positions: Charles Wick to the U.S. Information Agency (USIA) and William Casey to the Central Intelligence Agency (CIA).

Unlike past presidents, Reagan did not convene his Cabinet officers for a public presentation. The Cabinet officers were announced to the press by Meese as they were picked by Reagan. The Cabinet only met once as a group prior to the inauguration, in a rather informal meeting that served as an orientation program for new political executives. Meese used the talent of former political executives and career professionals to provide an overview of the federal government and the role of their departments.[23] Reagan also enlisted the talents of William Timmons, a prominent Washington lobbyist and director of the office of congressional liaison for President Ford, to develop very specific discussions of each department for the new Cabinet officers. Timmons developed an organizational blueprint of each agency and worked with each Cabinet nominee on the staffing and legislative mandates of their future department.[24]

Once the group sessions were over, the transition team moved quickly to bring the Cabinet designees into the presidential orbit. According to Martin Anderson, who worked for Meese on the transition team, the Cabinet orientation process designed by Meese was "basically an indoctrination course for Cabinet members, especially those who were not closely connected with the campaign or fully familiar with Ronald Reagan's positions on major policy issues. There were two primary things one wanted to indoctrinate the new Cabinet on: ideas and people."[25] The transition team worked with individual Cabinet officers to focus their agenda on Reagan's policy positions and to provide a list of personnel. Pendleton James was asked to head the transition team's personnel unit and to develop lists of politically acceptable people for the new administration.[26] The transition team endeavored to ensure a common sense of purpose among Cabinet officers during the recruitment process to unify the new political executives and to reduce the strains of what Hugh Heclo referred to as "a government of strangers."[27]

SELECTION OF THE WHITE HOUSE STAFF

As is true in most presidential campaign staffs, the senior campaign staff moved into the White House as the president's senior staff and they in turn brought in their own team. The White House staff was dominated by the three key players in the campaign: Edwin Meese, James Baker, and Michael Deaver.

The roles and responsibilities of the White House staff were clearly laid out at the onset of the administration. There would be no single chief of staff to insulate the president, as Richard Nixon had, nor would there be a spokes of the wheel system as Jimmy Carter had.[28] Rather, Reagan opted for a mixture of the two in which power was shared by three individuals at the highest level of the staff. The press quickly dubbed this three-man structure the "troika."

The Troika

Each of the three in the troika had free access to Reagan and each had a distinct area of responsibility. Jim Baker was given the somewhat misleading title of chief of staff, with Michael Deaver named deputy chief of staff, and Ed

Meese designated presidential counselor. In fact, each had equal power within the inner circle.

Jim Baker, George Bush's campaign manager in 1980, had proven during the campaign to be a stalwart Reagan supporter and brilliant political strategist. Ed Meese, a friend of the Reagans who had served as chief of staff during Reagan's two terms as Governor in California, had been the 1980 campaign manager. Michael Deaver, another longtime political supporter and personal friend of the Reagans, had also been a senior member of the 1980 campaign staff.

The responsibilities of the troika were clearly delineated from their first day in office. This, as were many facets of the Reagan administration, was quite different than the confusion that dominated the roles and responsibilities of both the Nixon and Carter White House staffs during the early months.

Baker took responsibility for political affairs, such as forging political coalitions within Congress and with outside constituencies to achieve support for administration proposals. A wide range of special assistants also reported to Baker, including the personnel office, legal office, speech writers, Congressional liaison, press office, and the public liaison. His role was viewed not as policy-making but as the chief coordinator of public and Congressional support.

Meese was to be the chief coordinator of policy formulation. He supervised both the domestic and foreign policy staffs within the White House and supervised the Cabinet Secretariat. This was another major departure from previous administrations in which both the domestic and foreign policy advisors had direct access to the president. One is hard pressed to imagine either Henry Kissinger or Zbigniew Brzezinski not marching into the oval office whenever they felt so compelled.

Deaver had day-to-day responsibility for the president's schedule, appointments, travel, the first lady's staff, and the administration of the White House. He met regularly with Baker and Meese to ensure that Reagan met with those people that they wanted him to. There was little infighting among the three or jockeying for a senior position.

Beneath this upper tier of White House staff were a host of special assistants who brought a depth of Washington knowledge and federal experience into the White House. Most had been in a variety of high-level posts in past administrations but none had been employed full-time by the campaign although all were relatively conservative Republicans. They brought to the White House an understanding of executive-legislative relations and a working knowledge of Washington, both of which had been lacking in the Nixon and Carter White House staffs. As were the Cabinet officers, each member of the White House staff had to be cleared through the White House Personnel Office, or at least through Lyn Nofziger's political operation in the White House.

White House Personnel Office

The White House personnel operation was set up under Pendleton James, who not only had gained Reagan's trust during the transition but had already served in the White House as Frederic Malek's deputy in the Nixon personnel office. After leaving government, James had set up an executive search personnel firm. His long-standing relationship with many members of Reagan's kitchen cabinet and his experience in personnel selection were ample credentials for his senior staff position in the White House. James's proximity to Reagan and his west wing office underscored the importance of the White House personnel operation, which traditionally had its offices only in the old executive office building.

Not surprisingly, James used the same criteria for White House staff as he had for the Cabinet officers: Are you a conservative who supports the Reagan agenda? White House staff thus had the same consistent philosophy that the Cabinet had. This was at the heart of the success of Reagan's strong Cabinet–White House relationship.

In 1980 and 1981 John Kessel of Ohio State University surveyed the entire upper tier of White House staff to poll the level of agreement between staff issue preferences and Reagan's issue preferences. He found that not only was there a strong degree of cohesion among staff members on policy issues but also between the staff and Reagan. In a similar study he found that neither the Nixon nor Carter staffs had either the internal degree of issue cohesion nor the degree of agreement with the president that the Reagan staff had.[29]

TABLE 3. Median Issue Positions of White House Staffs

Policy Area	Carter	Nixon	Reagan
International involvement	4.1	3.4	2.7
Economic management	3.1	2.0	1.3
Social benefits	3.6	3.3	1.9
Civil liberties	5.1	2.2	1.4
Agriculture	4.0	2.8	2.1

Note: scores of 1.0-2.4=conservative; 2.5-3.4=moderate conservative; 3.5-4.5=moderate liberal; 4.6-7.0=liberal
Source: John H. Kessel, "The Structures of the Reagan White House," *American Journal of Political Science,* Volume 28, May 1984, page 234.

STRUCTURING THE WHITE HOUSE–CABINET RELATIONSHIP

Once the Cabinet and White House staffs had been chosen, the first order of business was to structure a White House–Cabinet relationship that would facilitate a strong working relationship between the two. That working relationship depended on policy development by the Cabinet that focused on presidential political and programmatic needs.

For this White House–Cabinet relationship to succeed, Reagan had to develop a strong White House staff that could clearly articulate to the Cabinet officers what policies were important to the administration. This meant increasing the size of the White House staff, at least those staff members directly involved in policy matters, within the White House office. This did not refer to the broader definition of the White House staff such as the vice president's staff, the secret service, the military office, the residence staff, and the like.[30]

During the first year of the administration, the senior White House staff grew to a total of 51, 10 per cent higher than in the Carter White House. By the time Reagan left office, the senior White House staff had grown by another 50 per cent to a record high of 83. At mid-term in 1984–85 that number had reached an unprecedented high of 92. The principal growth area in staffing occurred at the Special Assistant Level, which included those staff responsible for policy development, implementation, and programmatic oversight. The numbers in Table 4 show the growth patterns throughout the eight years of the administration. Thus while Reagan was supporting decreases in bureaucracy, he was increasing his own staff to manage the bureaucracy.

TABLE 4. Changes in White House Staffing, 1981–89

	1981 –82	1982 –83	1983 –84	1984 –85	1985 –86	1986 –87	1987 –88	1988 –89
Counsellor to the president	1	1	1	1	0	0	0	0
Deputy counsellor	1	1	1	0	0	0	1	0
Assistant counsellor	1	1	1	1	0	0	0	0
Chief of staff	1	1	1	1	1	1	1	1
Deputy chief of staff	1	1	1	1	0	0	1	1
Assistant to the president	10	14	14	13	9	11	12	13
Counsel to the president	1	1	1	1	1	1	1	1
Deputy counsel to the president	2	1	1	1	1	1	2	1
Associate counsel to the president	0	5	5	6	5	4	4	6
Deputy assistant to the president	15	14	14	16	20	18	15	15
Special assistant to the president	18	39	47	49	39	46	46	45
Total	51	79	87	92	76	82	83	83

Source: U.S. Government Manual, 1981–1989

The sheer size of the White House staff was a critical ingredient in overseeing the policy development process, but it was not the only ingredient. The other critical ingredient was a structure that kept the Cabinet officers in tune with the goals and objectives of the president. The transition team needed to develop a process that guarded the Cabinet officers against their own bureaucracies and kept them within the presidential orbit. The key to this process was developing a system that allowed Cabinet officers to regularly meet with Reagan and have discussions with him. However, the Reagan team quickly determined that these meetings did not meet the needs of the Reagan team. They wanted a system that allowed for more frequent and more open discussions by Cabinet officers with the president and with each other.

Cabinet Councils Emerge

Two options for restructuring the Cabinet meetings were crafted by Ed Meese and Caspar Weinberger, also a member of the transition team and a former Cabinet secretary in the California Reagan administration. Both options were designed to keep the traditional Cabinet meeting system but to devise a supplemental meeting system.

Option one was to create a supercabinet composed of five or six Cabinet officers to oversee the programs developed by the entire Cabinet. The supercabinet would meet regularly with Reagan to discuss policy options. The entire Cabinet would then meet with Reagan in full Cabinet meetings but rarely in smaller groups. This concept was based on the system that Reagan had used as governor of California in which he met with all six Cabinet officers weekly to direct state agencies.[31] During these informal Cabinet meetings in Sacramento, Reagan heard debates by all members of the group on the agenda items. Cabinet members contributed to the discussions at will, bringing up any points they felt were relevant to the issues at hand. Reagan thrived on these open discussions, listening to the points made by all participants.

The idea of a supercabinet was quickly discarded, however, after comparing the sizes of the state and federal Cabinets. Creating a supercabinet at the federal level was deemed unacceptable since too many Cabinet officers would be kept out of the inner circle. This would have hurt White House efforts to keep Cabinet officers tied to the White House. Although the Ash Commission had recommended exactly this system during the Nixon administration, the Reagan transition team determined that it would not meet their needs. The Nixon administration had in the end made a similar determination.

Option two was to create a system of smaller working groups of Cabinet officers who would have the same informal relationship among themselves that the Cabinet in Sacramento had had. Reagan wanted to preserve the personal interaction that the smaller working groups created. Since the size of the president's Cabinet had grown to thirteen by 1981, Reagan saw the working groups as the more viable means of maintaining the "parrying," as Weinberger called it, among the Cabinet members.[32]   The working groups were to meet regularly but were not to take the place of full Cabinet meetings. Full Cabinet meetings would continue to be scheduled on a biweekly basis.

The small working group concept became known as Cabinet councils, designed to bring together Cabinet officers around issues that cut across jurisdictional lines. Since nearly every policy issue was multijurisdictional, the Reagan team believed that these small groups could manage the process more efficiently than either the Cabinet officers alone or the full Cabinet collectively. The cabinet council system allowed Cabinet officers to continue the types of discussions that Reagan felt had been so valuable both to him and to the Cabinet officers themselves in Sacramento. In addition, by bringing the Cabinet officers to the White House on a regular basis, Reagan gained valuable insights on the political support from both Congress and the public for various programs. One of the great failings of past administrations was that White House staff had been accused of insulating the president from the Cabinet and from using them as a political sounding board. In fact, the president himself (e.g., Nixon) had stipulated the rules governing access by his Cabinet subordinates.

Thus with only slight modification, the system that had served Reagan so successfully for eight years in California was reinstituted at 1600 Pennsylvania Avenue. Reagan became an active member of the cabinet councils and frequently attended council meetings. Cabinet council meetings during the first year of the administration were held at a rate of nearly twelve times per month.[33] Reagan attended 14 per cent of the meetings, and if he could not attend the meeting, frequently sought feedback on the meetings from Meese.

Not surprisingly, creation of the cabinet council system supported a widespread movement within the professional circles of political science and public administration to reduce the concentration of power within the White House and to increase the Cabinet's participation in policy-making. During the transition period, Ed Meese was given, and apparently read, two documents by the National Academy of Public Administration recommending just the sort of system that was being considered by the transition team.[34] It should be noted, however, that many of the other recommendations, such as to increase career employees in the White House, were not instituted.

Cabinet Membership in the Councils

The cabinet councils were structured in such a way as to have six to eight members, which was in line with the number in the Sacramento Cabinet. Reagan was comfortable with a group of that size and sought to replicate the structure in the new administration.[35] The structure was not designed to exclude members, only to ensure a small enough working group to facilitate active discussions. Cabinet officers were free to attend any of the other cabinet council meetings.

Although the cabinet council system that the Reagan team created was drawn primarily from the California experience, in some ways it parallelled a system that Jimmy Carter had set in place during his tenure in office. Carter had established the cluster system of Cabinet officers, in which groups of Cabinet officers met to discuss a wide range of issues. The clusters of the Carter administration had a constantly changing membership depending on the issue at hand. The Reagan cabinet council membership remained constant. (See below for a list of cabinet councils and members.) The Reagan system was similar to that of Nixon's Urban Affairs Council and, later, his Domestic Council.

Cabinet Councils During the First Term of the Reagan Administration

Cabinet Council on Economic Affairs
      * Secretary of the Treasury, chairman pro tempore
      * Secretary of State
      * Secretary of Commerce
      * Secretary of Labor
      * Secretary of Transportation
      * Director, Office of Management and Budget
      * U.S. Trade Representative
      * Chairman, Council of Economic Advisors
      (ex officio members — the Vice President, Counselor to the
      President, White House Chief of Staff, Assistant to the President for Policy
      Development)

Cabinet Council on Human Resources
      * Secretary of Health and Human Services, chairman pro tempore
      * Attorney General
      * Secretary of Agriculture
      * Secretary of Labor
      * Secretary of Housing and Urban Development
      * Secretary of Education
      (ex officio members — the Vice President, Counselor to the
      President, White House Chief of Staff, Assistant to the President for Policy
      Development)

Cabinet Council on Legal Policy
      * Attorney General, chairman pro tempore

    * Secretary of State
    * Secretary of Treasury
    * Secretary of Interior
    * Secretary of Commerce
    * Secretary of Labor
    * Secretary of Health and Human Services
    * Secretary of Housing and Urban Development
    * Secretary of Transportation
    * Director, Office of Management and Budget
    * White House Counsel
    * Chairman, Administration Conference of the U.S.
    (ex officio members — the Vice President, Counselor to the
President, White House Chief of Staff, Assistant to the President for Policy
Development)

Cabinet Council on Natural Resources and the Environment
    * Secretary of Interior, chairman pro tempore
    * Attorney General
    * Secretary of Agriculture
    * Secretary of Transportation
    * Secretary of Housing and Urban Development
    * Secretary of Energy
    * Chairman, Council of Environmental Quality
    * Chairman, Council of Economic Advisors
    (ex officio members — the Vice President, Counselor to the
President, White House Chief of Staff, Assistant to the President for Policy
Development)

Cabinet Council for Management and Administration
    * Counsellor to the President, chairman pro tempore
    * Secretary of Treasury
    * Secretary of Defense
    * Secretary of Commerce
    * Secretary of Health and Human Services
    * Secretary of Transportation
    * Secretary of Energy
    * Director, Office of Management and Budget
    * Administrator of General Services Administration
    * Director, Office of Personnel Management
    (ex officio members — the Vice President, White House Chief of
Staff, Assistant to the President for Policy Development)

Cabinet Council on Commerce and Trade
* Secretary of Commerce, chairman pro tempore
* Secretary of State
* Secretary of Treasury
* Attorney General
* Secretary of Labor
* Secretary of Transportation
* Secretary of Energy
* U.S. Trade Representative
* Chairman, Council of Economic Advisers
(ex officio members — the Vice President, Counselor to the
President, White House Chief of Staff, Assistant to the President for Policy
Development)

National Security Council
Note: the National Security Council was established by Congress in
the National Security Act of 1947 and has statutorily created members.
* President
* Vice President
* Secretary of Defense
* Secretary of State
Statutory observers:
* Director, Central Intelligence Agency
* Chairman, Joint Chiefs of Staff

Cabinet Councils During the Second Term of the Reagan Administration

Domestic Policy Council
Attorney General (chair)
Interior
HHS
HUD
Transportation
Energy
Education
OMB

Economic Policy Council
Treasury (chair)
State
Agriculture

Commerce
Labor
OMB
Trade Representative
CEA

Martin Anderson, who worked closely with Meese and Weinberger on the transition process, describes the deliberations over cabinet councils during the transition period:

> Meese had this idea that he wanted to have Cabinet councils. This was a good idea because only a small number of issues are possible for the whole Cabinet to deal with. But the whole government is so complex today that most issues require several departments to work together. The genius of the Cabinet council system was that councils were cabinet-level. You couldn't send substitutes, such as deputies, to the meetings. The Cabinet chair became a super-Cabinet member for their issues. . . .What really made the whole thing work was that all meetings had to be in the White House. The White House controlled what time the meeting would take place, where the meeting occurred, and the agenda.[36]

Five cabinet councils were subsequently created by executive order on February 26, 1981. As the White House press office noted, they were to "bring together every Cabinet member in the decision-making process."[37] These five councils, which were meant to complement the National Security Council, were focused around broad policy areas: economic affairs, commerce and trade, human resources, natural resources and the environment, and food and agriculture. The name council was specifically used to indicate that the domestic policy team was as important to the president as the National Security Council team.

As Anderson and Meese had envisioned, the cabinet councils met in the Roosevelt Room next to the oval office. If for any reason the Roosevelt Room was occupied, the Cabinet councils met in the Cabinet Room of the White House. Meetings were never held outside the White House. By meeting only in the White House, Meese guaranteed a constant flow of Cabinet officers to the White House. This well-crafted process was developed to benefit both the president and the Cabinet officers. Cabinet officers gained heightened status in their own departments by being seen as part of the president's inner circle and as key players in the policy process. The president's interests were well served by keeping in continual touch with his Cabinet. It provided one more reinforcement to the Cabinet that they represented the president to the departments, rather than they represented the departments to the president.

Cabinet council meetings, although formal by nature, were intended to foster a close working relationship among the Cabinet officers and to reinforce their sense of a shared vision for the administration. As one of the Cabinet officers described the meetings:

> Cabinet councils did work and they worked well. At each meeting we kind of hugged each other. The meetings were important because every one understood they we were part of a team and were the president's representatives to the constituencies and not the other way around.[38]

One of the more intangible rewards of this process was the behind-the-scenes negotiations that took place before every cabinet council meeting in the hallway outside the Roosevelt Room. Cabinet officers usually came early in order to talk informally about issues that mutually affected their departments. Many issues were worked out quietly among the Cabinet officers before they even were brought up at the cabinet council meetings. For example, one of these issues was a pact that the Agriculture Department wanted to make with Russia regarding long-term grain sales. Prior to one of the cabinet council meetings, Secretary of State George Shultz asked Agriculture Secretary John Block to wait a few months before completing the grain deal so that some sensitive arms negotiations could be completed. Block agreed and waited until Shultz gave him the green light to proceed.[39]   As another Cabinet officer noted, "It was the fact that the people got along so well that allowed the cabinet council system to be so successful."[40]

As was every other aspect of the cabinet councils, the structure of the councils had been carefully deliberated by Anderson and Meese. The meeting time, place, and agenda was regularly sent to all Cabinet officers for all council meetings. However, most Cabinet officers chose to attend only those council meetings of which they were formally a part. In addition to the Cabinet members, Edwin Meese, James Baker, and Vice President George Bush were named as members of all the councils. They attended the meetings sporadically, depending on the importance of the issues at hand.

Cabinet officers generally served on three or four cabinet councils, with one member serving on six. Only one member of the Cabinet, the Secretary of Education, sat on only one council. (Table 5 indicates the frequency of membership by Cabinet officer. The list is in order of the statutory creation of the agency, beginning with State in 1789 and ending with Education in 1979.) Because Cabinet officers sat on several councils, they interacted with most other members of the Cabinet frequently. This contributed to the comraderie among the Cabinet officers and the feeling of shared mission that the Reagan White House nurtured throughout the administration.

The cabinet council system was so successful during the first year of the administration that two more councils were created in 1982. On January 29, 1982, the Cabinet Council for Legal Policy was formed, and on September 22, 1982, the Cabinet Council on Management and Administration was established. Both operated in exactly the same format at their counterparts.

TABLE 5. Frequency of Membership by Cabinet Officers on Cabinet Councils

Agency	Frequency
Secretary of State	5
Secretary of Treasury	4
Secretary of Defense	2
Attorney General	4
Secretary of Interior	3
Secretary of Agriculture	4
Secretary of Commerce	5
Secretary of Labor	4
Secretary of HHS	3
Secretary of HUD	3
Secretary of Transportation	6
Secretary of Energy	3
Secretary of Education	1

Source: The White House, 1988, OPD internal memo

In early 1982 Anderson left the White House and returned to an academic post at Stanford University. The leadership of Reagan's domestic policy staff moved to Edwin L. Harper, a University of Virginia Ph.D., who had been David Stockman's deputy at OMB. Harper had played a major part in the domestic policy process through OMB, and regularly attended the 8:00 A.M. meetings of Reagan's inner circle. Harper, one of John Ehrlichman's deputies in the Nixon White House, had moved into the private sector during the 1970s with INA Corporation, Certain Teed Corporation, and Emerson Electric. He met the test of management expertise and party loyalty that Reagan was seeking for administration appointments.

Harper named Roger Porter as his deputy director. Porter also had political and managerial expertise, having served as executive secretary of the Economic Policy Board under President Ford. Porter had returned to Harvard after Ford's loss to Jimmy Carter, where he taught at the Kennedy School of Government.[41] When George Bush captured the White House,

Porter remained at the White House and advanced to become the president's chief domestic policy advisor.

In September 1982 John A. Svahn replaced Ed Harper as director of the Office of Policy Development (OPD), becoming the third director in as many years.   Svahn had recently moved from Social Security Commissioner (1981–82) to undersecretary of Health and Human Services. He was one of many who followed Reagan to Washington, D.C., from the California state house. Svahn continued the mold established by Anderson and Harper. He was clear on the Reagan agenda and saw the White House staff as the primary tool for maintaining that agenda throughout the departments. He used the cabinet councils as the vehicle for keeping departmental initiatives in line with presidential objectives.

Operating Structure of the Cabinet Councils

The operating structure of the cabinet council system was relatively simple. Three basic levels of operation were set in motion. At the top of the structure were the formal meetings chaired by the president. Formal meetings had the full council present and met for the primary purpose of discussing and debating the policy options that should be pursued by the council. At the middle level of the structure were the working groups of Cabinet officers, chaired by the lead department. The role of the working groups was to review the various policy proposals, legislative support, and implementation obstacles. The working groups were subsets of the full cabinet council. At the bottom level, or principal operating level as it was called, departmental staff from each of the departments in the working group and members of the White House staff worked out the fine details of the policy issue. This group, which was headed by a member of the White House staff, met at the White House to work out details of the policy proposals. Staff from OMB met regularly with the working group staff to ensure that the policy proposals met budgetary and legislative requirements.[42] This three-tiered structure for operating the cabinet councils brought the Cabinet into the policy process, yet provided strong White House direction. Ever wary of leaving the Cabinet officers without White House direction, Ed Meese described the cabinet councils as "a means of management communications and policy guidance from the President."[43]

In addition to the cabinet councils, a series of supplementary coordinating mechanisms were put in place. Among these were two coordinating mechanisms for economic policy. The first, and perhaps most important, was an informal group composed of the Treasury Secretary, Director of the Office of Management and Budget, Chairman of the Council of Economic Advisors, and the Director of the White House Office of Policy

Development. Every Monday morning the four would meet for an informal breakfast at Donald Regan's office at Treasury. They discussed economic strategies and developed modifications to any policies that were emerging from the cabinet councils.

Another coordinating mechanism in economic policy was the President's Economic Advisory Policy Board, created by executive order by Reagan during the first hundred days of the administration. The President's Economic Advisory Policy Board was designed to be the economic counterpart to the President's Foreign Policy Advisory Board, also created by executive order by Reagan, which was designed to give the president outside advice on strategic and diplomatic issues. The primary purpose of the Economic Advisory Policy Board was to serve as an institutional memory in economic policy for the administration. Members such as Arthur Burns, Alan Greenspan, Paul McCracken, Milton Friedman, Walter Wriston, and William Simon brought a wealth of experience to the policy process. In addition, they provided an unimpeachable line of support for Reagan's economic policies.

In each of these cases, the purpose of the coordinating mechanisms was to give the White House staff another layer of control over the policy process. At every stage of policy development, White House staff were an integral part of the process. At no time was there a structure for policy development that did not have members of the White House staff involved.

Reagan's cabinet council structure for policy development has encouraged a continuing dialogue among scholars on the virtue of the cabinet councils as a tool for presidential management of the executive branch. Viewed favorably, the council structure was seen as ensuring a sense of teamwork and contributing to the "orderly handling of business in the administration."[44] The council structure was praised for its ability "to facilitate the coordination of policy implementation"[45] and "to pull together executive branch and White House resources and facilitate coordinated action on a number of important issues."[46] It was also viewed as an integral part of White House management of domestic policy with the caveat that the structure only worked because of "the ties of cabinet and subcabinet appointees to the Reagan philosophy."[47]

Viewed less favorably the cabinet councils were seen as "preoccupied with details required to carry out Reagan's agenda. More than other forces, the budget initially drove other policy, not the reverse."[48] Another view was that the cabinet councils failed to control the "fratricidal disputes among executive agencies that have long characterized American national politics."[49] Certainly the debate will continue, but the success of the cabinet council system in focusing departmental priorities around the presidential agenda and strengthening interdepartmental coordination is evident.

THE WHITE HOUSE OFFICE OF POLICY DEVELOPMENT

Within the White House the unit assigned to guide the Cabinet's domestic policy initiatives was the Office of Policy Development (OPD). The Office of Policy Development managed the elaborate cabinet council process and provided staff for the council's working groups. This office was the Reagan administration's central point for the development of domestic policy initiatives. Working closely with Ed Meese and Jim Baker, Anderson's office kept the cabinet councils focused on the Reagan agenda.

At the heart of the Office of Policy Development was its director, Martin Anderson. He had been a key player throughout both the campaign and transition, and had developed the blueprint for the Office of Policy Development. During the 1980 presidential campaign Anderson had been the architect of Reagan's economic platform and a stalwart supporter of the conservative agenda.

However, it was Anderson's experience in the Nixon White House that led him to define a controlled relationship between the White House staff and the Cabinet. After serving on the Nixon campaign and transition team, Anderson joined the administration as Arthur Burns's assistant and later became a staff member for John Ehrlichman. Nixon's attempt at Cabinet government convinced Anderson that the president had to ensure White House participation in departmental policy-making.

Once Reagan had taken office, Anderson reshaped the image of the Office of Policy Development (OPD). His first move was to change the name of Carter's Domestic Policy Group to the Office of Policy Development to "serve notice that a new administration had taken over."[50] He then moved to frame the cabinet council system to ensure a major role for OPD. As the president's chief domestic policy advisor, the Office of Policy Development was given responsibility for guiding the cabinet councils. Every council working group was chaired by a member of Anderson's staff and their meetings were held in the OPD offices in the old executive office building. As were the cabinet council meetings, which were held in the White House, council working group meetings were held in White House office space rather than departmental office space. It is worth noting that Anderson's staff used offices in the old executive office building rather than the White House to minimize the perception of White House policy control. The constant participation of OPD in the cabinet councils provided "lots of different places to stop the policies we didn't like," as Anderson noted.[51]

Anderson then met daily with Meese to review the policy proposals being prepared by each council working group and every decision made by

the cabinet councils was approved by Meese. This was actually a two-
tiered process to ensure that a broad group of White House staff understood
and approved cabinet council decisions. Five days a week at 7:30 A.M. the
senior White House staff met in the Roosevelt room to discuss major issues
facing the administration. Senior staff included fifteen to twenty staffers,
such as Anderson, Meese, Jim Baker, David Gergen, Richard Darman, the
Congressional Liaison staff, and the press office staff. After the senior staff
meeting ended, Meese and the OPD staff would adjourn to Meese's office to
discuss policy issues evolving in the cabinet councils and the working groups.

The decisions that finally emerged from the cabinet councils were decisions that had been guided and refined at every step in the process by the
White House staff. Once a policy emerged from the Cabinet councils, it
emerged with the blessing of the White House. As a result, all the policy initiatives that emerged from the Cabinet council process, which Reagan eventually made decisions on, were initiatives that the White House itself had crafted.[52]

Staffing the Office of Policy and Development

In spite of Meese and Anderson's commitment to overseeing the policy
process, they realized that the OPD staff could not increase in size and should
actually decrease in size for political reasons. Reagan had campaigned on a
platform of reducing the size of government and on increasing his reliance on
the Cabinet, which meant a trimmed down OPD staff. As Table 6 indicates,
Meese and Anderson successfully trimmed the staff of the Office of Policy
Development below that of their predecessor. One of the techniques that
Anderson employed to reduce the need for staff was the computerization of his
office.[53] Computers were used to follow departmental proposals during policy development and to continue to follow them during implementation. The
computerization of the office helped to keep the OPD staff at a minimum and
strengthened the image of a trimmed down White House staff. The OPD size
was about half that of the Domestic Policy Group under Stuart Eizenstat in the
Carter Administration and about one-third that of the Domestic Council under
John Ehrlichman in the Nixon Administration. Yet the numbers are somewhat
deceiving. As Table 6 indicates, Reagan appeared to guide departmental policy with a significantly smaller percentage of his White House staff than either
Nixon or Carter. Reagan reduced the size of the Office of Policy Development
to give the appearance of a reduced White House presence in policy issues.
However, the original size of the White House staff was significantly
increased (see Table 6) and responsibility for policy development, implementation, and programmatic oversight was spread across the White House. For
example, during the first term Ed Meese (Counsellor to the President) and his

staff, Jim Baker (Chief of Staff) and his staff, and staff from the Counsel's Office, the Cabinet Secretary, Legislative Affairs, Political Affairs, Cabinet Affairs, and Intergovernmental Affairs, all contributed to discussions on policy issues. All of these staffs grew.

TABLE 6. Comparison of Domestic Policy Staffs

Size of Domestic Policy Staff		
Nixon	*Carter*	*Reagan*
74	41	20

Size of White House Staff		
Nixon	*Carter*	*Reagan*
344	464	435

Domestic Policy Staff As Percent of White House		
Nixon	*Carter*	*Reagan*
21%	8%	4%

Note: The White House staff includes only those that are considered the policy-making and administrative staff.

Source: U.S. Governmental Manual; White House staff phone directories

A classic example of the overlapping responsibility of White House staff in policy issues was the relatively simple decision to encourage federal employees to volunteer to tutor in literacy programs. Before the Federal Employees Literacy Training Program (FELT) was approved, the Office of Management and Budget, Presidential Personnel, Legislative Affairs, OPD, Intergovernmental Affairs, Office of Administration, and the Counsel's Office had to be consulted.[54]

Although Reagan successfully kept the OPD at relatively low staffing levels, the senior staff positions throughout the White House steadily grew, as they had under the Nixon, Ford, and Carter administrations.

The Notebooks: The OPD Guide to Policy Development

In order to ensure that each member of the OPD staff had a clear idea of the administration's domestic policy goals, Anderson assigned two staff members, Kevin Hopkins and Douglas Bandow, to prepare a series of notebooks that established Reagan's policy positions for the previous five years. These ten notebooks became the bibles of the OPD staff. When in doubt on policy direction, staff simply referred to the notebooks and quoted presidential positions to Cabinet officers.[55]   James Miller, who followed David Stockman as Reagan's director of the Office of Management and Budget, noted:

> Martin Anderson's books were the bibles. The president had a consistent ideology. The bibles provided a consistent framework and consistent ideas. I felt I could predict what Ronald Reagan would do in almost any circumstance from the statements in these notebooks.[56]

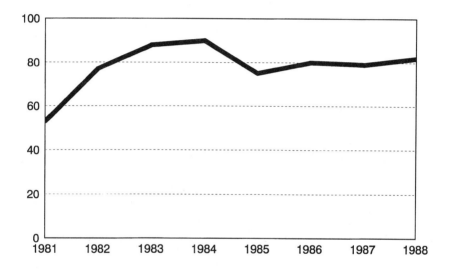

FIGURE 9. Total Senior White House Staff (Reagan)

Anderson's decision to prepare the notebooks was again the product of his experience in the Nixon administration. During the presidential transition period, Anderson served as Arthur Burns's deputy. Meeting in the Drake Hotel in New York City during the fall of 1968, Burns and Anderson were charged with putting together a book of action steps on all domestic and economic policy. These steps were based on the campaign statements made by Nixon.[57]

Anderson's staff differed not only in its size from previous administrations but in its personnel makeup as a result of its high rate of politicization. Most of the OPD staff were part of Reagan's California administration and had been active in the 1980 presidential campaign. Several were close associates of Anderson's. For example, Anderson's second in command,

Edwin J. Gray, had been Reagan's press secretary in Sacramento. Senior staff included Kevin Hopkins, a campaign speech writer; Douglas Bandow, a colleague of Anderson's at Stanford and campaign speech writer; and Barbara Honegger, Anderson's assistant at Stanford and a staff assistant on the campaign. This strengthened the OPD ability to guide the departments, for OPD staff were wed to the same goals and objectives as Reagan.

Guiding the Cabinet Councils

The cabinet council system worked well not only due to the continual direction that the White House provided it, but also due to the continual attention by Reagan. The Reagan White House went to great lengths to keep the Cabinet and sub-Cabinet officers within the presidential orbit. Simply by meeting regularly with Reagan in both Cabinet meetings and Cabinet council meetings, Cabinet officers felt a sense of kindred with the president and believed they were part of the presidential team. Ed Meese compared the Reagan system to past attempts at Cabinet Government by noting that "The difference is that Reagan has used his system so that Cabinet members all feel closer to him than they do to their departments. And he gives them a lot of opportunity to remember that."[58]

In an article in *Government Executive* in January 1983, Meese described in some detail Reagan's participation in the cabinet councils:

> The President doesn't like to make decisions based on memoranda. He always reads the back-ground papers, the working group report, before the final cabinet council meeting [on an issue]. Then, at that meeting [which President Reagan always chairs, himself, for every Council] he listens to the arguments and opinions right in front of him and knows what is behind the final policy recommendation when it reaches the Oval Office. He feels that face-to-face exchange is the way to make clear which alternative recommendations are likely to be the best.[59]

The overarching principle of the cabinet council system was to protect the Cabinet officers from being captured by their departments.

While there was a significant reliance on the cabinet councils for policy development, the White House nevertheless acted alone in many instances. Issues that were politically volatile crossed too many departmental turfs, or simply required immediate attention, were handled directly by the White House. White House senior staff analyzed a broad array of policy issues without cabinet council input, including such diverse issues as social security disability and hospice services.[60] Even a package of incentives to appease women's groups developed in 1983 by OPD were worked out directly with members of Congress and not with Cabinet officers.[61] However, the great bulk of issues were passed through the cabinet council system.

LEGISLATIVE STRATEGY GROUP

Although the White House worked with the departments to develop policies that met Reagan's political and programmatic needs, these policies were not always acceptable to Congress. Traditionally, the Congressional Liaison in the White House worked with the departments to modify proposals that could not pass muster in Congress. This, of course, took time.

And time was of the essence to the Reagan White House. Their answer to the problem was to revamp the policies internally without going back to the departments and through the Cabinet council system. James Baker headed a small group of senior White House staff known as the legislative strategy group, which developed the most advantageous means of securing Congressional support for administration programs.

The legislative strategy group was composed of OMB director David Stockman, Treasury Secretary Donald Regan, and senior staff members Meese and Baker. Baker also included from his staff Congressional lobbyist Max Friedersdorf, public liaison Elizabeth Dole (later to become Secretary of Transportation), communications director David Gergen, and his chief lieutenant Richard Darman. Their role was to develop the most appropriate public relations and legislative strategy for Cabinet council–developed proposals.

The effect of the legislative strategy group on Cabinet–White House relations was to bring another layer of White House control into the policy development process.

OFFICE OF MANAGEMENT AND BUDGET

As did the legislative strategy group, the Office of Management and Budget (OMB) played a major role in the development of the final product that went to Congress. As a member of every cabinet council, David Stockman's staff (and later James Miller's staff) was able to push options that cut programs and personnel. When the cabinet councils argued with OMB staff that certain programs simply could not be cut, Stockman overruled the councils. An example of the power that Stockman had over the departments was his decision to cut commodity price supports. The price supports had been developed through the cabinet council system and approved by Anderson's OPD staff, but Stockman wanted to see deeper cuts. Without consulting the cabinet council, or the Department of Agriculture, Stockman made further cuts and worked with the Legislative Strategy Group to push the bill through Congress. Assistant Agriculture Secretary for Economics William G. Lesher noted that the "cabinet council system broke down. Stockman and others had their ideas of what should be in a farm bill. . . . Much to our chagrin, that persuasion won out."[62]

Stockman was equally hard on individual Cabinet officers. When departmental policies did not meet the administration's budget-cutting goals, Stockman met with the Cabinet officers and reiterated Reagan's charge to cut the budget. In *Triumph of Politics*, Stockman writes,

> We had brow-beaten the Cabinet, one by one, into accepting the cuts. . . .We forced health research cuts on Dick Schweiker at HHS. We stiffed Jack Block with soil conservation cuts at USDA. We shackled Ted Bell with a sweeping retrenchment at the Education Department.[63]

Some Cabinet officers, such as Alexander Haig, felt that Stockman was interfering with policy decisions with the budget cuts that OMB recommended. Early in 1981 Haig declared that he was "mindful of the need for budgetary restraint," but he and "no one else was in charge of policy."[64] Yet in the end, OMB always won. As Samuel Pierce woefully remarked, "OMB always controlled the end product because they controlled the money."[65]

Stockman's role in the Cabinet–White House relationship cannot be underestimated. Not only could Stockman overrule Cabinet officers and effectively abrogate cabinet council decisions, but he could make policy decisions without ever bringing them to the Cabinet or cabinet council for debate. Perhaps the most significant example of his authority was the 1981 budget cuts. On February 18, 1981, Reagan went before a joint session of Congress to announce his "Program for Economic Recovery." The program presented to Congress a list of program cuts, most of which Stockman had single-handedly made without consulting any of the departments. Stockman allowed virtually no discussion by Cabinet officers on his proposals for cuts.[66]

PERSONNEL SELECTIONS FOR SUB-CABINET POSITIONS

Cabinet officers, as we have seen, had a significant amount of control from the White House. Another aspect of that control was the personnel selection system for sub-Cabinet staff. Not only were Cabinet officers chosen for their ideological commitment to the Reagan agenda, but all political appointees within the departments were as well. The strata of political appointees below the Cabinet were scrutinized for their ideological commitment to the Reagan agenda as thoroughly as the Cabinet officers themselves.

Unlike Nixon and Carter, Reagan did not allow his Cabinet officers single-handedly to choose their deputies or any of the other political appointments in the departments. Pendleton James's White House personnel operation controlled all departmental political jobs. All political positions, from deputy secretaries to personal secretaries, were controlled from the White House. Interviewed for the *Washington Post* in mid-1981, James said that "Nixon, like Carter, lost the appointments process. They lost control to the departments and the agencies. We have maintained control at the Oval Office."[67] Cabinet officers were discouraged from even recommending names to the White House, but if they did, the nominee had to meet a five-point test:

1. They had to have a philosophy in tune with the president.
2. They had to have a competency to pursue the philosophy of the president.
3. They had to have personal and professional integrity.
4. They had to be team players.
5. They had to be tough enough to take the abuse from the press, Congress, and constituent groups.[68]

There was a preoccupation by the Reagan staff that the career bureaucracy would actively oppose their agenda. They sought to place Reagan loyalists in management positions and not promote career staff. The Heritage Foundation prepared a blueprint for action for the Reagan administration prior to the inauguration, entitled *Mandate for Leadership,* in which it warned the administration how powerful the bureaucracy was. They noted:

> The political executive who is promoting significant policy change within his department should not be surprised by career bureaucratic subordinates engaging in . . . covert inter-bureaucratic struggle to block his initiatives. Bureaucratic opponents will lobby vigorously against the proposed policy change to client groups, congressional committee staffs, and the press. The bureaucracy's resources for defending its viewpoint, leaking discrediting material, and mustering outside allies are such that it could be correctly called the ultimate lobby.[69]

There is evidence to support efforts by career staff to thwart the Reagan team, which gave greater credence to the warnings of the Heritage Foundation. For example, two Reagan staff appointed to direct the Department of Justice's Office of Juvenile Justice and Delinquency Prevention found a small group of people who were opposed to what they were doing. The career staff let their opposition be known to crucial staff of the Senate and House committees and to many of the grantees. The solution of the Reagan appointees was to split up the career staff to minimize their influence over any one program.[70]

Throughout the first year, James cleared most, if not all, appointments with the "Big Three," as he called the Baker, Deaver, Meese troika, and many appointments he cleared directly with Reagan. According to James, "I met with the President twice a week and with the Big Three at 5:00 P.M. every day of the first year."[71] This continual oversight of personnel by senior staff and by the president himself reinforced the importance that the Reagan White House attached to controlling the bureaucracy.

The use of a personnel clearance system was refined by the Reagan staff, but in fact had been used by both the Nixon and Carter staffs late in their terms. Nixon had Frederic Malek and Carter had Tim Kraft run centralized personnel systems. The Reagan staff, however, tied personnel clearance to the entire structure of a strong Cabinet–White House relationship.

The personnel selection system was part of the grand design to minimize the career staff's influence over departmental policy decisions. Some Cabinet officers balked at the directive, and tried to bring in their own staff. For example, Caspar Weinberger tried to bring Frank Carlucci on as his principal deputy. The White House personnel operation refused to accept Carlucci, who had been serving as Deputy Director of the Central Intelligence Agency under Carter. The very mention of the Carter administration sent shutters up the spines of the personnel team. Weinberger eventually won, but Carlucci was one of the rare exceptions.

Most of the Cabinet quietly accepted the Reagan demand for approval over their sub-Cabinet appointments. Alexander Haig said of the process, "The names on this list, it was understood, were the ones which Reagan was comfortable."[72] At the top of the list for Deputy Secretary of State, the senior position in the department, was Judge William P. Clark of the California Supreme Court, a longtime Reagan friend, but not deeply involved in foreign policy. Clark was subsequently named to the post.

Cabinet Officers Respond to White House Control

Cabinet officers were given lists of names that were acceptable to the White House from which to choose their top staff. Most Cabinet officers found that they could easily find acceptable people on the lists. However, some Cabinet officers forged separate deals with Pendleton James that allowed them to put their own people in place. Such a case was Secretary of the Interior James Watt, whose entire staff was hand-picked by Watt himself. All of Watt's staff were former associates with whom he had previously worked and whom he knew shared the same agenda for the department.[73] But Cabinet secretaries were not completely discouraged from making recommendations to James for their sub-Cabinet positions. As one Cabinet officer noted, "If you were doing a good job and had a track record of picking good people, the White House personnel office approved your people."[74] Samuel Pierce, however, allowed James to place nearly all of the HUD senior staff.

It is worth adding that the personnel operation shrewdly coupled loyalty to the Reagan agenda with federal management experience in their quest for departmental staff. Unlike Jimmy Carter who pursued technical experts for managerial positions, Ronald Reagan pursued managers.

Some Cabinet officers, however, were quite bitter about the degree of control that the White House exerted over personnel selection. Terrel Bell, Secretary of Education, rather bitterly described the process by saying that:

> Even under normal circumstances, the selection and ultimate confirmation of a presidential appointee are very difficult, time-consuming, and frustrating for the Cabinet officer and for the candidate he or she has recruited. But when a fight simmers between the White House staff and a Cabinet secretary, the ensuing delay, confusion and behind-the scenes tactics can be discouraging to even the most dedicated. Given the determination of Ed Meese and his White House aides to stack my department and my equally fervent resolve to prevent this, it is not difficult to fathom the reasons for the inordinate delays in consummating subcabinet positions in Education. . . . How could I fight back? . . . . I was on my own during the first months of 1981.[75]

Yet in spite of often vigorous opposition to White House control of the personnel process, the White House pursued its goal of centralizing personnel decisions. Although Terrel Bell and others complained about the system, they were essentially forced into complying with it. Presidential scholar Bradley Patterson summed up the process when he said "The Presidential Personnel Office is thus part of the White House gateway, closing out those who don't measure up, beckoning in the select, doing the president's bidding to help him be chief executive in fact as well as in name."[76]

PERSONNEL MANAGEMENT FOR SUB-CABINET POSITIONS

Personnel selection was followed by personnel management. Once in office, political appointees were briefed on administration goals and on budgeting, policy development, and other key areas. This task fell to Craig Fuller, the Assistant to the President for Cabinet Affairs, who designed a two-pronged approach to personnel management.[77] Top-level presidential appointees met in small seminars of twenty to twenty-five persons, with faculty from the John F.

Kennedy School of Government at Harvard University on political and managerial strategies for both policy development and implementation.[78] All senior executive service (SES) officials participated in day and a half long seminars run by the Office of Personnel Management through the Federal Executive Institute.

The political appointees were invited to various receptions and dinners at the White House to emphasize their importance on the presidential team. Again, this was part of the effort to keep the Cabinet and their staff in the presidential orbit rather than the departmental orbit. At all times, Reagan wanted Cabinet officers to be the advocate for his policies and not the advocate for departmental policies.

Personnel management continued throughout the administration as sub-Cabinet appointments were regularly brought together by OMB staff to discuss policy issues in the old executive office building. The purpose of these regular meetings was twofold. On the one hand, the meetings served as mini-Cabinet council meetings in which interjurisdictional policy details could be further refined. On the other hand, and more importantly, it gave the White House another opportunity to reiterate the Reagan agenda and confirm that sub-Cabinet officials understood that agenda. Sub-Cabinet staff were continually reinforced with the idea that they were an integral part of the Reagan team, and that their mission was to reduce the number of departmental programs and to reduce the size of the departmental staff.[79]

MODIFICATIONS TO THE STRUCTURE: THE SECOND TERM

The Cabinet–White House relationship operated extremely successfully throughout Reagan's first term in office. The only significant modification to the system came during the early months of the term when the Cabinet Administration Office was created under Edwin Meese's jurisdiction. Its role was to ensure that Cabinet meetings were held regularly, to establish the agenda, and to circulate background information to each member of the Cabinet and to the president. The Cabinet Administration Office worked closely with the OPD representatives on each of the cabinet councils to obtain their agenda items.

However, changes in the system were inevitable with the changes in the White House senior staff during the second term of the administration. The top three staff left the White House following the 1984 reelection, with James Baker moving to the Treasury Department, Edwin Meese moving to the Justice Department, and Michael Deaver leaving to open a private consulting firm. The vacuum in the White House was quickly filled by former Treasury Secretary Donald Regan, who was named chief of staff after the 1985 inauguration.

Donald Regan Takes Control

With Regan came a new approach to Cabinet–White House relations and to the management of the White House internal structure. Regan sought to consolidate under his jurisdiction all the functions which the troika directly oversaw. Regan's first order of business was to tighten control of the policy development and implementation process of the cabinet councils. On April 11, 1985, through an executive order, Reagan merged the Meese and Baker operations into one unit directly under Donald Regan's control. The cabinet council system similarly underwent a dramatic change when Regan collapsed the seven domestic councils into two domestic cabinet councils: one for domestic policy and one for economic policy. Table 6 totals up the membership of each of the two new councils. The structure of the National Security Council, which was statutorily mandated, remained unchanged. When asked why these changes were made to the cabinet councils, the White House simply responded that "It was the Chief of Staff Don Regan organizing the White House policy shops the way he wanted them."[80] Each Cabinet officer, with the exception of the Secretary of Defense, was represented on one of the two new councils. As in the previous system, the vice president and the White House chief of staff were ex officio members of both. The Secretary of Defense, however, remained a statutory member of the National Security Council, and was invited to participate in any other cabinet council meeting he wanted to, as were all the Cabinet officers.

Regan not only reorganized the structure of the cabinet council system to reframe what he called a "cumbersome and redundant system,"[81] but also the entire operation of the system. Cabinet Government suffered a major setback under Regan's brief tenure in the White House. Not only did he reduce the number of councils, which reduced the access points of Cabinet officers to the president, but he reduced the president's participation in council meetings. Cabinet council recommendations, which had previously been presented to the president and discussed at length with him during the meetings, were handled by Regan. Regan directed that all council recommendations be sent to him and that he would present them directly to the president.

Regan's efforts were focused on centralizing the entire decision-making process, including policy development, through his office. Typical of Regan's efforts to change the former more collaborative system initiated by the troika were the economic policy meetings. Working on a tax reform package, for example, Regan carefully excluded two key players: Beryl Sprinkel, chairman of the Council of Economic Advisers, and Malcolm Baldrige, Secretary of Commerce.[82] Regan's approach to management was a return to the hierarchical policy development system that both the Nixon and Carter administrations had used, in which senior White House staff, not the Cabinet officers, met with the president to discuss policy options.

Regan created a new level of bureaucracy between the Cabinet officers and the president. Regan replaced the Cabinet Administration Office, created by Meese, with the Cabinet Affairs Office, and added the Office of Cabinet Secretary to oversee the Cabinet Affairs Office and the cabinet councils.

The new director of the Cabinet Affairs Office, Alfred Kingon, was a Regan protégé from Treasury. Kingon's office took over the role that OPD previously had of managing the cabinet councils. Kingon's staff prepared a "decision memorandum," a term carried over from the Carter administration's cabinet cluster system, for the president. The memorandum, usually two or three pages, presented the major arguments for and against a departmental policy proposal. Reagan approved or disapproved a council recommendation based on the decision memorandum.

During the two years that Regan served as chief of staff he restructured the system of Cabinet–White House relations that had been so carefully crafted in 1981. Cabinet officers did not meet regularly with Reagan, either through individual or cabinet council meetings, and were relegated to dealing with the Cabinet secretariat on policy matters. Cabinet officers became increasingly discontent with the structure that Regan had set in place, giving White House staff independent power.

One of the more vocal opponents of the centralized management style of Don Regan was Secretary of State George Shultz. Shultz was extremely dissatisfied with the power that Regan had given the National Security Council. In his memoirs, Shultz angrily described his view of the newly empowered NSC:

> My main fight was with an NSC staff that had developed an operational capability and a fervent will to use it—often unwisely. With authority, ambition, and power, the NSC staff would operate without anyone's full knowledge, even the president's, and was not subject to congressional oversight. . . .The NSC staff had turned into a "wildcat operation." [83]

Howard Baker Replaces Regan

The inevitability of a nearly totally centralized policy-making system subsided when Regan resigned as chief of staff after the Iran-Contra affair in 1986. He was replaced by Howard Baker, former Senate majority leader. Baker quickly restored the previously strong relationship between the Cabinet officers and the president, and reduced the power of the Cabinet Secretary to act as a go-between. Baker also replaced the Regan staff, particularly Alfred Kingon who was replaced by Nancy Risque. Risque had worked in a number of departments and was widely respected within the Cabinet. Further, Baker brought in a new communications director for the White House, Thomas

Griscom, to improve communications not only with the press but with the departments. Griscom, who followed Baker from the Senate, had been one of the majority leader's senior aides.[84]

The Cabinet overwhelmingly applauded the changes that Baker made to revitalize the cabinet council system. Reagan again became a regular participant in the cabinet council meetings, allowing the Cabinet officers to make presentations on their recommendations and to present opposing viewpoints. When Baker resigned in 1988 to return to Tennessee, stating that he had only joined the staff for a limited period of time, he was replaced by his deputy, Kenneth Duberstein. Duberstein continued the same system that Baker had established.

Although the strong Cabinet-White House relationship that existed during the first term was clearly jeopardized by Regan's changes, it remained in tact. Had Regan remained for the entire second term, the system may have fallen apart. Had Cabinet officers turned over, the system may have fallen apart. Had Reagan wanted major new programs, the system may have fallen apart. Had Ed Meese not continued to oversee the domestic policy agenda, the system may have fallen apart. But none of this happened and the structure survived the Regan era. The Regan era is, however, an indication of how well-developed the policy development structure had been during the first term and how, even with modification, the structure continued to operate smoothly.

THE NATIONAL SECURITY COUNCIL: IRAN-CONTRA

The careful structure that enabled the White House to control the domestic policy process through a web of process, personnel, and legislative management was not mirrored in the national security process. Unlike Edwin Meese and Martin Anderson, who developed a carefully orchestrated structure for policy formulation and coordination, Richard Allen and subsequent National Security Advisors never gained control over their own house.

The Iran-Contra scandal of 1986, which nearly brought down the Reagan administration, involved an overzealous national security staffer, Lt. Colonel Oliver North, who attempted to provide a funding source for the Contra "freedom fighters" in Nicaragua. Reagan had frequently spoken publicly of his support for the Contras and their noble cause. Congress, however, did not agree with Reagan and banned military aid to the Contras. The lack of Congressional support for the Contras led North to find alternate funding sources. His solution was to sell arms to Iran using Israel as an intermediary in spite of a Congressional ban on selling arms to Iran. North successfully accomplished the arms sale, including shipment of 508 TOW antitank missiles, and raised millions of dollars, which surreptitiously was given to the Contras.

The complex scenario that North created to circumvent Congress was soon discovered and vociferously condemned by Congress, the public, and the president. North resigned as did National Security Advisor John Poindexter. Chief of Staff Donald Regan was eventually driven from office in large part because of his failure to control North and his activities.

This brief overview of the Iran-Contra episode is worth noting because it highlights how easily the White House staff can lose control. The failure of the national security office to manage their policy process can be juxtaposed against the success of the domestic policy office. The domestic policy process was characterized by two leaders (both Meese and Anderson) who understood the Reagan agenda and framed administration objectives within that agenda. The process was further characterized by a policy structure that ensured all members of the White House staff understood the Reagan agenda and could communicate that agenda to departmental staff. The cabinet council system reinforced the specific details of the Reagan agenda and the sense of teamwork between the White House and the departments.

In contrast, the National Security Council staff never had the same organizational structure or oversight process that its counterpart in domestic affairs had. Neither Richard Allen nor his successors gained control over the staff.[85] Staff regularly were reassigned, policy was constantly redefined, and morale was consistently low in the NSC staff.[86] In addition, territorial squabbles over policy control between the NSC, the Department of State, and the Department of Defense reduced the NSC to primarily a paper-shuffling body rather than a policy coordinating body, as the National Security Act of 1947 had intended. The President's Foreign Intelligence Advisory Board (PFIAB) had not delved deeply enough into the NSC internal affairs to understand the structural and personnel problems that needed to be addressed. As the Tower Commission noted, "no periodic evaluation" was undertaken by these oversight agencies.[87] The recommendation to increase oversight was supported by the Congressional committees investigating the Iran-Contra issue. Both the House and Senate select committees further recommended revitalization of the President's Intelligence Oversight Board.[88]

The Iran-Contra case is brought to light here as a means of contrasting the two primary operating structures within the White House during the Reagan administration. The domestic policy operation was characterized by staff coherence and a clear understanding of administration objectives, close working relations with the departments, and continual oversight by the domestic policy advisor (Anderson) and the president's counselor on domestic affairs (Meese). In contrast, the national security office was characterized by staff infighting, morale problems, a lack of direction, and weak relations with the departments. In addition, the national security office had a succession of directors, including Allen, Robert McFarlane, and John Poindexter during the Iran-Contra process that added to problems in oversight and policy management.

The Tower Commission, convened by President Reagan to explore how the entire Iran-Contra scenario was able to progress, concluded that the primary issue was one of structure and accountability. Had the NSC operated with greater reliance on formal decision structures, Oliver North would not have had the same independent operating style. Yet, one of the paradigms of bureaucratic politics is that, as Graham Allison notes, "substantive problems are so inordinately difficult that differences about goals, alternatives, and consequences are inevitable."[89] Whether a more formal operating structure could have prevented Iran-Contra and Oliver North's activities is only speculation, but it certainly would have put up far more roadblocks to his activities.

CONCLUSION: THE WHITE HOUSE MAINTAINS CONTROL

Lou Cannon noted that "the modern presidency created by Franklin Roosevelt is of necessity a centralizing force."[90] More than any other President in modern history, Ronald Reagan centralized the policy-making process. The White House became the center of policy development, management, and Congressional implementation. Political personnel within the departments were cleared through the White House and their actions constantly monitored by the White House and the Executive Office of the President.

The legacy of the Reagan White House is that it built a system of control that the Nixon, Ford, and Carter administrations began but had not fully developed. Under Reagan, the system of controlling domestic policy development from the White House was finely tuned.

The Reagan White House was able to control Cabinet officers from moving in directions that were politically and programmatically unacceptable to the president. By constantly meeting in small groups with the Cabinet, White House staff were able to keep Cabinet officers within the presidential orbit and minimize cooption. Departmental policy initiatives could be focused around the goals and objectives outlined by the White House.

The principal failure of the three previous attempts at managing domestic policy from the White House was that the White House structures had focused around relatively narrow issues and had failed to bring Cabinet officers into discussions on the broader issues facing the administration. The Reagan White House succeeded in building a bridge between the White House and the departments that allowed Cabinet officers input into a broad array of policy issues. Cabinet officers considered themselves key players in the development of the administration's policy initiatives. The White House, however, maintained control over issues that were either politically volatile or required rapid turnover time.

Is there a lesson from the Reagan experience? Perhaps the most important lesson learned for future administrations is that the White House can develop a workable structure to manage departmental domestic policy-making. Presidents Nixon, Ford, and Carter each built part of the frame for the structure, which Reagan finally nailed together. The structure remains wobbly, however, for it was a structure that suited the Reagan agenda of cutting bureaucracy, privatizing programs, reducing federal regulations, and bringing down federal spending. Haynes Johnson summed up Reagan's agenda quite succinctly when he said, "Reagan's impulses were to abet creative impulses."[91]

It is unquestionably easier to foster strong relations between the Cabinet and the White House if reducing programs rather than increasing programs is central to the agenda. If an administration seeks to increase programmatic activities, the battle over limited resources will dominate the relationship among Cabinet officers. White House staff will be less successful in binding Cabinet officers together when the administration's policy direction is broader and forces competition for funding. The lesson, however, is not lost. Reagan successfully changed the way the White House dealt with the departments by fostering the sense that policy development was a team operation between the Cabinet officers and the White House.

SEVEN

THE BUSH YEARS

In 1988 George Bush defied the odds and became the first incumbent vice president since 1836 to win election to the presidency. His victory continued the Republican dominance of the White House that had ruled nearly continuously since 1969. Only Jimmy Carter's brief tenure interrupted the Republican hold on the executive branch during the previous twenty years.

The election of George Herbert Walker Bush to the presidency was predicated on a continuation of the policies of Ronald Reagan.[1] In essence, Bush promised to maintain the status quo and continue to move government down the road that Reagan had traveled. He promised that government would continue to shrink, that the deficit would continue to move downward, and that fewer regulations would be imposed on business. "George Bush didn't come to the presidency to make a 180-degree turn, he came to build upon the successes," was the campaign phrase.[2] The Bush policies were Reagan policies that the Bush team would move forward. As Ronald Reagan himself noted after the election, "the mandate of the Bush administration will be to make it possible not just to continue, but to build upon the achievements of the past eight years."[3]

At the heart of the 1988 presidential campaign was the promise by George Bush that the American people would pay "no new taxes." This was successfully intended to draw a sharp line between the policies of his opponent, Massachusetts Governor Michael Dukakis, and his own. Dukakis promoted a host of new government programs, which Bush inferred would require major tax increases. The keystone of the Bush campaign was the pledge to keep new taxes from being imposed. The Bush campaign worked diligently to minimize campaigning on specific issues, issues that could lead to expensive program initiatives. Once in office, Bush remained consistent with his campaign promises. In a brief interview with reporters in the oval office immediately after the inauguration, Bush was asked his goals for the next year. There were no domestic initiatives mentioned.[4]

The campaign focused on nonsubstantive issues such as his promise for a "kinder, gentler America." It was often a campaign of symbols, to reinforce the continuation of the Reagan agenda while focusing attention on a new style of leadership. Such language was not intended to be a repudiation of Reagan's leadership, only a refinement of his leadership style. Bush promised to be a more hands-on president with longer days and more attention to details.

However, unlike the 1980 campaign of Ronald Reagan against Jimmy Carter, there was little mention of the role of the White House staff in policy-making. The election rhetoric of 1988 did not include the role of the White House staff or of the Cabinet in the policy process. The term *Cabinet Government,* which had become intertwined in campaign speeches for nearly two decades, had suddenly disappeared. Neither the Bush nor the Dukakis camp used the phrase at any point in the election.

Although the 1988 election lacked a substantive debate on the Cabinet–White House relationship, as there had been in previous elections, the Bush camp had clearly delineated the powersharing structure. As candidate Bush had noted throughout the campaign, the Bush presidency would be managed in a different mode than had the Reagan presidency. There would be "a new leadership style." George Bush would not delegate blindly to his staff and would be actively involved in the decision-making process. The White House staff would not wield the power it had for eight years. The Cabinet would be the primary source of advice for the president.

The debate on Cabinet–White House relationships that had been publicly addressed under the rubric *Cabinet Government* for twenty years was now taking a different turn. Rather than refer to Cabinet Government to describe a reduced White House staff, the Bush team referred to a "new leadership style" in structuring the Cabinet–White House relationship.

The repudiation of the term *Cabinet Government* by the Bush campaign was a carefully crafted effort to redesign the Cabinet–White House relationship without focusing public attention on the Reagan presidency. Since the entire campaign was premised on a continuation of the Reagan era, attacks on Reagan's governing style would be detrimental to George Bush. The simple and nonthreatening phrase "new leadership style" sufficed to address the issue of centralization of power within the White House.

Not until the election had been secured did the Bush campaign begin to address the specific structure of the Cabinet–White House relationship and the role of the White House staff in decision-making. As was to be expected, the president-elect moved quickly toward a strong Cabinet system. The transition team was given primary responsibility for framing the organizational structure for the new administration.

Although the term *Cabinet Government* had been replaced by the term *new leadership style* in the 1988 campaign, the theme had remained constant. The White House staff had amassed too much power in the policy process. As had every candidate since 1969, George Bush promised the electorate that his administration would reframe the policy process and reduce the role of White House staff. The Bush campaign had simply repackaged the issue. In his first major interview after being named chief of staff, New Hampshire Governor John Sununu said that "he would try to stay in the background, encourage debate among advisors, and tailor the White House system to suit" the president's evolving style.[5] Sununu also offered that he would try to be "invisible for a while." Sununu, cognizant of the public outcry against such powerful chiefs of staff as Donald Regan and H.R. Haldeman, saw his role cast as a background player.

The Cabinet–White House relationship that Bush alluded to during the campaign was one of a strong role for the Cabinet and a trimmed down White House staff with far less influence than in previous administrations. The task of the transition team was to design a Cabinet and White House staff that could successfully operate within this theme.

THE TRANSITION

The transition team began operations within a week after the election in four floors of leased office space on Connecticut Avenue. Using $3.5 million of Congressionally appropriated funds,[6] the transition team immediately brought in 125 paid staff to manage the wide-ranging operations. Under the direction of Craig Fuller, Bush's vice presidential chief of staff, and Robert Teeter, a Republican strategist and pollster, the transition team began to focus their efforts around personnel selection and policy analysis. Unlike its predecessors, the Bush campaign had not developed a shadow transition team prior to the election. Chase Untermeyer, a senior member of the Bush campaign, had handled rudimentary planning for the transition, but had not developed an organization chart or discussed appointments. It was left to the transition team both to design the organizational process of Cabinet–White House interaction, and to choose both teams.[7]

With little hesitation, the transition team divided responsibilities around four key areas: choosing Cabinet and sub-Cabinet personnel, choosing White House staff, developing packets of information for Cabinet appointments, and preparing a 100-day plan for the new administration. Fuller and Baker focused on personnel selection while departmental management issues were managed by other staff.

An inordinate amount of the transition team's time was focused on departmental management reviews. As had the Reagan transition team, the Bush transition team wanted Cabinet nominees thoroughly versed in their departments before taking office. The transition team moved quickly to emulate the Reagan administration's successful briefing package prepared for new Cabinet officers. The transition team appointed transition office contacts (known as TOCs) for each department. Most of the TOCs were transition staff who had moved directly from the campaign policy staff and were familiar with departmental issues. Their objective was to prepare reports for incoming Cabinet officers on the statutory responsibilities of their departments, staff makeup, and current goals. Reminiscent of the Reagan administration, these reports were referred to as "the notebooks."

At the heart of the issues that the transition team dealt with was the personnel selection for the Cabinet. Unlike his predecessors, George Bush chose to place his closest associates in the Cabinet rather than on the White House staff. Top campaign staff and longtime associates moved to the departments, rather than to the White House. As a result, few on the White House staff had a long and established relationship with Bush, and the seniormost member of the White House staff, John Sununu, had worked with Bush for only months during the election. Most of those appointed to the White House staff were relatively young, in contrast to the decades-older Cabinet officers.

The Cabinet–White House relationship was never directly discussed nor was the issue of a revitalized Cabinet during the transition process. Perhaps the most important indication that Bush gave of his intention to reduce the influence of the White House staff came in his announcement of Brent Scowcroft as National Security Advisor. Bush firmly noted that James Baker (Secretary of State–designate) rather than Scowcroft, would be the chief spokesman for the administration on foreign affairs. Similarly, when Nicholas Brady was announced as Treasury Secretary, the formal announcement noted that Brady would be the chief economic spokesman for the administration.

The transition process continued without a clear discussion of the Cabinet–White House relationship. As the choices were named for Cabinet posts, the strength of the Cabinet as a policy-maker became evident. As had all recent presidents, George Bush was revitalizing his Cabinet and refocusing the policy development structure. But unlike recent presidents, George Bush was addressing the issue quietly and without a formal transition document to guide the process.

As the inauguration grew closer, rather than focus on the structure of the governing process, the transition team turned its attention to the policy process and the development of a "100-day plan" for the new administration. Since the campaign had chosen to be vague in its issue orientation, the transition team was forced to flush out specific objectives for the first one hundred days of the administration. Lobbyists inundated the transition team with policy proposals. For example, since the campaign had highlighted the environment as a key issue, environmental groups proposed more than seven hundred recommendations for the administration to pursue, including a 20 per cent increase in the budget of the Environmental Protection Agency.[8] As the executive director of the American Conservative Union noted, "We're trying to get the Bush people on record, so we can go back to them with the implementation of policy starts."[9] All the energies of the transition team were focused on a series of goals and objectives that the administration could develop for the first one hundred days.

The issue of the structure of the Cabinet–White House relationship became overshadowed by the need to create a policy package. As a result, Cabinet officers and White House staff moved into their jobs without a clear framework for policy interaction. As the administration moved into gear, the absence of either a structure for Cabinet–White House interaction in policy development or a series of well-developed policy proposals led to an administration that the public perceived as rudderless. By the end of his first four months in office, public approval ratings for Bush had fallen to just over 50 per cent from the 63 per cent approval he received in his first month in office.[10]

CABINET SELECTION

Indicative of his emphasis on a strengthened Cabinet, George Bush named the most powerful member of the administration first. Barely one day after the election, James Baker was nominated for Secretary of State. Within a week, Nicholas Brady, another close friend, was reappointed at Treasury. Not until November 17, after the two top Cabinet officials had been chosen, was the White House chief of staff, John Sununu, named.

The choice of James Baker for a Cabinet rather than White House position was the first of several indicators that the president-elect intended to use the Cabinet as his primary source of advice. Bush followed the selection of Baker and Brady with that of Robert Mosbacher to take the helm at the Commerce Department. Baker, Brady, and Mosbacher were all Texans with long relationships with Bush, both professional and personal. John Tower, another Texan, was nominated for Defense. When his nomination ran into problems during the Senate confirmation process, Bush chose Dick Cheney, another close friend from their years in the Ford administration, for the job.

The Cabinet selection process continued through the second week of January. The process was slower than most recent administrations: Ronald

Reagan completed his first Cabinet on January 8, 1981, while Dwight Eisenhower completed his first Cabinet on December 1, 1952. Most Presidents had completed their Cabinets by Christmas.

The choices for the Bush Cabinet were predicated on a sense of collegiality, experience, and managerial expertise. Ideology, which dominated the Reagan Cabinet, was not a factor. Bush sought a Cabinet of managers who could control the proliferation of government programs and focus on his efforts to reduce the federal budget deficit, strengthen ethics in government, control federal spending. Although loyalty to George Bush was a primary determinant in Cabinet selection, loyalty to an ideological direction was not. Craig Fuller noted that "We don't run around with a lot of litmus paper in our pockets. We want people [for the Cabinet] who are philosophically compatible, but we're really looking for the best people we can find. . . . We want people with expertise and qualifications for the job."[11]

When directly asked about the qualifications of his new Cabinet, Bush responded only that it would be a "brand new team" of officials that could "reinvigorate the process."[12] He made no reference to ideology or direction in his assessment of the credentials required for his Cabinet. The Cabinet that was subsequently assembled was not a "brand new team," as Bush had promised, with fresh faces from around the country, but rather a cadre of experienced Washington politicians. Ten of the fourteen nominees currently lived in Washington, D.C. Six of the nominees were holdovers from the Reagan administration who kept the same job; three were holdovers from the Reagan administration who moved to new jobs; four were former members of Congress; and only four were from outside the beltway.

TABLE 7. Bush Cabinet

Holdovers from Reagan — Kept Same Job
Brady (Treasury)
Thornburgh (Justice)
Cavazos (Education)

Holdovers from Reagan — Assigned New Job
Dole (Transportation 1983–87 to Labor)
Baker (Treasury to State)
Yeutter (Trade Rep to Agriculture)

Retired from Congress
Kemp
Lujan
Tower
Derwinski (at State since 1982)

(Continued on next page)

TABLE 7. Bush Cabinet *(continued)*

Beltway Outsiders
Skinner (Illinois)
Mosbacher (Texas)
Sullivan (Georgia)
Watkins (California)

The decision to form a Cabinet from experienced managers bolstered the campaign pledge to continue the direction embarked on by the Reagan administration. While the Reagan Cabinet framed the ideas for change, in many cases it would be the Bush Cabinet to move those ideas to fruition. In a lead article days before the inauguration, the *New York Times* analyzed the Bush Cabinet and concluded that it was, above all else, a Cabinet of managers, which resembled the parliamentary style of governing:

> The President-elect's 14 choices for the Cabinet, as well as those for the half dozen or so other jobs that strongly affect the substance and personality of an administration, resemble the selection of a parliamentary leader more than those of an American chief executive. Prime ministers choose ministers almost entirely from experience (and presumably wisdom) in prior governments. For all of his talk of new faces, Mr. Bush has done the same thing.[13]

By choosing a Cabinet of experienced managers, rather than ideologues, Bush endeavored to maximize his efforts toward reaping legislative rewards for his programmatic initiatives. Unlike the Reagan administration which had few programmatic initiatives, the Bush administration sought to move a series of initiatives on the environment, education, and foreign aid through Congress.

Balance in the Cabinet

The Cabinet selections, while based primarily on loyalty and government experience, ensured traditional balance in the Cabinet. As had every president since George Washington, George Bush continued the tradition of geographic balance in the Cabinet. Every region of the country was represented, although those regions that had provided strong electoral support to the Bush/Quayle ticket were weighted more heavily in the Cabinet selection process.

The northeast had only two selections representing the relatively weak support for the ticket: Jack Kemp from New York as Secretary of Housing and Urban Development, and Richard Thornburgh from Pennsylvania as Attorney General. In contrast, the midwest, the south, and the west all had significantly more nominees as a result of their electoral support for Bush/Quayle.

TABLE 8. 1988 Electoral Votes by Region

	Northeast	*South*	*Midwest*	*West*
Bush	*60*	*168*	*108*	*90*
Dukakis	*53*	*8*	*29*	*21*

Source: Statistical Abstract of the United States 1992, 112th edition (Washington, D.C.: U.S. Government Printing Office, 1992)

From the south were the nominees for Health and Human Services, Dr. Louis Sullivan from Atlanta, Georgia; and Texans James Baker for State, Nicholas Brady for Treasury, Lauro Cavazos for Education, and Robert Mosbacher at Commerce.   From the midwest were Elizabeth Dole at Transportation from Kansas and Clayton Yeutter at Agriculture from Nebraska. Rounding out the geographic balance on the Cabinet were James Watkins of California for Energy and Manuel Lujan of New Mexico for Interior.

Gender and racial balance were both considered in the Cabinet selection process, although not dwelled upon.   Fuller noted in a press conference that Bush would consider gender and race in the overall composition of the administration and would ensure that blacks and women were represented in it.[14] This was reiterated frequently throughout the transition. "The vice president has made it clear," noted one staffer, "that he will have men and women of excellence on his staff and in his Cabinet. He will keep that promise."[15]

Gender balance was considered one component to the Bush selection process, but not a priority component. The 1988 election had not focused on gender issues nor had there been a perceived gender gap. Women tended to view both Dukakis and Bush as responsive to gender problems, and thus split their vote equally. The transition team was comfortable allocating only one slot for gender balance. Most of the efforts of the new administration focused on sub-Cabinet rather than Cabinet appointments, which satisfied most women's groups. The Women's Political Caucus centered its energies on providing names for general counsels, deputy secretaries, and undersecretaries rather than Cabinet officers.

Only one woman was seriously considered for the Cabinet, Elizabeth Dole of Kansas. She provided managerial strength to the Cabinet, having served for four years as Reagan's Labor Secretary and provided gender balance. Dole brought the additional benefit of mending political fences within the Republican Party. Her husband, Senator Robert Dole of Kansas, had run against Bush in the 1988 Republican primaries. Dole had resigned her Labor post in 1987 to manage her husband's presidential aspirations. His current position as Senate Minority Leader would also be critical to moving the administration's legislative package forward.

Racial balance, as was gender balance, was considered important although not prioritized in the Cabinet selection process. Two Hispanic-Americans were brought into the Cabinet, Manuel Lujan and Lauro Cavazos. Cavazos was a Reagan holdover, but was popular in the Hispanic-American community. As the nation's first Hispanic in the Cabinet, he had built a politically significant following and actively sought to continue in his job. By choosing a second Hispanic for the Cabinet, Bush bolstered his standing among increasingly activist Hispanic-American voters. It was also a personal commitment based on his son's marriage to an Hispanic-American.

But as the Cabinet nominees were announced throughout November and early December, none were African-American. Although the transition team was sympathetic to calls for a more diverse Cabinet, they were reluctant to actively recruit a minority Cabinet member. Their reluctance largely reflected the nearly total repudiation of the Bush ticket by blacks: 92 per cent voted against the ticket.[16]

On December 9 Benjamin Hooks, executive director of the National Association for the Advancement of Colored People, met with Bush to express his concern and was assured that there would be an African-American in the Cabinet. On November 30 the head of the Chicago-based Rainbow Coalition, Rev. Jesse Jackson, met with Bush to pressure the administration for appointment of an African-American. Jackson, no stranger to party politics, had accused the Bush campaign of using racist overtones in its Willie Horton advertisements. (Horton had been a black prison inmate in Massachusetts who attacked a white woman while on prison furlough.) Bush responded to Jackson's attacks by referring to Jackson as the "hustler from Chicago."[17] Their meeting, however, was cordial and indicated a willingness by the Bush team to rebuild bridges with the black community. Although Jackson remained embittered, it was not lost to him that Bush had met more often with black leaders before his inauguration than Reagan had in eight years in office.

Two weeks later, on December 22, the transition team announced the selection of Dr. Louis Sullivan as Secretary of Health and Human Services. As the founder of the School of Medicine at Morehouse College in Atlanta, Sullivan had been an activist for improvements in minority health care. Although a slight wrinkle developed when Sullivan appeared to support abortion, he quickly refined his views to support those of Bush and the Republican platform. In addition to Sullivan, Thaddeus Garrett, Jr., a businessman and campaign advisor, and Alan Keys, who had served in the State Department and run unsuccessfully for the Senate from Maryland, were considered for Cabinet posts.

While there existed a concerted effort to ensure at least one Cabinet position for a woman and one for an Africa-American, the thrust of the effort went to broadening sub-Cabinet appointments for the two groups. Chase

Untermeyer, who ran the personnel selection operation for the transition team, assured both Hooks and Jackson that the Bush administration would have "more women and minorities than in the Reagan administration."[18]

   Building political bridges was a key determinate in Cabinet selection, second only to personal bonds. Four of the Cabinet nominees had served in Congress: Jack Kemp at Housing and Urban Development; Edward Derwinski at Veteran's Affairs; Manuel Lujan at Interior; and John Tower at Defense. When Tower's nomination was squashed by the Senate Judiciary Committee for reasons of both professional and personal misconduct, Bush chose Dick Cheney (R-Wyoming) for Defense.

   The only Cabinet position which ran into internal conflict was that of Energy Secretary and became the last position to be filled. James Baker was solidly behind Tom Loeffler, a former House member from Texas. Loeffler had managed the 1988 campaign in Texas for Bush/Quayle, had the support of Jim Baker, and was a longtime friend of Bush. Strong opposition mounted against more Texans in the administration. The U.S. Chamber of Commerce supported W. Henson Moore, a former House member from Louisiana. Senator James McClure (R-Idaho) urged the appointment of Peter Johnson, the former Bonneville Power Administration head. The nominee was finally a retired admiral with a strong background in nuclear power, James Watkins of California. Watkins met the criteria for strong managerial experience and had the background to manage a cleanup of nuclear weapons production facilities and the development a safe nuclear power program.[19]

   Only two members of the new cabinet were viewed as conservatives. All of the others held moderate or centrist views similar to those of the president-elect. Jack Kemp was an outspoken conservative who had questioned the conservative credentials of candidate Bush. Dick Thornburgh was less conservative than Kemp, although a clear friend of the right-wing of the Republican Party.

   The Cabinet that emerged in January 1989 was overwhelming white male, middle-aged (average age was 57), with moderate political views. Nearly all knew George Bush and many had long personal relationships with him. They were a Cabinet of managers, with broad experience in the ways of Washington, D.C. Parallels in composition were much stronger to the Carter Cabinet than the Reagan Cabinet. Nearly all were political moderates, reflecting the views of the new president.

WHITE HOUSE STAFF SELECTION

   While most White House staffs have been mirror images of the campaign, the Bush White House staff was not. In a protracted fight over who would land the key White House job, none of the senior Bush staff or key transition staff landed the prized position. The three senior members of the campaign did not move into top White House positions. Jim Baker, campaign manager, moved into the Cabinet. Craig Fuller, Baker's deputy and transition co-director, and Robert Teeter, key campaign advisor, both left the administration after losing the battle for chief of staff.

Conservative New Hampshire governor and national co-chairman of the Bush campaign, John Sununu became Bush's choice for chief of staff after a bitter fight with Craig Fuller for the post. One staffer politely referred to "considerable tension" and "jockeying" taking place for the position within the transition team.[20]   Sununu, 49, no stranger to politics, ended three two-year terms as governor on January 5, barely fifteen days before assuming his new duties in Washington. His ambition for national politics had been evident throughout recent years, including his own lobbying for the post of Energy Secretary in the Reagan administration.

The choice of Sununu for chief of staff was intended to bring the same strength of managerial experience to the White House that had been brought to the Cabinet. Craig Fuller, 37, had spent most of his career as Bush's chief of staff in the vice president's office. In contrast, Sununu, more than ten years his senior, had built a solid reputation in state and national politics. As one associate noted, "There was a difference in stature [between Fuller and Sununu]. In this particular environment, with Democrats gaining in Congress, we needed someone with stature. . . someone who can call up House Speaker Jim Wright and command attention."[21]

Sununu, who had a record as a hard negotiator, was credited with eliminating a $44 million deficit in New Hampshire and maintaining an unemployment rate consistently below the national average. As past chairman of the National Governors' Association, he had been an ardent defender of states' rights and government deregulation. He brought conservative political credentials to the job, which served to ameliorate conservative Republicans concerned about the number of moderates in the administration. Bush offered senior deputy positions to both Fuller and Teeter, with responsibility under Sununu, which both rejected.

The White House staff that emerged under John Sununu was one with numerous ties to Bush. Nearly all senior staff were directly tied to the campaign or the vice presidency, which was intended to mitigate Sununu's control of the White House.

Bush appointed General Brent Scowcroft as his National Security Advisor, a position he had held during the Ford administration. As Central Intelligence Director in the Ford administration, Bush had worked closely with Scowcroft. Personnel Director Chase Untermeyer, a Texan, had worked on both the campaign and on the vice presidential staff. Marlin Fitzwater, press secretary to President Reagan, had previously held the position for the vice president. Presidential Counsellor Boyden Gray had also held the same position for the vice president. Perhaps no one on the White House staff was closer to Bush than Gray, who was Bush's first presidential appointment the day after the election. Bush and Gray had deep personal ties, dating back to their childhoods when their fathers played golf together.

Other senior staff included Cabinet Secretary David Q. Bates, Jr., a Houston attorney, had been a longtime personal aide to Bush. Congressional Liaison Frederick McClure had been in both the Ford and Reagan administrations, and had been legislative director to Senator John Tower (R-Texas) before joining Texas Air Corp's Washington lobbying office. Roger Porter, the domestic policy advisor, had held the same position during the Reagan administration and also served in the Ford White House.

SUB-CABINET APPOINTMENTS

As were the Cabinet appointments, sub-Cabinet appointments were based primarily on competence and political connections. Political consistency rather than political ideology was the dominant theme. Rather than filling the thirty-seven hundred presidentially-appointed positions with ideologues, as Reagan had done, or technocrats, as Carter had done, Bush sought to reward longtime supporters. The result was an administration composed of administrators, many of whom lacked either an ideological compass or a depth of experience in their decision-making.[22]

The Bush administration reinstated the Jacksonian spoils system, rewarding friends and political allies for years of support. Texans flocked to Washington for political jobs. Bush was known to hire friends, the children of friends, and friends of his children. The White House was a gold mine used to reward loyalty.

Bush was also cognizant of rewarding those states that supported him during the 1988 election. New Hampshire received five times as many appointments as its population would allow under a strict apportionment system. Similarly, Wyoming, which had strongly supported the Bush/Quayle ticket, received a highly disproportionate number of appointments.

The appointments process was controlled to a limited extent by Chase Untermeyer, who had moved into the White House from the transition team as personnel director. The transition team gathered more than seventy thousand applications, including twenty-five hundred names that the conservative Heritage Foundation provided.[23] Untermeyer gathered the names and provided lists to the Cabinet officers for sub-Cabinet staff. Cabinet officers were not obligated to accept the names, and often provided their own names.

Untermeyer and the respective Cabinet officer together developed the final list. John Sununu reviewed senior appointments, with Bush providing the final nod.

Since most Cabinet officers wanted to control the appointments process for senior staff, most of the names generated by Untermeyer went to lower-level political appointments. Since neither political consistency nor technical expertise were viewed as key determinants in the appointments process, Untermeyer used ethics as part of the screening test for applicants. This conformed to Bush's frequent remarks that his administration would meet the highest ethical standards. All candidates for sub-Cabinet positions were originally asked by Untermeyer to fill out a form that included the question on voting. All applicants had to divulge whether or not they voted. Untermeyer noted that "It's a citizenship test, not a partisan test. Voting, after all, is the minimum qualification of good citizenship."[24] Eventually the question was deleted from the applications.

Although there was no concerted effort to develop an "administrative presidency" as both Richard Nixon and Ronald Reagan had attempted through sub-Cabinet appointments, George Bush knew the importance of these appointments in moving his agenda forward.[25] Less than a week after taking office, Bush met with thirty-seven hundred political appointees at Constitution Hall. He sought to assuage their egos and reinforce their importance to the administration. "You work hard, you sacrifice, and you deserve to be recognized, rewarded, and appreciated," he said.[26]

WHITE HOUSE ORGANIZATION

In essence, Bush had learned from his years in the Ford administration that the White House staff had to have a singular loyalty to the president. The divisiveness among the Ford White House staff had ultimately led to its downfall. With the addition of John Sununu, Bush endeavored to minimize any such divisiveness among the White House staff by making all senior appointments himself. Only Bonnie Newman, brought in by Sununu to run the White House administration office, had not worked previously with Bush.

Key senior staff were:

John Sununu	Chief of Staff
Brent Scowcroft	National Security Advisor
Chase Untermeyer	Personnel Director
Boyden Gray	Counsel to the President
David Q. Bates, Jr.	Cabinet Secretary

(Continued on next page)

Frederick McClure	Congressional Liaison
Bonnie Newman	Administration and Management
David Demarest	Communications Director
Roger Porter	Domestic Policy Advisor

Bush went one step further to control Sununu by naming his deputies. Andrew Card, named deputy chief of staff, was a senior campaign staffer to Bush and former Massachusetts legislator. James Cicconi, a lawyer with the Washington office of Akin, Gump, Strauss, Hauer, and Feld (a Dallas law firm) and former assistant to James Baker, was named staff secretary.

The structure of the senior White House staff was given little attention by the transition team, partly due to the pressure to name Cabinet secretaries and focus the agenda, but partly due to Craig Fuller's lack of interest in the White House staff after Sununu's appointment on November 18.

The only clear structure was that Sununu, as chief of staff, would be the first among equals. In announcing his appointment, Bush said "He's the right man for the job and I'm very pleased that he will lead the Bush team in the White House."[27] There would be no spokes of the wheel system, with access by all senior staff, as Jimmy Carter had done. Only Scowcroft, Sununu, and Gray were accorded direct access to Bush. Nor would there be a shared power relationship with other senior staff. Sununu would control the paperwork and the appointments of the president. Although the structure appeared to be somewhat authoritarian, Sununu struggled to ensure that the flow of paperwork to the president represented clear-cut options. As one former White House staffer noted, Sununu "wanted people's opinions and recommendations for dealing with problems and issues."[28]

Lack of organizational structure and clearly defined roles, other than job descriptions taken from the Reagan White House, was tempered by the collegiality that dominated the White House. As did most of the Cabinet officers, the White House staff were familiar with each other, shared a common mission, and were comfortable in the White House environment. Sununu was one of the few members of the senior White House staff never to have worked either in the president or vice president's office. One staff member said that "there are so many cross-relationships. Most of these people are good friends of mine who I've know for years. I'm not aware of any of them who don't get along."[29]

White House Organizational Structure

The task of developing the organizational structure fell to Sununu. Several organizational structures were developed, with Sununu, Deputy Chief of Staff Andrew Card, Budget Director Richard Darman, and McClure the primary determinants in the process. Since it was generally assumed that most of the job descriptions would remain the same, the key issues involved managing the domestic agenda and legislative maneuvers.

McClure quickly gained control of the legislative structure, ending the more broadly controlled legislative strategy group in the Reagan White House. In contrast, the domestic policy structure tended to fall more in line with the Reagan model. Domestic policy would be shared by Sununu, Bates, Richard Breeden (Assistant to the President for Issues Analysis), Cicconi, Darman, Gray, Porter, and others as necessary. Gray had been particularly eager to move out of the traditional role of counsel to the president and provide input into domestic issues such as regulatory policy, justice issues, and drug policy.[30] This followed the model created during the first Reagan administration in which the Baker-Deaver-Meese triumvirate handled domestic programs.

The focus by Sununu on domestic policy was not unexpected. In the press conference held by Bush to announce the Sununu appointment in November, Sununu outlined his role as chief of staff. Key to his role would be the opportunity "to give his opinion" to the president on domestic policy, on "budget items," and "some of the initiatives we might want to take."[31]

The picture that emerged of the White House staff was one of relative youth. As one observer noted, "Bush's senior aides . . . are probably more used to being second-level people" than decision-makers.[32] Nearly all were in their thirties. Sununu was the oldest of the White House with the exception of 63 year old Allan Bromley, the president's science advisor. Andrew Card and Roger Porter at 42 followed Sununu in age among the senior staff. In contrast, the Cabinet generally were in their fifties and sixties. Both Cabinet and White House staff were drawn from among a wide group of Bush loyalists, most of whom had deep bonds with the new president.

STRUCTURING THE CABINET–WHITE HOUSE RELATIONSHIP

The structure of the Cabinet–White House relationship was generally ignored by the transition team and by the president-elect. Meeting with reporters one week before the inauguration, it was clear that the Cabinet's role in decision-making had not been framed. Asked what he planned to tell his Cabinet at their first meeting, Bush said:

We'll outline my priorities. We'll just spell it all out on how I want them to work with Congress, how we'll work with each other, how I'd like to emphasize the very seriousness of the conflict of interest, ethical stand I talked about during campaign. I'll talk to these teammates of mine.[33]

Three days after the interview, Bush assembled his Cabinet to discuss their role in the new administration. Hours after filling the final Cabinet post for Energy on January 12, the Cabinet officers met for the first time as a group. The essence of the meeting was for Bush to give them their "marching orders," a phrase he coined. The list of marching orders was:

* Think big
* Challenge the system
* Adhere to the highest ethical standards
* Be on the record as much as possible
* Be frank
* Fight hard for your position
* When I make the call, we move as a team
* Work with Congress
* Represent the United States with dignity[34]

The marching orders gave no indication of policy orientation or of the Cabinet–White House relationship. The list only vaguely noted that they were to "think big," implying that policy development would focus in the Cabinet. There was no indication of priorities in policy direction.

The relationship of the Cabinet and the White House staff in policy development was not clearly discussed during either the informal Cabinet meeting or the first formal meeting held on January 24, 1989. The Cabinet officers were neither given control of the policy process nor told how policy interaction with the White House would be framed.

The Office of Policy Development

Domestic policy development became a reactive process in the Bush White House, a far cry from the highly structured and proactive process created by Martin Anderson in the Reagan White House.

As the Assistant to the President for Economic and Domestic Policy, Roger Porter was on record as the president's point person for domestic issues. Porter's role as the president's key domestic advisor was created in an ad hoc fashion, with little analysis during the transition. Neither the domestic agenda nor the operating structure within the White House was discussed with Porter prior to his taking the job. The transition team had ignored the internal structures of the White House in their deliberations. The absence of a clear role for the domestic policy office, officially named the Office of Policy Development (OPD), left Porter a free rein to gain control of the policy process.

But Porter failed to do so. Porter quickly became a manager whose primary responsibility was to coordinate the daily affairs of the OPD and its staff. He viewed himself as the "honest broker" rather than the policy formulator "who has the responsibility for looking at the problem from the vantage point of the president and making sure that the options developed are optimal from the standpoint of the president."[35] Porter's view of his job as an "honest broker" was similar to that of White House National Security Advisor Brent Scowcroft, who described his White House role as one "to make sure that the president has the benefit of all the options and is in the best possible position to make a decision."[36]

Porter viewed his own role as a facilitator rather than a creator. His expertise was in managing the players who sought to influence the policy process rather than in creating the policy.[37] In large part Porter supported the model of multiple adhocracy, which he used in his 1980 book entitled *Presidential Decision-Making*.[38] The model calls for departmental staff working in concert with White House staff in a collegial process to determine policy. The concept of multiple adhocracy supports a wide range of participants in the policy process. Porter, unlike Martin Anderson, was not an advocate of White House control of the policy process.

Porter essentially became the analyst who provided other White House staff studies on policy issues. Sununu, Card, Gray, and others became the catalysts for change. Porter provided their support staff, noting, "Nobody elected me to make policy. I'm here to provide my best advice."[39] Andrew Card added that Porter was a "good sponge and think piece; when squeezed he wrote memos."[40]

Porter's failure to break into the senior strata of the White House policy team was mirrored by his failure to gain control of his own office.[41] He became preoccupied with micromanaging the OPD staff and failed to give adequate responsibility for management to his deputies William Roper or Charles Kolb. Roper, a close friend of Porter's, was unable to move Porter out of micromanagement within the OPD.[42]

Although Porter viewed his role as an "honest broker," he began to increase the size of the OPD to meet the numerous requests from White House staff for information. At the outset of the administration in January 1989, Porter had a staff of 20 positions. Three months later in March, the staff had grown to 21 positions. By November the staff had grown to 24, by January 1991 to 26, and by October 1992 to 41 positions.

The original staff of twenty focused their attention around seven major areas:

1. Domestic economic policy
2. International economic policy
3. Environment

4. Energy
5. National resources
6. Health and human services
7. Administration.

By March, not only had the staff been increased but new areas of focus were added:

8. Education
9. Housing and urban development
10. Transportation
11. Legal policy

By 1992, as the election moved closer, not only was staff again increased but more areas of responsibility were added:

12. Agriculture
13. Policy coordinating group
14. Policy planning group[43]

The proliferation of staff and responsibility reflected the growing control that John Sununu and budget director Richard Darman (Office of Management and Budget) had over departmental policy initiatives. Rather than framing initiatives within the White House, Sununu and Darman used the OPD to review departmental proposals and ensure that they either cut programs or require no new funding. The OPD staff were policy reviewers, not policy setters. But the effect was to give the White House greater control over the policy process since Porter reviewed all major departmental programs. Although Sununu and Darman, rather than Porter, were the major players, the White House continued to be the clearinghouse for departmental policy.

The Cabinet Council Structure

As Bush had learned from the Reagan experience with policy development, close contact between the Cabinet and the White House staff worked to ensure that departmental policy-making was in line with administration goals and objectives. As a tool to nurture the Cabinet–White House relationship, the Domestic Policy Council (DPC) and the Economic Policy Council (EPC) were created on February 8, 1989. Their mandate was to serve "as the primary channels for advising [the president] on the formulation, coordination, and implementation of domestic and social policy."[44] The statement by Bush noted that the Domestic Policy Council "would produce effective decision-making and make available the best information from the [president's] senior advisors of various departments and agencies."[45] The creation of the the two policy councils was intended to revitalize the cabinet in the policy-making process.

The councils were a tool to build the collegial presidency. Bush frequently attended cabinet council meetings and participated in their discussions to bolster their sense of participation in the presidential team.[46] But unlike the Reagan council meetings which produced policy decisions, the primary benefit of the Bush cabinet council meetings was to allow Bush interaction with his Cabinet officers. Most policy matters were handled in one-on-one sessions between either Bush and the department head or Sununu and the department head.

The Domestic Policy Council

The Domestic Policy Council was formally referred to as a "cabinet council," as had the Reagan Domestic Policy Council. As in the Reagan administration, the Bush cabinet councils met in the Roosevelt Room of the White House and invited the president to all its meetings. In addition to the Cabinet officers, the director of the Office of Management and Budget, the vice president, and the White House chief of staff were members ex officio. However, unlike the Reagan administration, which viewed the cabinet councils as mandatory attendance for Cabinet officers, undersecretaries or deputy secretaries frequently represented their departments.

During its first year the Domestic Policy Council rapidly became the arbiter of policy conflicts rather than the focus of policy initiatives. Policy issues that were addressed by the Domestic Policy Council tended to focus on interjurisdictional policy issues that individual Cabinet officers had been unable to resolve. Richard Thornburgh, who chaired the DPC, noted that "the meetings usually consisted of Cabinet Secretaries debating and arguing over whose policy perspective would be better for the administration and for the respective department."[47]

The failure to use an executive order, as previous presidents had, to create the Economic Policy Council and the Domestic Policy Council, was a key indicator of the lack of influence that the cabinet councils would actually have in the policy process. The cabinet councils were created without fanfare in a simple statement released to the press noting that the Bush administration was continuing the Reagan cabinet councils.

Another indicator of the lack of importance of the Domestic Policy Council to the policy-making process was its limited membership. Of the fourteen Cabinet officers, only six were members: the Secretaries of Interior; Health and Human Services; Housing and Urban Development; Energy; Education; and Veterans Affairs.

Thornburgh's role was not to create policy but to manage interdepartmental conflict in policy areas. As he noted, "the principal task of [the DPC] was to deal in areas where more than one Cabinet officer was involved."[48] On issues that arose requiring coordination or conflict resolution, Thornburgh appointed an interagency task force called a "working group" to meet. These groups generally met in the Roosevelt Room of the White House, because "it was the most functional room for dealing with Cabinet affairs."[49] The final product was a policy option paper, referred to as a "decision memorandum," that went to the president.[50]

An average of fifteen different working groups dealt with policy issues at any time. The working groups were created to deal with specific problems, as the cabinet clusters had been during the Carter administration. Thornburgh designed the Cabinet membership of each working group to fit the issue, in the same fashion that the cabinet clusters had operated. This contrasted to the Reagan model, which had a fixed membership focused around broad issues.

Decision–Making in the White House

As part of his commitment to a more hands-on presidency, George Bush wanted briefings from his staff on key issues that faced the administration. Most of the briefings on issues that involved domestic policy recommendations from the Cabinet took the form of a decision memorandum. Once Bush had read the decision memorandum, Sununu, Porter, and various other White House staff discussed the options with him.

The recommendations presented in the decision memorandum included the various Cabinet-supported options and an analysis of those options by Porter's staff. Rarely did Porter present an additional option; he presented the pro's and con's of each Cabinet proposal. All Cabinet officers who had worked on the options in the decision memorandum were sent a copy for review before it went to the president. If they felt their position was not adequately reflected, the decision memorandum was rewritten. Bush chose between the various options and returned the material to Thornburgh directly, Porter, or to the Cabinet Affairs Office in the White House.

The Office of Policy Development under Porter did not attempt to sway the president in his policy-decision making. Porter wanted Bush to hear all the options (in his role as "honest broker"), and to formulate the final decision. Unlike the Carter and Reagan administrations, which used the White House staff to review Cabinet recommendations and provide political and programmatic comment for the president, the Office of Policy Development sought to provide objective information on the fiscal and often legislative constraints of a policy proposal.

Once Bush had made a decision on a policy issue, either through the decision memorandum or through direct consultation with Cabinet officers, Porter and his staff became lobbyists for the president. Porter spent a considerable portion of his day meeting with constituent groups, members of Congress, and others to sway them to the president's position.[51]

As a result of the process that Porter developed for policy analysis, the decision memoranda sent to Bush often lacked political input. The political options were generally brought to Bush's attention in private meetings in the oval office, without either the Cabinet officers or Porter attending, by Lee Atwater, former campaign manager and chairman of the Republican National Party, and John Sununu. When Atwater became ill from a brain tumor fifteen months into the administration, Sununu became the primary source for information on the political constraints. Sununu sought to broaden the political expertise of his own staff by naming David Carney, White House political director, deputy chief of staff. Carney had been Sununu's chief political advisor in New Hampshire. Richard Darman also provided political input to Bush, but focused his discussions around the fiscal constraints of policies and the election pledge to cut the deficit.

Surprisingly, for an administration with a significant number of political appointments, decision-making in the White House tended to place political considerations low on its priority list. Sununu and Darman provided the primary oversight for political consistency. The process set in motion during the early months of the administration for domestic policy-making was one that lacked a course or a direction. The Cabinet-based Domestic Policy Council saw their mission as one of conflict resolution for existing programs rather than as the innovator for new programs. The White House–based Office of Policy Development viewed their role as the "honest broker" for presidential decision-making. A great deal of Roger Porter's time and that of his staff was spent analyzing existing bills in Congress, such as the Clear Air Act and the Environmental Summit treaty, and providing well-researched options for Bush. Neither the Domestic Policy Council nor the Office of Policy Development viewed their role as the focus of policy development for the administration.

AGENDA SETTING BY THE CABINET

When George Bush was inaugurated on January 20, 1989, he promised not only a kinder, gentler nation but a kinder, gentler tone of government. He gave few specifics on what he meant nor did he provide substantially more depth on the agenda for the new administration. When he accepted the

Republican nomination for president, he declared that he longed for "missions defined and missions completed." What those missions were remained an enigma. His policies were shaped less by an agenda, or a White House staff, but by a slow change in direction by departmental personnel moving away from the conservative positions of the Reagan years to the more moderate positions of the Bush appointees. For example, the Energy Department was moving toward a national energy policy that included solar energy, the Environmental Protection Agency was reexamining conservation efforts, and the Justice Department's Civil Rights Division received broad praise from the executive director of the Leadership Conference on Civil Rights. Even the Department of Housing and Urban Development, under the direction of one the administration's most conservative members, was developing initiatives for low-income housing.

The departments, not the White House, were shaping the agenda. But the agenda clearly met the goals of the president: a moderate, incremental change in the role of government. The Cabinet, with their own moderate leanings and breadth of Washington experience, was moving government slowly in new directions.

With the departments dominating the policy-setting process, clashes in direction between the White House and the agencies were inevitable. Although Cabinet officers understood the mandate of the Bush administration—continue to cut the deficit and reduce the role of government—several sharp differences in policy direction emerged. Not surprisingly, all the clashes were between the White House and those Cabinet officers with the least personal relationship with Bush.

In every case, the clash focused on a departmental request to secure more funding for programs or to prevent cuts from existing departmental programs. Cabinet officers had moved out of the presidential orbit into the departmental orbit. The failure of the White House to maintain Cabinet officers within the presidential orbit is due primarily to Roger Porter, who failed to develop an organizational structure that kept the Cabinet fully attuned to presidential objectives. Maintaining Richard Thornburgh as chairman of the Domestic Policy Council may have ensured some procedural consistency, but it failed to ensure that Cabinet officers were repeatedly subject to the central theme of the administration: no new taxes. Thornburgh, a Reagan Cabinet holdover, lacked any commitment or understanding of the Bush agenda.

None of the clashes were as deep as those in the Carter or Nixon administrations, although they forced a rift in the collegial decision-making structure between the Cabinet and the White House. When Sununu or Darman were opposed to their initiatives, cabinet officers often sought other avenues of meeting departmental objectives.

CLASHES BETWEEN THE CABINET AND THE WHITE HOUSE

During the first year of the administration, several members of the Cabinet actively pursued policies that lacked White House support. Because these were policies which were not interjurisdictional in nature, they had not been subjected to White House staff review through the Domestic Policy Council. Additionally, since the White House had not established a process that essentially round-tabled every major departmental proposal, many departmental initiatives received little or no White House oversight.

White House clearance for many departmental programs occurred after the proposal had been publicly announced. Either John Sununu or Richard Darman met with the Cabinet officer to discuss why the proposal was not acceptable to the White House. In most cases, the issue focused on funding: the White House would not support new programmatic funding. Sununu and Darman reviewed departmental proposals to ensure that their budgets conformed to OMB objectives. Budgets were the controlling factor in domestic policy-making. If Sununu and Darman felt departmental proposals were out of line with overall administration goals, they moved against the department initiative.

During the first two weeks of the administration, Sununu, Darman, and Treasury Secretary Nicholas Brady clashed over the Treasury Department's proposal to levy a $0.25 fee on each $100 deposited in a savings account in a commercial bank or thrift association.[52] Brady argued that this was the most viable alternative for ensuring the solvency of the Federal Savings and Loan Insurance Corporation (FSLIC). Rocked by numerous bank failures during the Reagan era, the FSLIC was on the verge of collapse. Sununu and Darman saw the proposal as a new tax rather than a fee, as Brady insisted. Eventually, the Big Two, as Sununu and Darman were often referred to, forced Brady to seek other solutions to the FSLIC problem.

The following month Energy Secretary James Watkins sought increased funding for environmental clean-up programs. Again Sununu and Darman rejected the program. Watkins came back with proposals for new funding for burning coal. Sununu retorted that the administration was not pursuing programs on renewable energy in the 1990 budget. Watkins and Sununu continued to clash on funding issues, particularly as they related to Watkins' alignment with Environmental Protection Agency Director William Reilly. Both Watkins and Reilly supported a Treasury fund to pay for energy conservation projects.

In March 1989 Agriculture Secretary Clayton Yeutter entered into a public debate with Darman over the OMB proposal to cut agricultural subsidies. Yeutter argued that the farm bill would be reauthorized in 1990, and that any changes in the subsidies should be incorporated into a general revamping of the legislation. Darman disagreed and successfully won funding cuts.

In July 1989 Veterans Affairs Secretary Edward Derwinski sought additional Congressional funding for capital improvements at veterans' facilities. Derwinski had frequently promised his support for funding, including his confirmation hearing. However, Sununu and Darman opposed any new funding. Derwinski appealed directly to Bush, a World War II combat veteran, who supported the funding increases. In a carefully maneuvered lobbying effort, Derwinski secured $3.3 billion in additional funding for the 1990 budget.

The pattern continued into the fall when Secretary of Education Lauro Cavazos supported funding for magnet schools. Sununu not only argued against more funding, but noted to Cavazos that the priority of the administration was for school choice, not a burgeoning of the existing system.

In April 1990, Sununu and Darman had pushed their budget-cutting programs beyond the tolerance of the Democratically controlled Congress. Many of the departmental initiatives which were cut by OMB were supported in Congress. As a means to curb departmental budget cuts, the House Governmental Operations Committee, chaired by John Conyers (D-Michigan), threatened not to reauthorize the 1980 Paperwork Act, which gave OMB regulatory review authority. Sununu and Conyers reached an agreement that moderated OMB power.

Yet Congress continued to be frustrated with White House actions. In a rare move, 81 House Republicans sent a letter to Bush urging that he "declare war on our domestic ills." They urged Bush to use Jack Kemp to a greater extent in that effort.[53] This was unquestionably a political move to reinsert the conservative agenda, but it was also an attempt by Kemp to rein in Sununu and Darman. If Kemp could not succeed through the White House, he wanted Bush to know that he continued to have influence in Congress to support departmental objectives.

FOREIGN AFFAIRS DOMINATES POLICY–MAKING

As the White House was sorting out the Cabinet–White House relationship in domestic policy, a series of international events began to dominate the attention of the administration. In December 1989 the United States sent troops to invade Panama and remove General Manuel Noriega from power. Noriega surrendered on January 3, 1990. Eights months later Iraq invaded Kuwait, setting the stage for an international crisis. After repeated demands from the Bush administration for Iraq to withdraw from Kuwait, half a million American troops were sent to Saudi Arabia and surrounding areas to "liberate Kuwait." From January 17 to February 18, 1991, American troops, in concert with troops from the United Nations, pushed the Iraqi invaders back to their borders. Once the battles were over, American troops continued to monitor the Iraqis and protect the Kurdish population from reprisal.[54]

Thus for nearly two years, the Bush White House was preoccupied with foreign affairs. The president's approval-rating sky-rocketed to nearly 90 per cent as the American public showed overwhelming support for the Panamanian and Iraqi policies developed by the White House.

During the same period, the administration was actively involved in negotiations with the newly dissolved Soviet Union. Russia was seeking membership in the Group of Seven (G-7) economic summit and pursuing liberal loans from the international banking community. A host of former Soviet bloc countries were involved in similar financial support requests. One of the former Soviet bloc countries, Georgia, was involved in civil war. The Ukraine was trying to negotiate a deal to sell the United States nuclear warheads. By the end of the administration, famine was overtaking Somalia and war had broken out in the former Yugoslavia.

DOMESTIC POLICY RETURNS TO THE FOREFRONT OF PUBLIC ATTENTION

In spite of a record public approval rating for the administration in early 1991 after the successful Kuwait operation, the Democrats were drawing attention to the absence of a substantive domestic policy. If George Bush were going to be reelected in 1992, a clear domestic agenda had to be framed and at least partly implemented. The foreign policy events of 1990 and 1991 had dominated White House attention and eclipsed any domestic programs.

Only two major pieces of legislation were moved forward after the Panama invasion in 1990: the Clean Air Act and the Civil Rights Act, both in late 1991. Both bills, however, were reauthorizations of existing legislation and were not White House–based programs. The Clean Air Act, signed into law on November 15, consumed the attention of Roger Porter, who analyzed every line of the bill. The Civil Rights Act, signed into law November 21, consumed Sununu. Bush and the foreign policy team were focused on managing the fallout from the Iraqi invasion. Little else moved throughout the administration. Even the economic policy team failed to produce measurable change. They were castigated for continuing to focus on the message rather than "fixing the problem."[55]

By the end of 1991, the glow of the Iraq victory had faded. The public's attention was being increasingly drawn to the absence of substantive domestic initiatives on the part of the White House. The administration had failed to deliver either major education or environmental proposals, as the campaign had promised. One leading commentator noted that:

> Richard Nixon once told Theodore White that the "country could run itself domestically without a President." Bush seems to be governing on that model. If the Administration stays its present course, which is no course at all, it will not be because the Machiavellian Darman has seized power, but because the President prefers to let polls and powerbrokers generate policy at home, while he visits troops in distant climes.[56]

The media continued to lambast the administration. As *Business Week* headlined in 1990, "Bush Needs A Domestic Agenda."[57] The sentiment continued even after the foreign policy triumphs.

SUNUNU RESIGNS

In order to revitalize the domestic policy process, Bush changed his senior White House staff rather than Cabinet officers. Unlike the Carter administration, which changed Cabinet officers to refocus domestic problems, Bush changed the White House staff. This was consistent with the framework of the administration since its inception: the Cabinet commanded the president's trust. When the administration came under fire, the White House staff was the first to meet the guns.

Skinner as Chief of Staff

In December 1991, less one year before the 1992 election, Bush replaced John Sununu as chief of staff with Transportation Secretary Samuel Skinner. Skinner had deftly handled the Exxon Valdez oil spill in Alaska, the San Francisco earthquake, and crafted a national transportation strategy. Although not a member of Bush's inner circle when he joined the administration, he was perceived as both a loyalist and a skillful manager.

Skinner quickly moved to revamp White House decision-making for domestic policy, noting that Bush "clearly was not satisfied with the handling of the domestic agenda and is determined to have that rectified."[58] He brought in Henson Moore as deputy chief of staff and replaced a score of senior staff. Perhaps most significantly, he brought Clayton Yeutter (who had left Agriculture to chair the Republican National Committee) into the White House as the president's chief domestic advisor with the title "Counselor to the President for Domestic Policy."

Yeutter, appointed in early February, was charged with coordinating both economic and domestic policy and revamping the White House policy process. Roger Porter, who remained in the White House, lost power and became a subordinate of Yeutter's. Yeutter not only took over Porter's job, but his office. Porter moved out of his panelled west wing corner office and into a smaller one down the hall.

Yeutter and the Policy Coordinating Group

Yeutter, who accepted the job only under the condition that he gain control of Porter's office and the Domestic and Economic Policy Councils, redesigned the policy process as soon as he started work. He abolished both cabinet councils and established the Policy Coordinating Group (PCG) as the replacement. Attorney General William Barr, who had replaced Richard Thornburgh as chairman of the Domestic Policy Council, had no objections to the change. Treasury Secretary Nicholas Brady, who headed the Economic Policy Council, was reluctant to support the change but was convinced by Skinner to do so.

In a dramatic change of policy from the Sununu years, Skinner began daily meetings with Yeutter and Moore to discuss domestic policy initiatives. Every morning at 7:00 A.M. the three met to review departmental initiatives and to develop new White House proposals. Skinner next resurrected the legislative strategy group of the Reagan era, to focus on legislative programs. The legislative strategy group, which included Yeutter, met daily at 5:00 P.M.

The PCG was designed to bring economic and domestic policy under one umbrella, a design that Roger Porter had successfully fought against at the onset of the administration. The Cabinet officers, who comprised the membership of the PCG, were broken into working groups, as they had been under both the Domestic and the Economic Policy Council. The White House called together the working groups, which varied in membership, as issues dictated. Sub-Cabinet staff, known as the deputies committee, managed the majority of the work.[59]

Working groups were fluid, with Yeutter deciding "the chairmanship, membership, and mandate" of each working group.[60] The working groups were charged with developing policy options for new domestic policy initiatives. Since Yeutter determined the agenda for the working groups, he was now providing clear direction on issues to be addressed. For the first time in the administration, the White House was taking control of the domestic policy agenda and the creation of new programs.

Skinner Fails to Revitalize the Domestic Policy Process

Skinner's efforts to revitalize the domestic policy process from, as the *Washington Post* referred to it, its "moribund" status, proved unsuccessful.[61]

Nearly nine months to the day after his appointment as chief of staff, Skinner was removed. On August 13, 1992, as the Republican convention was ending, the announcement came that major changes were being made in the White House staff. Longtime Bush confidant James Baker was moved from the helm of the State Department to the helm of the White House. Skinner, as Sununu before him, was elevated to Counselor to the President.

The interregnum of Sam Skinner had failed to produce an organizational structure to develop and refine policy initiatives. His operating style had antagonized senior staff. Senior staff, who were never quite sure whether their jobs were secure, were cut from staff meetings almost immediately. The twenty-five senior staffers who regularly met with Sununu were cut from the daily staff meetings in favor of a smaller group of ten, mostly Skinner appointees. When Skinner indicated that he wanted to remove many top White House staff, Bush personally intervened to protect staff.

Skinner's problems with staff were compounded with the appointment of Clayton Yeutter to manage domestic policy. Yeutter's appointment was seen by senior staff as an effort to put another management layer between them and the president, and an attempt by Skinner to reduce their influence.

The failure of Skinner to establish a workable domestic policy process in the White House and to mitigate staff unrest was compounded by his failure to provide Bush appropriate political advice. One of the primary roles of the White House staff has been to quickly respond to crisis events, a response that has become known as "firefighting" in the White House. One of Skinner's earliest mishaps was his inability to manage the Los Angeles riots after the Rodney King verdict in May 1992. In the hours after the riots began in Los Angeles, Skinner's staff provided no clear direction to the president. The debate emerged between OMB Director Richard Darman, who argued that Bush should take a hard law-and-order stand, and HUD Secretary Jack Kemp who argued for a personal appeal for less violence in Los Angeles.

Skinner eventually took the position with Darman that "this was a time above all when you have people being killed and a city burning, and you have to talk about the absolute inadmissibility of that."[62] Skinner's credibility as either manager or as Bush stalwart was further damaged when two key White House staff opposed Skinner's position on the riots. Marlin Fitzwater, the White House press secretary, argued that the President should ensure that his speeches and his actions focus on compassion and "a recognition that things had gone wrong" in Los Angeles.[63] One of the White House speechwriters, Anthony Snow, went even further by arguing for Bush to seize the moment and issue a major speech on racial problems in the United States. David Demarest, Assistant to the President for Communications, also argued for a major speech that would heal rather than castigate.

The inability of either Skinner or Yeutter to take control of the riots and the national crisis in confidence that resulted from the riots was the beginning of the end for Skinner. As Democratic candidate Bill Clinton continued to hammer the Bush administration for its failure to improve the economy and establish a domestic agenda, Skinner was unable to prop up the sagging popularity of the president. In August 1992, after having to rebuff a primary challenge from within his own party, Bush again changed the White House staff leadership.

When James Baker took over as chief of staff on August 24, 1992, Skinner moved to the position of Counselor to the President. Soon after Baker's arrival, however, both Skinner and Yeutter resigned. The White House staff's dislike for Skinner was evident in a joke passed around the White House. Skinner's resignation was accompanied by a statement that he was returning to Chicago, where he had previously served as U.S. Attorney, to assume the $500,000 a year presidency of Commonwealth Edison. Staffers began circulating memos with mock urgency advising anyone who owned Commonwealth Edison stock to "sell short, for God's sake, sell short!".[64]

The Baker era began a return to a fast-paced, invigorated White House with clear goals and objectives. Baker established a crisis management team, prepared to move into operation as any major national event or controversy arose. His message for the president became more focused: the Bush administration did not need to make apologies for concentrating on the "historic opportunities" in international affairs during the past four years, but that the time was now right to concentrate on domestic issues.[65] Baker continued the Reagan/Bush themes of low taxes, less regulation, and less government.

Baker's success at managing the White House was short-lived. Two and a half months later George Bush was defeated at the polls and the Bush presidency came to an end. Whether Baker could have made a difference to the domestic policy process in the long run is problematical. Although White House staff were eager to rid themselves of Skinner, Baker may not have brought continuity to either the process or the staff. Most White House staff were shut out from the decision-making process, as a small cadre of Baker loyalists from the State Department moved to control the information and policy process. Whether Baker would have been successful at redesigning the domestic policy process is not at all clear. Baker's task in the long run would have been to frame policies that met the test of fiscal restraint with restoring the view that Republicans were compassionate and thoughtful stewards of the public trust.[66] Neither Sununu nor Skinner had been successful in that endeavor.

CONCLUSION

George Bush entered office in 1989 with a promise to reduce federal spending, cut the deficit, and build a "kinder, gentler nation." His campaign had not only promised to cut spending, but to move toward significant changes in education, the environment, crime, and drug policy. The failure of the Bush administration was ultimately its failure to reconcile these two contrasting goals: on the one hand, cut spending; on the other hand, increase spending.

The Cabinet–White House relationship that Bush set in motion to manage domestic policy was as confused by these contradictory goals as the electorate proved to be. The Cabinet felt their role was to move the agenda forward; the White House staff, particularly Sununu and Darman, felt their role was to protect the campaign promise of "no new taxes."

These contradictory goals were not impossible to manage had an adequate White House management process been in place.[67] The White House needed to establish a structure that guided Cabinet development of domestic policies and satisfied the campaign agenda without significant increases in funding. The cabinet council structure set in motion was charged primarily with managing interjurisdictional conflict. Not until Samuel Skinner took over as chief of staff was a management process established that encouraged departmental initiatives within the fiscal constraints outlined by the OMB.

George Bush entered office promising to have a strong Cabinet and a trimmed down White House staff. He succeeded in his goal, but it was a goal that proved fatal to his administration. The White House staff, particularly the domestic and economic policy office, was never given the authority to adequately manage domestic policy. John Sununu, although a powerful chief of staff, failed to understand the importance of nurturing the Cabinet and ensuring their understanding of the president's agenda.

The lesson learned from the Bush experience is that without strong direction from the White House, the Cabinet will eventually become coopted and oriented toward departmental rather than presidential objectives. Certainly the Bush Cabinet was as loyal to the president as is possible, yet they still moved in their own direction. This was not due to lack of loyalty, but rather a lack of consistent signals from the White House on priorities.

Presidents need a strong White House staff to manage the executive branch. George Bush, John Sununu, and Roger Porter failed to understand the importance of White House control of the domestic policy process. Whether Samuel Skinner had changed the course of decision-making enough to build a consistent domestic policy agenda is a moot point. Bill Clinton won the 1992 election.

EIGHT

THE CLINTON YEARS

After twelve years of continuous Republican control of the White House, the Democrats triumphantly returned to power in the election of 1992. Arkansas Governor Bill Clinton captured the presidency from George Bush and ushered in a new generation of leaders committed to economic security. With the cold war over and the arms race won, the nation turned out its foreign policy president and elected a domestic policy president. George Bush's commanding 90 per cent popular support after the Persian Gulf War could not salvage his image as someone insensitive to mounting domestic problems.

The election of 1992 focused around the 46-year-old William Jefferson Clinton, born after World War II, who sought to recapture the excitement of Camelot and his hero, John F. Kennedy.[1] As Kennedy himself noted after taking the mantle of leadership from Dwight D. Eisenhower, "the torch has passed to a new generation of Americans."[2] This generation would focus on peace, not war. If elected, Clinton promised to revitalize the economy and rebuild America's domestic strength.

The Clinton theme was the simple "We can do better," urging a return to policies centering on middle-class America. Clinton continuously targeted the economy, hammering at the Bush administration's failure to stimulate growth and increase jobs. Clinton referred to himself as a "New Democrat," committed to economic prosperity for the nation and a renewed emphasis on education, the environment, and health care.

The American public overwhelmingly rejected a continuation of Republican leadership and dealt George Bush a commanding defeat, handing him only 38 per cent of the vote. Although the election was somewhat skewed by Ross Perot, who ran as a third party candidate and won 19 per cent of the popular vote, Clinton's electoral vote was a commanding 357 to 168 for Bush and 0 for Perot. The nation had clearly chosen to move away from the conservatism of the Reagan/Bush years toward the more centrist positions of the Clinton New Democrats.

The nation had also rejected George Bush personally and what was perceived as his lack of principle. During the 1980 campaign for president, Bush charged Ronald Reagan with supporting voodoo economics, yet easily moved into the vice presidency when Reagan offered the position to him. Eight years later during the presidential campaign he promised to veto any tax increases with the pledge "read my lips." A year later, he capitulated on his principles and approved such increases. Abortion was a similar issue. Although he had supported Planned Parenthood in Texas, once he moved into the national spotlight, he opposed abortion. Bush appeared to abandon his principles when they became politically inconvenient.

Although George Bush was turned out of office for his lack of leadership, the election of Bill Clinton was not a mandate to return to the liberal policies of past Democratic administrations. Rather it was a mandate to refocus government to solve domestic problems in ways that did not broaden government programs or increase the federal bureaucracy. The mandate of the Clinton administration was to use the federal government as an agent for change without new taxes, new programs, or new bureaucracies. The conservatism of the 1980s was moderated in the 1990s, but not abandoned. The task for Bill Clinton was how to frame a government around change with relatively few changes.

CAMPAIGN PROMISES: THEMES FOR A NEW DEMOCRAT

Throughout the campaign of 1992 Clinton targeted the declining economy and the absence of a clear Republican policy to improve domestic economic conditions. The national debt had quadrupled in the Reagan-Bush years to over $4 trillion. The savings and loan industry was in shambles and banks were crushed by bad debts. Ten per cent of the population was on food stamps and one in eight was living below the poverty line. Over a quarter of the nation had lived through unemployment.

Clinton's campaign director, James Carville, wrote on a slip of paper "the economy, stupid" and pinned it over his desk. That simple phrase became the central theme of the campaign, with Clinton hammering the theme of past economic failure and a promise of economic revitalization. As Clinton himself noted, the campaign would focus "like a laser beam" on the economy.

The campaign, however, had been through a series of crises as both the crowd of primary opponents and Bush himself attempted to center the election around Clinton's character. His rivals had repeatedly cast Clinton as a womanizer and attempted to focus the election around moral values. The Clinton campaign staff moved to regain the momentum. Meeting in secret in what they termed the Manhattan Project, named after the atomic bomb research project, the Clinton team targeted the general election around broader issues. They successfully refocused the electorate around Clinton's middle-class values and his economic objectives.

The Manhattan Project divided Clinton's message into four themes:

1. The People First, investing in the American people to secure the economic future;
2. Opportunity With Responsibility, stressing "no more something for nothing";
3. The Middle Class, a populism of the center, not the left;
4. Reinventing Government, not a revolution but a plan to make the system work for you.[3]

Each of these themes tried to position the Democratic Party around the centrist goals of the New Democrats. The Republican victories over the past twelve years had clearly shown that the electorate supported moderation in government. The election would be won or lost by the candidate who could convince the nation that the economy could be stimulated without increasing government.

With the on-again, off-again candidacy of Ross Perot challenging the Clinton campaign's economic proposals, and with the Bush campaign focusing on Clinton's character, little time was left for the Clinton team to address the issue of governance if elected. No plan was developed during the campaign for managing the transfer of power to a Clinton presidency. All the energies of the campaign were devoted to the election itself.

The Manhattan Project paid off. In a stunning defeat for both Ross Perot and George Bush, Bill Clinton captured the election. Clinton dominated the west, the midwest, New England, and the mid-Atlantic states. Perot failed to win a single state. Bush garnered his strongest support in states with few electoral votes: North Dakota, South Dakota, Wyoming, Idaho, and Oklahoma. Only one major state, his home state of Texas, with its 32 electoral votes, and only one industrial state, Indiana, home of vice president Dan Quayle, went to Bush. Even half the south, a Republican stronghold, switched to the Democratic ticket.

The Democratic victory reflected in part a public outcry against the last-minute negative tactics of both Bush and Perot. Bush had called the Democrats "bozos" and vice presidential candidate Al Gore the "Ozone man."

Perot attacked the Republicans for "dirty tricks" and spent millions of his own funds on made-for-television "infomercials". The Democrats continued to hammer on the economy, ignoring the attacks and launching a blitz of advertising to "Put People First."

THE TRANSITION: A PLAN FOR GOVERNANCE

When the cheering was over, the Clinton campaign staff was faced with a new task: designing a government. With all their attention focused on the election, the task of governance had only minimally been included in the campaign efforts to win the White House. Campaign chairman Mickey Kantor had secretly convened a group to design a White House structure. At the same time, Kantor began working with the Democratic Leadership Council who were preparing a formal document on policy proposals.

Kantor provided relatively little guidance to the transition once an operational staff emerged. As one columnist described the process, "the transformation from campaign to governance has seemed especially awkward."[4] While the campaign had been a well-oiled machine, the transition was, in comparison, in chaos. Not only had the process of governance been generally ignored during the campaign, the transition process itself had been ignored during the campaign. No one seemed positioned to move into a leadership role for the transition. James Carville, Clinton's closest advisor, returned to his consulting work. Mickey Kantor, the campaign chairman, became the obvious choice to manage the transition. But Kantor was quickly told he would not be transition director.

Clinton loyalists began jockeying for power. Infighting began as a broad array of campaign staff and Clinton associates (known as FOBs, for Friends of Bill) tried to move into key positions on the transition staff.

For several days, chaos reigned. Finally, nearly a week after the election, Clinton appointed codirectors of the transition: Washington lawyer Vernon Jordan and veteran State Department official/Los Angeles lawyer Warren Christopher. Neither had been involved in day-to-day campaign activities, but were general campaign advisors. Christopher had been Clinton's coordinator for the vice presidential search, and had strongly recommended Al Gore. Jordan had been quietly working with the campaign through Ron Brown, chairman of the Democratic National Committee.

After the senior transition jobs had been established, campaign staff and a host of Clinton loyalists emerged. Key members included Mark Gearan, moving from the campaign headquarters to transition deputy director; Roy Neel, from Gore's staff to deputy director; Mickey Kantor, campaign chairman to transition advisor; George Stephanopoulos, campaign communications director to transition communications director; Dee Dee Myers campaign press secretary to transition press secretary; Sandy Berger and Tony Lake, campaign advisors on foreign policy to transition advisors on foreign policy; Bruce Lindsey, campaign advisor and Clinton confidant to personnel director; Bruce Reed, campaign domestic policy advisor to transition domestic policy advisor; Richard Riley, campaign advisor on education policy to transition coordinator for sub-Cabinet positions. James Carville, Mandy Grunwald, and Stan Greenberg, all of whom were paid consultants to the campaign, chose to remain outside the official transition team.

Once in place, the transition staff moved quickly to develop a series of goals for the transition. At the top of the list for attention were departmental reviews. The transition staff sought to examine each of the fourteen executive departments and analyze their programmatic and budgetary responsibilities. In addition, the transition team pursued a path of legislative initiatives and executive orders that could immediately implement promises made during the campaign.

The structure of government was to be focused around the concept of teams, a concept that Clinton himself engineered. Teams would be the center of the transition, with teams focusing on both the organization and the staffing of the new administration. Teams would later form the cornerstone of White House–Cabinet relations.

Ten teams, or "agency cluster groups," were created by the end of November to study agency budgets and personnel as the first step to hit the ground running. Cluster groups included:

1. Economics/International Trade: chaired by Franklin Raines, vice chairman of the Federal National Mortgage Association
2. State/National security: chaired by Sandy Berger, Washington lawyer and Carter administration State Department staff
3. Transportation: chaired by Federico Pena, mayor of Denver from 1983 to 1991
4. Science/Space: chaired by Sally Ride, director of the California Space Institute at the University of California at San Diego and former astronaut
5. Natural Resources/Environment/Energy/Agriculture: chaired by James Speth, environmental activist
6. Education/Arts/Humanities: chaired by Johnnetta Cole, President of Spelman College
7. Health/Human Services: chaired by Thomas J. Downey, defeated in 1992 for reelection after nine terms in the U.S. House of Representatives
8. Justice/Civil Rights: co-chaired by Peter Edelman, professor of constitutional law at Georgetown University
9. Justice/Civil Rights: co-chaired by Bernard Nussbaum, corporate lawyer
10. Government Relations: chaired by Dietra L. Ford, staff of the House Committee on the District of Columbia.[5]

In choosing the directors for the cluster teams, Clinton required broad gender and racial diversity, resulting in cluster directors that included seven men and three women, six whites, three blacks, and one Hispanic.

The agency cluster groups, whose members were all volunteers, were charged with preparing a forty-to sixty-page report divided into eight chapters: an overview; description of major programs, Fiscal Year 1993 budget authority and full-time employment level; ongoing and imminent policy, regulatory, and program issues recruiting high level attention with ninety days, highest priority positions to fill, budget and procurement issues; legislation due to expire and current legislative initiatives; observations and areas of concern; and background materials.[6]

The material assembled by the cluster groups was designed to be used by the Cabinet officers as a blueprint for running their departments. The principal objective for creating the reports was to ensure that Cabinet nominees had the requisite information for management. Cluster groups were not responsible for recommending policy initiatives or for recommending how departmental policies meshed with campaign promises. Their task was primarily information gathering.

In addition to the agency cluster groups, a team of lawyers was assembled to prepare executive orders for Clinton to use immediately after the inauguration. The cluster groups were directed to funnel proposals for executive orders to the legal team throughout their activities. As one transition member noted, "Clinton wants to be able to hit the ground running and demonstrate some presidential leadership."[7]

As the agency cluster groups were developing overviews of the departments for the Cabinet nominees, yet another team was developing names for sub-Cabinet appointments. Under the direction of Washington lawyer James Hamilton, more than a hundred Washington insiders, primarily lawyers, developed a list of names for sub-Cabinet positions. Referred to as the "vetters," the search teams divided into subgroups focused around specific departments.[8]

The numerous parts of the transition team remained scattered, with little coordination from the center. Transition team members had little in common and only basic knowledge of the campaign. Neither Christopher nor Jordan provided direction to the various teams, which operated relatively autonomously. The result was a transition process that produced mounds of assorted pieces of information, but little focus for the new administration. The principal accomplishment of the transition was its emphasis on ethnic and gender diversity within the agency cluster groups, providing early evidence that the campaign promise for an administration that "looks like America" would be honored. This provided a foundation for ensuring the nation that campaign promises were not idle rhetoric but serious commitments.

The lack of direction and coordination within the transition had immediate implications for the new administration. Someone in the transition requested the Bush administration to require all presidential appointments to resign. They agreed and sent out a form letter to all full-time presidential appointees subject to Senate confirmation (not including U.S. attorneys, federal marshals, and ambassadors) that "it is the pleasure of the president" that they leave by noon on inauguration day.[9] The transition team reversed their decision and asked that the Bush appointments stay because "people will be needed for an interim period to help with the transition."[10] The Bush appointees honored the president's original letter and resigned. While the original decision to remove all Bush appointees was perhaps the correct decision, the impact was to diminish public approval for the fledgling administration.

CABINET SELECTION

As the transition teams were assembling their various parts of the puzzle at transition headquarters in Washington, D.C., the president-elect was assembling his part of the puzzle, the Cabinet, in Little Rock. Clinton viewed the Cabinet as vital members of the decision-making team, and, as such, wanted to be intimately involved in the Cabinet selection process. For Clinton, the Cabinet officers were essential members, but not the only members, of the decision process. He made no attempt to revitalize Cabinet Government, as recent administrations had, in which policy-making was focused in the departments. Clinton had a distinct view of a strong White House–Cabinet relationship in which the Cabinet members actively contributed to, but did not control, the decision process. Subsequently, choices for Cabinet nominees were predicated on their ability to work collegially and as part of a team, with the White House staff managing team decision-making.

The Cabinet selections were handled in several waves, first the economic policy team, next the foreign policy team, and finally the domestic policy team, with the entire process completed on Christmas eve. The selection process itself signaled an effort to use a team approach to policy-making, with each Cabinet team focused on a specific part of the policy process.

Clinton Manages the Selection Process

The small team assembled by Clinton for the Cabinet selection process included Hillary Clinton, Al Gore, Warren Christopher, Roy Neel, and Bruce Lindsey. It was primarily Clinton himself, however, who framed the Cabinet. The group's self-directed task was threefold: to ensure gender, racial, and geographic diversity; to mend political fences within the Democratic Party; and to ensure collegiality among the Cabinet members. "I don't want a Cabinet of strangers," Clinton said at a news conference, "but neither do I want people whose only criteria for having a job was that they had somehow been involved with me before."[11]

At the center of Clinton's Cabinet selection strategy was a Cabinet that "looks like America." The Cabinet that Clinton ultimately chose reflected the gender and ethnic diversity he had often pledged throughout the campaign. For the fourteen Cabinet officers, Clinton nominated four blacks, three women, and two Hispanics. Three other women were named to positions that Clinton pledged to elevate to Cabinet level.[12]

Ensuring Diversity

Ethnic diversity was perhaps the most critical to the search, but proved to be the most difficult. Pressured by Jesse Jackson to fulfill his campaign pledge to appoint more minorities, Clinton actively pursued minority Cabinet officers. His efforts were hindered by the lack of black participants in either the campaign or the transition. Clinton had only two senior advisors who were black: Ron Brown, chair of the Democratic National Committee, and Vernon Jordan. Both were offered administration jobs. Brown, who sought the State Department post, was offered Commerce. Jordan was offered the Attorney General's post, but declined after press reports of his ties to a tobacco company.

Although Clinton promised to keep his pledge for minorities in his Cabinet, his relationship with Jesse Jackson was sufficiently damaged during the campaign that any Cabinet nominee could not be aligned with Jackson. As a result, the other three minorities brought into the administration were virtual unknowns to Clinton and most of the nation: Hazel O'Leary, a Minnesota energy executive tapped for the Energy Department; Jesse Brown, executive director of the Disabled Veterans of America; and Mike Espy, a relatively obscure Congressman from Mississippi. The only large minority group not represented in the Cabinet were Asian-Americans, who complained about the problem but were promised sub-Cabinet positions.

Gender diversity proved to be equally as difficult. As Jesse Jackson had on behalf of minorities, women's groups fervently lobbied Clinton for women in the Cabinet. Three women were ultimately nominated to the Cabinet: Donna Shalala, a friend of Hillary Clinton's for Health and Human Services; Hazel O'Leary; and Zoe Baird, legal counsel for a Connecticut insurance company and protégé of Warren Christopher.[13] Clinton had only met the latter two in their Cabinet interviews. Although women's groups had sought a greater number of women in the Cabinet, they were clearly satisfied. As Eleanor Smeal, president of the Fund for the Feminist Majority and former head of

NOW noted, the women in the Cabinet "were a step forward for women in breaking the glass ceiling in public leadership."[14]

While the quest for ethnic and gender diversity dominated the selection process, Clinton carefully considered other factors in building his Cabinet. Geographic diversity was ensured, ranging from the west (Warren Christopher, California) to the midwest (Les Aspin, Wisconsin) to the south (Lloyd Bentsen and Henry Cisneros, Texas) to the deep south (Mike Espy, Mississippi) to the northeast (Robert Reich, Massachusetts). Not one of his Cabinet members was from Arkansas, a signal to the nation that his advisors would be from every corner of America.

Political diversity was also carefully considered. In an effort to mend fences with the Democratic Party after a volatile primary process, Clinton chose leading members of the more conservative wing of the party (Lloyd Bentsen and Les Aspin), of the moderate wing of the party (Warren Christopher), and of the more liberal wing of the party (Donna Shalala and Bruce Babbitt). Although he attempted to fulfill a campaign pledge to bring a Republican into the administration, he did not. Only one Republican, Hewlett-Packard chairman John Young, was approached for the Cabinet and he declined the offer.[15]

Another consideration for the Cabinet was its familiarity with state and local issues. As the nation's senior governor, Clinton viewed state and local officials as uniquely qualified to influence federal programs and manage departmental budgets and personnel. Nearly one-third of his Cabinet was composed of state and local elected officials, including two governors (Babbitt and Riley) and two mayors (Pena and Cisneros). As he presented his Cabinet choices to the nation, he noted that they came "from all across America. From the state capitals and the U.S. capitol, from the city halls and the board rooms, and the class rooms. They come from diverse backgrounds and we will all be better and strong for that diversity."[16]

Clinton's quest for a Cabinet with diverse backgrounds included the nomination of two academics: Donna Shalala, chancellor of the University of Wisconsin, and Robert Reich, an economics professor at Harvard University. Both had been active in the campaign and had long-standing personal relationships with both Clinton and his wife. Shalala, active in children's rights, had taken over from Hillary Clinton as chair of the Children's Defense Fund. Reich had known Clinton since their days together as Rhodes scholars in England.

Unlike his predecessors, however, Clinton did not seek to stack the Cabinet from states that had given him electoral mandates. Texas, the home of George Bush and which had supported the Republican ticket, provided two nominees to the Cabinet. Similarly, Arizona, South Carolina, and Mississippi supported Bush but received appointments to the Cabinet.

Although most of the Cabinet had been assembled by Clinton, Al Gore successfully brought in Carol Browner at the Environmental Protection Agency and Bruce Babbitt at Interior. The nomination of Browner, a former Gore staffer, was a major victory for Gore who sought to influence administration environmental policy. Gore's first choice for Interior, former Senator Timothy Wirth of Colorado, had been denied the job due to rumblings in the Senate over his role in a savings and loan. Gore also convinced Clinton not to nominate World Bank chief economist Lawrence Summers as chairman of the Council of Economic Advisors, because of Summers's support for dumping toxins in third world countries. Laura D'Andrea Tyson, an economics professor and campaign advisor, eventually was nominated to the post.

Emphasis on Education

Perhaps the single most defining feature of the Clinton Cabinet was its emphasis on education. The Cabinet selection process had produced a group of highly educated insiders, most of whom shared Clinton's moderate political views. Jack Watson, former chief of staff to Jimmy Carter, noted that "in the Clinton administration, it is education, more than birth, wealth, or previous experience in government that defines the people Clinton has chosen to serve with him."[17]

The educational backgrounds of the fourteen Cabinet and four Cabinet level appointees included 89 per cent with advanced degrees, including 67 per cent with law degrees and 22 per cent with Ph.D. degrees. Most had either held elected office or a senior-level appointed position. There was a striking absence of the corporate community in the Cabinet, a further reflection of Clinton's own background. According to Clinton, three criteria were used for selecting his Cabinet: "people who share my vision . . . greater diversity . . . and a personal relationship with my Cabinet members."[18] Clinton clearly satisfied his goals for Cabinet selection. The Cabinet, with its emphasis on experience in government and establishment educational credentials, mirrored Clinton's own background. Clinton's calculated structure for his Cabinet produced what he hoped would be a collegial environment for teamwork and decision-making.

WHITE HOUSE STAFF SELECTION

Selection of White House staff did not formally begin until the Cabinet selection process had been completed. This was intended to indicate the importance of the Cabinet in the Clinton administration. Clinton, as had every president since the Watergate affair, pledged to reduce the power of the White

House staff. Not until January 14, 1993—six days before the inauguration and three weeks after the last Cabinet appointment—were most White House staff appointments announced.

Clinton's promise to ensure a reduced role for the White House staff was further supported by his announcement less than a month after taking office that he would cut the White House staff by twenty-five per cent by the end of the fiscal year. This involved reducing the staff from 1,394, the total complement under Bush, to 1,044 by October 1.[19] However, once the cuts were completed, relatively little had changed. Most of the staffing cuts involved a major downsizing of the National Drug Control Policy office and the Council on Environmental Quality. The primary policy offices in the White House suffered no staffing losses.

As he had with the Cabinet, Clinton personally took control of the White House staff selection process. Every position was reviewed by Clinton and those selected for the position met with him to discuss what role that position played in the White House structure. Even relatively junior staff members met with Clinton to discuss their roles.

Ensuring Diversity

The decision-making process for White House staff was less complicated than that for the Cabinet, but significantly more detailed than in previous administrations. Rather than move campaign staff into the White House, Clinton sought to ensure the same gender and ethnic diversity on the White House staff as he had in the transition teams and Cabinet.

Since most senior staff on the campaign were white males, a more diversified group was sought for White House staff positions. This proved more difficult than it had for the Cabinet. Even after the final choices were made, eleven of the sixteen top positions went to white males, although the next level of appointments was considerably more diverse. Nearly one-third of the sixty White House jobs, top - and middle-level, went to women.

Of the five senior women on the White House staff, only one, Carol Rasco, had a policy position. Rasco was Clinton's second choice for the domestic policy director. Bruce Reed, the campaign domestic policy advisor, was Clinton's first choice but was a white male. Rasco's appointment was part of Clinton's pledge to increase the policy-making roles of women on the White House staff. Reed was later chosen deputy director of domestic policy for the White House.

The top position on the White House staff went to longtime Clinton friend Thomas "Mack" McLarty III, chairman of an Arkansas natural gas company who had known Clinton since childhood. McLarty, with no previous Washington experience, was chosen primarily for his intense personal loyalty to Clinton. Although his name was not officially released to the press until December 12, McLarty was Clinton's only choice for chief of staff. As a result, McLarty became a key member of the transition team and a major advisor to Clinton as he designed the White House structure.[20]

In his role as chief of staff, Mclarty sought to encourage an open door policy for senior staff and ensure that Clinton received a broad range of advice as he made his decisions. McLarty noted that,

> The chief of staff role is supportive to the President and to Cabinet members. In a business sense, it is the role of maintaining a strong working relationship between the top management and the line management, which in this case will be the White House and the Cabinet members. The job will be to organize the work day and to organize the workers in a professional, collegial manner and to get information to the President in a timely, efficient manner.[21]

McLarty's view of his role mirrored the description given by Clinton, who said that as an honest broker the chief of staff would supervise the staff and organize the "president's time, paperwork, and information so that an open and forward-looking culture can thrive here." Clinton further noted that McLarty would be responsible for building a team in the White House "whose voices would be heard before decisions were made." [22] McLarty viewed the White House staff as the "line management" and the Cabinet as the "top management," and sought to focus the White House staff in a support, not a policy-making, position. Unfortunately, this position was somewhat at odds with Clinton's own view of using the team approach to policy development, with both White House and departmental staff working as a team for policy development. McLarty, who was eventually replaced as chief of staff, was unable to focus a White House structure that ensured strong White House direction.

In shaping his role in the White House, McLarty bought a copy of a 1986 symposium,[23] in which eight chiefs of staff discussed their White House roles. His conclusion was that he would not serve as an aggressive chief of staff or gatekeeper. Clinton, he said, would be the decision maker as to what he sees and what is put on his desk.[24]

The senior White House staff were as follows:

Chief of Staff	Thomas McLarty III
Deputy Chief of Staff	Mark D. Gearan
Deputy Chief of Staff	Roy Neel
Staff Secretary	John Podesta
Legislative Liaison	Howard Paster

Communications Director	George Stephanopoulos
Press Secretary	Dee Dee Myers
Counsel	Bernard Nussbaum
Cabinet Secretary	Christine A. Varney
Presidential Personnel	Bruce Lindsey
Domestic Policy Advisor	Carol Rasco
Economic Policy Advisor	Robert Rubin
National Security Advisor	Anthony Lake
Intergovernmental Affairs	Regina Montoya
Public Liaison	Alexis Herman
Political Affairs	Rahn Emmanuel

Nearly all the senior White House staff had been key members of the campaign. Exceptions included Roy Neel, who had been Gore's chief of staff during the campaign and a former Gore Senate staffer; Howard Paster, a Washington lobbyist; Robert Rubin, a Wall Street investment banker; Anthony Lake, a professor of international affairs at Mount Holyoke College; and Alexis Herman, deputy director of the Democratic National Committee. Each of the non-Clinton campaign staff, however, had worked closely with the campaign and were considered Clinton loyalists.

Spokes-of-the-Wheel Structure

The list of senior staff was considerably larger than in past administrations, reflecting Clinton's desire for broad access to the oval office. In keeping with Clinton's spokes-of-the-wheel governing style, each of the senior staff had direct access to Clinton. McLarty did not attempt to schedule senior staff or to review those memos that were sent to the president. Clinton's strategy for decision-making was to have a broad array of opinions, even conflicting opinions, from his staff before making a policy decision. McLarty encouraged staff to meet with the president and discuss their views on issues.

This process of presidential decision-making was hands-on. Clinton rejected the short briefing sheet as Reagan had had, choosing instead to have discussions with staff on each issue, more in the manner that Carter used. He frequently had detailed discussions with staff on policy issues before reaching a decision. This was particularly true of domestic and economic policy issues at the early stages of the administration, when international issues were less volatile than later in the administration.

SUB-CABINET SELECTION

Although Clinton did not manage the sub-Cabinet selection process as closely as he had the Cabinet selection process, he established a framework for selection based on loyalty. "Carter's problem," Clinton noted, "was that he gave little thought to how his appointees would work together. He went for the best people without thinking about their loyalty to him or to his program, and he avoided getting involved with choosing the second-tier people, who are the ones who really run things on a day to day basis."[25] As a result, the patronage positions at the sub-Cabinet level were managed through the White House by Bruce Lindsey, a Little Rock lawyer who had close ties to Clinton.

White House Control

Cabinet nominees were told that the decision process for sub-Cabinet appointments would be jointly managed by Lindsey and the departments, with the White House being the managing partner. Lindsey would provide the departments names that met White House political criteria. If the departments felt their own choices were more appropriate for a particular position, they would be reviewed by the White House. Clinton did not follow Carter's model of allowing Cabinet control of departmental positions, nor did he follow the Reagan model of White House control. Rather, he sought a blend of the two models and provided names to the departments that had White House support, but was willing to discuss departmental names. Subsequently, most appointments to sub-Cabinet positions were White House nominees.[26]

Clinton's efforts to gain control of sub-Cabinet positions was strongly supported by the Democratic Leadership Council (DLC), the heart of the New Democratic movement. The DLC produced a document after the election entitled *Mandate for Change*, based on the Heritage Foundation's *Mandate for Leadership* written for Presidents Reagan and Bush. Among the proposals for leadership called for the *Mandate for Change* was the necessity of placing "people loyal to his [the president's] agenda in the key positions needed to carry out that mandate."[27]

Ensuring Diversity

The sub-Cabinet personnel search included the same diversity check that had been used in the transition, White House staff, and Cabinet searches. Every nominee was scrutinized in terms of ethnicity, gender, and geographic (EGG) diversity criteria.[28] Cabinet officers were told that any names submitted directly through the department had to meet the EGG standards. Deputy Secretary of State Clifton R. Wharton, Jr., who battled with Lindsey over departmental positions, was unable to garner White House support for several nominees for ambassadorial positions because of the abundance of white male names submitted. Although Wharton argued that most of the names came from the ranks of the career staff and the foreign service, as they had traditionally, Lindsey required more diversity.

Lindsey was extremely successful in diversifying the top political appointments. Of the appointments made during the first six months of the administration, 34 per cent went to women, 15 per cent to blacks, 8 per cent to Hispanics, and 2 per cent to Asian-Americans.[29]

STRUCTURING A POLICY PROCESS IN THE WHITE HOUSE

As he had for every other decision-making process, Clinton developed a team approach for policy development. Teams were created both among White House policy groups and between the White House and the departments. Within the White House, the structure for policy development focused around policy groups analyzing issues and presenting a series of options to Clinton. Three primary policy groups, or councils as they were known, were established: the National Security Council, the Domestic Policy Council, and the National Economic Policy Council. Each was responsible for establishing the administration's policy orientation and working toward the execution of that policy with the departments.

National Security Council

Of the three policy councils in the White House, the National Security Council was the least complicated to move immediately into operation, given the nature of its mandate and its staff. Its mandate had been prescribed by Congress with the National Security Act of 1947 and its staff tended to be highly qualified, nonpolitical, career employees. Campaign advisors Anthony Lake and Sandy Berger immediately took control of coordinating foreign policy and managing the National Security Council.

Office of Policy Development

In contrast, the domestic policy unit, with no official title and no Congressional mandate, lacked the institutionalization of the National Security Council. Its staff turned over with every new administration and its mandate was at the discretion of each president through the authorizing executive order.

The transition team chose to create an umbrella unit for domestic policy called the Office of Policy Development. Within that unit, two distinct subsections were created: the Domestic Policy Council and the National Economic Policy Council. This was a divergence from previous administrations in which all domestic policy was controlled in one unit. Only the Ford administration, which separated economic policy from domestic policy, sought to divide domestic policy into distinct policy units for economic and domestic policy.

The functions of the Domestic Policy Council were developed by Carol Rasco, who had served in the governor's office in Little Rock managing health and welfare policy; Bruce Reed, the campaign's domestic policy advisor; and William Galston, a campaign advisor and University of Maryland professor. Rasco later was named director of the office, with Reed and Galston serving as deputy directors.

Similarly, the functions of the National Economic Policy Council were developed by Wall Street investment banker Robert Rubin, chairman of Goldman Sachs & Co. Top staff to Rubin included Gene Sperling, deputy transition director and the coordinator for the campaign's economic policy; and W. Bowman Cutter, a senior partner in Coopers & Lybrand and associate director of OMB under the Carter administration.

In addition, a major subunit of the Domestic Policy Council evolved, focusing solely on health care. Ira Magaziner, an activist involved in a series of advocacy groups, managed the health care reform proposal. Although Magaziner technically reported to Carol Rasco, in reality he reported directly to Hillary Clinton, who became the president's point person for health care reform.

The National Security Council continued to have essentially the same relationship with the departments of State and Defense that it had had in previous administrations. However, the Domestic Policy Council and the National Economic Policy Council created new operating relationships both with Cabinet officers and within the White House itself.

The Domestic Policy Council became the primary tool for managing Clinton's domestic agenda, including education reform, welfare reform, veteran's programs, housing, and the myriad of other programmatic areas. The National Economic Policy Council had a narrower agenda focused on creating new jobs in the economy, including spurring industrial output and restructuring trade relations.

CABINET–WHITE HOUSE RELATIONS: MANAGING THE DOMESTIC POLICY PROCESS

The Domestic Policy Council, composed of White House staff and

Cabinet officers, had the widest responsibility for policy development. The membership of the Domestic Policy Council was itself a statement on the team approach that Clinton sought in his policy development process. Unlike past administrations, which built the Domestic Council solely from the Cabinet, the new Domestic Policy Council was officially composed of both White House staff and Cabinet officers and several agency directors. White House staff were, according to Carol Rasco, "a genuine working part" of the policy process "and had to be included."[30] This approach to policy development officially brought White House staff into the policy process. In prior administrations only Cabinet officers were, according to the executive order, members of the Domestic Council.

The executive order creating the Domestic Policy Council named the president, vice president, and the Secretaries of Agriculture, Commerce, Education, Health and Human Services, Housing and Urban Development, Interior, Energy, Labor, Transportation, Veterans Affairs, Treasury, and the Attorney General. Every Cabinet officer except State and Defense was included. In addition, the Environmental Protection Agency, Office of Management and Budget, the National Drug Control Policy agency, and the National AIDS Policy coordinator were represented, as were the President's assistants for domestic policy, economic policy, and the director of the Office of National Service.[31] The official list of members of the Domestic Policy Council was significantly larger than in any administration since the inception of a White House domestic policy unit in 1970.

According to the executive order, the functions of the Domestic Policy Council included the coordination of the domestic policy process, the coordination of domestic policy advice to the president, ensuring that domestic policy-decision and programs met the president's goals, and monitoring the president's domestic agenda. Power for managing the domestic policy process fell primarily to the White House staff, not the Cabinet officers. Unlike the Reagan and Bush administrations, which placed one Cabinet officer in charge of a cabinet council, the Clinton approach was to place presidential assistants directly in charge. White House–Cabinet interaction for policy development was purposely structured to ensure that the White House staff controlled the process. As such, meetings of the Domestic Policy Council were held biweekly in the White House, in the Roosevelt Room, only doors down from the oval office. The White House constantly sought to reinforce its role as team leader through both symbolic terms, such as meeting in the White House, and concrete terms, such as positioning its staff in leadership positions.

The regular biweekly meetings of the Domestic Policy Council served as a forum for information sharing and for focusing policy issues. Key to this policy structure was ensuring that Cabinet officers understood the president's policy agenda and worked within that agenda. As one White House staffer noted of the process, the "primary purpose of the DPC was to allow the Cabinet Secretaries who implement and oversee policy the opportunity to communicate with and comment to the White House staff inside the gates that design the policy."[32]

The team that developed domestic policy was focused squarely in the oval office. As he had throughout the transition, Clinton was determined to be involved in the decision-making apparatus. Not Jimmy Carter had there been a president so involved in understanding policy details. Although Clinton rarely attended the Domestic Policy Council meetings, he met regularly with Rasco to discuss domestic policy issues emerging in the council. Usually twice a week, Rasco met with Clinton for general reviews of departmental policy issues. When detailed discussions were called for, Rasco brought in one of her staff to answer specific questions.[33]

White House Staff Participation in Policy Development

Clinton's concept of team participation in policy development included not only White House–Cabinet team efforts, but a team effort within the White House itself. All senior staff to the president were invited to the biweekly Domestic Policy Council meetings. Either they or a member of their staffs usually joined the meetings, with George Stephanopoulos and Mack McLarty being the most frequent attendees.

In addition to their participation at the DPC meetings, White House staff were briefed daily on policy issues emerging through the departments. White House staff provided their input, noting political consequences and legislative stumbling blocks in policy implementation.

Rasco's frequent meetings with White House senior staff provided broad-based guidance to the policy process emerging through her office. While the Reagan White House had used campaign speeches to guide the domestic policy office, framed in the "notebooks" prepared by Martin Anderson's staff, the Clinton White House used the daily staff meetings to guide the domestic policy office. Rasco's staff prepared "notebooks" similar to those of Anderson's staff, but far less detailed. The staff based most of their policy decisions on a combination of their own knowledge of Clinton's goals, the objectives outlined in the Democratic Leadership Council's *Mandate for Change,* and the input of the larger White House staff.

Working Groups

The formal structure for White House–Cabinet deliberation on policy issues was a series of "working groups." These were ad hoc groups of Cabinet officers brought together to deal with specific policy issues, similar to the "cabinet clusters" designed by the Carter White House. Their membership was fluid, depending on the issue at hand. As Bruce Reed noted, the working groups were "formed with a specific goal in mind and to come up with legislation to accomplish that goal. Once that goal is reached and the legislation is passed, the working group will cease to exist."[34]

The primary task of the working groups was to develop the details of a general policy goal established by the White House. The White House created the working groups and assigned the departments to work with them. Generally three or four departments were assigned to the working groups. Cabinet officers were then asked to assign their senior staff to the working groups, which were chaired by Rasco's staff.

Once the working group had developed a series of options for moving a policy forward, the entire Domestic Policy Council reviewed them. Typically, several options were developed by the working group rather than only one. Once approved by the Domestic Policy Council, those options were presented to Clinton by Rasco. Clinton reviewed the options and often reviewed those options not only with Rasco, but other senior staff. Bruce Reed noted that because of Clinton's total immersion in the domestic policy process, he was "the prime policy maker on any given issue." [35]

The implementation process moved forward once Clinton had made a decision. Rasco reported Clinton's decision to the Domestic Policy Council, which in turn moved toward legislative action.[36] Clinton's level of involvement was so detailed that he personally decided the number of precollege to postcollege slots to be included in the national service program that Eli Segal was developing. The departments then took the lead role in developing specific language for the legislative proposal before returning the proposal to the White House.

WHITE HOUSE CONTROL OF POLICY-MAKING: THE TEAM APPROACH

At the heart of the administration's structure for decision-making was the concept of team work. From the outset of the administration, teams had been a key component of the decision structure. Transition teams were established to review departmental structures and to review sub-Cabinet personnel appointments. Perhaps the most visible team was that established to review the Cabinet, a team assembled by Clinton himself.

Once in office, the administration continued to pursue the team approach to decision-making. Major policy issues were debated through teams, known as policy councils, composed of both White House and departmental staff. Within the White House, teams from the various policy units were brought together to develop policy objectives. The National Security Council, National Economic Policy Council, and Domestic Policy Council worked in tandem to focus key proposals.

Less official teams were also convened when necessary. Before the election, Clinton gathered a team of experts to advise him on the economy.[37] Similarly, Hillary Clinton held a series of task forces to advise her on health-care policy. Teamwork became the operative phrase in the Clinton adminis-tration.

Benefits to Teamwork

The team approach served several functions for the administration. Perhaps its most significant benefit was to strengthen the bridge between the Cabinet and the White House. By involving the Cabinet officers in the decision-making process with White House staff, Cabinet officers were kept in the presidential orbit and had less reason to "marry the natives." They believed they were part of the president's team and carried his message to the departments. Cabinet officers had far less chance of being coopted by their departments if they regularly met with the president and the White House staff, and considered themselves part of the decision-making team.

The bridge between the Cabinet and the White House was further strengthened because all the relevant players were able to input into the policy decision. Both Cabinet officers and White House staff, through the council and working group structure, thrashed out policy alternatives. Decisions were made through consensus and compromise. The process led to broader support across the agencies. As Robert Rubin noted, "If everyone is involved when a decision is made, everyone buys into it."[38]

Turf battles were also minimized through the White House–Cabinet team approach to policy making. The *territorial imperative* was minimized by departments working together to solve problems. Fewer crises developed as a result of constant coordination efforts in the departmental working groups, leading to smoother working relations between the departments.

The White House itself benefited from the team approach to policy-making. Not only were working groups established for White House–Cabinet interaction, but for policy discussions among White House staff. Staff from the National Economic Policy Council and the National Security Council worked on international economic issues. Similarly, staff from the Domestic Policy Council worked with the health care task force on health care and with the National Economic Policy Council on inner city revitalization. The team approach produced less friction among the units within the White House, improved policy coordination, and encouraged innovation and creativity to broad-based solutions.

Problems with Teamwork

But the teamwork concept that permeated the Clinton administration had several drawbacks. Principal among those was that too many agenda items were addressed in the working groups, both the White House–Cabinet groups and the intra–White House groups. Clinton had noted to his senior White House staff and Cabinet at a retreat at Camp David soon after the inauguration that he wanted a "flat organization." That phrase was taken literally by many members of the White House staff, who allowed a "flat," or nonhierarchial, process of decision-making. Rather than convene discussions around White House developed policy, signaling a hierarchial decision structure, White House staff often allowed the group to focus the policy proposal, rather than the policy specifics.

The absence of a strong decision system in the White House was large-ly the product of vaguely framed campaign goals. The goals outlined by the Manhattan Project early in the campaign were thematic in nature rather than specific policy objectives. During the campaign, the goals became somewhat more specific: increasing growth and investment, reducing the deficit, reform-ing health care, instituting national service, and reforming campaign finance.[39] But none of these objectives easily fit into the framework of the working groups. The working groups, therefore, had to develop specific policy objec-tives from the broad themes of the campaign and to give life to the New Democratic movement. The team approach to policy development was an attempt to operationalize thematic endeavors.

The process proved extremely slow. When the working groups failed to define objectives, Cabinet officers developed their own objectives to meet departmental needs. As a result, Henry Cisneros supported increased funding for housing subsidies, Donna Shalala supported increased funding for chil-dren's health programs, Richard Riley supported stronger federal standards for secondary education, Jesse Brown urged increased funding for Persian Gulf disabled veterans, and Bruce Babbitt sought to broaden the nation's public land-holdings. The result was a Cabinet that often appeared to be moving in disparate directions, leaving a public impression that the administration lacked focus.

The team approach also fractured the collegiality that Clinton had hoped to build in his Cabinet. In the absence of strong White House guidance on pol-icy, Cabinet officers often sought to frame the administration's policy. This led to bitter disagreements within the Cabinet. Social Security became a major source of contention, as Secretary of the Treasury Lloyd Bentsen and Office of Management and Budget Director Leon Panetta took the side of major Social Security cuts, while Labor Secretary Robert Reich and Health and Human Services Secretary Donna Shalala opposed such cuts.[40] Trade policy became another problem as Mickey Kantor, the Trade Representative, was often at odds with Commerce Secretary Ron Brown. Kantor shrugged off the difference in policy viewpoints by saying that he had no particular point of view on trade. "I don't claim to be anything," he said "I claim to be a good lawyer representing a terrific President. . . . Free-traders, protectionists, managed-traders, all those labels don't apply." [41]

Other problems emerged from the team approach to policy development. The Clinton administration was often criticized for its failure to move rapidly on key campaign promises. Health care and welfare reform, in particular, were criticized for the extremely slow pace that they moved, in large part because of the numerous task forces and constant consultations involved in producing a legislative proposal.

The principal legislative successes of the first year and a half of the Clinton administration were bills that were already in the cauldron of Congress. Passage of the family and medical leave bill, crime bill, and the North American Free Trade Agreement (NAFTA) were not dependent on a Clinton proposal. The only significant bill to emerge from Congress that was Clinton-initiated was the tax reform legislation, restructuring the personal income tax.

The failure of the administration to develop major legislative initiatives was rooted in the campaign itself. Clinton's campaign agenda for domestic and economic revitalization had few specific proposals. It was focused around eight broad themes in what was known as the national economic strategy:

* supporting free trade
* supporting scientific research and development
* retraining for workers
* rebuilding the industrial infrastructure
* funding for education, health care, and social services
* tax increases for the wealthy
* reinventing government
* modernizing the nation's infrastructure.[42]

The program was designed to appeal to Republicans in both the business community and the middle class without losing traditional working-class Democratic base. Because the campaign sought such broad-based appeal, few specifics were included that might jeopardize support. As *Newsweek* described the economic strategy:

> As a vote-getting strategy, it worked: he convinced many people that he understood their concerns and had thought hard and developed specific ideas about what to do. But now he is bumping into the fact that some

of his pledges were contradictory and others were easier to voice than fulfill."[43]

The campaign, however, simply reflected the candidate. Clinton's overarching goal was for long-term change in economic and social patterns. He wanted to change the foundation of relationships between the government and its citizenry. This was a long-term endeavor, based on a conceptual rather than a specific framework. Clinton noted that his "enduring legacy" was that he taught the people of Arkansas to "think long term. It's what I want most to do nationwide. It won't be easy and it will require a constant dialogue with the country, but it has to be done and I mean to do it."[44]

Once in office, Clinton was faced with forming a government around broadly based campaign promises. Since the transition team did not focus on developing specific policy initiatives, that task fell to the White House staff and the newly formed White House–Cabinet working groups. Their job became first to prioritize administration goals and then to provide detailed proposals.

Working groups of White House and department staff started to develop programs in welfare reform, national service, health care reform, job retraining, education reform, inner city revitalization, and government operations. But the process was slow and often frustrating to Cabinet officers who believed that they had been given a mandate by Clinton to move the principles of the New Democrats forward. The team approach to decision–making was painstaking slow as numerous participants became involved in policy discussions. Only the national service program moved forward during the first year of the administration. Eli Segal, who had been brought into the White House to manage creation of an independent agency for national service, operated out of the working group structure and spearheaded successful legislation.

In general, the process of a "flat organization" in the policy process stymied major proposals, which remained buried in the working groups. Neither the cabinet, as they had in the Ford and Carter administrations, nor the White House, as they had in the Nixon and Reagan administrations, was controlling the policy process.

The Clinton administration had by the middle of 1994, eighteen months after taking office, neither a structure of cabinet government nor a centralized White House policy structure. The Cabinet had returned to its traditional role of departmental spokesman, speaking to the president for the department rather than for the president to the department. Federico Pena, for example, was captured by his department early in the administration. When Vice President Al Gore and his National Performance Review urged the deregulation of the maritime industry and elimination of maritime subsidies, Pena supported the maritime industry and its unions.[45]

Clinton's concept of teamwork failed to include the Cabinet as a body. Although Cabinet officers were included in small working groups on select policy issues, Cabinet officers almost never met in larger groups. This strategy of policy development ignored some of the key lessons learned from past presidents. By rarely holding Cabinet meetings (Clinton held only seven Cabinet meetings during his first year in office) and by using the Cabinet meetings for show-and-tell, Clinton ignored the opportunity to reinforce the central themes of his administration. Rather than use the Cabinet meetings to promote individual Cabinet themes, such as AIDs czar Christine Gebbie's recitation on how Cabinet secretaries could raise AIDs awareness,[46] Clinton could have focused discussion around key policy initiatives.

In addition, the Cabinet meetings could have reinforced the concept of Cabinet members being part of the president's team and their overarching commitment to presidential goals. There is less chance of interdepartmental warfare over jurisdictional or programmatic issues if Cabinet secretaries are not strangers. A personal relationship among cabinet officers goes a long way in interdepartmental dealings.

Clinton's structure for dealing with his Cabinet was as unstructured as every other facet of his leadership style. There was no regularity to Cabinet meetings, no central theme to those meetings, no effort to forge a presidential team within the Cabinet. It was not surprising that cabinet officers easily moved into their departmental orbits and became coopted by departmental and constituent goals. Even Education Secretary Richard Riley, a friend of Clinton's since 1979 when they were both moderate southern governors, became a solider of his department rather than a commander in Clinton's legion.

Panetta Takes Control

After eighteen months in office Clinton's public opinion polls were falling rapidly, hovering at the 45 per cent approval level. More people disapproved of the president's handling of his job than approved. Only Ronald Reagan with a 41 per cent approval rating at the same point in time had a lower rating of the last nine presidents polled. Reagan's rating reflected the nation's recession, but Clinton's rating, in the middle of a national economic upswing, reflected growing disapproval of his total presidency.

In June 1994, in a move to redefine his presidency and regain control over the policy process, Clinton restructured his White House staff. OMB director Leon Panetta was moved to chief of staff and Mack McLarty was moved to the traditional position of ex-chief of staffs as Counsellor to the President. Clinton's decision to impose a more structured organization on the White House came only after, as Fred Greenstein notes, "outside forces had humbled him."[47]   His free-wheeling White House staff structure reflected his own undisciplined style of leadership, a style of leadership that was rapidly losing favor with the public.

Clinton had been his own chief of staff, his own domestic advisor, his own national security advisor. Clinton became involved in the largest decisions and the smallest decisions. Such minutia as choosing which scholars would come for lunch to how a speech on ethanol should be worded was included in his daily activities.[48]   The essence of the decision process lacked discipline and organization. As early as his first one hundred days in office, Clinton's presidency was being assessed by the public and the press as completely unfocused.

The selection of a strong chief of staff (Panetta) and the move toward a centralized and ordered policy-making structure marked a major redesign of the Clinton presidency. The White House staff was moving to gain control of the wide-ranging policy initiatives being brought to the president. Under the Panetta structure, options that rose to the oval office were consistent with the original theme of the administration. Policy options brought before Clinton under the new structure were not only thematically consistent, but consistent with the political reality of a difficult 1996 election.

Panetta's fiscal conservatism and skillful management of the budget process had gained him broad support both among other members of the administration and within Congress. Within days after Clinton's June 27 announcement of Panetta's new White House role, Panetta met with Senate Finance Committee Chairman Daniel Patrick Moynihan (D-NY) to discuss health care. The battle over health care had mounted throughout the spring of 1994 as Moynihan's committee seemed to be moving in different directions from the White House. However, after the Panetta-Moynihan meeting, the committee unveiled a draft health care bill that bore a striking resemblance to Clinton's.[49]   Panetta's personal stock immediately rose and his dominance in White House decision-making began.

Soon after moving into the west wing of the White House on July 17, into an office far less sumptuous than his office in the old executive office building but with far more proximity to the center of power, Panetta began to restructure the White House staff. In his meeting with Clinton and Vice President Gore at Camp David on the weekend of June 25–26, Panetta had insisted on wide-ranging authority in the White House. Panetta was assured of such authority. McLarty's aides were reshuffled in the White House and top OMB staff moved into key positions on Panetta's staff. Press Secretary DeeDee Myers, who was asked to leave by Panetta, fought back, seeking redress from Clinton. Myers argued that her lack of effectiveness, as Panettta had referred to it, was due to McLarty's refusal to include her in senior staff meetings and the overall decision process. Clinton agreed and Myers kept her job. But by the end of the year she had resigned, replaced by Panetta's choice of Michael McCurry, chief spokesman for the State Department.[50]

Clinton's spokes-of-the-wheel decision structure under McLarty had failed and resulted in the chaotic decision process that consumed the White House. Panetta quickly moved to consolidate the policy process under his office, endeavoring to establish a more orderly system for presidential review of policy issues. Under the old system, staff walked in and out of the oval office at will, presenting different ideas on issues. Under the new structure, Panetta sought to reduce the number of staff with direct access to the president and to provide systematic analysis of policy issues. Although staff were uncomfortable with the changes, everyone had to go through Panetta to see the president.[51]

No material was brought to Clinton that Panetta had not cleared first, including National Security Council material. (This was largely a result of the Iran-Contra affair, in which the chief of staff had not seen the material discussed with Reagan by his National Security Advisor.) Panetta also moved to end the free-wheeling roles of top staff. Stephanopoulos became a spokesman to Congress, McLarty a spokesman to business, and Lindsey a legal counsel. In a similar vein, Panetta moved to limit the access of the cadre of consultants, such as Stanley Greenberg and Paul Begala, who regularly moved in and out of the oval office.

The New Democrats Return

Panetta's move to the west wing signaled not only a tightening of the internal workings of the White House but also a return to the roots of the Clinton presidency: the themes of the New Democrats. Although Panetta had never taken up the mantle of the New Democrats, his actions consistently supported their objectives. Panetta's House career had been built on fiscal restraint and deficit reduction. In his four years as chairman of the House Budget Committee, he mastered budget intricacies and consistently supported reduced spending.

His tenure at OMB had been similarly marked by often Darmanesque moves to reduce spending and restrain departmental initiatives. He quickly became the ambassador to conservative Democrats, a role that McLarty had promised but not delivered on. Panetta's early roots as a Republican who worked in Nixon's Department of Health, Education and Welfare added further credence to his conservative leanings.

His primary asset to the president was his ability to manage the paper flow into the oval office and to ensure that major policy initiatives met the test of both fiscal restraint and consistency with presidential objectives. Panetta's first major task was totally internal: to reestablish for White House staff

Clinton's commitment to reducing the deficit, cutting government spending, and providing tax relief to the middle class. The health care program, adamantly moved forward by Ira Magaziner and Mrs. Clinton, was viewed by an overwhelming percentage of the public as a new government program that would increase government spending. Panetta's first task, therefore, was to remove health care from the center of political attention and refocus public attention on efforts to address Clinton's key objectives.

By the summer of 1994 health care had all put disappeared from the political dialogue. The White House had pulled back and was no longer holding highly publicized meetings with members of Congress on health care. The national focus moved to foreign policy, as the Bosnia crisis continued to escalate as the United Nations bombed Serbian nationals. North Korea heightened a military alert when it refused to open its nuclear facilities for international inspection. Thousands of Cuban and Haitian refugees fled their homeland on makeshift boats, seeking asylum in the United States. American troops were sent to Haiti to oust the dictator and restore the democratically elected leader.

Panetta reined in the White House staff and kept the focus on foreign affairs. Throughout the summer and early fall of 1994 the White House focused on developing a tax relief package for the middle class. Cabinet members were restrained from public interviews. The only visible cabinet member was Secretary of Transportation Federico Pena, who sought to assure the nation that, in spite of three major airline crashes, the airline industry was safe.

The domestic policy office and the economic policy office, which had actively pursued new programs during the first year and a half of the administration, were silenced, handling primarily "firefighting" issues. White House staff became involved in such diverse "firefighting" issues as the baseball strike, the refugee crisis, and disaster relief. The Paula Jones lawsuit and the Whitewater hearings enveloped the counsel's office.

The only significant legislative package moved forward by the White House was the crime bill, a revised package first put forward during the Reagan administration. On August 21, the bill passed, providing the president a major legislative victory. Although it was not part of Clinton's original legislative agenda, by embracing the bill Clinton signaled a return to the core of his support in middle America. While liberals eschewed the bill as failing to deal with the root issues of crime, both moderate Democrats and moderate Republicans hailed the bill as an important step forward in the war on crime in America.

Panetta's primary objective was to refocus the White House within the narrow agenda framed by Clinton at the outset of the administration. That agenda involved developing:

1.   a stimulus program to reinvigorate the job base

2. an economic program that reduced the deficit and shifted priorities from consumption to investment
3. a political reform bill, including reform of campaign financing and new restrictions on lobbying
4. a national service bill
5. welfare reform
6. health care reform.[52]

Only two of the items on the agenda had been accomplished: a stimulus program and a national service bill. Health care reform was all but dead. For Panetta, the logical direction to move was welfare reform and deficit reduction. These were two areas that he could control, based on his OMB stint and ties in Congress. Panetta was determined not to let future initiatives suffer the same fate that health care had. As one commentator noted, "Ira Magaziner, the big-thinking adviser who ran the policy making on health care, designed a humdinger of a grand construct for reform, in isolation of the legislators who had to enact it."[53]

Midterm Elections of 1994: The Republicans Take Congress

The public's repudiation of the policies of the Clinton presidency was dramatically felt in the midterm elections of November 1994. In landslide victories across the nation, the Republicans gained control of both the Senate and the House for the first time in forty years. Exit polls consistently showed that voters supported Republicans as a message to the president.

Although Panetta had initiated changes in the White House policy structure to narrow the agenda and reduce departmental initiatives, it had been too late to counter the growing national perception of Clinton as a "traditional liberal" eager to spend the public coffer. The health care proposal had largely created this view of the administration.

In separate meetings after the election with the nation's Democratic governors and with the Democratic Leadership Council, Clinton was barraged with the same advice: narrow the agenda and return to a centrist theme.[54] By mid-December, barely one month after the election, Clinton was moving back toward the precepts of his administration and the fundamental principles of his New Democrat stalwarts. On December 8, 1994, Clinton announced a major expansion of his efforts to control government spending. In the first major attempt to reorganize the cabinet since Richard Nixon first proposed it with the supercabinet concept in 1973, Clinton proposed to dismantle HUD, Energy, and revamp Transportation.[55]

By the end of December two cabinet officers had resigned, Lloyd Bentsen at Treasury and Mike Espy at Agriculture. They were replaced by

White House economic advisor Robert Rubin at Treasury and former Democratic congressman Dan Glickman at Agriculture.

The test of the Clinton administration in 1995 and 1996 will be whether the White House can restructure the policy-making process to focus on those key policies that captured the public's attention in 1992. The public voted for a New Democrat in 1992 but by November 1994 thought they had gotten an old Democrat. Clinton's task for the remainder of his term will be to build a domestic policy structure that controls departmental independence in policy-making and frames the administration's policy objectives within the 1992 agenda.

CONCLUSION: A RETURN TO THE PROMISE OF THE NEW DEMOCRATS

The task of the Clinton White House for its remaining two years is to gain greater control over the policy process and focus the departments around clearer objectives. The team approach has led to a public perception that the administration lacks leadership. Policies are too slow to emerge and those that have emerged appear too costly. Bill Clinton will have to reduce the emphasis on joint White House–Cabinet policy development and refocus policy development within the White House.

The promise of the New Democrats to rebuild the Democratic Party around centrist principles of governmental action had the support of the American people in 1992. Through a clear electoral mandate, the public gave Bill Clinton the authority to use the power of the national government to stimulate the economy and enhance the lives of its citizenry through educational opportunities, job training, cleaner air and water, and universal health care. Few of the promises targeted by the administration have been accomplished, in large part because each of the programs has been subjected to extensive team analysis. Perhaps less team work and more direction from the White House would yield higher numbers of programmatic initiatives and build public confidence in the leadership skills of the president.

The White House staff changes in the summer of 1994, eighteen months into the administration, may provide tighter White House control of the policy process. With Leon Panetta moving from the Office of Management and Budget to replace Mack McLarty as chief of staff, and tightening the circle around the president, the entire policy process should undergo a reevaluation. Panetta is likely to refocus policy initiatives in the White House and ensure that campaign promises are moved forward in a more systematic way. With the 1996 election rapidly closing in, Panetta should close the broad-based structure in which policy is developed. Departmental participation in policy development will likely be reduced and Panetta's staff more involved in guiding White House decision-making. The team approach within the White House will also likely be reduced, with both the Domestic Policy Council and the National Economic Policy Council moving more independently and less collaboratively in policy development.

Team work is essential in any administration. However, the task for the Clinton administration is to reduce the necessity for team work in decision-making among the fourteen Cabinet departments and move toward team work in implementation. Leadership in policy development has to be focused in the White House.

Part of the explanation for the vacuum in policy leadership is that in its eight years of hibernation as the party out of power, the Democrats failed to unite behind a set of closely defined objectives. Although the Democratic Party was crippled by indecisiveness, Clinton's New Democrats were reluctant to develop policy specifics that would alienate conservative Democrats. Conservative Democrats had been Republican voters for the past three national elections and remained on the fence throughout most of the campaign of 1992. As a result, Clinton moved into the White House with few policy initiatives. Neither the campaign staff nor the transition staff attempted to narrow the agenda or focus policy proposals. Once in office, the task fell to the White House staff and its team of advisors to create the requisite policy initiatives.

The process has been slow and cumbersome. The absence of clearly defined objectives has led to a dwindling approval record. Public support for the president hovers between 45 and 50 per cent in 1995. During the mid-term elections, Democratic candidates shunned White House support in campaigning. The White House will have to gain control of the policy process and gain the confidence of the nation that Bill Clinton is indeed a leader.

NINE

POWERSHARING: CAN IT WORK?

This book began with the premise that powersharing between the Cabinet and the White House staff is a very difficult proposition. Cabinet officers must deal with a host of nonpresidential relationships that divide their loyalties and lead to policy development that often ignore presidential political and programmatic objectives. On the other hand, the federal government is too large, diverse, and at times enigmatic for the White House staff to guide without the substantial support of the Cabinet.

Where, then, does this seeming paradox leave the president? What is the most sensible way to structure the policy development process? Neither the Cabinet nor the White House staff alone appear to be the appropriate mechanism for policy development. The answer would seem to lie in a well-structured system of powersharing in which both the Cabinet and the White House staff share policy development responsibility. The Cabinet provides the president the technical expertise in policy development and implementation, while the White House staff provides the president the assurance that departmental policies meet administration goals and objectives, and are in concert with presidential political ends.

The problem, obviously, is how to establish a workable system in which the Cabinet and White House staff share policy-making power. Power, after all, is a very difficult commodity to share, and one that each actor wants to dominate. Presidents Nixon, Carter, and Reagan each understood, to a greater or lesser degree, that in spite of the problems that could develop, such sharing of policy-making responsibility was the only viable way to structure the decision-making process. By means of a quick refresher on how much government has grown in recent years, the federal budget was $9.5 billion in 1940, $42.6 billion in 1950, $92.2 billion in 1960, $195.6 billion in 1970, $590.9 billion in 1980, $979.9 billion in 1986, and $1.1 trillion in 1988. The growth in the budget reflects the growth in legislative mandates on the federal government and the programmatic responsibilities that emerge from such mandates.

The essence of this book has been to examine how Nixon, Ford, Carter, Reagan, Bush and Clinton established the powersharing relationship between the Cabinet and the White House staff. Ford, Bush and Clinton did not succeed at all at powersharing. Nixon and Carter experimented with a White House staff that had minimal policy responsibilities and found the system unsatisfactory. Ronald Reagan was the only one of the six presidents who attempted a powersharing relationship. What did Reagan do to structure the White House–Cabinet relationship in a more workable fashion than his predecessors? And, more importantly, is that relationship one that can be replicated by future presidents?

REAGAN'S STRUCTURE FOR POWERSHARING

The issue that plagued most presidential experiments with Cabinet Government, as they called it, was the Cabinet's failure to provide policy initiatives that met the president's political and policy objectives. This can be attributed to four general problems.

The first problem was the lack of direction that presidents generally give to their Cabinet officers. Most fail to establish a clear set of goals and objectives for the Cabinet. Reagan, however, gave his Cabinet officers from the very beginning of the administration a list of both general goals and specific objectives. The goals were encompassed in the famous "one hundred day plan" presented to the Cabinet at the first Cabinet meeting. The plan laid out four points that every Cabinet member should focus their departments on:

* reducing agency budgets as a means of reducing the federal budget
* cutting regulations
* cutting taxes
* stabilizing monetary policy

The objectives were discussed by the White House staff with each Cabinet member. Martin Anderson, director of the White House Office of Policy Development, had his staff prepare a list of campaign promises that the president wanted the departments to begin implementing. In addition, Reagan attended numerous cabinet council meetings to ensure that departmental policy initiatives were satisfactory.

The second problem for most presidents is their failure to build a

Cabinet that is committed to presidential goals. Most used the cabinet-building process to ameliorate the dissident wings of their own parties and to bring some geographic and professional diversity to the Cabinet. Carter and Clinton went one step further by using the Cabinet to ensure racial, religious, gender, and ethnic diversity in the administration.

Reagan took another course in cabinet-building by choosing a group who were economically and culturally homogenous (middle-aged, white, well-to-do males) and who were representative of the conservative wing of the Republican Party. As a result, policies which emanated out of the other presidential Cabinets often failed to represent presidential goals.

The third problem was the staffing of sub-Cabinet positions. Most presidents gave their Cabinet officers carte blanche in choosing their subordinates. This quickly proved to be a disaster in other administrations, for policies were developed that ignored presidential goals. Reagan tried very successfully to avoid this problem by requiring all sub-Cabinet officials to be approved by the White House personnel office. All Reagan appointees had to satisfy the White House that they understood the goals of the Reagan administration and that they were committed to those goals. The White House continued throughout the administration to ensure that sub-Cabinet personnel remained committed to the Reagan agenda by holding regular meetings on goals and objectives. This was a calculated move to ensure that the entire senior departmental staff remained ideologically committed and understood the administration's primary goals.

The fourth problem involved executive-legislative relations. Few White House staffs made any attempt to promote a positive working relationship with Congress. During his first six months in office, Nixon essentially ignored Congress and concentrated on foreign policy. He made two major trips out of the country and immersed himself with the National Security Advisor, Henry Kissinger, in finding solutions to the Vietnam war. He paid minimal attention to domestic affairs and rarely met with members of Congress on departmental initiatives. His relations with Congress further deteriorated in June 1969 when the Senate passed the "national commitments resolution" condemning Nixon for committing U.S. troops to the defense of Vietnam without Congressional approval.

Carter fared just as badly with Congress. He too ignored Congress and simply assumed that a Democratically-controlled House and Senate would rubber-stamp presidential initiatives.

As Charles O. Jones noted of Carter, "He seemed genuinely surprised and perplexed by the extent of Congressional involvement in public policy making. One wonders where he had been in the decade before the election."[1]

Carter's naivety on the executive-legislative relationship was at times comical. For example, rather than using engraved presidential pens for bill signings, which were traditionally given out to the sponsors of the bill, Carter used a felt-tip pen which he himself kept after the signing. Similarly, he sold the presidential yacht *Sequoia,* which had been used by past presidents to entertain members of Congress when administration-sponsored legislation was close to a vote. He also seemed to have a total ignorance of Congressional procedures. The barrage of departmental initiatives during the first nine months of the administration resulted in Cabinet secretaries competing for limited space on the Congressional docket and seeking priority for their own programs. This became a major problem during the first year of the administration when the House Ways and Means Committee was considering welfare reform, income tax reform, hospital cost containment, and energy legislation at the same time.

Reagan proved more adept at dealing with Congress than did any of the other five presidents examined here. He began his presidency by calling on senior members of the House and Senate at the Capitol, and pledged to work with them to arrive at mutually acceptable proposals. This was in stark contrast to Jimmy Carter, for instance, who had firmly stated that "I don't know how to compromise on any principle I believe is right."[2]

Reagan met frequently with both Democratic and Republican leaders of Congress during his terms, holding informal breakfast and lunch meetings in the White House to discuss policy issues. He then reinforced his desire to build collegial relations with Congress by regularly inviting members of Congress to state dinners, to share the presidential box at the Kennedy Center, to use the *Sequoia,* to attend Rose Garden ceremonies, and other such events. Reagan was constantly attuned to the personal prestige and political rewards that members of Congress attributed to presidential perks.

POWERSHARING: CAN IT WORK?

Where then does this leave us with regard to establishing a workable system of powersharing between the Cabinet and White House staff? The most important fact at this point is that as long as the federal government continues to grow, the Cabinet will have to be an integral part of the policy-making process. But the White House staff will have to continue to forge the policy direction, to ensure programmatic coordination, and to operate as the president's "firefighters."

Presidents in the future will have to carefully examine the power that they give to their White House staffs in order to avoid abuse of power within the White House. They, after all, have constant access to the president, control his schedule, and know his priorities. They will always have the potential for being the president's primary advisors. Such a system could eventually isolate the president from other sources of advice and result in a failed presidency.

Powersharing is a system that is here to stay. Presidents must give their Cabinet officers primary responsibility for building the administration's policy initiatives in light of the need for technical expertise and legislative support. But the White House staff must share responsibility for policy development with the Cabinet by providing consistent and clearly defined policy objectives for the departments.

The line that both sides are walking, of course, is a difficult one. Where does the White House staff stop? How detailed should their policy objectives be? How involved should they become in refining departmental initiatives? How much authority should they have? Should they stop departmental proposals from going to the president?

The president and his senior advisors must establish the level of authority of the White House staff in regard to policy development at the outset of the administration. Both they and the Cabinet officers must understand the parameters of their respective policy roles. Unless this is clearly and unequivocally defined from the beginning of their relationship, powersharing will fail. The White House staff will seek to dominate the policy process, and Cabinet officers will retreat to their departments and seek to implement their own policy agenda.

It is, after all is said and done, a fragile relationship between the White House staff and the Cabinet. The White House staff, whose loyalty is totally to the president, does not understand the nonpresidential pressures on the Cabinet officers and the Cabinet officers view the White House staff as isolated from the realities of institutional and political demands.

This is not to argue for a right way to structure the White House–Cabinet relationship. Rather it is to argue that the president must be cognizant of the role of both the Cabinet and the White House staff in the advisory system and must ensure that they work in tandem to achieve presidential goals. It is a balance that must be carefully established and one that all of the participants understand. Both the Cabinet and the White House staff have an important role in presidential policy-making, which is the legacy of the ultramodern presidency. Neither can dominate the policy-making process. The future of successful presidential policy-making is premised on a well-structured relationship between the Cabinet officers and the White House staff.

It is doubtful that the term Cabinet Government will continue in future presidencies. It was a term of convenience for Nixon and Carter, and does not reflect the public's view of presidential government. There is no doubt that the Cabinet will continue to play a powerful role in presidential decision-making, but the White House staff will share that role. It is critical that the White

House staff play the lead role in policy development and forge the basic poli-cy options that departments build their initiatives on. Cabinet Government is not a workable organizational structure and the term should be struck from our current political vocabulary.

Presidents should initiate a structure in which the White House staff work closely with their Cabinets and build a team approach to policy-making. The team's quarterback, however, must remain the White House staff.

The Nixon Cabinet
1969–1974

Name	Date of Appointment
Secretary of State	
William P. Rogers	1969
Henry A. Kissinger	1973
Secretary of the Treasury	
David M. Kennedy	1969
John B. Connally	1971
William P. Shultz	1972
William E. Simon	1974
Secretary of Defense	
Melvin R. Laird	1969
Elliot L. Richardson	1973
James R. Schlesinger	1973
Attorney General	
John N. Mitchell	1969
Richard G. Kleindienst	1972
Elliot L. Richardson	1973
William B. Saxbe	1974
Secretary of the Interior	
Walter J. Hickel	1969
Rogers C.B. Morton	1971
Secretary of Agriculture	
Clifford M. Hardin	1969
Earl L. Butz	1971
Secretary of Commerce	
Maurice H. Stans	1969
Peter G. Peterson	1972
Frederick B. Dent	1973
Secretary of Labor	
George P. Shultz	1969

| James D. Hodgson | 1970 |
| Peter J. Brennan | 1973 |

Secretary of Health, Education and Welfare

Robert H. Finch	1969
Elliot L. Richardson	1970
Caspar W. Weinberger	1973

The White House Staff 1969–70

Counselor to the President	Arthur F. Burns
Assistant to the President	Donald Rumsfeld
Counsel to the President	John D. Ehrlichman
Assistant to the President	Peter M. Flanigan
Special Consultant to the President	Leonard Garment
Assistant to the President	H.R. Haldeman
Assistant to the President	Bryce N. Harlow
Special Assistant to the President	James Keogh
Assistant to the President for National Security Affairs	Henry A. Kissinger
Director of Communications for the Executive Branch	Herbert G. Klein
Assistant to the President for Urban Affairs	Daniel P. Moynihan
Secretary to the Cabinet	John C. Whitaker
Special Consultant to the President	Charles B. Wilkinson
Press Secretary	Ronald L. Ziegler
Science Advisor to the President	Lee A. Dubridge
Deputy Assistant to the President for Congressional Relations	Kenneth E. Belieu
Deputy Assistant to the President	Alexander P. Butterfield
Deputy Assistant to the President for Urban Affairs	Stephen Hess
Deputy Assistant to the President for Congressional Relations	William E. Timmons
Deputy Assistant to the President	Darrell M. Trent
Deputy Press Secretary	Gerald L. Warren
Military Assistant to the President	Col. James D. Hughes, USAF
Special Assistant to the President	Martin Anderson
Special Assistant to the President	James D. Atwater
Special Assistant to the President	Robert J. Brown
Special Assistant to the President	Patrick J. Buchanan
Deputy Counsel to the President	Richard T. Burress
Special Assistant to the President	Dwight L. Chapin
Deputy Counsel to the President	Henry C. Cashen II

Special Assistant to the President	Kenneth R. Cole, Jr.
Special Assistant to the President	John S. Davies
Deputy Counsel to the President	Harry S. Dent
Special Assistant to the President	Harry S. Flemming
Special Assistant to the President	H. Dale Grubb
Special Assistant to the President for Consumer Affairs	Mrs. Virginia H. Knauer
Deputy Counsel to the President	Egil Krogh, Jr.
Deputy Counsel to the President	Edward L. Morgan
Special Assistant to the President	Raymond K. Price, Jr.
Special Assistant to the President	William L. Safire
Special Assistant to the President for Liaison with Former Presidents	Robert L. Schulz
Personal Secretary to the President	Rose Mary Woods
Press Secretary to the First Lady	Mrs. Gerry Van Der Heuvcl
Social Secretary	Mrs. Lucy Alexander Winchester
Physician to the President	Col. Walter R. Tkach, USAF, MC
Executive Assistant	William J. Hopkins
Chief Usher	Rex W. Scouten

The White House Staff 1970–71

Counselor to the President.	Robert F. Finch
Counselor to the President.	Bryce N. Harlow
Counselor to the President.	Robert P. Mayo
Counselor to the President.	Dr. Daniel P. Moynihan
Assistant to the President.	Donald Rumsfeld
Assistant to the President for Domestic Affairs.	John D. Ehrlichman
Assistant to the President	Peter M. Flanigan
Assistant to the President	H.R. Haldeman
Assistant to the President for National Security Affairs	Dr. Henry A. Kissinger
Assistant to the President for Congressional Relations	William E. Timmons
Special Consultant to the President	Leonard Garment
Advisor to the President on Manpower Mobilization	Gen. Lewis B. Hershey, USA
Special Assistant to the President	James Keogh
Director of Communications for the Executive Branch	Herbert G. Klein
Special Consultant to the President	Charles B. Wilkinson
Science Advisor to the President	Dr. Lee A. Dubridge
Press Secretary to the President	Ronald L. Ziegler
Military Assistant to the President	Brig. Gen. James D. Hughes, USAF

Special Consultant to the President for Systems Analysis	Dr. Martin Anderson
Deputy Assistant to the President for Senate Relations	Kenneth E. Belieu
Deputy Assistant to the President for Domestic Affairs	Richard T. Burress
Deputy Assistant to the President	Alexander P. Butterfield
Deputy Assistant to the President for Domestic Affairs	Henry C. Cashen II
Special Counsel to the President	Murray M. Chotiner
Deputy Assistant to the President for Domestic Affairs	Kenneth R. Cole, Jr.
Special Counsel to the President	Charles W. Colson
Special Counsel to the President	Harry S. Dent
Deputy Assistant to the President for Domestic Affairs	Egil Krogh, Jr.
Deputy Assistant to the President for Domestic Affairs.	Edward L. Morgan
Deputy Assistant to the President for Congressional Relations	Franklyn C. Nofziger
Deputy Assistant to the President	Darrell M. Trent
Deputy Press Secretary	Gerald L. Warren
Deputy Assistant to the President for Domestic Affairs	John C. Whitaker
Personal Secretary to the President.	Miss Rose Mary Woods
Special Assistant to the President	James D. Atwater
Special Assistant to the President	Robert J. Brown
Special Assistant to the President	Patrick J. Buchanan
Special Assistant to the President	Dwight L. Chapin
Special Assistant to the President	Charles Clapp
Special Assistant to the President	Jack T. Cole
Special Assistant to the President	Richard K. Cook
Special Assistant to the President	Eugene S. Cowen
Special Assistant to the President	John S. Davies
Special Assistant to the President	Harry S. Flemming
Special Assistant to the President	Edwin L. Harper
Special Assistant to the President for Consumer Affairs	Mrs. Virginia H. Knauer
Special Assistant to the President	Jeb S. Magruder
Special Assistant to the President	John R. Price, Jr.
Special Assistant to the President	Raymond K. Price, Jr.
Special Assistant to the President	William L. Safire

Special Assistant to the President for
    Liaison with Former Presidents.   Robert L. Schulz
Special Assistant to the President   Clay T. Whitehead
Staff Director for Mrs. Nixon   Mrs. Constance Stuart
Social Secretary   Mrs. Lucy Alexander
Physician to the President   Brig. Gen. Walter R. Tkach, USAF, MC
Executive Assistant   William J. Hopkins
Chief Usher   Rex W. Scouten

The White House Staff 1971–72

Counselor to the President   Robert H. Finch
Counselor to the President   Donald Rumsfeld
Assistant to the President for Domestic Affairs   John D. Ehrlichman
Assistant to the President   Peter M. Flanigan
Assistant to the President   H.R. Haldeman
Assistant to the President for National
    Security Affairs   Dr. Henry A. Kissinger
Counsel to the President for Congressional Relations   Clark MacGregor
Assistant to the President for International
    Economic Affairs   Peter G. Peterson
Assistant to the President for Congressional
Relations   William E. Timmons
Science Advisor to the President   Edward E. David, Jr.
Special Consultant to the President   Leonard Garment
Special Consultant to the President
    for Narcotics and Dangerous Drugs   Dr. Jerome H. Jaffe
Special Consultant to the President   John A. Scall
Advisor to the President on
Manpower   MobilizationGen. Lewis B. Hershey, USA
Director of Communications for the
    Executive Branch   Herbert G. Klein
Special Assistant to the President   Raymond K. Price, Jr.
Press Secretary to the President   Ronald L. Ziegler
Military Assistant to the President   Brig. Gen. James D. Hughes, Usaf
Deputy Assistant to the President   Alexander P. Butterfield
Deputy Assistant to the President   Dwight L. Chapin
Special Counsel to the President   Charles W. Colson
Counsel to the President   John Wesley Dean III
Special Counsel to the President   Harry S. Dent
Special Counsel to the President   Richard A. Moore
Special Assistant to the President   Frederic V. Malek

Deputy Assistant to the President for National Security Affairs	Brig. Gen. Alexander Meigs Haig, Jr.
Deputy Assistant to the President	John C. Whitaker
Deputy Assistant to the President	Henry C. Cashen II
Deputy Press Secretary	Neal Ball
Deputy Press Secretary	Gerald L. Warren
Personal Secretary to the President	Miss Rose Mary Woods
Special Assistant to the President	George T. Bell
Special Assistant to the President	Patrick J. Buchanan
Special Assistant to the President	Richard K. Cook
Special Assistant to the President	Eugene S. Cowen
Special Assistant to the President	John S. Davies
Special Assistant to the President	Max L. Friedersdorf
Special Assistant to the President	William L. Gifford
Special Assistant to the President	Mark I. Goode
Special Assistant to the President	Jon M. Huntsman
Special Assistant to the President	Roger E. Johnson
Special Assistant to the President	Daniel T. Kingsley
Special Assistant to the President for Consumer Affairs	Mrs. Virginia H. Knauer
Special Assistant to the President	Tom C. Korologos
Special Assistant to the President	William L. Safire
Special Assistant to the President for Liaison with Former Presidents	Robert L. Schulz
Staff Director for Mrs. Nixon	Mrs. Constance Stuart
Social Secretary	Mrs. Lucy Alexander Winchester
Physician to the President	Brig. Gen. Walter R. Tkach, USAF, MC
Chief Usher	Rex W. Scouten

The White House Staff 1972–73

Counselor to the President	Robert H. Finch
Counselor to the President	Donald Rumsfeld
Assistant to the President for Domestic Affairs	John D. Ehrlichman
Assistant to the President	Peter M. Flanigan
Assistant to the President	H.R. Haldeman
Assistant to the President for National Security Affairs	Dr. Henry A. Kissinger
Assistant to the President for Congressional Relations	William E. Timmons
Science Advisor to the President	Edward E. David, Jr.

Special Consultant to the President on Aging	Arthur S. Flemming
Special Consultant to the President	Leonard Garment
Special Consultant to the President for Narcotics and Dangerous Drugs	Dr. Jerome H. Jaffe
Special Consultant to the President	William M. Magruder
Special Consultant to the President	John A. Scali
Advisor to the President on Manpower Mobilization	Gen. Lewis B. Hershey, USA
Director of Communications for the Executive Branch	Herbert G. Klein
Special Assistant to the President	Raymond K. Price, Jr.
Press Secretary to the President	Ronald L. Ziegler
Military Assistant to the President	Brig. Gen. Brent Scowcroft USAF
Deputy Assistant to the President	Alexander P. Butterfield
Deputy Assistant to the President	Dwight L. Chapin
Special Counsel to the President	Charles W. Colson
Counsel to the President	John Wesley Dean III
Special Counsel to the President	Harry S. Dent
Special Counsel to the President	Richard A. Moore
Special Assistant to the President	Frederic V. Malek
Deputy Assistant to the President for National Security Affairs	Maj. Gen. Alexander Meigs Haig, Jr., USA
Deputy Assistant to the President for Congressional Relations	Richard K. Cook
Deputy Assistant to the President for Congressional Relations	Tom C. Korologos
Deputy Assistant to the President	John C. Whitaker
Deputy Assistant to the President	Henry C. Cashen II
Deputy Press Secretary	Neal Ball
Deputy Director of Communications for the Executive Branch	Ken W. Clawson
Deputy Press Secretary	Gerald L. Warren
Personal Secretary to the President	Rose Mary Woods
Special Assistant to the President	Desmond J. Barker, Jr.
Special Assistant to the President	George T. Bell
Special Assistant to the President	Patrick J. Buchanan
Special Assistant to the President	Michael J. Farrell
Special Assistant to the President	Max L. Friedersdorf
Special Assistant to the President	William L. Gifford
Special Assistant to the President	Mark I. Goode
Special Assistant to the President	Wallace H. Johnson
Special Assistant to the President	Daniel T. Kingsley

Special Assistant to the President for Consumer Affairs   Virginia H. Knauer
Special Assistant to the President   Jonathan C. Rose
Special Assistant to the President   William L. Safire
Special Assistant to the President for
    Liaison with Former Presidents   Robert L. Schulz
Special Assistant to the President   Ronald H. Walker
Staff Director for Mrs. Nixon   Constance Stuart
Social Security   Lucy Alexander Winchester
Physician to the President   Maj. Gen. Walter R. Tkach, USAF, MC
Chief Executive Clerk   Noble M. Melencamp
Chief Usher   Rex W. Scouten

The White House Staff 1973–74

Counselor to the President   Anne L. Armstrong
Counselor to the President   Bryce N. Harlow
Counselor to the President for Domestic Affairs   Melvin R. Laird
Assistant to the President   Dr. Henry A. Kissinger
Assistant to the President   Peter M. Flanigan
Assistant to the President   Gen. Alexander Meigs Haig, Jr., USA (Ret.)1
Special Advisor to the President   John B. Connally
Assistant to the President for Legislative Affairs   William E. Timmons
Assistant to the President and Press Secretary   Ronald L. Ziegler
Counsel to the President   Leonard Garment
Special Consultant to the President   Raymond K. Price, Jr.
Military Assistant to the President   Brig. Gen. Brent Scowcroft, USAF
Special Assistant to the President   William J. Baroody, Jr.
Special Counsel to the President   Richard A. Moore
Special Counsel to the President   J. Fred Buzhardt, Interim
Special Consultant to the President   Patrick J. Buchanan
Special Consultant to the President   Charles J. Dibona
Deputy Assistant to the President   John Charles Bennett
Deputy Assistant to the President for
    Legislative Affairs   Tom C. Korologos
Deputy Assistant to the President for
    Legislative Affairs   Max I. Friedersdorf
Executive Assistant and Personal Secretary
to the President   Rose Mary Woods
Deputy Press Secretary   Gerald L. Warren
Deputy Press Secretary   Ken W. Clawson
Deputy Press Secretary   Andrew T. Falkiewicz
Special Assistant to the President   Virginia H. Knauer

Special Assistant to the President for Legislative Affairs	Wilburn Eugene Ainsworth, Jr.
Special Assistant to the President	Michael J. Farrell
Special Assistant to the President	Lyndon K. Allin
Special Assistant to the President	Stephen B. Bull
Deputy Counsel to the President	Fred F. Fielding
Special Assistant to the President	David R. Gergen
Special Assistant to the President	W. Richard Howard
Special Assistant to the President	Lee W. Huebner
Special Assistant to the President	Jerry H. Jones
Special Assistant to the President	Bruce A. Kehrll
Special Assistant to the President	David N. Parker
Special Assistant to the President	Stanley S. Scott
Special Assistant to the President for Legislative Affairs	James M. Sparling, Jr.
Special Assistant to the President for Legislative Affairs	Frederick L. Webber
Social Secretary	Lucy Alexander Winchester
Physician to the President	Maj. Gen. Walter R. Tkach, USAF, MC
Chief Executive Clerk	Robert D. Linder
Chief Usher	Rex W. Scouten

The Ford Cabinet 1974–1977

Name	Date of Appointment
Secretary of State	
Henry Kissinger	1973
Secretary of Treasury	
William E. Simon	1974
Secretary of Defense	
James R. Schlesinger	1974
Donald H. Rumsfeld	1975
Attorney General	
William B. Saxbe	1974
Edward H. Levi	1975
Secretary of the Interior	
Rogers C.B. Morton	1971
Stanley K. Hathaway	1975
Thomas S. Kleppe	1975
Secretary of Agriculture	
Earl L. Butz	1971
John A. Knebel	1976
Secretary of Commerce	
Frederick B. Dent	1973
Rogers C.B. Morton	1975
Elliot L. Richardson	1975
Secretary of Labor	
Peter J. Brennan	1973
John T. Dunlop	1975
W.J. Usery, Jr.	1976
Secretary of Health, Education and Welfare	
Caspar W. Weinberger	1973
Forrest D. Mathews	1975

Secretary of Housing and Urban Development
James T. Lynn	1973
Carla Anderson Hills	1975

Secretary of Transportation
Claude S. Brinegar	1973
William T. Coleman, Jr.	1975

The White House Staff 1974–75

Counselor to the President	Anne L. Armstrong
Counselor to the President	Dean Burch
Counselor to the President	Robert T. Hartmann
Counselor to the President	John O. Marsh, Jr.
Counselor to the President for Economic Policy	Kenneth Rush
Assistant to the President	Roy L. Ash
Assistant to the President for Domestic Affairs	Kenneth R. Cole, Jr.
Assistant to the President	Gen. Alexander M. Haig, Jr., USA (Ret.)
Assistant to the President	Dr. Henry A. Kissinger
Assistant to the President	William E. Timmons
Counsel to the President	Philip W. Buchen
Press Secretary to the President	J.F. TerHorst
Special Consultant to the President	William J. Baroody, Jr.
Military Assistant to the President	Maj. Gen. Richard L. Lawson, USAF
Deputy Press Secretary to the President	Andrew T. Falkiewicz
Deputy Assistant to the President	Max L. Friedersdorf
Deputy Press Secretary to the President	John W. Hushen
Deputy Assistant to the President	Sidney L. Jones
Deputy Assistant to the President	Tom C. Korologos
Deputy Assistant to the President for National Security Affairs	Lt. Gen. Brent Scowcroft, USAF
Special Assistant to the President	Virginia H. Knauer
Special Assistant to the President	Wilburn Eugene Ainsworth, Jr.
Special Assistant to the President	Fernando E.C. Debaca
Assistant Press Secretary to the President	Thomas P. Decair
Special Assistant to the President	Roland L. Elliott
Special Assistant to the President	Michael J. Farrell
Special Assistant to the President	David R. Gergen
Special Assistant to the President	William Henkel, Jr.
Assistant Press Secretary to the President	James R. Holland
Special Assistant to the President	David C. Hoopes
Special Assistant to the President	Jerry H. Jones

Special Assistant to the President	Lt. Col. George A. Joulwan, USA
Special Assistant to the President	Vernon C. Loen
Special Assistant to the President	Charles M. Lichenstein
Special Assistant to the President	Theodore C. Marrs
Special Assistant to the President	Paul A. Miltich
Special Assistant to the President	John E. Nidecker
Special Assistant to the President	Patrick E. O'Donnell
Special Assistant to the President	Terrence O'Donnell
Appointments Secretary to the President	Warren S. Rustand
Special Assistant to the President	Stanley S. Scott
Special Assistant to the President	W.J. Usery, Jr.
Special Assistant to the President	David J. Wimer
Social Secretary	Lucy Alexander Winchester
Director, Office of Presidential Messages	Eliska A. Hasek
Deputy Staff Secretary to the President	David C. Hoopes
Personal Photographer to the President	David Hume Kennerly
Personal Assistant to the President	Mildred V. Leonard
Special Assistant for Legislative Affairs (House)	Charles Leppert, Jr.
Special Assistant for Legislative Affairs (Senate)	Patrick E. O'Donnell
Aide to the President	Terrence O'Donnell
Assistant Press Secretary	John W. Roberts
Executive Assistant to the Counselor to the President	Russell A. Rourke
Director, Scheduling Office	Warren S. Rustand
Assistant Press Secretary (Foreign Affairs)	Edward J. Savage
Assistant Press Secretary	Larry M. Speakes
Director, Research Office	Agnes M. Waldron
Deputy Director, Office of Public Liaison	Donald A. Webster
Deputy Director, Presidential Personnel Office	M. Alan Woods
Social Secretary	Nancy Ruwe
Press Secretary to the First Lady	Sheila Rabb Weidenfeld
Physician to the President	Rear Adm. William M. Lukash, Mc, USN
Chief Executive Clerk	Robert D. Linder
Chief Usher	Rex W. Scouten

The White House Staff 1975–76

Counsel to the President	Philip W. Buchen
Counselor to the President	Robert T. Hartmann
Assistant to the President	Henry A. Kissinger
Counselor to the President	John O. Marsh, Jr.
Assistant to the President	Donald H. Rumsfeld
Assistant to the President for Management and Budget	James T. Lynn

Press Secretary to the President	Ronald H. Nessen
Assistant to the President for Economic Affairs	L. William Seidman
Assistant to the President for Domestic Affairs	James M. Cannon
Assistant to the President for Public Liaison	William J. Baroody, Jr.
Assistant to the President for Legislative Affairs	Max L. Friedersdorf
Counsel to the President	Roderick M. Hills
Deputy Assistant to the President	Richard B. Cheney
Deputy Press Secretary to the President	William I. Greener, Jr.
Deputy Press Secretary to the President	John W. Hushen
Deputy Assistant to the President for National Security Affairs	Lt. Gen. Brent Scowcroft, USAF
Counsel to the President	William E. Casselman II
Special Consultant to the President	Robert A. Goldwin
Deputy Press Secretary to the President	Gerald L. Warren
Deputy Assistant to the President for Legislative Affairs (Senate)	William T. Kendall
Deputy Assistant to the President for Legislative Affairs (House)	Vernon C. Loen
Secretary to the Cabinet	James E. Connor
Special Assistant to the President for Hispanic Affairs	Fernando E.C. Debaca
Staff Secretary to the President	Jerry H. Jones
Special Assistant to the President for Consumer Affairs	Virginia H. Knauer
Military Assistant to the President	Capt. Leland S.Kollmorgen, USN
Associate Counsel to the President	Kenneth A. Lazarus
Associate Counsel to the President	James A. Wilderotter
Special Assistant to the President for Women	Patricia S. Lindh
Special Assistant to the President for Human Resources	Theodore C. Marrs
Special Assistant to the President for Minority Affairs	Stanley S. Scott
Executive Editor, Editorial Office	Paul A. Theis
Special Assistant to the President for Labor-Management Negotiations	W.J. Usery
Director, Presidential Personnel Office	William N. Walker
Assistant Press Secretary to the President	Margareta E. White
Deputy Executive Assistant to the Counselor to the President	Gwen A. Anderson
Special Assistant for Legislative Affairs (House)	Douglas P. Bennett
Executive Assistant to the Counselor to the President	John T. Calkins
Director, Advance Office	Byron M. Cavaney, Jr.
Assistant Press Secretary (Domestic Affairs)	John G. Carlson

Assistant Press Secretary to the President	Thomas P. Decair
Associate Counsel	Dudley H. Chapman
Personal Secretary to the President	Dorothy E. Downton
Director, Correspondence Office	Roland L. Elliott
Director, Office of White House Visitors	Michael J. Farrell
Deputy Editor, Editorial Office	Milton A. Friedman
Director, Office of Presidential Messages	Eliska A. Hasek
Deputy Staff Secretary to the President	David C. Hoopes
Personal Photographer to the President	David Hume Kennerly
Personal Assistant to the President	Mildred V. Leonard
Special Assistant for Legislative Affairs (House)	Charles Leppert, Jr.
Special Assistant for Legislative Affairs (Senate)	Patrick E. O'donnell
Aide to the President	Terrence O'donnell
Assistant Press Secretary	John W. Roberts
Executive Assistant to the Counselor to the President	Russell A. Rourke
Director, Scheduling Office	Warren S. Rustand
Assistant Press Secretary (Foreign Affairs)	Edward J. Savage
Assistant Press Secretary	Larry M. Speakes
Director, Research Office	Agnes M. Waldron
Deputy Director, Office of Public Liaison	Donald A. Webster
Deputy Director, Presidential Personnel Office	M. Alan Woods
Social Secretary	Nancy Ruwe
Press Secretary to the First Lady	Sheila Rabb Weidenfeld
Physician to the President	Rear Adm. William M. Lukash, MC, USN
Chief Executive Clerk	Robert D. Linder
Chief Usher	Rex W. Scouten

The White House Staff 1976–77

Counsel to the President	Philip W. Buchen
Counselor to the President	Robert T. Hartmann
Counselor to the President	John O. Marsh, Jr.
Assistant to the President	Richard B. Cheney
Assistant to the President for Public Liaison	William J. Baroody, Jr.
Assistant to the President for Domestic Affairs	James M. Cannon
Assistant to the President for Legislative Affairs	Max L. Friedersdorf
Assistant to the President for Management and Budget	James T. Lynn
Assistant to the President for National Security Affairs	Lt. Gen. Brent Scowcroft, USAF (Ret.)
Assistant to the President for Economic Affairs	L. William Seidman
Press Secretary to the President	Ronald H. Nessen
Deputy Press Secretary to the President	John G. Carlson

Deputy Assistant to the President for Domestic Affairs James H. Cavanaugh
Deputy Assistant to the President for Urban Affairs   Arthur A. Fletcher
Deputy Assistant to the President for Economic Affairs   William F. Gorog
Deputy Assistant to the President for
    National Security Affairs   William G. Hyland
Deputy Assistant to the President for
    Legislative Affairs (Senate)   William T. Kendall
Deputy Assistant to the President for
    Legislative Affairs (House)   Charles Leppert, Jr.
Deputy Counsel to the President   Edward C. Schmults
Secretary to the Cabinet and Staff
    Secretary to the President   James E. Connor
Special Consultant to the President   Robert A. Goldwin
Director, Presidential Personnel Office   Douglas P. Bennett
Special Assistant to the President for Minority Affairs   John C. Calhoun
Special Assistant to the President   Byron M. Cavaney, Jr.
Special Assistant to the President   Milton A. Friedman
Special Counsel to the President   David R. Gergen
Special Assistant to the President
    for Women   Maj. Gen. Jeanne M. Holm, USAF (RET.)
Special Assistant to the President   Jerry H. Jones
Special Assistant to the President for Consumer Affairs   Virginia H. Knauer
Military Assistant to the President   Capt. Leland S. Kollmorgen, USN
Special Assistant to the President for Ethnic Affairs   Myron B. Kuropas
Associate Counsel to the President   Kenneth A. Lazarus
Special Assistant to the President for
    Intergovernmental Affairs   Stephen G. Mcconamey
Special Assistant to the President
    for Human Resources   Theodore C. Marrs
Special Assistant to the President   Robert Orden
Special Counsel to the President   Michael Raoul-Duval
Assistant Press Secretary to the President   Larry M. Speakes
Assistant Press Secretary to the President   Margareta E. White
Editor, Presidential Messages and Research   Gwen A. Anderson
Director, Press Advance Office   Douglass C. Blaser
Personal Secretary to the President   Dorothy E. Downton
Director, Correspondence Office   Roland L. Elliott
Director, Office of White House Visitors   Michael J. Farrell
Director, Office of Presidential Messages   Eliska A. Hasek
Director, Office of Presidential Spokesmen   Warren K. Hendriks, Jr.
Deputy Staff Secretary to the President   David C. Hoopes
Special Assistant for Legislative Affairs (Senate)   Joseph S. Jenckes V

Associate Counsel	Barbara G. Kilberg
Personal Photographer to the President	David Hume Kennerly
Personal Assistant to the President	Mildred V. Leonard
Special Assistant for Legislative Affairs (House)	Thomas L. Loeffler
Director, Research Office	Charles H. Mccall
Deputy Director, Presidential Personnel Office	Peter M. Mcpherson
Director, Scheduling Office	William W. Nicholson
Aide to the President	Terrence O'Donnell
Special Assistant for Legislative Affairs (House)	J. Patrick Rowland
Executive Secretary, Economic Policy Board	Roger B. Porter
Assistant Press Secretary	John W. Roberts
Executive Assistant to the Counsellor to the President	Russell A. Rourke
Deputy to the Assistant to the President for Legislative Affairs	Robert K. Wolthuis
Social Secretary	Maria Downs
Press Secretary to the First Lady	Sheila Rabb Weidenfeld
Physician to the President	Rear Adm. William M. Lukash, MC USN
Chief Executive Clerk	Robert D. Linder
Chief Usher	Rex W. Scouten

The Carter Cabinet, 1977–1981

Name	*Date of Appointment*
Secretary of State	
Cyrus R. Vance	1977
Edmund S. Muskie	1980
Secretary of Treasury	
W. Michael Blumenthal	1977
G. William Miller	1979
Secretary of Defense	
Harold Brown	1977
Attorney General	
Griffin B. Bell	1977
Benjamin R. Civiletti	1979
Secretary of the Interior	
Cecil D. Andrus	1977
Secretary of Agriculture	
Bob Bergland	1977
Secretary of Commerce	
Juanita M. Kreps	1977
Philip M. Klutznick	1979
Secretary of Health Education and Welfare	
Joseph A. Califano, Jr.	1977
Patricia Roberts Harris	1979
Secretary of Health and Human Services	
Patricia Roberts Harris	1979
Secretary of Education	
Shirley Hufstedler	1979
Secretary of Housing and Urban Development	
Patricia Roberts Harris	1977
Moon Landrieu	1979

Secretary of Transportation
Brock Adams   1977
Neil Goldschmidt   1979

Secretary of Energy
James R. Schlesinger   1977
Robert W. Duncan, Jr.   1979

The White House Staff 1977–78

Assistant to the President for National Security Affairs	Zbigniew Brzezinski
Assistant to the President for Public Liaison	Margaret Costanza
Assistant to the President for Domestic Affairs and Policy	Stuart E. Eizenstat
Assistant to the President	Hamilton Jordan
Counsel to the President	Robert J. Lipshutz
Assistant to the President for Congressional Liaison	Frank B. Moore
Assistant to the President for Reorganization	Richard A. Pettigrew
Press Secretary to the President	Joseph L. Powell
Assistant to the President	James R. Schlesinger
Secretary to the Cabinet and Assistant to the President for Intergovernmental Affairs	Jack H. Watson, Jr.
Special Assistant to the President	Joseph W. Aragon
Special Assistant to the President for Health Issues	Peter G. Bourne
Special Assistant to the President for Administration	Hugh A. Carter, Jr.
Special Assistant to the President for Budget and Organization	Richard M. Harden
Special Assistant to the President for Media and Public Affairs	Barry Jagoda
Special Assistant to the President for Personnel	James B. King
Special Assistant to the President for Appointments	Timothy E. Kraft
Special Assistant to the President for Special Projects	Martha M. Mitchell
Special Assistant to the President for Consumer Affairs	Esther Peterson
Personal Assistant/Secretary to the President	Susan S. Clough
Press Secretary to the First Lady and East Wing Coordinator	Mary Finch Hoyt
Personal Assistant to the First Lady	Madeline F. Macbean
Social Secretary	Gretchen Poston
Social Assistant to the President	Maxie Wells
Deputy Assistant for National Security Affairs	David L. Aaron

Deputy Assistant for Intergovernmental Affairs	Lawrence A. Bailey
Deputy Assistant	Landon Butler
Deputy Assistant for Congressional Liaison (House)	William H.Cable
Deputy Director, Domestic Council	Bertram W. Carp
Deputy Secretary to the Cabinet	Jane L. Frank
Deputy Press Secretary	Rex L. Granum
Deputy Counsel	Margaret A. Mckenna
Deputy Assistant for Public Liaison	Robert A. Nastanovich
Deputy Assistant for Domestic Affairs and Policy	David M. Rubenstein
Director, White House Projects	Gregory S. Schneiders
Deputy Associate for Congressional Affairs (Senate)	Danny C. Tate
Deputy Press Secretary	Walter W. Wurfel
Deputy Press Secretary to the First Lady	Ann M. Anderson
Senior Associate Counsel	Michael H. Cardozo V
Associate Press Secretary	Walter E. Duka
Chief Speechwriter	James M. Fallows
Special Assistant for Congressional Liaison (Legislative Projects)	Leslie C. Francis
Special Assistant for Congressional Liaison (House)	James C. Free
Deputy Special Assistant for Personnel	James F. Gammill, Jr.
Senior Associate Counsel	Douglas B. Huron
Staff Secretary	Richard G. Hutcheson III
Associate for Intergovernmental Affairs	Bruce Kirschenbaum
Associate for Intergovernmental Affairs	Thomas M. Parham, Jr.
Special Assistant for Congressional Liaison (House)	Valerie F. Pinson
Deputy Assistant for Research	Elizabeth A. Rainwater
Special Assistant for Congressional Liaison (Administration)	Robert K. Russell, Jr.
Special Assistant for Congressional Liaison (Senate)	Robert Thomson
Associate for Public Liaison	S. Stephen Selig III
Deputy Assistant for Policy Analysis	Mark A. Siegel
Deputy Special Assistant for Appointments	Timothy G. Smith
Director of Scheduling	Frances M. Voorde
Associate Counsel	Patrick Apodaga
Associate Press Secretary	Patricia Y. Bario
Director of Projects/Issues/Research for the First Lady	Kathryn E. Cade
Associate Special Assistant for Personnel (Operations)	Michael Cushing
Speechwriter	Jerome H. Doolittle
Associate Press Secretary	William Drummond
Appointments Secretary to the First Lady	Jane S. Fenderson
Associate Special Assistant for Personnel (Financial, Regulatory, Legal Agencies)	Lisbeth K. Godley

Associate Special Assistant for Appointments   J. William Heckman, Jr.
Speechwriter   Achsah P. Nesmith
Deputy Special Assistant for Media
    and Public Affairs   Richard M. Neustadt
Associate Special Assistant for Personnel (Advisory
    Boards and Non-Salaried Appointments)   Peggy E. Rainwater
Associate Special Assistant for Personnel
    (Human Services, International Transportation)   Diana Rock
Associate Press Secretary   Jerrold Schecter
Deputy Staff Secretary   William D. Simon
Speechwriter   Griffin Smith, Jr.
Director, Research Office   Stephen M. Travis
Editor, News Summary   Claudia M. Townsend
Coordinator, Visitors Office   Nancy A. Willing
Director of Advance   Ellis A. Woodward
Director, White House Military Office   Warren L. Gulley
Physician to the President   Rear Adm. William M. Lukash, MC USN
Chief Executive Clerk   Robert D. Linder
Chief Usher   Rex W. Scouten

The White House Staff 1978–79

Assistant to the President for
National Security Affairs   Zbigniew Brzezinski
Assistant to the President for Public Liaison   Margaret Costanza
Assistant to the President for
    Domestic Affairs and Policy   Stuart E. Eizenstat
Assistant to the President   Hamilton Jordan
Assistant to the President   Timothy E. Kraft
Counsel to the President   Robert J. Lipshutz
Assistant to the President for Congressional Liaison   Frank B. Moore
Assistant to the President for Reorganization   Richard A. Pettigrew
Press Secretary to the President   Joseph L. Powell
Secretary to the Cabinet and Assistant
    to the President for Intergovernmental Affairs   Jack H. Watson, Jr.
Assistant to the President   Anne Wexler
Special Assistant to the President   Joseph W. Aragon
Special Assistant to the President for
    Health Issues   Peter G. Bourne
Special Assistant to the President for Administration   Hugh A. Carter, Jr.
Special Assistant to the President for
    Information Management   Richard M. Harden

Special Assistant to the President for Media and Public Affairs	Barry Jagoda
Special Assistant to the President for Special Projects	Martha M. Mithcell
Special Assistant to the President for Consumer Affairs	Esther Peterson
Appointments Secretary to the President	Phillip J. Wise, Jr.
Counsellor to the President on Aging	Nelson Cruikshank
Personal Assistant/Secretary to the President	Susan S. Clough
Press Secretary to the First Lady and East Wing Coordinator	Mary Finch Hoyt
Personal Assistant to the First Lady	Madeline F. Macbean
Social Secretary	Gretchen Poston
Deputy Assistant for National Security Affairs	David L. Aaron
Deputy to the Assistant to the President	Landon Butler
Deputy Assistant for Congressional Liaison (House)	William H. Cable
Deputy Assistant for Domestic Affairs and Policy	Bertram W. Carp
Deputy to the Assistant to the President	Michael H. Chanin
Deputy Secretary to the Cabinet	Jane L. Frank
Deputy Press Secretary	Rex L. Granum
Deputy Counsel	Margaret A. Mckenna
Deputy Assistant for Domestic Affairs and Policy	David M. Rubenstein
Director, White House Projects	Gregory S. Schneiders
Deputy Assistant for Congressional Liaison (Senate)	Danny C. Tate
Deputy Assistant for Public Liaison	Seymour Wishman
Deputy Press Secretary	Walter W. Wurfel
Director, White House Military Office	Marvin L. Beaman, Jr.
Special Assistant for Congressional Liaison (House)	Robert G. Beckel
Senior Associate Counsel	Michael H. Cardozo V
Chief Speechwriter	James M. Fallows
Appointments Secretary to the First Lady	Jane S. Fenderson
Special Assistant for Congressional Liaison (Legislative Projects)	Leslie C. Francis
Special Assistant for Congressional Liaison (House)	James C. Free
Director of the Presidential Personnel Office	James F. Gammill, Jr.
Director, White House Operations	Valerio L. Giannini
Associate for Intergovernmental Affairs	Lawrence D. Gilson
Senior Associate Counsel	Douglas B. Huron
Staff Secretary	Richard G. Hutcheson III
Associate for Intergovernmental Affairs	Bruce Kirschenbaum
Special Assistant for Congressional Liaison (House)	Valerie F. Pinson
Deputy Assistant for Research	Elizabeth A. Rainwater
Special Assistant for Congressional Liaison	Robert K. Russell, Jr.
Deputy Assistant	S. Stephen Selig III

Special Assistant for Congressional Liaison (Senate)	Robert Thomson
Associate Press Secretary	Claudia M. Townsend
Deputy Appointments Secretary	Frances M. Voorde
Counsel to the Intelligence Oversight Board	Burton V. Wides
Deputy Press Secretary to the First Lady	Ann M. Anderson
Associate Counsel	Patrick Apodaca
Associate Press Secretary	Patricia Y. Bario
Editor, News Summary	Patricia E. Bauer
Director of Projects/Issues/Research for the First Lady	Kathryn E. Cade
Director, Office of Presidential Messages	Eliska Hasek Coolidge
Speechwriter	Jerome H. Doolittle
Associate Press Secretary	Marc T. Henderson
Special Assistant to the Assistant for Domestic Affairs and Policy	Joanne K. Hurley
Speechwriter	Achsah P. Nesmith
Associate Director, Presidential Personnel Office	Peggy E. Rainwater
Associate Director, Presidential Personnel Office	Diana Rock
Associate Press Secretary	Jerrold Schecter
Speechwriter	Griffin Smith, Jr.
Director, Visitors Office	Nancy A. Willing
Director of Advance	Ellis A. Woodward
Physician to the President	Rear Adm. William M. Lukash, MC USN
Chief Executive Clerk	Robert D. Linder
Chief Usher	Rex W. Scouten

The White House Staff 1979–80

Assistant to the President for National Security Affairs	Zbigniew Brzezinski
Assistant to the President for Domestic Affairs	Stuart E. Eizenstat
Assistant to the President	Hamilton Jordan
Advisor to the President on Inflation	Alfred E. Kahn
Assistant to the President	Timothy E. Kraft
Counsel to the President	Robert J. Lipshutz
Assistant to the President for Congressional Liaison	Frank B. Moore
Assistant to the President for Reorganization	Richard A. Pettigrew
Press Secretary to the President	Joseph L. Powell
Assistant to the President for Communications	Gerald M. Rafshoon
Secretary to the Cabinet and Assistant to the President for Intergovernmental Affairs	Jack H. Watson, Jr.
Assistant to the President	Anne Wexler
Special Assistant to the President for Administration	Hugh A. Carter, Jr.

Special Assistant to the President for Information Management	Richard M. Harden
Special Assistant to the President	Louis E. Martin
Special Assistant to the President for Consumer Affairs	Esther Peterson
Special Assistant to the President	Sarah C. Weddington
Appointments Secretary to the President	Phillip J. Wise, Jr.
Counselor to the President on Aging	Nelson H. Cruikshank
Deputy Assistant for National Security Affairs	David L. Aaron
Deputy Press Secretary	Patricia Y. Bario
Deputy Assistant to the President	Landon Butler
Deputy Assistant for Congressional Liaison (House)	William H. Cable
Deputy Assistant for Domestic Affairs and Policy	Bertram W. Carp
Deputy to the Assistant to the President	Michael H. Chanin
Deputy Assistant to the President for Intergovernmental Affairs and Deputy Secretary to the Cabinet	Eugene Eidenberg
Deputy Assistant for Congressional Liaison Coordination	Leslie C. Francis
Deputy Press Secretary	Rex L. Granum
Deputy Assistant for Political Liaison	Joel Mccleary
Deputy Counsel	Margaret A. McKenna
Deputy Assistant for Domestic Affairs and Policy	David M. Rubenstein
Deputy to the Assistant to the President for Communications	Gregory S. Schneiders
Deputy Assistant for Congressional Liaison (Senate)	Danny C. Tate
Special Assistant for Congressional Liaison (House)	Robert G. Beckel
Senior Associate Counsel	Michael H. Cardozo V
Personal Assistant/Secretary to the President	Susan S. Clough
Associate for Congressional Liaison Coordination	James M. Copeland, Jr.
Special Assistant for Congressional Liaison (House)	James C. Free
Associate for Intergovernmental Affairs	Lawrence D. Gilson
Deputy Assistant for Political Liaison	Richard Hernandez
Press Secretary to the First Lady and Staff Coordinator	Mary Finch Hoyt
Senior Associate Counsel	Douglas B. Huron
Staff Secretary	Richard G. Hutcheson III
Associate for Intergovernmental Affairs	Bruce Kirschenbaum
Special Assistant for Congressional Liaison (House)	Robert W. Maher
Director of the Presidential Personnel Office	Arnie Miller
Special Assistant for Congressional Liaison (House)	Valerie F. Pinson
Deputy Assistant for Research	Elizabeth A. Rainwater
Special Assistant for Congressional Liaison	Robert K. Russell, Jr.
Deputy Assistant (Jordan)	S. Stephen Selig III

Special Assistant for Congressional Liaison (House)	Terrence D. Straub
Special Assistant for Congressional Liaison (Senate)	Robert Thomson
Deputy Appointments Secretary	Frances M. Voorde
Deputy Special Assistant for Administration—Military Office	Marvin L. Beaman, Jr.
Deputy Special Assistant for Administration	Valerio L. Giannini
Deputy Special Assistant for Administration—White House Operations	Daniel Malachuk, Jr.
Personal Assistant to the First Lady	Madeline F. Macbean
Social Secretary	Grethcen Poston
Deputy Director of the Presidential Personnel Office	Harley Frankel
Associate Assistant (Wexler)	Jane D. Hartley
Chief Speechwriter	Hendrik Hertzberg
Counsel to the Intelligence Oversight Board	Gilbert L. Kujovich
Associate Press Secretary	Claudia M. Townsend
Associate Director, Presidential Personnel Office	Peggy E. Rainwater
White House Fellow	James H. Scott
Associate Press Secretary	Marc T. Henderson
Special Assistant to the Assistant for Domestic Affairs and Policy	Joanne K. Hurley
Director, Office of Presidential Messages	Eliska Hasek Coolidge
Deputy to the Assistant to the President	Thomas V. Beard
Director of Projects for the First Lady	Kathryn E. Cade
Director of Community Liaison (First Lady)	Jane S. Fenderson
Director of Advance	Ellis A. Woodward
Director, Visitors Office	Nancy A. Willing
Deputy Press Secretary (First Lady)	Faith A. Collins
Editor, News Summary	Patricia E. Bauer
Curator	Clement E. Conger
Chief Executive Clerk	Robert D. Linder
Physician to the President	Rear Adm. William M.Lukash, MC USN
Chief Usher	Rex W. Scouten

The White House Staff 1980–81

Assistant to the President	Hamilton Jordan
Assistant to the President for National Security Affairs	Zbigniew Brzezinski
Counsel to the President	Lloyd N. Cutler
Staff Director for the First Lady	Edith J. Dobelle
Senior Adviser to the President	Hedley Donovan
Assistant to the President for Domestic Affairs & Policy	Stuart E. Eizenstat
Advisor to the President on Inflation	Alfred E. Kahn

Assistant to the President and
Staff Director Alonzo Lowry McDonald, Jr.
Assistant to the President for Congressional Liaison Frank B. Moore
Press Secretary to the President Joseph L. Powell
Secretary to the Cabinet and Assistant
to the President for Intergovernmental Affairs Jack H. Watson, Jr.
Assistant to the President Sarah C. Weddington
Assistant to the President Anne Wexler
Special Assistant to the President for Ethnic Affairs Stephen R. Aiello
Special Assistant to the President for Administration Hugh A. Carter, Jr.
Special Assistant to the President
for Information Management Richard M. Harden
Special Assistant to the President C. Ray Jenkins
Special Assistant to the President Louis E. Martin
Special Advisor to the President Alfred H. Moses
Special Assistant to the President for Consumer Affairs Esther Peterson
Special Assistant to the President for Hispanic Affairs Esteban E. Torres
Appointments Secretary to the President Phillip J. Wise, Jr.
Counselor to the President on Aging Harold L. Sheppard
Deputy Assistant for National Security Affairs David L. Aaron
Deputy Press Secretary Patricia Y. Bario
Deputy Assistant to the President Landon Butler
Deputy Assistant for Congressional Liaison (House) William H. Cable
Deputy Counsel Michael H. Cardozo V
Deputy Assistant for Domestic Affairs and Policy Bertram W. Carp
Deputy to the Assistant to the President Michael H. Chanin
Deputy Appointments Secretary Robert H. Dunn
Deputy Assistant to the President for Intergovernmental
Affairs and Deputy Secretary to the Cabinet Eugene Eidenberg
Deputy Assistant for Congressional
Liaison (Legislative Coordination) James M. Copeland, Jr.
Deputy Press Secretary Rex L. Granum
Deputy Counsel Joseph N. Onek
Deputy Assistant for Domestic Affairs and Policy David M. Rubinstein
Deputy Assistant for Congressional Liaison (Senate) Danny C. Tate
Deputy Assistant to the President William E. Albers
Special Assistant for Congressional Liaison (House) Robert G. Beckel
Personal Assistant/Secretary to the President Susan S. Clough
Special Assistant for Congressional Liaison (House) James C. Free
Deputy Assistant for Political Liaison Richard Hernandez
Chief Speechwriter Hendrik Hertzberg
Press Secretary to the First Lady Mary Finch Hoyt

Senior Associate Counsel	Douglas B. Huron
Staff Secretary	Richard G. Hutcheson III
Associate for Intergovernmental Affairs	Bruce Kirschenbaum
Special Assistant for Congressional Liaison (House)	Robert W. Maher
Director of the Presidential Personnel Office	Arnie Miller
Special Assistant for Congressional Liaison (House)	Valerie F. Pinson
Deputy Assistant for Research	Elizabeth A. Rainwater
Deputy to the Staff Director	Michael James Rowny
Special Assistant for Congressional Liaison	Robert K. Russell, Jr.
Associate Assistant (Wexler)	John Ryor
Deputy Assistant to the President	William G. Simpson
Special Assistant for Congressional Liaison (House)	Terrence D. Straub
Deputy Assistant to the President	Linda Tarr-Whelan
Deputy Assistant for Congressional Liaison	Robert Thomson
Deputy Appointments Secretary	Frances M. Voorde
Deputy Special Assistant for Administration-Military Office	Marvin L. Beaman, Jr.
Deputy Special Assistant for Administration-White House Operations	Daniel Malachuk, Jr.
Personal Assistant to the First Lady	Madeline F. Macbean
Social Secretary	Gretchen Poston
Deputy Director of the Presidential Personnel Office	Harley Frankel
Special Assistant for Congressional Liaison (Legislative Coordination)	Ronna Freiberg
Associate Assistant (Wexler)	Jane D. Hartley
Deputy Chief Speechwriter	Gordon C. Stewart
Counsel to the Intelligence Oversight Board	James V. Dick
Associate Press Secretary	Claudia M. Townsend
Associate Director, Presidential Personnel Office	Peggy E. Rainwater
Associate Press Secretary	Marc T. Henderson
Special Assistant to the Assistant for Domestic Affairs and Policy	Kathleen A. Reid
Director, Presidential Messages	Eliska Hasek Coolidge
Special Assistant for Hispanic Affairs	Raul Robert Tapia
Deputy to the Assistant to the President	Thomas V. Beard
Director of Projects for the First Lady	Kathryn E. Cade
Director of Scheduling (First Lady)	Jane S. Fenderson
Director, Visitors Office	Nancy A. Willing
Deputy Press Secretary (First Lady)	Faith A. Collins
Editor, News Summary	Janet E. Mcmahon
Curator	Clement E. Conger
Physician to the President	Rear Adm. William M. Lukash, MC USN
Chief Usher	Rex W. Scouten

The Reagan Cabinet, 1981–1989

Name	Date of Appointment
Secretary of State	
Alexander M. Haig, Jr.	1981
George P. Shultz	1982
Secretary of Treasury	
Donald T. Regan	1981
James A. Baker III	1985
Nicholas F. Brady	1988
Secretary of Defense	
Caspar W. Weinberger	1981
Frank C. Carlucci	1987
Attorney General	
William French Smith	1981
Edwin Meese III	1985
Richard Thornburgh	1988
Secretary of Interior	
James G. Watt	1981
William P. Clark	1983
Donald P. Hodel	1985
Secretary of Agriculture	
John R. Block	1981
Richard E. Lyng	1986
Secretary of Commerce	
Malcolm Baldrige	1981
C. William Verity, Jr.	1987
Secretary of Labor	
Raymond J. Donovan	1981
William E. Brock	1985
Ann D. McLaughlin	1987
Secretary of Housing and Urban Development	
Samuel R. Pierce, Jr.	1981

Secretary of Transportation
Andrew L. Lewis, Jr.	1981
Elizabeth Hanford Dole	1983
James H. Burnley	1987

Secretary of Energy
James B. Edwards	1981
Donald P. Hodel	1982
John S. Herrington	1985

Secretary of Health and Human Services
Richard S. Schweiker	1981
Margart M. Heckler	1983
Otis R. Bowen	1985

Secretary of Education
Terrel Bell	1981
William J. Bennett	1985
Lauro F. Cavazos	1988

The White House Staff 1981–82

Counselor to the President	Edwin Meese III
Chief of Staff and Assistant to President	James A. Baker III
Deputy Chief of Staff and Assistant to the President	Michael K. Deaver
Assistant to the President for National Security Affairs	Richard V. Allen
Assistant to the President for Policy Development	Martin Anderson
Assistant to the President and Press Secretary	James Scott Brady
Assistant to the President for Public Liaison	Elizabeth Hanford Dole
Counsel to the President	Fred F. Fielding
Assistant to the President for Legislative Affairs	Max L. Friedersdorf
Assistant to the President and Staff Director	David R. Gergen
Assistant to the President	Edwin L. Harper
Assistant to the President for Presidential Personnel	E. Pendleton James
Assistant to the President for Political Affairs	Franklyn C. Nofziger
Assistant to the President for Intergovernmental Affairs	Richard Salisbury Williamson
Deputy Counselor to the President	Robert M. Garrick
Deputy Assistant to the President and Assistant to the Deputy Chief of Staff	Joseph W. Canzeri
Deputy Assistant to the President for Public Liaison	Red Cavaney
Deputy Assistant to the President and Deputy to the Chief of Staff	Richard G. Darman

Deputy Assistant to the President for	
Legislative Affairs	Kenneth M. Duberstein
Deputy Assistant to the President and	
Director of the Office of Cabinet Administration	Craig L. Fuller
Deputy Assistant to the President and	
Director of the Office of Policy Development	Edwin J. Gray
Deputy Assistant to the President and	
Director of Special Support Services	Edward V. Hickey, Jr.
Deputy Assistant to the President and	
Deputy to the Chief of Staff	Francis S.M. Hodsoll
Deputy Assistant to the President for	
Intergovernmental Affairs	Alan F. Holmer
Deputy Assistant to the President	
and Director of Staff for the First Lady	Peter McCoy
Deputy Assistant to the President	
for Legislative Affairs	Powell Allen Moore
Deputy Assistant to the President	
for National Security Affairs	James W. Nance
Deputy Assistant to the President for Political Affairs	Edward Rollins
Deputy Assistant to the President	
and Deputy Press Secretary	Karna Small Stringer
Deputy Assistant to the President for	
Communications and Director of the	
Office of Communications	Frank A. Ursomarso
Assistant Counsellor to the President	Edwin W. Thomas, JR.
Deputy Counsel to the President	Herbert E. Ellingwood
Deputy Counsel to the President	Richard A. Hauser
Deputy Press Secretary to the President	Larry M. Speakes
Special Assistant to the President	
for Policy Development	Douglas Leighton Bandow
Special Assistant to the President	
for Public Liaison	Aram Bakshian, Jr.
Special Assistant to the President	Richard Smith Beal
Special Assistant to the President for Public Liaison	Morton C. Blackwell
Special Assistant to the President for Public Liaison	Robert F. Bonitati
Special Assistant to the President for Public Liaison	John F. Burgess
Special Assistant to the President	David C. Fischer
Special Assistant to the President	
for Policy Development	Kevin Randall Hopkins
Special Assistant to the President	
for Public Liaison	Virginia H. Knauer
Special Assistant to the President and	
Deputy Director of Special Support Services	Dennis E. Leblanc

Special Assistant to the President for Public Liaison   Diana L. Lozano
Special Assistant to the President
    for Intergovernmental Affairs   J. Steven Rhodes
Special Assistant to the President
for Intergovernmental Affairs   Judy F. Peachee
Special Assistant to the President for Administration   John F.W. Rogers
Special Assistant to the President
    and Director of the Advance Office   Stephen M. Studdert
Special Assistant to the President for Public Liaison   Wayne H. Valis
Special Assistant to the President   Helene A. Von Damm
Special Assistant for Scheduling   Gregory Newell
Curator   Clement E. Conger
Physician to the President   Daniel Ruge, M.D.
Chief Usher   Rex W. Scouten

The White House Staff 1982–83

Counselor to the President   Edwin Meese III
Chief of Staff and Assistant to the President   James A. Baker III
Deputy Chief of Staff and Assistant to the President   Michael K. Deaver
Assistant to the President and Press Secretary   James S. Brady
Assistant to the President for National Security Affairs   William P. Clark
Assistant to the President and
    Deputy to the Chief of Staff   Richard G. Darman
Assistant to the President for Public Liaison   Elizabeth H. Dole
Assistant to the President for Legislative Affairs   Kenneth M. Duberstein
Counsel to the President   Fred F. Fielding
Assistant to the President for Cabinet Affairs   Craig L. Fuller
Assistant to the President for Communications   David R. Gergen
Assistant to the President for Policy Development   Edwin L. Harper
Assistant to the President and Director
    of Special Support Services   Edward V. Hickey, Jr.
Assistant to the President for Presidential Personnel   E. Pendleton James
Deputy Counselor to the President   James E. Jenkins
Assistant to the President for Political Affairs   Edward J. Rollins
Assistant to the President for
    Intergovernmental Affairs   Richard S. Williamson
Deputy Assistant to the President for Political Affairs   Lee Atwater
    Deputy Assistant to the President and
    Director of Speechwriting   Aram Bakshain, Jr.
Deputy Assistant to the President and
    Director of Public Affairs   Michael Baroody

Deputy Assistant to the President for Public Liaison	Red Cavaney
Assistant Counselor to the President	T. Kenneth Cribb, Jr.
Deputy Assistant to the President and	
Director of the Office of Policy Information	Edwin J. Gray
Deputy Counsel to the President	Richard A. Hauser
Deputy Assistant to the President	
for Intergovernmental Affairs	Alan F. Holmer
Deputy Assistant to the President	
for National Security Affairs	Robert C. Mcfarlane
Deputy Assistant to the President and	
Deputy to the Deputy Chief of Staff	Michael A. Mcmanus
Deputy Assistant to the President	
for Legislative Affairs (House)	M.B. Oglesby
Deputy Assistant to the President for	
Policy Development and Director of	
the Office of Policy Development	Roger B. Porter
Deputy Assistant to the President for Management	
and Director of the Office of Administration	John F.W. Rogers
Deputy Assistant to the President	James S. Rosebush
Deputy Assistant to the President and	
Deputy Press Secretary to the President	Larry M. Speakes
Deputy Assistant to the President and	
Director of Media Relations and Planning	Karna Small Stringer
Deputy Assistant to the President for	
Legislative Affairs (Senate)	Pamela J. Turner
Deputy Assistant to the President for	
National Security Affairs	Charles P. Tyson
Deputy Assistant to the President and	
Director of Presidential Personnel	Helene A. Von Damm
Deputy Press Secretary to the President	Lyndon K. Allin
Special Assistant to the President and	
Director of Planning and Evaluation	Richard S. Beal
Special Assistant to the President for Communications	Joanna E. Bistany
Special Assistant to the President for Public Liaison	Morton C. Blackwell
Special Assistant to the President for	
Policy Development	Danny J. Boggs
Special Assistant to the President for Public Liaison	Robert F. Bonitati
Special Assistant to the President for Public Liaison	Wendy H. Borcherdt
Special Assistant to the President for	
Policy Development	Melvin B. Bradley
Special Assistant to the President for Public Liaison	
and Deputy Director of the Office of Public Liaison	John F. Burgess

Special Assistant to the President for Policy Development	Robert B. Carleson
Special Assistant to the President and Special Assistant to the Chief of Staff	James W. Cicconi
Special Assistant to the President for Legislative Affairs	Sherrie M. Cooksey
Special Assistant to the President and Chief Speechwriter	Anthony Dolan
Special Assistant to the President for Legislative Affairs	John H. Dressendorfer
Special Assistant to the President and Director, Office of Cabinet Affairs	Becky Norton Dunlop
Personal Photographer to the President	Michael A.W. Evans
Special Assistant to the President	David C. Fischer
Special Assistant to the President for Policy Development	Wendell W. Gunn
Special Assistant to the President and Director of Correspondence	Anne Higgins
Special Assistant to the President for Policy Development	Kevin R. Hopkins
Special Assistant to the President for Legislative Affairs	Robert J. Kabel
Special Assistant to the President for Public Liaison	Virginia H. Knauer
Special Assistant to the President and Deputy Director of Special Support Services	Dennis E. Leblanc
Special Assistant to the President for Public Liaison and Deputy Director of the Office of Public Liaison	Diana Lozano
Special Assistant to the President for Political Affairs	A. Morgan Mason
Special Assistant to the President for Intergovernmental Affairs	James M. Medas
Special Assistant to the President for Private Sector Initiatives	J. Upsher Moorhead
Special Assistant to the President for International Affairs	Rick Neal
Special Assistant to the President and Director of Scheduling	Gregory J. Newell
Special Assistant to the President for Legislative Affairs	Nancy J. Risque
Special Assistant to the President for Intergovernmental Affairs	J. Steven Rhodes

Deputy Press Secretary to the President	Peter H. Roussel
Special Assistant to the President for Political Affairs	Paul A. Russo
Special Assistant to the President for Legislative Affairs	John F. Scruggs
Special Assistant to the President and Assistant to the Deputy Chief of Staff	William J. Sittmann
Special Assistant to the President and Director of Presidential Advance	Stephen M. Studdert
Special Assistant to the President for Legislative Affairs	David L. Swanson
Special Assistant to the President for Legislative Affairs	Robert J. Thompson
Special Assistant to the President and Executive Assistant to the Chief of Staff	Margaret D. Tutwiler
Special Assistant to the President for Policy Development	Michael M. Uhlmann
Special Assistant to the President for Public Liaison	Wayne H. Valis
Special Assistant to the President for Legislative Affairs	David L. Wright

The White House Staff 1983–84

Counselor to the President	Edwin Meese III
Chief of Staff and Assistant to the President	James A. Baker III
Deputy Chief of Staff and Assistant to the President	Michael K. Deaver
Assistant to the President and Press Secretary	James S. Brady
Assistant to the President for NationalSecurity Affairs	William P. Clark
Assistant to the President and Deputy to the Chief of Staff	Richard G. Darman
Assistant to the President for Legislative Affairs	Kenneth M. Duberstein
Counsel to the President	Fred F. Fielding
Assistant to the President for Cabinet Affairs	Craig L. Fuller
Assistant to the President for Communications	David R. Gergen
Assistant to the President for Policy Development	Edwin L. Harper
Assistant to the President for Presidential Personnel	John S. Herrington
Assistant to the President and Director of Special Support Services	Edward V. Hickey, Jr.
Deputy Counselor to the President	James E. Jenkins
Assistant to the President and Deputy to the Deputy Chief of Staff	Michael A. McManus

Assistant to the President for Management and Administration and Director of the Office of Administration	John F.W. Rogers
Assistant to the President for Political Affairs	Edward J. Rollins
Assistant to the President for Intergovernmental Affairs	Lee Verstandig
Assistant to the President for Public Liaison	Faith Ryan Whittlesey
Deputy Assistant to the President for Political Affairs	Lee Atwater
Deputy Assistant to the President and Director of Speechwriting	Aram Bakshian, Jr.
Deputy Assistant to the President and Director of Public Affairs	Michael Baroody
Assistant Counselor to the President	T. Kenneth Cribb, Jr.
Deputy Assistant to the President for Presidential Personnel	Becky Norton Dunlop
Deputy Counsel to the President	Richard A. Hauser
Deputy Assistant to the President for National Security Affairs	Robert C. Mcfarlane
Deputy Assistant to the President for Intergovernmental Affairs	Rick J.Neal
Deputy Assistant to the President for Legislative Affairs (House)	M.B. Oglesby
Deputy Assistant to the President for Policy Development and Director of the Office of Policy Development	Roger B. Porter
Deputy Assistant to the President	James S. Rosebush
Deputy Assistant to the President and Deputy Press Secretary to the President	Larry M. Speakes
Deputy Assistant to the President and Director of Media Relations and Planning	Karna Small Stringer
Deputy Assistant to the President for Legislative Affairs (Senate)	Pamela J. Turner
Deputy Assistant to the President for National Security Affairs	Charles P. Tyson
Deputy Assistant to the President for Public Liaison	Jonathan Vipond III
Deputy Press Secretary to the President	Lyndon K. Allin
Special Assistant to the President for National Security Affairs	Norman A. Bailey
Special Assistant to the President and Deputy Director of Public Affairs	Pamela G. Bailey
Special Assistant to the President for National Security Affairs	Richard S. Beal

Special Assistant to the President for Communications   Joanna E. Bistany
Special Assistant to the President for Public Liaison   Morton C. Blackwell
Special Assistant to the President and
   Executive Secretary of the Cabinet
   Council on Management and Administration   Ralph C. Bledsoe
Special Assistant to the President
   for Policy Development   Danny J. Boggs
Special Assistant to the President
   for Policy Development   Melvin B. Bradley
Special Assistant to the President
   for Public Liaison   Judith A. Buckalew
Special Assistant to the President
   for Policy Development   Robert B. Carleson
Special Assistant to the President
   and Special Assistant to the Chief of Staff   James W. Cicconi
Associate Counsel to the President   Sherrie M. Cooksey
Special Assistant to the President
   for Private Sector Initiatives   James K. Coyne
Special Assistant to the President for Legislative Affairs   Randall E. Davis
Special Assistant to the President
   and Chief Speechwriter   Anthony Dolan
Special Assistant to the President
   for Legislative Affairs   John H. Dressendorfer
Personal Photographer to the President   Michael A.W. Evans
Special Assistant to the President   David C. Fischer
Special Assistant to the President
   for National Security Affairs   Donald R. Fortier
Special Assistant to the President
for Intergovernmental Affairs   Robert R. Gleason
Associate Counsel to the President   Harold P. Goldfield
Special Assistant to the President
   for Policy Development   Wendell W. Gunn
Special Assistant to the President
   for Intergovernmental Affairs   Edmund S. Hawley
Special Assistant to the President and
   Director of Presidential Advance   William Henkel
Special Assistant to the President and
   Director of Correspondence   Anne Higgins
Special Assistant to the President for
   Policy Development   Kevin R. Hopkins
Special Assistant to the President for
   Intergovernmental Affairs   C.A. Howlett

Special Assistant to the President for Public Liaison   Mary Jo Jacobi
Special Assistant to the President for Public Liaison   Dee Ann Jepsen
Special Assistant to the President for Legislative Affairs   Robert J. Kabel
Special Assistant to the President for
    National Security Affairs   Geoffrey T.H. Kemp
Special Assistant to the President for
    Legislative Affairs   Nancy M. Kennedy
Special Assistant to the President for
    National Security Affairs   Robert M. Kimmitt
Special Assistant to the President for
    National Security Affairs   Ronald F. Lehman
Special Assistant to the President and
    Director of the Office of Presidential Messages Mary Jo T. Livingston
Special Assistant to the President for
    Intergovernmental Affairs   James M. Medas
Special Assistant to the President for
    National Security Affairs   Walter Raymond, Jr.
Special Assistant to the President for
    Legislative Affairs   Nancy J. Risque
Associate Counsel to the President   John G. Roberts, Jr.
Deputy Press Secretary to the President   Peter H. Roussel
Special Assistant to the President for Public Liaison   John H. Rousselot
Associate Counsel to the President   Peter J. Rusthoven
Special Assistant to the President
    and Director of Scheduling   Frederick J. Ryan, Jr.
Special Assistant to the President
    for Legislative Affairs   John F. Scruggs
Special Assistant to the President
    for National Security Affairs   Gaston J. Sigur, Jr.
Special Assistant to the President
    for National Security Affairs   Robert B. Sims
Special Assistant to the President
    and Assistant to the Deputy Chief of Staff   William F. Sittmann
Special Assistant to the President
    for Legislative Affairs   David L. Swanson
Special Assistant to the President
    for Drug Abuse Policy   Carlton E. Turner
Special Assistant to the President   Robert H. Tuttle
Special Assistant to the President and
    Executive Assistant to the Chief of Staff   Margaret D. Tutwiler
Special Assistant to the President
    for Policy Development   Michael M. Uhlmann

Special Assistant to the President
    for Public Liaison   Catalina Villalpando
Senior Associate Counsel to the President   David B. Waller
Associate Counsel to the President   D. Edward Wilson, Jr.
Special Assistant to the President
    for Legislative Affairs   David L. Wright

The White House Staff 1984–85

Counselor to the President   Edwin Meese III
Chief of Staff and Assistant to the President   James A. Baker III
Deputy Chief of Staff and Assistant to the President   Michael K. Deaver
Assistant to the President and Press Secretary   James S. Brady
Assistant to the President and
    Deputy to the Chief of Staff   Richard G. Darman
Counsel to the President   Fred F. Fielding
Assistant to the President for Cabinet Affairs   Craig L. Fuller
Assistant to the President for Presidential Personnel   John S. Herrington
Assistant to the President and Director
    of Special Support Services   Edward V. Hickey, Jr.
Assistant to the President for
    National Security Affairs   Robert C. McFarlane
Assistant to the President and Deputy
    to the Deputy Chief of Staff   Michael A. Mcmanus
Assistant to the President for Legislative Affairs   M.B. Oglesby
Assistant to the President for Management
    and Administration and Director of
    the Office of Administration   John F.W. Rogers
Assistant to the President and Principal
    Deputy Press Secretary   Larry M. Speakes
Assistant to the President for Policy Development   John A. Svahn
Assistant to the President for Intergovernmental Affairs   Lee Verstandig
Assistant to the President for Public Liaison   Faith Ryan Whittlesey
Deputy Assistant to the President
    and Director of Public Affairs   Michael Baroody
Deputy Assistant to the President and
Director of the Office of Planning and Evaluation   Bruce Chapman
Assistant Counselor to the President   T. Kenneth Cribb, Jr.
    Deputy Assistant to the President for Public Liaison Frank J. Donatelli
Deputy Assistant to the President
    for Presidential Personnel   Becky Norton Dunlop

Deputy Assistant to the President and Director of Speechwriting	Bently T. Elliott
Deputy Assistant to the President for National Security Affairs	Donald R. Fortier
Deputy Counsel to the President	Richard A. Hauser
Deputy Assistant to the President and Director of the Presidential Advance Office	William Henkel
Deputy Assistant to the President for Policy Development	Charles D. Hobbs
Deputy Assistant to the President for National Security Affairs	Robert M. Kimmitt
Deputy Assistant to the President for Intergovernmental Affairs	Rick J. Neal
Deputy Assistant to the President for National Security Affairs	John M. Poindexter
Deputy Assistant to the President for Policy Development and Director of the Office of Policy Development	Roger B. Porter
Deputy Assistant to the President	James S. Rosebush
Deputy Assistant to the President for National Security Affairs and Senior Director, Public Affairs, National Security Council	Karna Small
Deputy Assistant to the President for Legislative Affairs (House)	W. Dennis Thomas
Deputy Assistant to the President for Legislative Affairs (Senate)	Pamela J. Turner
Special Assistant to the President and Director of the Office of Communications Planning	Pamela G. Bailey
Special Assistant to the President	Richard S. Beal
Special Assistant to the President for Policy Development	Ralph C. Bledsoe
Special Assistant to the President for Policy Development	Melvin L. Bradley
Special Assistant to the President for Public Liaison	Marshall J. Breger
Special Assistant to the President for Public Liaison	Judith A. Buckalew
Special Assistant to the President for Intergovernmental Affairs	Andrew H. Card, Jr.
Special Assistant to the President and Special Assistant to the Chief of Staff	James W. Cicconi
Associate Counsel to the President	Sherrie M. Cooksey

Special Assistant to the President
  for Private Sector Initiatives   James K. Coyne
Special Assistant to the President
  for Policy Development   Randall E. Davis
Special Assistant to the President
  for National Security Affairs   Kenneth E. Degraffenreid
Special Assistant to the President and
  Chief Speechwriter   Anthony Dolan
Special Assistant to the President for
  Legislative Affairs   Thomas R. Donnelly, Jr.
Personal Photographer to the President   Michael A.W. Evans
Special Assistant to the President   David C. Fischer
Special Assistant to the President and
  Deputy Press Secretary for Domestic Affairs   Max Marlin Fitzwater
Associate Counsel to the President   H. Lawrence Garret III
Special Assistant to the President for
  Intergovernmental Affairs   Robert R. Gleason
Special Assistant to the President for
  Policy Development   Wendell W. Gunn
Special Assistant to the President for
  Intergovernmental Affairs   Edmund S. Hawley
Special Assistant to the President and
  Director of Correspondence   Anne Higgins
Special Assistant to the President for
  Intergovernmental Affairs   C.A. Howlett
Special Assistant to the President for Legislative Affairs   John M. Hudson
Special Assistant to the President for Public Liaison   Mary Jo Jacobi
Special Assistant to the President for Legislative Affairs   Robert J. Kabel
Special Assistant to the President for
  National Security Affairs   Geoffrey T.H. Kemp
Special Assistant to the President for
  Legislative Affairs   Nancy M. Kennedy
Special Assistant to the President for
  National Security Affairs   Christopher M. Lehman
Special Assistant to the President for
  National Security Affairs   Ronald F. Lehman
Special Assistant to the President for
  Policy Development   Burleigh C.W. Leonard
Special Assistant to the President and
Director of the Office of Presidential Messages   Mary Jo T. Livingston
Special Assistant to the President for

National Security Affairs	William F. Martin
Special Assistant to the President for	
National Security Affairs	Jack F. Matlock, Jr.
Special Assistant to the President for	
National Security Affairs	Constantine C. Menges
Special Assistant to the President for	
Legislative Affairs	Richard H. Prendergast
Special Assistant to the President for	
National Security Affairs	Walter Raymond, Jr.
Special Assistant to the President for	
Public Liaison	Douglas A. Riggs
Special Assistant to the President for	
Legislative Affairs	Nancy J. Risque
Associate Counsel to the President	John G. Roberts, Jr.
Special Assistant to the President for Health Policy	William L. Roper
Special Assistant to the President and	
Deputy Press Secretary	Peter H. Roussel
Associate Counsel to the President	Peter J. Rusthoven
Special Assistant to the President and	
Director of Scheduling	Frederick J. Ryan, Jr.
Special Assistant to the President for	
National Security Affairs	Gaston J. Sigur, Jr.
Special Assistant to the President and	
Deputy Press Secretary for Foreign Affairs	Robert B. Sims
Special Assistant to the President and	
Assistant to the Deputy Chief of Staff	William F. Sittmann
Special Assistant to the President and	
Director of the Office of Media Relations	Merrie Spaeth
Special Assistant to the President for Drug Abuse Policy	Carlton E. Turner
Special Assistant to the President	Robert H. Tuttle
Special Assistant to the President and	
Executive Assistant to the Chief of Staff	Margaret D. Tutwiler
Special Assistant to the President for	
Policy Development	Michael M. Uhlmann
Special Assistant to the President for Public Liaison	Catalina V. Villalpando
Senior Associate Counsel to the President	David B. Waller
Associate Counsel to the President	Wendell L. Wilkie
Special Assistant to the President for Legislative Affairs	David L. Wright

The White House Staff 1985–86

Chief of Staff to the President	Donald T. Regan
Assistant to the President and Press Secretary	James Scott Brady

Assistant to the President and
 Director of Communications   Patrick J. Buchanan
Counsel to the President   Fred F. Fielding
Assistant to the President and Legislative
 Strategy Coordinator   Max L. Friedersdorf
Assistant to the President and Director
 of Special Support Services   Edward V. Hickey, Jr..
Assistant to the President for
 National Security Affairs   Robert C. Mcfarlane
Assistant to the President for Legislative Affairs   M.B. Oglesby
Assistant to the President for Political
 and Governmental Affairs   Edward J. Rollins
Assistant to the President and
Principal Deputy Press Secretary   Larry M. Speakes
Assistant to the President for Policy Development   John A. Svahn
Deputy Assistant to the President and
 Director of the Office of Planning and Evaluation   Bruce Chapman
Deputy Assistant to the President and
 Director of the Office of Public Liaison   Linda Chavez
Staff Secretary and Deputy Assistant to the President   David L. Chew
Deputy Assistant to the President and
 Director, Office of Intergovernmental Affairs   Mitchell E. Daniels, Jr.
Executive Assistant to the Chief of Staff and
 Deputy Assistant to the President   Thomas C. Dawson
Deputy Assistant to the President
 and Director of Speechwriting   Bently T. Elliott
Deputy Assistant to the President for
 National Security Affairs   Donald R. Fortier
Deputy Counsel to the President   Richard A. Hauser
Deputy Assistant to the President and
 Director of the Presidential Advance Office   William Henkel
Deputy Assistant to the President for Administration   Christopher Hicks
Deputy Assistant to the President for
 Policy Development   Charles D. Hobbs
Cabinet Secretary and Deputy Assistant to the President   Alfred H. Kingon
Deputy Assistant to the President for
 Legislative Affairs (House)   Alan M. Kranowitz
Deputy Assistant to the President and
 Director, Office of Political Affairs   William B. Lacy
Deputy Assistant to the President for
 National Security Affairs   Vice Adm. John M. Poindexter
Deputy Assistant to the President for
 Policy Development and Director of

the Office of Policy Development | Roger B. Porter
Deputy Assistant to the President | James S. Rosebush
Deputy Assistant to the President | Frederick J. Ryan, Jr.
Deputy Assistant to the President for
National Security Affairs and Senior Director
for Public Affairs, National Security Council | Karna Small
Deputy Assistant to the President for
Drug Abuse Policy | Carlton E. Turner
Deputy Assistant to the President for
Legislative Affairs (Senate) | Pamela J. Turner
Deputy Assistant to the President and
Director of Presidential Personnel | Robert H. Tuttle
Special Assistant to the President for
Intergovernmental Affairs | Ronald L. Alvarado
Special Assistant to the President and
Deputy Director of the Office of Public Liaison | Linda L. Arey
Special Assistant to the President for
Political Affairs | Haley Barbour
Special Assistant to the President and
Executive Secretary of the Cabinet Council | Ralph C. Bledsoe
Special Assistant to the President for
Policy Development | Melvin L. Bradley
Special Assistant to the President and
Deputy Press Secretary for Domestic Affairs | Albert R. Brashear
Special Assistant to the President for Public Liaison | Marshall J. Breger
Special Assistant to the President for Political Affairs | Helen R. Cameron
Special Assistant to the President for
Intergovernmental Affairs | Andrew H. Card Jr.
Associate Counsel to the President | Sherrie M. Cooksey
Special Assistant to the President for
National Security Affairs | James P. Covey
Special Assistant to the President for
National Security Affairs | Kenneth E. Degraffenreid
Special Assistant to the President and
Chief Speechwriter | Anthony Dolan
Special Assistant to the President for
Legislative Affairs | Thomas Donnelly, Jr.
Special Assistant to the President for
Policy Development | Michael A. Driggs
Special Assistant to the President for
Legislative Affairs | Henry M. Gandy
Associate Counsel to the President | H. Lawrence Garrett III

Special Assistant to the President for Legislative Affairs	Bryce L. Harlow
Special Assistant to the President and Director of Correspondence	Anne Higgins
Special Assistant to the President for Legislative Affairs	John M. Hudson
Special Assistant to the President for Public Liaison	Mary Jo Jacobi
Special Assistant to the President for Legislative Affairs	Nancy M. Kennedy
Special Assistant to the President	James F. Kuhn
Special Assistant to the President for National Security Affairs	Christopher M. Lehman
Special Assistant to the President for National Security Affairs	Ronald F. Lehman
Special Assistant to the President for Legislative Affairs	Frederick D. McClure
Special Assistant to the President for National Security Affairs	William F. Martin
Special Assistant to the President for National Security Affairs	John F. Matlock, Jr.
Special Assistant to the President for National Security Affairs	Constantine C. Menges
Special Assistant to the President for Presidential Speechwriting	Margaret Noonan
Associate Counsel to the President	Deborah K. Owen
Special Assistant to the President for Legislative Affairs	Richard Prendergast
Special Assistant to the President for National Security Affairs	Walter Raymond Jr.
Special Assistant to the President for Public Liaison	Robert R. Reilly
Special Assistant to the President for Legislative Affairs	Nancy J. Risque
Associate Counsel to the President	John G. Roberts, Jr.
Special Assistant to the President for Health Policy	William L. Roper
Special Assistant to the President and Deputy Press Secretary	Peter H. Roussel
Special Assistant to the President for National Security Affairs	Gaston J. Sigur, Jr.
Special Assistant to the President and Director of the Office of Policy Development	Paul B. Simmons
Special Assistant to the President and Deputy Press Secretary for Foreign Affairs	Robert B. Sims

Physician to the President   T. Burton Smith, M.D.
Special Assistant to the President for Public Liaison   Catalina Villalpando
Senior Associate Counsel to the President   David B. Waller
Special Assistant to the President for Legislative Affairs   Lyn M. Withey
Special Assistant to the President and
    Director of Presidential Advance   James L. Hooley

The White House Staff 1986–87

Chief of Staff to the President   Donald T. Regan
Assistant to the President and Press Secretary   James S. Brady
Assistant to the President and
    Director of Communications   Patrick J. Buchanan
Assistant to the President for
    Political and Intergovernmental Affairs   Mitchell E. Daniels, Jr.
Counsel to the President   Peter J. Wallison
Assistant to the President   William Henkel
Cabinet Secretary and Assistant to the President   Alfred H. Kingon
Assistant to the President for Legislative Affairs   William L. Ball III
Assistant to the President for
    National Security Affairs   Vice Adm. John M. Poindexter, USA
Assistant to the President and
    Principal Deputy Press Secretary   Larry M. Speakes
Assistant to the President for
    Policy Development   John A. Svahn
Assistant to the President   W. Dennis Thomas
Assistant to the President and
    Chief of Staff to the First Lady   Jack L. Courtemanche
Staff Secretary and Deputy Assistant to the President   David L. Chew
Executive Assistant to the Chief of
    Staff and Deputy Assistant to the President   Thomas C. Dawson
Deputy Assistant to the President
    and Director of Speechwriting   Bently T. Elliott
Deputy Assistant to the President
    for National Security Affairs   Donald R. Fortier
Deputy Assistant to the President for
    Policy Development   Charles D. Hobbs
Deputy Assistant to the President and
    Director of the Office of
    Intergovernmental Affairs   Gwendolyn S. King
Deputy Assistant to the President for
    Legislative Affairs (House)   Alan M. Kranowitz

Deputy Assistant to the President and
Director, Office of Political Affairs — William L. Lacy
Deputy Assistant to the President for
National Security Affairs — Ronald F. Lehman II
Deputy Assistant to the President and
Director of the Office of Public Liaison — Mari Maseng
Deputy Assistant to the President for Administration — Jonathan S. Miller
Deputy Assistant to the President and
Director of the White House Military Office — Richard P. Riley
Deputy Assistant to the President for Legislative Affairs — Nancy J. Risque
Deputy Assistant to the President for
National Security Affairs — Peter W. Rodman
Deputy Assistant to the President,
Director of Presidential Appointments
and Scheduling, and Director of
Private Sector Initiatives — Frederick J. Ryan, Jr.
Deputy Assistant to the President for
National Security Affairs and Senior
Director, Public Affairs, National Security Council — Karna Small
Deputy Counsel to the President — Jay B. Stephens
Deputy Assistant to the President for Drug Abuse Policy — Carlton E. Turner
Deputy Assistant to the President for
Legislative Affairs (Senate) — Pamela J. Turner
Deputy Assistant to the President and
Director of Presidential Personnel — Robert H. Tuttle
Special Assistant to the President for Public Liaison — Carl A. Anderson
Special Assistant to the President and
Deputy Director of the Office of Public Liaison — Linda L. Arey
Special Assistant to the President for Political Affairs — Haley Barbour
Special Assistant to the President for
Policy Development — Ralph C. Bledsoe
Special Assistant to the President and
Director of the Television Office — Elizabeth I. Board
Special Assistant to the President for
Legislative Affairs — David A. Bockorny
Special Assistant to the President for
Policy Development — Melvin L. Bradley
Special Assistant to the President and
Deputy Press Secretary for Domestic Affairs — Albert R. Brashear
Special Assistant to the President for Public Liaison — Merlin P. Breaux
Special Assistant to the President for
National Security Affairs — Raymond F. Burghardt

Special Assistant to the President for
    Intergovernmental Affairs   Andrew H. Card, Jr.
Special Assistant to the President and
    Deputy Director of the Office of Cabinet Affairs   Donald A. Clarey
Special Assistant to the President for
    Political and Intergovernmental Affairs   Cecilia Cole- Mcinturff
Special Assistant to the President for
    National Security Affairs   James P. Covey
Senior Associate Counsel to the President   C. Christopher Cox
Special Assistant to the President for
    National Security Affairs   Stephen I. Danzansky
Special Assistant to the President for
    National Security Affairs   Kenneth E. Degraffenreid
Special Assistant to the President and
    Deputy Press Secretary for Foreign Affairs   Edward P. Djerejian
Special Assistant to the President
    and Chief Speechwriter   Anthony Dolan
Special Assistant to the President
    for Policy Development   Michael A. Driggs
Special Assistant to the President
    for Legislative Affairs   J. Edward Fox
Special Assistant to the President and
    Director of Public Affairs   Thomas F. Gibson III
Special Assistant to the President and
    Director of Correspondence   Anne Higgins
Special Assistant to the President and
    Director of Presidential Advance   James L. Hooley
Special Assistant to the President for Legislative Affairs   John M. Hudson
Special Assistant to the President
    for Legislative Affairs   Nancy M. Kennedy
Special Assistant to the President for Public Liaison   Linas J. Kojelis
Associate Counsel to the President   Robert M. Kruger
Special Assistant to the President   James F. Kuhn
Special Assistant to the President for
    National Security Affairs   Robert E. Linhard
Special Assistant to the President for
    Legislative Affairs   Frederick D. McClure
Special Assistant to the President for
National Security Affairs and Executive
    Secretary of the National Security Council   Rodney B. McDaniel
Special Assistant to the President for
    National Security Affairs   William F. Martin

Special Assistant to the President for National Security Affairs	Jack F. Matlock, Jr.
Special Assistant to the President and Executive Secretary of the Economic Policy Council	Eugene J. McAllister
Special Assistant to the President for National Security Affairs	Constantine C. Menges
Special Assistant to the President for Presidential Speechwriting	Margaret Noonan
Special Assistant to the President	Kathleen Osborne
Special Assistant to the President for Legislative Affairs	Richard Prendergast
Associate Counsel to the President	Alan Charles Raul
Special Assistant to the President for National Security Affairs	Walter Raymond, Jr.
Special Assistant to the President and Director of Media Relations	Susan Mathis Richard
Associate Counsel to the President	John G. Roberts, Jr.
Special Assistant to the President for Health Policy	William L. Roper
Special Assistant to the President and Deputy Press Secretary	Peter H. Roussel
Special Assistant to the President for National Security Affairs	Ronald K. Sable
Special Assistant to the President for National Security Affairs	James A. Kelly
Physician to the President	T. Burton Smith, M.D.
Special Assistant to the President for Legislative Affairs	John C. Tuck
Special Assistant to the President and Director of Research	Agnes M. Waldron
Special Assistant to the President for Legislative Affairs	Lyn M. Withey

The White House Staff 1987–88

Chief of Staff to the President	Howard H. Baker Jr.
Deputy Chief of Staff	Kenneth M. Duberstein
Assistant to the President for Legislative Affairs	William L. Ball III
Assistant to the President for Policy Development	Gary L. Bauer
Assistant to the President and Press Secretary	James S. Brady
Assistant to the President for National Security Affairs	Frank C. Carlucci
Assistant to the President for Domestic Affairs	T. Kenneth Cribb, Jr.
Counsel to the President	Arthur B. Culvahouse, Jr.
Assistant to the President for Operations	Rhett B. Dawson

Assistant to the President for Political and Intergovernmental Affairs	Frank J. Donatelli
Assistant to the President for Press Relations	M. Marlin Fitzwater
Assistant to the President for Communications and Planning	Thomas Griscom
Assistant to the President	William Henkel
Assistant to the President	Charles Hobbs
Cabinet Secretary and Assistant to the President	Nancy J. Risque
Deputy Assistant to the President and Chief of Staff to the First Lady	Jack L. Courtemanche
Staff Secretary and Deputy Assistant to the President	David L. Chew
Deputy Assistant to the President and Director of Speechwriting	Anthony Dolan
Deputy Assistant to the President and Director of the Office of Intergovernmental Affairs	Gwendolyn S. King
Deputy Assistant to the President for Legislative Affairs (House)	Alan M. Kranowitz
Deputy Assistant to the President and Director, Office of Political Affairs	Franklin L. Lavin
Deputy Assistant to the President and Director of the Office of Public Liaison	Mari Maseng
Deputy Assistant to the President for Management and Administration	(Vacancy)
Deputy Assistant to the President for National Security Affairs	Lt. Gen. Colin L. Powell, USA
Deputy Assistant to the President and Director of the White House Military Office	Richard P. Riley
Deputy Assistant to the President, Director of Presidential Appointments and Scheduling, and Director of Private Sector Initiatives	Frederick J. Ryan, Jr.
Deputy Counsel to the President	Jay B. Stephens
Deputy Special Counselor to the President	William B. Lytton
Deputy Assistant to the President for Legislative Affairs	John C. Tuck
Deputy Assistant to the President for Legislative Affairs (Senate)	Pamela J. Turner
Deputy Assistant to the President and Director of Presidential Personnel	Robert H. Tuttle
Deputy Assistant to the President, Office of the Chief of Staff	Danny L. Crippen
Special Assistant to the President for Public Liaison	Carl A. Anderson

Special Assistant to the President and Deputy Director of the Office of Public Liaison	Linda L. Arey
Special Assistant to the President and Deputy Press Secretary	Leslye A. Arsht
Special Assistant to the President for Intergovernmental Affairs	Cristena L. Bach
Special Assistant to the President for Intergovernmental Affairs	Judy A. Black
Special Assistant to the President for Policy Development	Ralph C. Bledsoe
Special Assistant to the President and Director of the Television Office	Elizabeth I. Board
Special Assistant to the President for Legislative Affairs	David A. Bockorny
Special Assistant to the President for Policy Development	Melvin L. Bradley
Special Assistant to the President and Deputy Press Secretary for Domestic Affairs	Albert R. Brashear
Special Assistant to the President and Deputy Director of the Office of Cabinet Affairs	(Vacancy)
Special Assistant to the President for National Security Affairs	William A. Cockell, Jr.
Special Assistant to the President for National Security Affairs	Herman J. Cohen
Special Assistant to the President for Political and Intergovernmental Affairs	Lisa Stoltenberg
Senior Associate Counsel to the President	C. Christopher Cox
Special Assistant to the President for Public Liaison and Director, Economic Division	Donald A. Danner
Special Assistant to the President for National Security Affairs	Stephen I. Danzansky
Special Assistant to the President for National Security Affairs	Robert W. Dean
Special Assistant to the President for Policy Development	Michael A. Driggs
Special Assistant to the President for National Security Affairs	Fritz W. Ermarth
Special Assistant to the President for National Security Affairs	Alison B. Fortier
Special Assistant to the President and Director of Public Affairs	Thomas F. Gibson III
Special Assistant to the President for	

National Security Affairs and
Executive Secretary of the National
Security Council   Grant S. Green, Jr.
Special Assistant to the President for
Legislative Affairs   Bryce L. Harlow
Special Assistant to the President and
Director of Correspondence   Anne Higgins
Special Assistant to the President and
Director of Presidential Advance James L. Hooley
Physician to the President Col. John E. Hutton, Jr., M.D., MC, USA
Special Assistant to the President for
National Security Affairs   David Barry Kelly
Special Assistant to the President for
National Security Affairs   James A. Kelly
Special Assistant to the President for
Legislative Affairs   Nancy M. Kennedy
Special Assistant to the President for
Public Liaison   Linas J. Kojelis
Associate Counsel to the President Robert M. Kruger
Special Assistant to the President   James F. Kuhn
Special Assistant to the President for
Administration and Deputy Director
of the Office of Administration Charles M. Kupperman
Special Assistant to the President for
National Security Affairs   Robert E. Linhard
Special Assistant to the President for
Drug Abuse Policy and Director of
the White House Drug Abuse Policy Office Donald Ian McDonald
Associate Counsel to the President C. Dean McGrath
Special Assistant to the President and
Executive Secretary of the
Economic Policy Council   Eugene J. McAllister
Special Assistant to the President for
National Security Affairs   Robert B. Oakley
Special Assistant to the President   Kathleen Osborne
Special Assistant to the President for
Legislative Affairs   Richard Prendergast
Special Assistant to the President for
Intergovernmental Affairs   Karen Kae Rairdin
Associate Counsel to the President Alan Charles Raul
Special Assistant to the President and
Director of Media Relations   Susan Mathis Richard

Special Assistant to the President for
   National Security Affairs   Peter W. Rodman
Special Assistant to the President for
   Legislative Affairs (Senate)   Ronald K. Sable
Special Assistant to the President for
   National Security Affairs   Jose S. Sorzano
Special Assistant to the President for
   National Security Affairs   Paul S. Stevens
Special Assistant to the President for
   Agricultural Trade and Food Assistance   Alan T. Tracy
Special Assistant to the President and
   Director of Research   Agnes M. Waldron
Special Assistant to the President for
   Legislative Affairs   Lyn M. Withey

The White House Staff 1988–89

Chief of Staff to the President   Howard H. Baker Jr.
Deputy Chief of Staff   Kenneth M. Duberstein
Assistant to the President for Policy Development   Gary L. Bauer
Assistant to the President and Press Secretary   James S. Brady
Assistant to the President for Domestic Affairs   T. Kenneth Cribb, Jr.
Counsel to the President   Arthur B. Culvahouse, Jr.
Assistant to the President for Operations   Rhett B. Dawson
Assistant to the President for
   Political and Intergovernmental Affairs   Frank J. Donatelli
Assistant to the President for Press Relations   M. Marlin Fitzwater
Assistant to the President for Communications
   and Planning   Thomas C. Griscom
Assistant to the President   Charles Hobbs
Assistant to the President for Legislative Affairs Alan M. Kranowitz
Assistant to the President for
   National Security Affairs   Lt. Gen. Colin L. Powell
Assistant to the President and
   Cabinet Secretary   Nancy J. Risque
Assistant to the President, Director of Presidential
   Appointments and Scheduling, and
   Director of Private Sector Initiatives   Frederick J. Ryan, Jr.
Assistant to the President and
   Director of Presidential Personnel   Robert H. Tuttle
Deputy Assistant to the President
   for Legislative Affairs   David S. Addington

Deputy Counsel to the President	Phillip D. Brady
Deputy Assistant to the President and Chief of Staff to the First Lady	Jack L. Courtemanche
Deputy Assistant to the President	Dan L. Crippen
Deputy Assistant to the President and Director of Speechwriting	Anthony Dolan
Deputy Assistant to the President for Legislative Affairs (House)	James W. Dyer
Deputy Assistant to the President and Director of Presidential Advance	James L. Hooley
Deputy Assistant to the President	James F. Kuhn
Deputy Assistant to the President and Director, Office of Political Affairs	Franklin L. Lavin
Deputy Assistant to the President and Director of the White House Military Office	James C. McKinney
Deputy Assistant to the President for National Security Affairs	John D. Negroponte
Deputy Assistant to the President	Kathleen Osborne
Deputy Assistant to the President and Director of Public Liaison	Rebecca G. Range
Deputy Assistant to the President and Director of the Office of Administration	Gordon G. Riggle
Deputy Assistant to the President and Executive Assistant to the Chief of Staff	John C. Tuck
Deputy Assistant to the President for Legislative Affairs (Senate)	Pamela J. Turner
Special Assistant to the President and Deputy Press Secretary	Leslye A. Arsht
Associate Counsel to the President	Michael J. Astrue
Special Assistant to the President for Intergovernmental Affairs	Cristena L. Bach
Special Assistant to the President for Intergovernmental Affairs	Judy A. Black
Special Assistant to the President and Director of Public Affairs	Marion C. Blakey
Special Assistant to the President for Policy Development	Ralph C. Bledsoe
Special Assistant to the President for Media and Broadcast Relations	Elizabeth I. Board
Special Assistant to the President and Director of Economic Development	Roger Bolton

Special Assistant to the President for Policy Development	Melvin L. Bradley
Associate Counsel to the President	Patricia M. Bryan
Special Assistant to the President for National Security Affairs	William A. Cockell, Jr.
Associate Counsel to the President	Benedict S. Cohen
Special Assistant to the President for National Security Affairs	Herman J. Cohen
Special Assistant to the President and Deputy Press Secretary	B. Jay Cooper
Special Assistant to the President for National Security Affairs	Stephen I. Danzansky
Special Assistant to the President for National Security Affairs	Robert W. Dean
Special Assistant to the President for Legislative Affairs (House)	Nancy P. Dorn
Special Assistant to the President for Policy Development	Michael A. Driggs
Special Assistant to the President for Public Liaison	Juanita D. Duggan
Special Assistant to the President for National Security Affairs	Alsion B. Fortier
Special Assistant to the President for Legislative Affairs (House)	Charles Greener
Special Assistant to the President and Deputy Director, Political Affairs	Carlyle Gregory
Special Assistant to the President for Legislative Affairs	Bryce L. Harlow
Special Assistant to the President and Director of Correspondence	Anne Higgins
Physician to the President	Col. John E. Hutton, Jr., M.D., MC, USA
Special Assistant to the President for National Security Affairs	David Barry Kelly
Special Assistant to the President for National Security Affairs	James A. Kelly
Special Assistant to the President for Legislative Affairs	Nancy M. Kennedy
Associate Counsel to the President	Robert M. Kruger
Special Assistant to the President and Director of the White House Secretariat	Katherine D. Ladd
Associate Counsel to the President	William J. Landers
Special Assistant to the President for	

National Security Affairs   Nelson C. Ledsky
Special Assistant to the President for
    National Security Affairs   Robert E. Linhard
Special Assistant to the President and
    Executive Secretary of the Economic Policy Council   William Maroni
Special Assistant to the President for
Drug Abuse Policy and Director of
    the White House Drug Abuse Policy Office   Donald Ian MacDonald
Associate Counsel to the President   C. Dean McGrath
Special Assistant to the President for
    Domestic Affairs   David M. McIntosh
Special Assistant to the President for
    National Security Affairs   Robert B. Oakley
Special Assistant to the President for
    White House Operations   Claire M. O'donnell
Special Assistant to the President and
    Deputy Press Secretary   Roman Popadiak
Special Assistant to the President for
    Intergovernmental Affairs   Karen Kae Rairdin
Special Assistant to the President and Speech Writer   Peter M. Robinson
Special Assistant to the President for
    National Security Affairs   Peter W. Rodman
Special Assistant to the President for
    National Security Affairs   Charles N. Rostow
Special Assistant to the President for
    National Security Affairs   Jose S. Sorzano
Special Assistant to the President for
National Security Affairs and Executive Secretary of the
    National Security Council   Paul S. Stevens
Special Assistant to the President for
    Political and Intergovernmental Affairs   Lisa Stoltenberg
Special Assistant to the President for
    Legislative Affairs (House)   John C. (Jay) Stone
Special Assistant to the President for
    Agricultural Trade and Food Assistance   Alan T. Tracy
Special Assistant to the President and
    Director of Research   Agnes M. Waldron
Special Assistant to the President and
    Assistant Press Secretary   Mark D. Weinberg
Special Assistant to the President and
    Director of the Office of Cabinet Affairs   Kay W. Woodward

The Bush Cabinet, 1989–1993

Name	Date of Appointment
Secretary of State	
James A. Baker III	1989
Lawrence S. Eagleburger	1992
Secretary of Treasury	
Nicholas F. Brady	1989
Secretary of Defense	
Richard B. Cheney	1989
Attorney General	
Richard Thornburgh	1989
William P. Barr	1991
Secretary of the Interior	
Manuel Lujan	1989
Secretary of Agriculture	
Clayton K. Yeutter	1989
Edward Madigan	1991
Secretary of Commerce	
Robert A. Mosbacher	1989
Barbara H. Franklin	1992
Secretary of Health and Human Services	
Louis W. Sullivan	1989
Secretary of Education	
Lauro F. Cavazos	1989
Lamar Alexander	1991
Secretary of Housing and Urban Development	
Jack F. Kemp	1989
Secretary of Transportation	
Samuel K. Skinner	1989

Andrew H. Card   1992

Secretary of Energy
    James D. Watkins   1989

Secretary of Veterans Affairs
    Edward J. Derwinski   1989

The White House Staff 1989–90

Chief of Staff to the President	John H. Sununu
Assistant to the President and Deputy to the Chief of Staff	Andrew H. Card, Jr.
Assistant to the President and Deputy to the Chief of Staff	James W. Cicconi
Assistant to the President and Secretary to the Cabinet	David Q. Bates
Assistant to the President for Issues Analysis	Richard C. Breeden
Assistant to the President for Communications	David F. Demarest Jr.
Assistant to the President and Press Secretary	Max Marlin Fitzwater
Counsel to the President	C. Boyden Gray
Assistant to the President for Legislative Affairs	Frederick D. McClure
Assistant to the President for Management and Administration	J. Bonnie Newman
Assistant to the President for Economic and Domestic Policy	Roger B. Porter
Assistant to the President for National Security Affairs	Gen. Brent Scowcroft, USAF, (Ret.)
Assistant to the President for Special Activities and Initiatives	Stephen M. Studdert
Assistant to the President and Director of Presidential Personnel	Charles G. Untermeyer
Deputy Assistant to the President and Director of the Office of Intergovernmental Affairs	Debra Anderson
Deputy Assistant to the President for Management and Director, Office of Administration	Paul W. Bateman
Deputy Assistant to the President and Director, Office of Cabinet Affairs	Philip D. Brady
Deputy Assistant to the President for Legislative Affairs (House)	Nicholas E. Calio
Deputy Assistant to the President and Deputy Press Secretary	B. Jay Cooper
Deputy assistant to the President for National Security Affairs	Robert M. Gates
Deputy Assistant to the President for	

Appointments and Scheduling   Joseph W. Hagin II
Deputy Assistant to the President for
Legislative Affairs (Senate)   E. Boyd Holingsworth, Jr.
Deputy Assistant to the President for
Presidential Personnel   Ronald C. Kaufman
Deputy Assistant to the President and
Director of Presidential Advance   John G. Keller
Deputy Assistant to the President for Public Liasion   Barbara G. Kilberg
Deputy Assistant to the President and
Director, Office of National Service   C. Gregg Petersmeyer
Deputy Assistant to the President for
Policy Planning   James P. Pinkerton
Deputy Assistant to the President and
Deputy Press Secretary   Roman Popadiuk
Deputy Assistant to the President   Patricia Presock
Deputy Assistant to the President and
and Executive Assistant to the Chief of Staff   Edward M. Rogers, Jr.
Deputy Assistant to the President for
Domestic Policy and Director,
Office of Policy Development   William L. Roper
Deputy Assistant to the President and
Chief of Staff to the First Lady   Susan Porter Rose
Deputy Counsel to the President   John P. Schmitz
Deputy Assistan to the President for Public Liasion   Sichan Siv
Deputy Assistant to the President and
Deputy Director of Presidential Personnel   Roscoe B. Starek III
Deputy Assistant to the President for
Communications   Chriss Winston
Deputy Assistant to the President and
Director, Office of Political Affairs   James Wray
Special Assistant to the President for
Legislative Affairs (House)   Gary J. Andres
Special Assistant to the President for
National Security Affairs   Robert D. Blackwill
Special Assistant to the President for
National Security Affairs   Everett E. Briggs
Special Assistant to the President for
Intergovernmental Affairs   William Canary
Special Assistant to the President and
Deputy Director for Political Affairs   David M. Carney
Special Assistant to the President for National Service   Paul Collins, Jr.
Special Assistant to the President for
Legislative Affairs (House)   Nancy P. Dorn
Special Assistant to the President for Cabinet Affairs   Junanita Duggan

Special Assistant to the President and
 Associate Director of Presidential Personnel   Robert A. Estrada
Special Assistant to the President for
 Agricultural Trade and Food Assistance   Cooper Evans
Special Assistant to the President and
 Assistant Staff Secretary   John S. Gardner
Special Assistant to the President and
 Deputy Press Secretary   Alixe R. Glen
Special Assistant to the President and
 Associate Director of Presidential Personnel   Martha H. Goodwin
Special Assistant to the President for
 Presidential Messages and Correspondence   Shirley M. Green
Special Assistant to the President for
 Intergovernmental Affairs   George O. Griffith, Jr.

The White House Staff 1990–91

Chief of Staff to the President   John H. Sununu
Assistant to the President and Deputy
 to the Chief of Staff   Andrew H. Card, Jr.
Assistant to the President and Deputy
 to the Chief of Staff   James W. Cicconi
Assistant to the President and Secretary to the Cabinet   David Q. Bates, Jr.
Assistant to the President for Science and Technology   D. Allan Bromley
Assitant to the President for Communications   David F. Demarest, Jr.
Assistant to the President and Press Secretary   Max Marlin Fitzwater
Assistant to the President and Deputy
 for National Security Affairs   Robert M. Gates
Counsel to the President   C. Boyden Gray
Assistant to the President for
 Legislative Affairs   Frederick D. McClure
Assistant to the President for Management
 and Administration   J. Bonnie Newman
Assistant to the President for Economic
 and Domestic Policy   Roger B. Porter
Assistant to the President for Public
 Events and Initiatives   Sigmund Rogich
Assistant to the President for National
 Security   Gen. Brent Scowcroft, USAF, (Ret.)
Assistant to the President and Director
 of Presidential Personnel   Charles G. Untermeyer
Deputy Assistant to the President and
 Director, Office of Intergovernmental Affairs   Debra Anderson

Deputy Assistant to the President for
Management and Director, Office of Administration Paul W. Bateman
Deputy Assistant to the President for
Legislative Affairs   Nicholas E. Calio
Deputy Assistant to the President and
Director, Office of Cabinet Affairs   Stephen I. Danzansky
Deputy Assistant to the President for
Appointments and Scheduling   Joseph W. Hagin II
Deputy Assistant to the President for
Legislative Affairs (Senate)   E. Boyd Hollingsworth, Jr.
Deputy Assistant to the President for
Presidential Personnel   Ronald C. Kaufman
Deputy Assistant to the President and
Director of Presidential Advance   John G. Keller, Jr.
Deputy Assistant to the President for Public Liasion   Barbara G. Kilberg
Deputy Assistant to the President and
Director, Office of National Service   C. Gregg Petersmeyer
Deputy Assistant to the President for
Policy Planning   James P. Pinkerton
Deputy Assistant to the President and
Deputy Press Secretary   Roman Popadiuk
Deputy Assistant to the President for
Legislative Affairs   Robert J. Portman
Deputy Assistant to the President   Patricia Presock
Deputy Assistant to the President and
Executive Assistant to the Chief of Staff   Edward M. Rogers, Jr.
Deputy Assistant to the President and
Chief of Staff to the First Lady   Susan Porter Rose
Deputy Counsel to the President   John P. Schmitz
Deputy Assistant to the President for Public Liasion   Sichan Siv
Deputy Assistant to the President and
Deputy Director of Presidential Personnel   Roscoe B. Starek III
Deputy Assistant to the President for
Communications and Director of Speechwriting   Chriss Winston
Deputy Assistant to the President and
Director, Office of Political Affairs   James Wray
Special Assistant to the President for Communications Deborah A. Amend
Special Assistant to the President for
Legislative Affairs (House)   Gary J. Andres
Special Assistant to the President for
National Security Affairs   Robert D. Blackwill
Special Assistant to the President for
Intergovernmental Affairs   William J. Canary

Special Assistant to the President and Deputy Direcor, Office of Political Affairs	David M. Carney
Special Assistant to the President for Political Affairs	Paul J. Collins, Jr.
Special Assistant to the President for National Security Affairs	Timothy E. Deal
Special Assistant to the President for Cabinet Affairs	Juanita D. Duggan
Special Assistant to the President for Agricultural Trade and Food Assistance	Cooper Evans
Special Assistant to the President for Policy Development	Stephen Farrar
Special Assistant to the President and Assistant Staff Secretary	John S. Gardner
Special Assistant to the President and Deputy Press Secretary	Alixie R. Glen
Special Assistant to the President and Associate Director of Presidential Personnel	Martha H. Goodwin
Special Assistant to the President for Policy Development	Theresa A. Gorman
Special Assistant to the President for Presidential Messages and Correspondence	Shirley M. Green
Special Assistant to the President for Intergovernmental Affairs	George O. Griffith, Jr.
Special Assistant to the President and Associate Director of Presidential Personnel	Anne B. Gwaltney
Special Assistant to the President for National Security Affairs	Richard N. Haass
Special Assistant to the President and Deputy Press Secretary	Stephen T. Hart
Special Assistant to the President for Legislative Affairs (House)	John W. Howard
Executive Secretary of the National Security Council	G. Philip Hughes
Special Assistant to the President and Deputy Director, Office of Administration	Hector F. Irastorza, Jr.
Special Assistant to the President for National Security Affairs	Arnold Kanter
Special Assistant to the President for National Security Affairs	Virginia A. Lampley
Physician to the President	Burton Lee III, M.D.
Associate Counsel to the President	Lee S. Liberman
Special Assistant to the President for Policy Development	Lawrence Lindsey
Associate Counsel to the President	Nelson Lund

Special Assistant to the President and Associate Director of Presidential Personnel	Jose Martinez
Special Assistant to the President	Timothy J. McBride
Special Assistant to the President for Intergovernmental Affairs	Mary A. McLure
Special Assistant to the President for Policy Development	Marianne McGettigan
Special Assistant to the President for National Security Affairs	David C. Miller, Jr.
Special Assistant to the President and Associate Director of Presidential Personnel	Nancy F. Miller
Special Assistant to the President and Associate Director of Presidential Personnel	Jeannette L. Naylor
Special Assistant to the President and Associate Director of Presidential Personnel	Thomas F. Needles
Associate Counsel to the President	Frederick D. Nelson
Special Assistant to the President for Legislative Affairs	Frances McNurtray Norris
Special Assistant to the President for Legislative Affairs	Penelope Payne
Special Assistant to the President for National Security Affairs	William T. Pryce
Special Assistant to the President for National Security Affairs	Peter W. Rodman
Special Assistant to the President for National Security Affairs	Charles Nicholas Rostow
Associate Counsel to the President	Amy L. Schartz
Special Assistant to the President for Legislative Affairs (Senate)	David P. Sloane
Special Assistant to the President and Director of the White House Military Office	Richard G. Tefry
Special Assistant to the President for Legislative Affairs	Brian K. Waidmann
Special Assistant to the President for Public Liasion	R. Doughlas Wead
Special Assistant to the President and Executive Secretary, Economic Policy Counsel	Olin Lewis Wethington
Special Assistant to the President for National Security Affairs	William W. Working
Special Assistant to the President and Executive Secretary , Domestic Policy Council	Kenneth Yale
Special Assistant to the President and Director of White House Operations	Rose M. Zamaria

The White House Staff 1991-92

Chief of Staff to the President	John H. Sununu
Assistant to the President and Deputy Chief of Staff	Andrew H. Card
Assistant to the President and Staff Secretary	Philip Brady
Assistant to the President for Science and Technology	D. Allan Bromley
Assistant to the President for Communications	David F. Demarest, Jr.
Assistant to the President and Press Secretary	Max Marlin Fitzwater
Assistant to the President and Deputy for National Security Affairs	Robert M. Gates
Counsel to the President	C. Boyden Gray
Assistant to the President and Secretary of the Cabinet	Edith E. Holiday
Physician to the President	Burton J. Lee III, M.D.
Assistant to the President for Legislative Affairs	Frederick D. McLure
Assistant to the President and Director, Office of National Service	C. Gregg Petersmeyer
Assistant to the President for Economic and Domestic Policy	Roger B. Porter
Assistant to the President for Public Events and Initiatives	Sigmund Rogich
Assistant to the President for National Security Affairs	Gen. Brent Scowcroft, USAF
Assistant to the President for Media Affairs	J. Dorrance Smith
Assistant to the President for Presidential Personnel	Charles G. Untermeyer
Deputy Assistant to the President and Director, Office of Intergovernmental Affairs	Debra Anderson
Deputy Assistant to the President for Management and Director, Office of Administration	Paul W. Bateman
Deputy Assistant to the President for Legislative Affairs (House)	Gary J. Andres
Deputy Assistant to the President and Director, Office of Cabinet Affairs	Stephen I. Danzansky
Deputy Assistant to the President for Legislative Affairs (Senate)	James W. Dyer
Deputy Assistant to the President for	

Political Affairs	Ronald C Kaufman
Deputy Assistant to the President for Public Liasion	Bobbie G. Kilberg
Deputy Assistant to the President for Domestic Policy	Charles E.M. Kolb
Deputy Assistant to the President and Deputy Director of Presidential Personnel	Jeannette L. Naylor
Deputy Assistant to the President for Policy Planning	James P. Pinkerton
Deputy Assistant to the President and Deputy Press Secretary	Roman Popadiuk
Deputy Assistant to the President	Patricia Presock
Deputy Assistant to the President and Executive Assistant to the Chief of Staff	Edward M. Rogers, Jr.
Deputy Assistant to the President and Chief of Staff to the First Lady	Susan Porter Rose
Deputy Counsel to the President	John P. Schmitz
Deputy Assistant to the President for Public Liasion	Sichan Siv
Deputy Assistant to the President for Cabinet Liasion	Gary R. Blumenthal
Deputy Assistant to the President for Communications and Director of Speechwriting	Robert Anthony Snow
Deputy Assistant to the President for Appointments and Scheduling	Katherine Super
Deputy Assistant to the President and Director of White House Operations	Rose M. Zamaria
Special Assistant to the President for Communications	Deborah A. Amend
Special Assistant to the President for Legislative Affairs (House)	Arnold I. Havens
Special Assistant to the President for Intergovernmental Affairs	William J. Canary
Special Assitant to the President and Director, Office of Political Affairs	David M. Carney
Special Assistant to the President for Political Affairs	Paul J. Collins, Jr.
Special Assistant to the President for National Security Affairs	Timothy E. Deal
Special Assistant to the President for Policy Development	Stephen Farrar
Special Assistant to the President and Assistant Staff Secretary	John S. Gardner

Special Assistant to the President for Presidential Press Advance	Spencer E. Geissinger
Special Assistant to the President and Senior Director for European and Soviet Affairs	David C. Gompert
Special Assistant to the President and Associate Director of Presidential Personnel	Martha H. Goodwin
Special Assistant to the President for Policy Development	Teresa A. Gorman
Special Assistant to the President for Presidential Messages and Correspondence	Shirley M. Green
Special Assistant to the President for Intergovernmental Affairs	George O. Griffith, Jr.
Special Assistant to the President and Associate Director of Presidential Personnel	Anne B. Gwaltney
Special Assistant to the President for National Security Affairs	Richard N. Haass
Special Assistant to the President and Deputy Press Secretary	Stephen T. Hart
Special Assistant to the President for National Security Affairs	Edward A. Hewett
Associate Counsel to the President	Jeffery R. Holmstead
Special Assistant to the President for Legislative Affairs (House)	John W. Howard
Special Assistant to the President and Deputy Director, Office of Administration	Hector F. Irastorza, Jr.
Special Assistant to the President and Executive Secretary for Cabinet Liasion	Michael P. Jackson
Special Assistant to the President for National Security Affairs	Arnold Kanter
Special Assistant to the President for National Security Affairs	Virginia A. Lampley
Associate Counsel to the President	Lee S. Lieberman
Special Assistant to the President for Policy Development	Lawrence Lindsay
Associate Counsel to the President	Nelson Lund
Special Assistant to the President and Associate Director of Presidential Personnel	Jose E. Martinez
Special Assistant to the President for Intergovernmental Affairs	Mary A. McClure
Special Assistant to the President for Policy Development	Marianne McGettigan
Special Assistant to the President for Public Liasion	Leigh Ann Metzger

Special Assistant to the President and Associate
   Director of Presidential Personnel   Nancy Miller
Special Assistant to the President for
   Legislative Affairs   Frances McMurtray Norris
Special Assistant to the President for
   National Security Affairs   Douglas Paal
Special Assistant to the President and Director
   of Presidential Advance   Jake L. Parmer
Special Assistant to the President for
   Legislative Affairs   Nell Payne
Special Assistant to the President and Executive
   Secretary, Domesic Policy Council   Richard W. Porter
Special Assistant to the President for
   National Security Affairs   William T. Pryce
Special Assistant to the President for
   National Security Affairs   C. Nicholas Rostow
Associate Counsel to the President   Gene C. Schaerr
Executive Secretary, National Security Council   William F. Sittmann
Special Assistant to the President for
   Legislative Affairs (Senate)   Shawn H. Smeallie
Special Assistant to the President and Deputy
   Press Secretary   Judy A. Smith
Military Assistant to the President and Director,
   White House Military Office   Lt. Gen. Richard Tefrey, USA (Ret.)
Special Assistant to the President for
   Legislative Affairs   Brian K. Waidmann
Associate Counsel to the President   Gregory S. Walden
Special Assistant to the President and Executive
   Secretary, Economic Policy Council   Olin Lewis Washington
Special Assistant to the President for
   National Security Affairs   William W. Working

The White House Staff 1992–93

Chief of Staff to the President   Samuel K. Skinner
Deputy Chief of Staff to the President   W. Henson Moore
Assistant to the President and Staff Secretary   Philip D. Brady
Assistant to the President for Science
   and Technology   D. Allan Brady
Assistant to the President for Legislative Affairs   Nicholas E. Calio
Assistant to the President for Communications   David F. Demarest, Jr.
Counselor to the President and
   Press Secretary   Max Marlin Fitzwater

Counsel to the President	C. Boyden Gray
Assistant to the President and Secretary of the Cabinet	Edith E. Holiday
Assistant to the President and Director of Presidential Personnel	Constance Horner
Physician to the President	Burton J. Lee III, M.D.
Assistant to the President for Management and Administration	Timothy J. McBride
Assistant to the President and Director of the Office of National Service	C. Gregg Petersmeyer
Assistant to the President for Economic and Domestic Policy	Roger B. Porter
Assistant to the President for Public Events and Initiatives	Sigmund Rogich
Assistant to the President for Public Liasion and Intergovernmental Affairs	Sherrie S. Rollins
Assistant to the President for National Security Affairs	Gen. Brent Scowcroft, USAF (Ret.)
Assistant to the President for Media Affairs	J. Dorrance Smith
Counselor to the President for Domestic Policy	Clayton Yeutter
Deputy Assistant to the President for Legislative Affairs (House)	Gary J. Andres
Deputy Assistant to the President for Cabinet Liasion and Special Assistant to the President for Agricultural Trade and Food Assistance	Gary R. Blumenthal
Deputy Assistant to the President and Director of the Office of Legislative Affairs	Joshua Bolten
Deputy Assistant to the President for Legislative Affairs (Senate)	James W. Dyer
Deputy Assistant to the President and Counselor to the Chief of Staff	D. Cameron Finlay
Deputy Assistant to the President and Director of the White House Military Office	John A. Gaughan
Deputy Assistant to the President for National Security Affairs	Adm. Jonathan T. Howe, USN
Deputy Assistant to the President for Political Affairs	Ronald Kaufman
Deputy Assistant to the President and Director of the Office of Intergovernmental Affairs	Bobbi G. Kilberg

Deputy Assistant to the President for Domestic Policy	Charles E.M. Kolb
Deputy Assistant to the President and Director of the Office of Public Liasion	Cecile B. Kremer
Deputy Assistant to the President for Public Liasion	Leigh Ann Metzger
Deputy Assistant to the President and Director of Presidential Advance	Edward D. Murname
Deputy Assistant to the President and Deputy Director of Presidential Personnel	Jeannette L. Naylor
Deputy Assistant to the President and Deputy Press Secretary	Roman Popadiuk
Deputy Assistant to the President	Patricia Presock
Deputy Assistant to the President and Chief of Staff to the First Lady	Susan Porter Rose
Deputy Counsel to the President	John P. Schmitz
Deputy Assistant to the President for Public Liasion	Sichan Siv
Deputy Assistant to the President for Media Affairs	Robert Anthony Snow
Deputy Assistant to the President for Appointments and Scheduling	Katherine Super
Deputy Assistant to the President for Policy Development	Gail R. Wilensky
Deputy Assistant to the President and Director of White House Operations	Rose M. Zamaria
Special Assistant to the President and Executive Secretary, Policy Coordinating Group	J. French Hill
Associate Counsel to the President	Jeffrey R. Holmstead
Special Assistant to the President for Legislative Affairs (House)	John W. Howard
Special Assistant to the President for National Security Affairs	Virginia A. Lampley
Associate Counsel to the President	Lee S. Liberman
Associate Counsel to the President	Nelson Lund
Special Assistant to the President for Intergovernmental Affairs	Mary A. McClure
Special Assistant to the President and Deputy Director of Speechwriting	Daniel B. McGroarty
Special Assistant to the President for Legislative Affairs (House)	Kim F. McKernan
Special Assistant to the President and Senior Director for International Programs	Thomas E. McNamara
Special Assistant to the President and Associate Director of Presidential Personnel	Nancy F. Miller

Special Assistant to the President for
  National Security Affairs   Douglas Pal
Special Assistant to the President for
  National Security Affairs   William T. Pryce
Special Assistant to the President for
  National Security Affairs   C. Nicholas Rostow
Associate Counsel to the President   Gene C. Schaerr
Executive Secretary of the National Security Counsel   William F. Sittmann
Special Assistant to the President for
  Legislative Affairs (Senate)   Shawn H. Smeallie
Special Assistant to the President and
  Deputy Press Secretary   Judy A. Smith
Special Assistant to the President for
  Intergovernmental Affairs   James J. Snyder
Special Assistant to the President for
  Legislative Affairs (Senate)   Linda E. Tarplin
Special Assistant to the President for
  Legislative Affairs (Senate)   Brian K. Waidmann
Associate Counsel to the President   Gregory S. Walden
Special Assistant to the President for
  National Security Affairs   William W. Working
Special Assistant to the President for
  Intergovernmental Affairs   David J. Beightol
Special Assistant to the President and
  Deputy Director for Scheduling   Antonio Denedi
Special Assistant to the President for Political Affairs   Paul J. Collins Jr.
Special Assistant to the President and
  Associate Director of Presidential Personnel   Les T. Csorba
Special Assistant to the President for
  National Security Affairs   Timothy E. Deal
Special Assistant to the President and
  Deputy Press Secretary   Gary L. Foster
Special Assistant to the President and
  Deputy Staff Secretary   John S. Gardner
Special Assistant to the President and Senior Director
  for European and Soviet Affairs   David C. Gompert
Special Assistant to the President and
  Associate Director of Presidential Personnel   Martha H. Goodwin
Special Assistant to the President for
  National Security Affairs   John A. Gordon
Special Assistant to the President for
  Policy Development   Teresa A. Gorman

Special Assistant to the President for
    Presidential Messages and Correspondence   Shirley M. Green
Special Assistant to the President and
    Associate Director of Presidential Personnel   Anne B. Gwaltney
Special Assistant to the President for
    National Security Affairs   Richard N. Haass
Special Assistant to the President for
    Legislative Affairs (House)   Arnold I. Havens
Special Assistant to the President for Advance   John F. Herrick
Special Assistant to the President for
    National Security Affairs   Edward A. Hewett

The Clinton Cabinet, 1992–1994

Name	Date of Appointment
Secretary of State Warren Christopher	1992
Secretary of Treasury Lloyd Bentsen	1992
Secretary of Defense Les Aspin William Perry	1992 1993
Attorney General Janet Reno	1992
Secretary of the Interior Bruce Babbitt	1992
Secretary of Agriculture Mike Espy	1992
Secretary of Commerce Ron Brown	1992
Secretary of Labor Robert Reich	1992
Secretary of Health and Human Services Donna Shalala	1992
Secretary of Housing and Urban Development Henry Cisneros	1992
Secretary of Transportation Federico Pena	1992
Secretary of Education Richard Riley	1992

Secretary of Energy
   Hazel O'Leary   1992

Secretary of Veterans Affairs
   Jesse Brown   1992

The White House Staff 1992–93

Chief of Staff to the President	Thomas (Mack) McLarty III
Deputy Chief of Staff to the President	Mark D. Gearan
Deputy Chief of Staff to the President	Roy Neel
Assistant to the President and Staff Secretary	John Podesta
Assistant to the President for Science and Technology	John H. Gibbons
Assistant to the President for Legislative Affairs	Howard Paster
Special Assistant for Legislative Affairs	Steve Richetti
Assistant to the President for Communications	George Stephanopoulos
Press Secretary	Dee Dee Myers
Counsel to the President	Bernard Nussbaum
Deputy Assistant to Clinton and Cabinet Secretary	Christine A. Varney
Assistant to the President and Director of Presidential Personnel	Bruce Lindsey
Assistant to the President for Management and Administration	David Watkins
Assistant to the President and Director of the Office of National Service	Eli J. Segal
Special Assistant for Domestic Policy	Shirley Sagawa
Assistant for Domestic Policy	Carol H. Rasco
Economic Policy Czar	Robert E. Rubin
Deputy Assistant for Economic Policy	Gene Sperling, W. Bowman Cutter
Director of Public Liaison	Alexis M. Herman
Director of Intergovernmental Affairs	Regina Montoya
National Security Advisor	Anthony Lake
Deputy Assistant for National Security Affairs	Samuel Berger
Deputy Assistant to the President and Deputy Press Secretary	Lorraine A. Voles
Director of Media Affairs	Jeff Eller
Deputy Director of Legislative Affairs	Susan Brophy
Assistant to the President and Director of Political Affairs	Rahn Emmanuel
Deputy Director of Public Liaison	Doris Matsui

Deputy Assistant for Appointments and Scheduling	Nancy Hernreich
Deputy Assistant for Legislative Affairs	Lorraine Miller
Director of Scheduling and Advance	Isabelle Rodriquez Tapia
Director of Speechwriting	David Kusnet
Chief of Staff to the First Lady	Margaret A. Williams
Deputy Counsel to the President	Vince Foster
Deputy Communications Director	Ricki Seidman
Special Assistant for Policy Coordination	Bob Boorstin
Associate Counsels	Ronald Klain & Cheryl Mills
Special Assistant for Speech Writing	David Kusnet
Special Assistants for Public Liaison	Mike Lux & Amy Zisook
Special Assistant to the President for Political Affairs	Elaine Weiss
Assistant to the President for Communications	Sara M. Pines
Planning Director	David Dreyer

[3]General Haig's retirement effective August 1, 1973.
[4]Resigned September 8, 1974.

Notes

Chapter 1

1. Richard F. Fenno, Jr., *The President's Cabinet* (New York: Vintage Books, 1959), 6.

2. Fenno, *The President's Cabinet*

3. Bradley H. Patterson, *The President's Cabinet* (Washington, D.C.: Basic Books, 1976).

4. Thomas E. Cronin, *The State of the Presidency* (Boston: Little Brown and Company: 1980). See also Louis W. Koenig, The Chief Executive (New York: Harcourt Brace Jovanovich, 1986).

5. Louis Koenig, *The Chief Executive* (New York: Harcourt Brace Jovanovich, 1986).

6. Harold M. Barger, *The Impossible Presidency: Illusions and Realities of Executive Power* (Glenview, Illinois: Scott, Foresman and Company, 1984).

7. Hugh Heclo, "One Executive Branch or Many?," *Both Ends of the Avenue: The Presidency, The Executive Branch, and Congress in the 1980's,* Anthony King, ed. (Washington, D.C.: American Enterprise Institute, 1983).

8. Lester Salamon, "The Presidency and Domestic Policy," *Analyzing the Presidency*, Robert DiClerico, editor (Guilford, Ct.: The Dushkin Group, 1985).

9. G. Calvin Mackenzie, *The Politics of Presidential Appointments* (New York: Free Press, 1981).

10. Paul C. Light, *The President's Agenda: Domestic Policy Choice from Kennedy to Carter* (Baltimore: Johns Hopkins University Press, 1983); Matthew R. Kerbel, *Beyond Persuasion: Organizational Efficiency and Presidential Power* (Albany: State University of New York Press, 1991); John P. Burke, *The Institutional Presidency* (Baltimore: Johns Hopkins University Press, 1994).

11. Bradley H. Patterson, *Ring of Power: The White House Staff and Its*

Expanding Role in Government (New York: Basic Books, 1988); John Hart, *The Presidential Branch: From Washington to Clinton,* second edition (Chatham, New Jersey: Chatham House, 1995); James P. Pfiffner, *The Modern Presidency* (New York: St. Martin's Press, 1994).

12. Richard P. Nathan, *"The Reagan Presidency in Domestic Affairs,"* The 'Reagan Presidency: An Early Assessment (Baltimore: Johns Hopkins University Press, 1983); Joseph Pika and Norman Thomas, "The President as Institution Builder: The Reagan Years," paper presented at the annual meeting of the American Political Science Association, 1989; Chester A. Newland, "A Mid-Term Appraisal—The Reagan Presidency: Limited Government and Political Administration," *Public Administration Review*, Volume 43, Number 1, January/February 1983.

CHAPTER 2

1. Henry Barrett Learned, *The President's Cabinet: Studies in the Origin, Formation, and Structure of an American Institution* (New York: Burt Franklin, 1912; reprint, New York: Burt Franklin, 1972), 13 (page references are to reprint edition).

2. John P. Macintosh, *The British Cabinet,* 2d ed. (London: Stevens and Sons, Limited, 1968), 38.

3. Karl Loewenstein, *British Cabinet Government* (New York: Oxford University Press, 1967), 84.

4. Walter Bagehot, *The English Constitution,* rev. ed. (Ithaca, New York: Cornell University Press, 1963, first published in 1867), 61.

5. Malcolm Townsend, *Handbook of United States Political History,* rev. ed. (Boston: Lothrop, Lee and Shepard Co., 1910), 318.

6. Learned, *Cabinet,* 53.

7. Edward Channing, *A History of the United States*, vol. 2 (New York: MacMillian Company, 1938), 43.

8. Alexander Hamilton, James Madison, and John Jay, *The Federalist Papers,* No. 70 (New York: Mentor Books, 1961), 428–29.

9. Woodrow Wilson, *George Washington* (New York: Schocken Books, 1969, first published 1896), 273.

10. Robert Jones, "George Washington and the Establishment of a Tradition," *Power and the Presidency*, 15. Also see James MacGregor Burns, *Presidential Government, The Crucible of Leadership* (Boston: Houghton Mifflin Company, 1965).

11. Hamilton, *Federalist Papers*, No. 72, 436.

12. R. Gordon Hoxie, "The Cabinet in the American Presidency, 1789–1984,"

Presidential Studies Quarterly 14 (Spring 1984): 214.

13. Learned, *Cabinet,* 136–37.

14. Hoxie, *"Cabinet,"* 214.

15. The population of the United States increased from 3,929,214 in 1790 to 9,638,453 in 1820 to 23,191,876 in 1850.

16. Robert A. Diamond, ed., *Origins and Development of Congress,* (Washington, D.C.: Congressional Quarterly, Inc., 1976), 193.

17. Thomas Bonaventure Lawler, *Essentials of American History,* rev. ed. (Boston: Lothrop, Lee and Shepard, Co., 1910), 247–48.

18. Townsend, *Handbook,* 127–28.

19. Wilfred E. Binkley, *President and Congress,* 3d. ed., rev. (New York: Vintage Books, 1962), 152–53.

20. Stephen Horn, *The Cabinet and Congress* (New York: Columbia University Press, 1960), 54.

21. Woodrow Wilson published *Congressional Government* in 1885, which proposed a British-style Cabinet Government with the president and his Cabinet sharing responsibility for policy initiatives. To accommodate Wilson's proposals, two constitutional amendments were required: changes in Article I, Section 6 to allow Cabinet officers to sit in Congress and changes in Article I, sections 2 and 3 and Article II, Section 1 to change the length of House, Senate, and presidential terms to coincide. Wilson substantially changed his view on the value of collective responsibility for decision-making by the time he entered the presidency, but retained his high esteem for the Cabinet as a participant in the decision-making process.

22. Arthur S. Link, *Woodrow Wilson and the Progressive Era, 1910–1917* (New York: Harper and Row, 1954), 32.

23. Hoxie, *"Cabinet,"* 222.

24. Hamilton, *Federalist Papers,* No. 72, 436.

25. Clinton Rossiter, *The American Presidency,* 2d ed. (New York: Time, Inc., Book Division, 1960), 135.

26. James MacGregor Burns, *Presidential Government* (Boston: Houghton Mifflin Company, 1965), 129.

27. Larry Berman, *The Office of Management and Budget* (Princeton, New Jersey: Princeton University Press, 1979), 13.

28. President's Committee on Administrative Management, Report of the Committee, Submitted to the President and the Congress in Accordance with Public Law no. 739, 74th Congress, 2nd session, 1937.

29. Edward S. Corwin, *The President: Office and Powers, 1787–1984*, rev. ed. (New York: New York University Press, 1984), 538.

30. Stephen Hess, *Organizing the Presidency*, rev. ed. (Washington, D.C.: Brookings Institution, 1988), 30.

31. Brownlow Committee Report, 2 and 5.

32. Emmette S. Redrod and Richard T. McCulley, *White House Operations* (Austin, Texas: University of Austin Press, 1986), 5.

33. Harry S. Truman, *Memoirs, Volume 1* (Garden City, New York: Doubleday, 1955), 12–13.

34. Margaret Truman, *Harry S. Truman* (New York: Pocket Books, 1974), 276.

35. Hess, *Organizing the Presidency*, 47.

36. "Study of the 1960–61 Presidential Transition," November 11, 1960, Brookings Institution, Washington, D.C.

37. Adams, who became the most powerful member of the White House staff, hardly knew Eisenhower. Adams's first association with Eisenhower came at the Republican convention of 1952 where he operated as a floor manager for Eisenhower. His first working relationship with Eisenhower came when the newly elected president brought him into the transition headquarters at the Commodore Hotel to organize the outpouring of mail and calls. See Herbert Brownell, *Advising Ike* (Lawrence, Kansas: University of Kansas Press, 1993).

38. Stephen Ambrose notes that Eisenhower "set about picking his principal White House aides and organizing them along lines taken from both the SHAEF example and that of the British War Cabinet." Stephen E. Ambrose, *Eisenhower, Volume 11* (New York: Simon and Schuster, 1984), 25.

39. For one of the most detailed discussions of the Eisenhower Cabinet Secretariat, see Bradley H. Patterson, Jr., *Ring of Power: The White House Staff and Its Expanding Role in Government* (New York: Basic Books, 1988).

40. Bradley H. Patterson, *Ring of Power*. 31.

41. Arthur M. Schlesinger, Jr., *A Thousand Days* (Greenwich, Connecticut: Fawcett Crest Books, 1965), 631–32.

42. Ibid., 631.

43. Patrick Anderson, *The President's Men* (Garden City, New York: Doubleday and Company, Inc., 1965), 233.

44. Anderson, *President's Men*, 266.

45. Schlesinger, *Thousand*, 851.

46. Doris Kearns, *Lyndon Johnson and the American Dream* (New York: Signet

Books, 1976), 255.

47. R. Gordon Hoxie, ed., *The White House: Organization and Operation* (New York: Center for the Study of the Presidency, 1971), 72–73.

48. Norman C. Thomas and Harold L. Wolman, "The Presidency and Policy Formulation: The Task Force Device," *Public Administration Review* 24 (September-October 1969): 461–62.

49. Don K. Price and Rocco C. Siciliano, *A Presidency for the 1980's* (Washington, D.C.: National Academy of Public Administration, 1980), 32.

50. Jack Valenti, *A Very Human President* (New York: W.W. Norton and Company, Inc., 1975), 62.

51. Rossiter, *Presidency*, 277.

CHAPTER 3

1. Dan Rather and Gary Paul Gates, *The Palace Guard* (New York: Warner Paperback Library, 1975), 81.

2. Richard Nixon, *R.N., The Memoirs of Richard Nixon* (New York: Grosset and Dunlop, 1978), 337–38. See also H.R. Haldeman, *Ends of Power* (New York: Dell Books, 1979), 84.

3. Rowland Evans, Jr., and Robert D. Novak, *Nixon in the White House* (New York: Random House, 1971), 48.

4. Another view of why the White House staff was kept small was furthered by columnists Evans and Novak. In their view, the White House staff was kept small for another reason: Nixon's need for privacy. The structure reduced the amount of time Nixon needed to spend with his Cabinet officers. He preferred, according to Evans and Novak, "long periods alone. . . for reading, writing and just plain thinking." Evans and Novak, *Nixon*, 48.

5. For an overview of Nixon's search for a bipartisan Cabinet, see Nixon, *R.N.*, 338.

6. The Post Office Department was a Cabinet position until 1970 when the Postal Reorganization Act replaced the department with the Postal Service, an independent federal agency.

7. Maurice Stans's appointment to the Department of Commerce was a compromise. The banking community adamantly refused to accept Stans as Treasury Secretary, Nixon's original choice of a Cabinet position for him.

8. Lyndon Johnson was extraordinarily proud of his success in creating the Department of Housing and Urban Development. He notes in *The Vantage Point:*

"Three-quarters of a century after the farmers had been given a voice at the Cabinet table, the cities still had none. Our urban programs had grown into a network of separate fiefdoms. We pulled them all together by establishing a new Department of Housing and Urban Development, headed by the first Negro to serve in a President's Cabinet, Secretary Robert C. Weaver." Lyndon Johnson, *The Vantage Point: Perspectives of the Presidency, 1963–1969* (New York: Holt, Rinehart, and Winston, 1971), 329.

9. Nixon, *R.N.*, 338–39.

10. Dom Bonafede, "Nixon's First Year Appointments Reveal Pattern of his Administration," *National Journal*, January 24, 1970, 190.

11. Ibid., 190–91.

12. Chalmers M. Roberts, "Rogers Picked by Nixon for Secretary of State," *Washington Post*, December 11, 1968, A7.

13. "Excerpts from a National Radio Speech by Richard Nixon," *New York Times*, September 20, 1968, A1.

14. Martin Anderson, *Welfare: The Political Economy of Welfare Reform in the United States* (Stanford, California: Hoover Institution Press, 1978) 6.

15. Interview with H. R. Haldeman. See also Nixon, *R.N.*, 342.

16. Interview with Bryce Harlow.

17. "Excerpts from a National Radio Speech by Richard Nixon," *New York Times*, December 20, 1968, A1.

18. "Nixon, On Television, Presents His Cabinet," *Washington Post*, December 12, 1969, A8.

19. Carol Kilpatrick, "Nixon and Cabinet Meet, Set Drive on Crime, Inflation," *Washington Post*, January 23, 1969, A1.

20. Theodore H. White, *The Making of the President 1968* (New York: Atheneum, 1969), 504.

21. The Urban Affairs Council included the seven domestic Cabinet officers: the Attorney General, Secretary of Agriculture, Secretary of Commerce, Secretary of Labor, Secretary of Health, Education & Welfare, Secretary of Housing and Urban Development, and the Secretary of Transportation. In addition, both the president and vice president were members of the council, with the president the presiding officer. Executive Order 11452, July 23, 1969.

22. Daniel Patrick Moynihan, *Maximum Feasible Misunderstanding* (New York: Free Press, 1970), 79.

23. Daniel Patrick Moynihan, *The Politics of a Guaranteed Income* (New York: Vintage Books, 1973), 74.

24. Roger Porter, *Presidential Decision-Making: The Economic Policy Board* (Cambridge, England: Cambridge University Press, 1980), 92.   The Cabinet Committee on Economic Policy consisted of the president, vice president, Arthur Burns, the Chairman of the Council of Economic Advisors, the Director of the Bureau of the Budget, and the Secretaries of Treasury, Agriculture, Commerce, and Labor.

25. Public Papers of the President, "Presidential Directives on Domestic Issues," February 10, 1969, 209.

26. Seymour M. Hersh, *The Price of Power, Kissinger in the White House* (New York: Summit Books, 1983), 32.

27. Chart, May 14, 1974, "Domestic Policy Committees," Box 69, James Cannon File, Gerald R. Ford Presidential Library, Ann Arbor, Michigan.

28. Interview with John Ehrlichman. See also John Ehrlichman, *Witness to Power* (New York: Simon and Schuster, 1982), 82–83.

29. Richard P. Nathan, *The Plot That Failed* (New York: John Wiley and Sons, Inc., 1975), 47.

30."The President's Message to Congress Transmitting Reorganization Plan 2 of 1970, Implementing Recommendations of the President's Advisory Council on Executive Organization," March 12, 1970. *Public Papers of the President*, 353.

31. Office of the White House Press Secretary, December 14, 1972. "Delegation of Certain Functions to the Executive Director of the Domestic Council."

32. *Congressional Quarterly Almanac* 1969, volume 25, 115.

33. Paul C. Light, *The President's Agenda: Domestic Policy Choice from Kennedy to Carter* (Baltimore: Johns Hopkins University Press, 1982), 45.

34. Ronald Randall, "Presidential Power versus Bureaucratic Intransigence: The Influence of the Nixon Administration on Welfare Policy," *American Political Science Review* 73 (June 1979): 795.

35. James L. Sundquist, *Politics and Policy: The Eisenhower, Kennedy, and Johnson Years* (Washington, D.C.: Brookings Institution, 1968), 415.

36. Louis Fisher, *President and Congress — Power and Policy* (New York: Free Press, 1972), 213.

37. See Henry Kissinger, *White House Years* (Boston: Little, Brown and Company, 1979), 73ff., and Nixon, R.N., 394.

38. "President Lists Plans for Domestic Legislation," *Congressional Quarterly Almanac 1969*, April 14, 1969, A39.

39. Roger H. Davidson, "The Presidency and Congress," in *The Presidency and the Political System*, ed. Michael Nelson (Washington, D.C.: Congressional Quarterly Press, 1984), 374.

40. Nixon's concern that the career staff was Democratically oriented was supported in a 1970 study by Joel Aberbach and Bert Rockman, who examined the partisan affiliations of senior members of the bureaucracy. They determined that the top career staff was predominantly non-Republican (either Democratic or Independent) and had a liberal approach to the role of government in the delivery of social services. They did not, however, assess whether or not the career staff was directly opposed to specific policies proposed by Nixon. See Joel D. Aberbach and Bert A. Rockman, "Clashing Beliefs Within the Executive Branch: The Nixon Administration Bureaucracy," *American Political Science Review*, 70 (June 1976): 467. Six years later, as part of a larger study on personal management during the Nixon years, Richard Cole and David Caputo concluded that the top career staff were generally willing to support specific presidential policies. See Richard L. Cole and David A. Caputo, "Presidential Control of the Senior Civil Service: Assessing the Strategies of the Nixon Years," *American Political Science Review* 73 (June 1979): 402.

41. Ibid., 267.

42. Ibid., 761.

43. Nathan, *Plot*, 82.

44. Ibid., 228.

45. Finch appointed James Allen as Assistant Secretary of Education, described by Richard Nathan as "the liberal New York State Education Commissioner." See Nathan, *Plot*, 50. Finch also appointed Leon Panetta, a liberal Republican from California who was committed to federal enforcement of school desegregation, as Director of the Office of Civil Rights.

46. During his second term, Nixon abandoned the idea that Cabinet officials choose their own personnel. Nixon endeavored to implement a strategy in which all sub-Cabinet personnel were cleared by the White House and were supportive of administrative goals. In his memoirs Nixon states, "In some cases I planned to transfer White House staff members into Cabinet departments to see to it that our policies would be followed. See Nixon, *R.N.*, 769. For a description of this process, see Nathan and Fred Malek, *Washington's Hidden Tragedy* (New York: Free Press, 1978).

47. Francis Rourke argues that because of "the nature of their mission or the dedication of their personal, some agencies generated a good deal more energy than others." See Francis E. Rourke, "Variations in Agency Power," *Bureaucratic Power in National Politics*, ed. Francis E. Rourke, 3d ed. (Boston: Little, Brown and Company, 1978), 224.

48. Ehrlichman, *Witness*, 105.

49. Dennis R. Judd, *The Politics of the American Cities* (Boston: Little, Brown and Company, 1979), 308ff.

50. Walter J. Hickel, *Who Owns America?* (Englewood Cliffs, New Jersey: Prentice-Hall, Inc., 1971).

51. Moynihan, *Misunderstanding*, 182.

52. "Executive Office Staff Expanding Despite Decentralization Pledge," *National Journal*, April 25, 1970, 858.

53. For excellent discussions of the supercabinet concept, see A. James Reichley, *Conservatives in An Age of Change: The Nixon and Ford Administrations* (Washington, D.C.: Brookings Institution, 1981), 246; and Joan Hoff, *Nixon Reconsidered* (New York: Basic Books, 1994), 73–76.

54. Jeffrey E. Cohen, *The Politics of the U.S. Cabinet* (Pittsburgh: University of Pittsburgh Press, 1988), 36.

55. John Ehrlichman, *Witness*, 111.

CHAPTER 4

1. Whitehead, who had an office down the hall from Buchen's, had been in government since the Johnson administration. As a young Harvard-educated Ph.D., Whitehead began his career in the Budget Bureau under Johnson and then moved into the Nixon White House personnel operation with Peter Flannigan. Whitehead created the Office of Telecommunications Policy after serving under Flannigan.

2. A. James Reichley, *Conservatives in An Age of Change: The Nixon and Ford Administrations* (Washington, D.C.: Brookings Institution, 1981), 291.

3. Robert Hartmann, *Palace Politics, An Inside Account of the Ford Years* (New York: McGraw-Hill, 1980), 165.

4. Jerald F. terHorst, *Gerald Ford and the Future of the Presidency* (New York: The Third Press, 1974), 184–85.

5. Gerald R. Ford, *A Time to Heal* (New York: Harper & Row, 1979), 130.

6. The transition group consisted of not only the four formal members, but also less formal members. Assembled were Whyte, Harlow, Buchen, Morton, Scranton, Griffin, Hartmann, Marsh, terHorst, Clay Whitehead, Leon Parma, Rumsfeld, Haig, and Ford.

7. Memorandum for the President, transition team, August 10, 1974, Box 62, Philip Buchen files, Gerald R. Ford Library, Ann Arbor, Michigan.

8. Ibid.

9. Memorandum to the President from Alexander M. Haig, Jr., "Meeting with the Cabinet, August 10, 1974," Box 9, Presidential Handwriting File, Gerald R. Ford Library, Ann Arbor, Michigan.

10. Ford, *Time to Heal*, 131–32.

11. Ibid., 132.

12. "Transition Team Report to the President," August 20, 1974, folder, "Transition," Box 63, Philip Buchen files, Gerald R. Ford Library, Ann Arbor, Michigan

13. Kenneth W. Thompson, ed., *The Ford Presidency: Twenty-Two Intimate Perspectives of Gerald Ford* (Lanham, Md.: University Press of America, 1988), 58–59

14. Juan Cameron, "The Management Problem in Ford's White House," *Fortune,* July 1975, 77.

15. Ford, *Time to Heal,* 133.

16. John T. Casserly, *The Ford White House* (Boulder, Colorado: Colorado Associated University Press, 1977), 19.

17. Press Release, White House Press Secretary, September 30, 1974, "Press Conference of Donald Rumsfeld, Assistant to the President," Gerald R. Ford Library, Ann Arbor, Michigan.

18. For an overview of this relationship, see Kenneth Thompson, *Ford,* 59.

19. Reichley, *Conservatives,* 314.

20. Casserly, *Ford,* 18.

21. Handwritten working paper, Jerry Jones, undated (approximately December 1974), Jerry Jones Files, Box 33, "White House Organization," Gerald R. Ford Library, Ann Arbor, Michigan.

22. Roger Porter, *Presidential Decision Making: The Economic Policy Board* (Cambridge, England: Cambridge University Press, 1980), 41.

23. Memo, Ken Cole to Gerald Ford, 10/25/74, folder "FG 6–13 6–15 10/3/74, Box 58, FG 6–13 National Goals Research Staff to FG 6–15 Domestic Council 1/9/75, Gerald R. Ford Library, Ann Arbor, Michigan.

24. Cole's letter was short and did not address any of the issues he had noted in his memo of October 25. Cole simply said he was leaving with "mixed regret and thanks and anticipation." Letter, Ken Cole to Gerald Ford 12/13/74, folder "Domestic Council Organization May 14-December 1, 1974," Box 69, James Cannon Files, Gerald R. Ford Library, Ann Arbor, Michigan.

25. Ford, *Time to Heal,* 234.

26. Interview of Nelson Rockefeller by Robert Hartmann, December 2, 1977, Gerald R. Ford Presidential Library, Ann Arbor, Michigan.

27. Memo, Gerald Ford to Nelson Rockefeller et al, 2/13/75, folder "Transition-Domestic Council Book December 1976," Box 21, James Cannon Papers, Gerald R. Ford Library, Ann Arbor, Michigan.

28. Reichley, *Conservatives,* 308.

29. Memo, Nelson Rockefelller to Domestic Council Departments, 2/75, folder "Study of National Domestic Needs, February 1975," Box 85, James Cannon Files, Gerald R. Ford Library, Ann Arbor, Michigan.

30. Casserly, *Ford,* 55.

31. Talking points for meeting with Gerald Ford, 3/75/ folder "Domestic Council Organization January - March 1975," Box 69, James Cannon Files, Gerald R. Ford Library, Ann Arbor, Michigan.

32. Memo, James Cannon to Nelson Rockefeller, 3/21/75, folder "Vice Presidential Memos, March 21-30, 1975," Box 86, James Cannon Files, Gerald R. Ford Library, Ann Arbor, Michigan.

33. Memo, Dick Cheney to Don Rumsfeld, 6/9/75, folder "Domestic Council Meeting 6/19/75": Box 3, Michael Duval Files, Gerald R. Ford Library, Ann Arbor, Michigan.

34. Memo, James M. Cannon for the President, 5/13/75, Folder "Local Government-New York City (1)", Presidential Handwriting File, Box 28, Gerald R. Ford Library, Ann Arbor, Michigan.

35. *Presidential Documents: Gerald R. Ford,* 1975, volume 11, no. 44, 512.

36. Charles J. Orlebeke, "Saving New York: The Ford Administration and the New York City Fiscal Crisis," paper presented at the Gerald R. Ford Conference, Hofstra University, April 6–8, 1989, 8.

37. *Presidential Documents,* 1202.

38. Memo, Nelson Rockefeller to Gerald Ford, December 16, 1975, folder "Domestic Council Organization June-December, 1975," Box 64, James Cannon Files, Gerald R. Ford Library, Ann Arbor, Michigan.

39. Eizenstat described Cannon's view of the Domestic Council in an exit interview. Cannon had met with Eizenstat during the transition from the Ford to Carter presidencies. Exit Interview of Stuart Eizenstat, page 9, Jimmy Carter Presidential Library, Atlanta, Georgia.

40. Memo, The President to the Vice President and Members of the Domestic Council, January 8, 1975, Box 76, James Cannon Papers, Gerald R. Ford Presidential Library, Ann Arbor, Michigan.

41. Staff meeting minutes, 1/21/76, 5:30 p.m., Folder "Domestic Council Staff Meeting (2)", Box 14, James Cannon File, Gerald R. Ford Library, Ann Arbor, Michigan.

42. The Federal Energy Administration (FEA) was signed into legislation by Gerald Ford on October 11, 1974, as part of the Federal Energy Administration Act of 1974. The Federal Energy Administration replaced the Federal Energy Office, which

had been created by Nixon on December 4, 1973. The Federal Energy Office itself replaced the Energy Policy Office, also created by Nixon (June 29, 1973). Each of these three programs was designed to respond to the instability of the oil market as a result of warring factions in the Middle East. The issue came to the forefront with the Yom Kippur War in late 1973 and a subsequent shutdown of the Middle East pipeline of oil to the United States. The Federal Energy Administration operated as a Cabinet-level agency in a fashion similar to the Environmental Protection Agency. The FEA's director was appointed by the president and the staff was predominantly civil service. The Federal Energy Administration and the Energy Research and Development Administration were abolished when Congress created, at President Carter's initiative, the Department of Energy on August 4, 1977.

43.   Richard Reeves, *A Ford, Not A Lincoln* (New York: Harcourt Brace Jovanovich, 1975), 137.

44.   Ford, *Time to Heal,* 157.

45.   Ibid., 161.

46.   Memo From Dudley Chapman to Jim Cannon, July 3, 1975, "Coyote Paper: Intermediate Options," Box 10, Philip Buchen Files, Gerald R. Ford Library, Ann Arbor, Michigan.

47.   Press Release, Office of the White House Press Secretary, July 18, 1975, "Executive Order, Environmental Safeguards on Activities for Animal Damage Control on Federal Lands," Box 18, Domestic Council Folder, George W. Humphreys Files, Gerald R. Ford Library, Ann Arbor, Michigan.

48.   Memo for the President from James Cannon, undated, "Predator Control," "Domestic Council—Memoranda," Box 10, Philip Buchen Files, Gerald R. Ford Library, Ann Arbor, Michigan.

CHAPTER 5

1. Carter garnered 40,828,929 votes to Ford's 39,148,940.

2. Neal Pierce, "The Democratic Nominee – 'If I Were President'. . . ," *National Journal* 8 (17 July 1976): 997.

3. "Carter: Ford Has Been a Dormant President," interview with Jimmy Carter in *U.S. News and World Report,* September 13, 1976, 25.

4. Jimmy Carter, "Policy Forum," *National Journal* 8 (9 October 1976): 1449.

5. Pierce, "Nominee," 997. This interview provides one of the best compilations of Carter's views on the Cabinet and the presidency available prior to his election.

6. Ibid.

7. Nelson Polsby, "Presidential Cabinet Making: Lessons For the Political System," *Political Science Quarterly* 93 (Spring 1978): 20–23.

8. Jimmy Carter, *Keeping Faith* (New York: Bantam Books, 1982), 66.

9. Jimmy Carter, *Why Not the Best?* (New York: Bantam Books, 1976), 170. Also see Nelson Polsby, "Lessons," 22.

10. Lawrence Stroup, *The Carter Presidency and Beyond* (Palo Alto, California: Ramparts Press, 1980), 43.

11. The AFL-CIO wanted John Dunlop, Ford's Secretary of Labor, to be returned to the post, but his nomination was vigorously opposed by consumer groups, women's groups, and the Congressional Black Caucus. They argued that Dunlop had been lax in enforcing equal opportunity requirements in federal contracts.

12. Carter, *Keeping Faith*, 49.

13. Arthur M. Schlesinger, Jr., *A Thousand Days* (Greenwich, Connecticut: Fawcett Publications, Inc., 1965), 650.

14. David Kucharsky, *The Man From Plains* (New York: Harper and Row, 1976), 111.

15. Jules Witcover, *Marathon: The Pursuit of Presidency*, 1972-1976 (New York: Viking Press, 1977), 635.

16. Pierce, "Nominee," 998.

17. Memo, Greg Schneiders to Hamilton Jordan, Jack Watson, Stu Eizenstat, Stephen Hess, November 26, 1976, "Organization of White House Staff and Executive Office of the President," Jimmy Carter Presidential Library, Atlanta, Georgia.

18. Interview with Stephen Hess. Carter invited Mr. Hess to meet with him to discuss the organizational structure of the White House. For a description of the staff structures used by previous administrations, see Stephen Hess, *Organizing the Presidency* (Washington D.C.: Brookings Institution, 1976).

19. *Public Papers of the President*, January 23, 1977, "Cabinet Swearing In Ceremony."

20. Ibid., 1105.

21. Interview with Benjamin Heineman, Jr. See also Joseph A. Califano, Jr., *Governing America* (New York: Simon and Schuster, 1981), 26.

22. Interview with Jack Watson by Peter Sienkiewicz as part of research project for author.

23. Text of Carter's Reorganization Plan No. 1 of 1977, *1977 Congressional*

Quarterly Almanac, volume 33, page 38E.

24. James Reston, "Half-Speed Ahead," *New York Times*, December 15, 1976, 25(A).

25. *Washington Post*, February 3, 1977, 1(A).

26. The one-third reduction in staff he sought, however, was a reference to the 583 staff in the White House that Gerald Ford inherited in August 1974. Ford subsequently reduced the number to 542 by 1976. Carter sought to further reduce the staff below 500, which he successfully accomplished.

27. "Carter Proposes White House Reorganization," *National Journal*, July 23, 1977, 1165.

28. Interview with Stuart Eizenstat.

29. Letter, Bert Carp, Deputy Director of the Domestic Council, to John Helmer, April 22, 1977, FG-6–7, Jimmy Carter Presidential Library, Atlanta, Georgia.

30. Stephen J. Wayne, The *Legislative Presidency* (New York: Harper and Row, 1978), 209-210.

31. Interview with Eizenstat.

32. Exit interview with Stuart Eizenstat, January 10, 1981, page 10. Jimmy Carter Presidential Library, Atlanta, Georgia.

33. David Broder, "Shaping the Administration's Policy," *Washington Post*, February 12, 1978, 14(A).

34. Roger B. Porter, *Presidential Decision Making* (Cambridge, England: Cambridge University Press, 1980). 41. Under Gerald Ford, economic policy had been managed by the Economic Policy Board, a separate unit within the White House that Ford had created by executive order. Although Carter never rescinded Ford's executive order, he collapsed the functions of the Economic Policy Board into the Domestic Policy Group.

35. Interviews with Eizenstat and with his assistant, Joe Onek (who later became Deputy Counsel to the President).

36. The Presidential Review Memorandum (PRM) had been used by the National Security Advisor to transmit information to the president in the Carter as well as previous administrations. The Domestic Policy Group adopted the same procedure. For an overview of how Carter's NSC used the Presidential Review Memorandum system, see Zbigniew Brzezinski, *Power and Principle*, 51–52.

37. The phrase "weak spots" was used first in a memo from Hamilton Jordan to President Carter in a memo outlining the need for a meeting between the president and the Cabinet.

38. Califano, *America*, 406.

39. Griffin B. Bell, *Taking Care of the Law* (New York: William Morrow and Company, Inc., 1982), 46.

40. Exit interview of Robert Lipshutz, September 29, 1979, page 29, Jimmy Carter Presidential Library, Atlanta, Georgia.

41. Terrence Smith, "Jordan Appointed Chief of Staff; Aides Will Be Rated," *New York Times*, 19 July 1979, A16.

42. Ibid.

43. Interview with Benjamin Civiletti.

44. "1977 Farm Bill Raises Crop Price Supports," *1977 Congressional Quarterly Almanac*, volume 33, 417.

45. Carter proposed target prices of $2.60 a bushel for wheat, $1.75 per bushel for corn, 47.5 cents for a pound of cotton, and $8.40 per hundredweight for rice. The final bill, $275, passed on September 16, 1977, set the target price for wheat as $2.90 per bushel, $2 per bushel for corn, 52 cents per pound for cotton, and $8.00 per hundredweight for rice.

46. Lawrence E. Lynn, Jr. and David F. Whitman, *The President as Policy Maker* (Philadelphia: Temple University Press, 1981), 111.

47. The Family Assistance Plan, Nixon's welfare reform proposal, was approved by the House of Representatives but died in committee in the Senate.

48. "Senate Passes Mass Transit Bill," *1977 Congressional Quarterly Almanac*, volume 33, 530.

49. Califano, *America*, 181.

50. Ibid., 188.

51. Bell, *Law*, 27.

52. Ibid., 41.

53. Clyde H. Farnsworth, "Eizenstat is Helping to Fill a Vacuum," *New York Times*, December 3, 1978, 2(F).

54. Ibid., 13.

55. In April Carter abandoned the $50 rebate stating that the economy was recovering satisfactorily without it.

56. Califano, *America*, 54.

57. Ibid., 84.

58. Bell, 42-43. The Tellico Dam was constructed by the Tennessee Valley Authority to provide electricity to southeastern Tennessee and western North Carolina

in the Tellico River basin.

59. Although the Clinch River breeder-reactor was a nuclear project, Carter objected to continued federal funding due to the possibility that the plutonium waste material could be used by foreign governments for the construction of nuclear weapons. It was, therefore, a foreign policy issue.

60. "Carter vs. Congress – At War Over Water," *Congressional Quarterly* 35 (March 19, 1977): 481.

61. "Carter 1978 Budget Revision," text of the presidential massage, *1977 Congressional Quarterly Almanac*, volume 33, 12E.

62. "Carter vs. Congress," 482.

63. Ibid.

64. Califano, *America*,405.

65. Charles O. Jones,"Presidential Negotiation with Congress," *Both Ends of the Avenue*, ed. Anthony King (Washington.D.C.: American Enterprise Institute, 1983), 121.

66. Eric L. Davis, "The Congressional Liaison – The People and the Institutions," *Both Ends of the Avenue,* Anthony King, ed. (Washington, D.C.: American Enterprise Institute, 1983), 77.

67. James Schlesinger controlled the Development of the Energy Plan. Although he was technically a White House staff member, Carter considered Schlesinger a Cabinet Secretary–designate and therefore assigned him the responsibility for the plan's development. In Carter's view, the Energy Plan was developed by the Cabinet officer responsible for its implementation and was not a violation of the principle of Cabinet Government.

CHAPTER 6

1. For an excellent overview of the election process, see Lou Cannon, *Reagan* (New York: G.P. Putnam's Sons, 1982), 185–227.

2. S. Weisman, "Reagan Dissipates Heat by Delegating Authority," *New York Times*, October 11, 1981, E4.

3. Richard Nathan, *The Plot That Failed: Nixon and the Administrative Presidency* (New York: John Wiley and Sons, 1975).

4. Peter M. Benda and Charles H. Levine, "Reagan and the Bureaucracy: The Request, the Promise, and the Legacy," in *The Reagan Legacy,* Charles O. Jones, ed. (Chatham, New Jersey: Chatham House Publishers, 1988), 107.

5. Cannon, *Reagan*, 317.

6. For a description of his battle with the White House personnel office, see Terrel Bell, *The Thirteenth Man: A Reagan Cabinet Memoir* (New York: Free Press, 1988).

7. Interview with Martin Anderson

8. Interviews with James Miller and Charles Hobbs (Deputy Director, Office of Policy Development). Also note material on the Executive Forum from *Public Papers of the President*, January 20, 1984, "Remarks by the Reagan Administration Executive Forum."

9. Steven Weisman, "The President as Chairman of the Board," *New York Times Magazine,* January 10, 1982, 1.

10. Herbert Brownell and John P. Burke, *Advising Ike: The Memoirs of Attorney General Herbert Brownell* (Lawrence, Kansas: University of Kansas Press, 1993), 134.

11. Lou Cannon, *President Reagan: The Role of a Lifetime* (New York: Simon and Schuster, 1991), 372.

12. Cannon, *The Role of a Lifetime,* 187 and 424–32. Among the many descriptions of these power struggles are those written by the principles themselves, including Nancy Reagan, *My Turn: The Memoirs of Nancy Reagan* (New York: Random House, 1989); Michael K. Deaver, *Behind the Scenes* (New York: William Morrow, 1987); Donald Regan, *For the Record* (New York: Harcourt Brace Jovanovich, 1988).

13. Reagan won by 8,417,992 votes.   He garnered 50.7 per cent of the vote (43,901,812) to Carter's 41 per cent (35,483,820) and John Anderson's 6.6 per cent (5,719,722). The electoral margin for Reagan was dramatic: 489 for Reagan and 44 for Carter.

14. David Hoffman and Lou Cannon, "The Reagan Cabinet," *Washington Post,* July 18, 1982, A1.

15. Drew Lewis, Reagan's Secretary of Transportation, had run for governor of Pennsylvania in 1974 against the incumbent governor, Milton Shapp, but lost the election.

16. Interview with E. Pendleton James (Director, White House Office of Personnel).

17. Dom Bonafede, "Reagan and His Kitchen Cabinet Are Bound By Friendship and Ideology," *National Journal,* April 11, 1981, 608.

18. Laxalt was such a close friend of the Reagans' that he was the only person (except for two secret service agents and Mrs. Reagan) allowed to see Reagan after the assassination attempt in March 1981 by John Hinkley. See N. Reagan, *My Turn*, 4.

19. Interview with James Watt.

20. Interview with John Block.

21. Cannon, *The Role of a Lifetime*, 85.

22. Interview with Block.

23. Members of the National Academy of Public Administration and the American Society of Public Administration participated in this session. Bradley Patterson was one of those involved and provided information on this process.

24. Original document prepared by William Timmons, Washington, D.C. Personal copy of author.

25. Martin Anderson, *Revolution: The Reagan Legacy* (Stanford, California: Hoover Institution Press, 1988, updated 1990), 197.

26. Interview with James. See also Wallace Earl Walker and Michael R. Roepel, "Strategies for Governance: Transition and Domestic Policy Making in the Reagan Administration," *Presidential Studies Quarterly* (Fall 1986): 742.

27. Hugh Heclo, *A Government of Strangers* (Washington, D.C.: Brookings Institution, 1977).

28. Gerald Ford had a single chief of staff first in Donald Rumsfeld and then in Richard Cheney in fact, if not in title.

29. John Kessel, "The Structures of the Reagan White House," *American Journal of Political Science*, 28 (May 1984): 234–37.

30. For a thorough description of the components of the White House staff in its entirety, see Bradley H. Patterson, Jr., *The Ring of Power: The White House Staff and Its Expanding Role in Government*, pp. 339ff.

31. Interview with Ralph Bledsoe. Also see Caspar W. Weinberger, *Fighting for Peace* (New York: Warner Books, 1990), 28.

32. Weinberger, *Fighting*, 28.

33. Carl M. Brauer, *Presidential Transitions: Eisenhower Through Reagan* (New York: Oxford University Press, 1986), 241.

34. National Academy of Public Administration, "Watergate: Its Implications for Responsible Government" (Washington, D.C.: National Academy of Public Administration, 1974) and "A Presidency for the 1980's" (Washington, D.C.: National Academy of Public Administration, 1980). Chester Newland, a former director of the Federal Executive Institute and a past president of the American Society of Public Administration discusses the cabinet council process in "A Mid-term Appraisal: The Reagan Presidency," *Public Administration Review*, 43 (January-February 1983).

35. Newland, "Appraisal," 7. Also see Anderson, *Revolution,* 224–25.

36. Interview with Anderson.

37. Office of the Press Secretary, the White House, February 26, 1981, 1.

38. Interview with Miller.

39. Interview with Block.

40. Interview with Watt.

41. For an excellent summary of staff backgrounds, see Dick Kirschten, "Decision-Making in the White House: How Well Does It Serve the President?," *National Journal*, April 3, 1982, 585.

42. Interview with Bledsoe. See also Edwin Meese III, *With Reagan: The Inside Story* (Washington, D.C.: Regnery Gateway, 1992).

43. Lou Cannon and David Hoffman, "The Inner Circle Decides and the Outer Circle Ratifies," *Washington Post*, July 19, 1982, A8. See also Dick Kirschten, "Decision Making in the White House: How Well Does It Serve the President?", *National Journal*, April 3, 1983, 588.

44. Colin Campbell, *Managing the Presidency: Carter, Reagan, and the Search for Executive Harmony* (Pittsburgh: University of Pittsburgh Press, 1986), 73.

45. Joseph Pika and Norman Thomas, "The President as Institution Builder: The Reagan Years," paper presented at the annual meeting of the American Political Science Association, Atlanta, August 30-September 3, 1989.

46. Peter M. Benda and Charles H. Levine, "Reagan and the Bureaucracy: The Bequest, the Promise, and the Legacy," *The Reagan Legacy: Promise and Performance*, Charles O. Jones, ed. (Chatham, New Jersey: Chatham House, 1988), 110.

47. Richard P. Nathan, "The Reagan Presidency in Domestic Affairs," *The Reagan Presidency: An Early Assessment* (Baltimore: Johns Hopkins University Press, 1983), 73.

48. Chester A. Newland, "Executive Office Policy Apparatus: Enforcing the Reagan Agenda," *The Reagan Presidency and the Governing of America*, Lester M. Salamon and Michael S. Lund, editors (Washington, D.C.: Urban Institute Press, 1986, 153. See also a similar view by Newland in Chester A. Newland, "A Mid-Term Appraisal—The Reagan Presidency: Limited Government and Political Administration," *Public Administration Review*, volume 43, number 1, January/February 1983.

49. Francis E. Rourke, "Executive Responsiveness to Presidential Policies: The Reagan Presidency," *Congress and the Presidency*, volume 17, number 1, spring 1990.

50. Kirschten, *Decision,* 588.

51. Interview with Anderson.

52. Patricia Dennis Witherspoon, *Within These Walls: A Study of*

Communication Between Presidents and Their Senior Staffs (New York: Praeger Publishers, 1991), 178.

53. Interview with Bledsoe.

54. White House Staffing Memorandum, September 28, 1984, Document #261658CS, folder Education 261500–261689, Box 14, Subject File, White House Office of Records Management, Ronald Reagan Library, Simi Valley, California.

55. Dick Kirschten, "Reagan Sings of Cabinet Government, and Anderson Leads the Chorus," *National Journal*, May 9, 1981, 827.

56. Interview with Miller.

57. Interview with Anderson.

58. Anderson, *Revolution*, 197ff. Also see Kirschten, "Decision Making at the White House," 588.

59. "Cabinet Councils of Government: Effectively Running the Federal Machine," *Government Executive* (January 1983), 20.

60. Ed Harper to Bob Carleson, May 26, 1983, Document #139239PD, folder Education 115900–140569, Box 4, White House Office of Records Management, Ronald Reagan Library, Simi Valley, California.

61. Because of an apparent gender gap in voting behavior, the Reagan White House wanted to shore up support from women and women's groups. OPD staff worked with Senate minority leader Robert Dole (R-Kan), Barber B. Conable, Jr. (R-NY), ranking member of the House Ways and Means Committee, and women in the House and Senate to develop a package of initiatives, which included programs for dependent-care tax credits, increases in the amount of money that nonworking spouses can contribute to an Individual Retirement Account, and pension equity proposals. See Dick Kirschten, "Don't Look for Sparks to Fly from White House Domestic Policy Office," *National Journal*, December 11, 1983, 2567.

62. Kirschten, "Decision-Making in the White House," 588.

63. David Stockman, *Triumph of Politics* (New York: Avon Books, 1986), 123.

64. Ibid., 128.

65. Interview with Samuel Pierce

66. Colin Campbell, *Managing the Presidency: Carter, Reagan and the Search for Executive Harmony* (Pittsburgh: University of Pittsburgh Press, 1986), 197–98.

67. "Personnel Office Grinds Out Names of Toilers in Reagan Vineyard," *Washington Post*, June 18, 1981, A13.

68. Interviews with Watt and James.

69. Stuart Butler, Michael Sanera, and W. Bruce Weinrod, *Mandate For*

Leadership II (Washington, D.C.: Heritage Foundation, 1984), 491.

70. Robert Rector and Michael Sanara, *Steering the Elephant: How Washington Works* (New York: Universe Books, 1987), 300.

71. Dom Bonafede, "Presidential Appointments: The Human Dimension," in *The Insiders and Outsiders,* Calvin Mackenzie, ed. (Baltimore: Johns Hopkins University Press, 1987), 50.

72. Alexander Haig, *Caveat* (New York: MacMillan Co., 1984), 64.

73. Interview with Watt.

74. Interview with Miller.

75. Terrel Bell, *The Thirteenth Man: A Reagan Cabinet Memoir* (New York: Free Press, 1988), 43.

76. Patterson, *Ring,* 258–59.

77. Edward Preston, "Developing Managers: Orientating Presidential Appointees," *The Bureaucrat* (Fall 1984), 40–44.

78. James Pfiffner,"Strangers in a Strange Land: Orienting New Presidential Appointees," in *The Insiders and Outsiders,* Calvin MacKenzie, ed. (Baltimore: Johns Hopkins University Press, 1987), 150.

79. Campbell, *Managing,* 266–67.

80. Office of the Press Secretary, the White House, April 11, 1985.

81. Donald Regan, *For the Record* (New York: Harcourt Brace Jovanovich, 1988), 235.

82. Dick Kirschten, "Once Again, Cabinet Government Beauty Lies in Being No More Than Skin Deep," *National Journal,* June 15, 1985, 1418.

83. George Shultz, *Turmoil and Triumph* (New York: MacMillan, 1993), 822.

84. I am endebted to Tom Griscom for reviewing this material and contributing to its accuracy.

85. Former National Security Advisor Zbigniew Brzezinski noted that his mode of operation in the Carter White House had been to review every member's activities at the end of the day. Each staff member was required to prepare a one page summer of all of his/her actions of the day, including phone calls and media contacts. Brzezinski stayed at work until 10-11:00 p.m. every night reading these summaries to ensure that he knew every activity of NSC staff. In addition, Brzezinski sought to coordinate and frame national security policy within the NSC rather than react to State or Defense proposals. In discussing the Iran-Contra incident, Brzezinski noted that he told Richard Allen at the outset of the Reagan administration how he had operated the NSC and recommended that Allen follow the same procedure to ensure that individuals were operating within acceptable guidelines. Discussion by Zbigniew Brzezinski

on November 9, 1994 with students and faculty from Gettysburg College and Johns Hopkins University, Baltimore, Maryland.

86. Colin Campbell, *Managing the Presidency: Carter, Reagan, and the Search for Executive Harmony* (Pittsburgh, Pa.: University of Pittsburgh Press, 1986), 107.

87. John Tower, Edmund Muskie, and Brent Scowcroft, *The Tower Commission Report* (New York: Random House, 1987), 62.

88. Daniel K. Inouye and Lee H. Hamilton, *Report of the Congressional Committees Investigating the Iran-Contra Affair* (New York: Random House, 1988), 368.

89. Graham H. Allison, *Essence of Decision: Explaining the Cuban Missile Crisis* (Boston: Little Brown and Company, 1971), 162.

90. Cannon, *The Role of A Lifetime*, 184.

91. Haynes Johnson, *Sleepwalking Through History* (New York: Doubleday Books, 1991), 50.

CHAPTER 7

1. See George Bush, *Looking Forward: An Autobiography* (New York: Doubleday, 1987).

2. Janet Hook and Chuck Alston, "Mixed Signals, Agenda Gap' Plague Bush's First Year," *Congressional Quarterly*, November 4, 1989, 2922.

3. Gerald M. Boyd, "Bush Names Baker and Hails Voter Support for 'My Principles,'" *New York Times*, November 10, 1988, B3.

4. David E. Rosenbaum, "Experts on Budget Voicing Optimism on Goal on Deficit", *New York Times*, January 26, 1989, A1.

5. Maureen Dowd, "Sununu Sees Himself in Background," *New York Times,* November 29, 1988, B9.

6. New legislation was passed in August, 1988 which increased the transition funds from $2 million to $3.5 million (HR 3932 — PL 100–398).

7. In addition to Fuller, Teeter, and Untermeyer, other campaign staff to join the transition team were J. Michael Ferren as deputy director, James Pinkerton as research director, C. Boyden Gray as legal advisor, David Demarest, as public affairs director, and Sheila Tate as press secretary.

8. David Shribman, "Lobbying of Bush Transition Office is Turning to Matters of Policy from Personnel Choices," *Wall Street Journal*, January 3, 1989, A14.

9. Ibid.

10. Arvind Raichur and Richard W. Waterman, "The Presidency, the Public, and the Expectations Gap," *The Presidency Reconsidered*, Richard W. Waterman, editor (Itasca, Illinois: F.E. Peacock, 1993), 13.

11. Burt Solomon, "Bush Promised Fresh Faces But He's Hiring Old Friends," *National Journal,* January 21, 1989, 142.

12. Gerald M. Boyd, "Bush Names Baker as Secretary of State: Hails 40-State Support for 'My Principles,'" *New York Times*, November 10, 1988, A1.

13. R.W. Apple, Jr., "Bush's Beltway Team," *New York Times,* January 13, 1989, A1.

14. "President-Elect Meets with Old Critics, Rivals," *Congressional Quarterly*, December 3, 1988, 3453.

15. Jean Becker, "Women Push for a Share of Bush Jobs," *USA Today*, November 22, 1988, A1.

16. Hooks realized that there would be a minimal number of black appointees to the Cabinet. His meeting on November 9 focused less on appointees than securing a pledge from Bush to convene a White House conference on race and poverty.

17. Bernard Weinraub, "Bush Meets Jackson in Bid to Heal Rift," *New York Times,* December 1, 1988, B17.

18. Ibid.

19. Joseph A. Davis and Nadine Cohodas, "Watkins, Bennett Complete Bush's Cabinet," *Congressional Quarterly*, January 1, 1989, 88.

20. Bernard Weinraub, "Amid Tension, Two Vie for White House Chief," *New York Times*, November 15, 1988, B10.

21. Owen Ullman and Charles Green, "Bush Names Sununu as Chief of Staff," *Philadelphia Inquirer*, November 18, 1989, A1.

22. For an overview of the sub-Cabinet selection process, see Charles L. Heatherly and Burton Yale Pines, editors, *Mandate for Leadership III: Policy Strategies for the 1990s* (Washington: Heritage Foundation, 1989).

23. James Pfiffner, "Establishing the Bush Presidency," *Public Administration Review*, January/February 1990, 68.

24. "A Citizenship Test for Job Applicants," *New York Times*, December 13, 1988, B12.

25. For an overview of executive-bureaucratic relations, see Charles T. Goodsell, *The Case for Bureaucracy* (Chatham, New Jersey: Chatham House Publishers, Inc., 1994).

26. See text in *The Bureaucrat,* 18 (Spring 1989): 3.

27. "Transcript of Bush and Sununu Remarks at News Conference," *New York Times*, November 18, 1988, D18.

28. Interview with Jack Howard.

29. Burt Solomon, "For Now, At Least, Collegiality Reigns Supreme Among Bush Staff", *National Journal*, February 2, 1989, 299.

30. Burt Solomon, "A Southern Conciliator Was Bush's First Choice," *National Journal*, November 26, 1988, 3022.

31. "Transcript of Bush and Sununu Remarks at News Conference." *New York Times*, November 18, 1988, D18.

32. Burt Solomon, "Collegiality Reigns," 298.

33. "Interview with Vice President," *USA Today*, January 9, 1988, A11.

34. Excerpts from news conference, *New York Times*, January 13, 1989, A1.

35. For a description of the phrase "honest broker," see Roger Porter, *Presidential Decision-Making* (Baltimore: Johns Hopkins University Press, 1980). See also an article by Pat Bodnar, "The President's Honest Broker," *Christian Science Monitor*, September 6, 1989, 14.

36. Christopher Madison, "No Sharp Elbows," *National Journal*, May 26, 1990, 1281.

37. Maureen Dowd, "Bush's Adviser on Domestic Policy," *New York Times*, March 29, 1990, A18.

38. Roger Porter, *Presidential Decision-Making* (Baltimore: Johns Hopkins University Press, 1980).

39. Michael McQueen, "Presidential Policy Adviser Faces Complaints That His Idea Menu Offers Leftovers and No Punch," *Wall Street Journal*, June 20, 1989, A20.

40. Interview with Andrew Card.

41. Charles Kolb, *The White House Dazed: The Unmaking of Domestic Policy in the Bush Years* (New York: Free Press, 1984).

42. Interview with William Roper.

43. Staff complement and responsibilities taken from the White House phone books, Office of Policy Development, 1989–1993. Provided by the White House Library.

44. *Public Papers of the President* (Washington, D.C.: Office of the Federal Register, 1990), George Bush, 1989, 71.

45. Ibid.

46. Interview with Andrew Card.

47. Interview with Richard Thornburgh. The Domestic Policy Council was chaired by Attorney General Richard Thornburgh, who had chaired the council during the Reagan administration and continued in the same role during the Bush administration. Thornburgh's tenure as DPC chair stemmed from interadministration politics under Reagan. Reagan's first chairman of the Domestic Policy Council, Ed Meese, did not want to relinquish his control over domestic policy after leaving the White House to assume the Attorney General post in the second term. When Meese left the White House, rather than have the chairmanship move to Donald Regan or someone of Regan's choice, Meese simply took the DPC with him to Justice. When Meese was replaced at Justice by Thornburgh, the chairmanship of the DPC remained at the Justice Department.

48. Interview with Richard Thornburgh.

49. Interview with Andrew Card.

50. Interview with Andrew Card. See also Spencer Rich, "Domestic Forum Can Sway a President," *Washington Post,* August 15, 1990, A19.

51. Burt Solomon, "A Day in the Life," *National Journal,* July 7, 1990, 1654.

52. For an overview of the savings and loan crisis, see "Bailouts for S&Ls and Foreign Debtors," *President Bush — The Challenge Ahead,* Hoyt Gimlin, editor (Washington: Congressional Quarterly Inc., 1989), 21.

53. Maureen Dowd, "For Bush, the Kemp Thing Reappears," *New York Times,* November 26, 1991, A1.

54. For an overview of the decision-making process during the Iraq War, see Bob Woodward, *The Commanders* (New York: Simon & Schuster, 1991). See also Fred R. Harris, *Deadlock or Decision* (New York: Oxford University Press, 1993), 237, and Cecil V. Crabb and Kevin V. Mulcahy, *American National Security* (Pacific Grove, California: Brooks/Cole Publishing Co., 1991), 162.

55. John E. Yang and Ann Devroy, "Winning It In Economic Turbulence," *Washington Post,* November 21, 1991, A1.

56. "Can This Administration Be Saved," *National Review,* December 17, 1990, 16.

57. Douglas Harbrecht and Howard Gleckman, "Bush Needs a Domestic Agenda, But He's Getting a Domestic Squabble," *Business Week,* December 3, 1990, 47.

58. Burt Solomon, "Send in the Clones," *National Journal,* March 21, 1992, 678.

59. "Policy Coordinating Committee" discussion paper, February 26, 1992, The White House.

60. Ibid.

61. Ann Devroy, "Skinner Still Courting Yeutter for Domestic Policy Post," *Washington Post*, January 31, 1992, C4.

62. Andrew Rosenthal, "Bush Tries to Shift to Active Style on Domestic Policy," *New York Times*, May 10, 1992, A22.

63. Ibid.

64. John Podhoretz, "Beaten and Bushed: The Black Comedy of a White House on the Verge of a Nervous Breakdown," *Washington Monthly*, October 1993, 37.

65. Marshall Ingwerson, "Baker's Impact at White House is Already Clear," *Christian Science Monitor*, September 10, 1992, A1.

66. James Pinkerton, "Life in Bush Hell," *The New Republic*, December 14, 1992, 27.

67. For an excellent overview of Bush's management style, see Colin Campell, S.J., "The White House and Presidency under the `Let's Deal' President," *The Bush Presidency: First Appraisals*, Colin Campell, S.J. and Bert A. Rockman, editors (Chatham, New Jersey: Chatham House Publishers, Inc., 1991).

CHAPTER 8

1. As a 16-year-old, Clinton had traveled to Washington, D.C. with the Boy's Nation to meet with John F. Kennedy in 1963. Clinton shook hands with Kennedy in the Rose Garden.

2. Inaugural address, John F. Kennedy, January 20, 1961.

3. Howard Fineman, "The Torch Passes," *Newsweek*, special election edition, November/December 1992, 42.

4. Tom Matthews, "Warm Up Lesson," *Newsweek*, January 25, 1993, 30.

5. "Clinton's Cluster Coordinators: Who's Who," *Washington Post*, November 26, 1992, A27.

6. "Making Contact at the Agency Level," *Washington Post*, November 25, 1992, A19.

7. "Helping a Jogger Hit the Ground Running," *Washington Post*, December 4, 1992, A29.

8. Burt Solomon, "The True Secrets of Clintonites Linger Behind the 'Vetting' Veil," *National Journal*, March 13, 1993, 645.

9. Robert Pear, "Bush Asks Hundreds to Quit the Day Clinton Starts," *New York*

Times, January 16, 1992, A1.

10. Ibid.

11. Gwen Ifill, "Clinton's High-Stakes Shuffle to Get the Right Cabinet Mix," *New York Times*, December 21, 1992, A1.

12. Four positions were added to Cabinet-level rank by Clinton: the administrator of the Environmental Protection Agency; the chairman of the Council of Economic Advisors; the United Nations Ambassador; and the U.S. Trade Representative.

13. Zoe Baird withdrew her nomination after admitting failure to pay Social Security taxes on a nanny. Janet Reno, a Florida prosecutor, was subsequently named to the post.

14. Gwen Ifill, "Clinton Completes Cabinet and Points to Its Diversity," *New York Times*, December 24, 1992, A1.

15. Gwen Ifill, "Clinton's High Stakes Shuffle to Get the Right Cabinet Mix," *New York Times*, December 21, 1992, A1.

16. Gwen Ifill, "Clinton Completes Cabinet and Points to Its Diversity," *New York Times,* December 25, 1992, A1.

17. Jack Watson, "The Clinton White House," *Presidential Studies Quarterly*, volume 23, number 3, Summer 1992, 43.

18. Gwen Ifill, "Clinton's High-Stakes Shuffle to Get the Right Cabinet Mix," *New York Times*, December 21, 1992, A1.

19. "Remarks on Reduction and Reorganization of the White House Staff," February 9, 1992, *Presidential Papers.* See also Ann Devroy, "Clinton Announces Cut in White House Staff," *Washington Post*, February 19, 1993, A1. Also an analysis of the final staffing cuts in Ann Devroy, "Adding Up Clinton's Cuts," *Washington Post,* September 30, 1993, A1.

20. Interview with Mark Middleton.

21. Michael Kelly, "Clinton's Chief of Staff Ponders Undefined Post," *New York Times*, December 14, 1992, B6.

22. Ann Devroy, "Clinton Picks Brown for Commerce Post," *Washington Post*, December 13, 1992, A1.

23. Samuel Kernell and Samuel Popkin, *Chief of Staff: Twenty-Five Years of Managing the Presidency* (Berkeley, California: University of California Press, 1986).

24. Michael Kelly, "Clinton's Chief of Staff Ponders Undefined Post," *New York Times*, December 14, 1992, B6.

25. Michael Kramer, "What He Will Do," *Time*, November 16, 1992, 34.

26. Interview with Mark Middleton.

27. Will Marshall and Martin Chram, ed., *Mandate for Change* (New York: Berkley Books, 1992), 322.

28. Al Kamen, "Administration Still Walking on EGG Shells," *Washington Post*, April 19, 1993, 21.

29. Burt Solomon, "Clinton's Meritocracy," *National Journal,* June 16, 1993, 1453.

30. Interview with Carol Rasco.

31. Executive Order #12895, August 17, 1993.

32. Interview with Bruce Reed.

33. Interview with Carol Rasco.

34. Interview with Bruce Reed.

35. Interview with Bruce Reed.

36. Interview with William Galston.

37. Clinton convened a two-day conference on the economy on December 13–14, 1992. Four hundred people were invited, with two primary sessions held. One session was entitled "Assessment of the Domestic Economy" and the other session was entitled "Assessment of the International Economy."

38. "Who Makes Policy," *The Economist*, January 8, 1994, 25.

39. Michael Duffy, "Ready or Not," *Time,* January 25, 1993, 29.

40. George Church, "Clinton's Lucky Numbers," *Time,* February 15, 1993, 22.

41. Brit Hume, "Trading Policies," *National Review*, April 26, 1993, 20.

42. Theodore J. Lowi and Benjamin Ginsberg, *Democrats Return to Power* (New York: W.W. Norton & Company, 1994), 10.

43. George Church, "His Seven Most Urgent Decisions," *Newsweek,* January 25, 1993, 25.

44. Michael Kramer, "Moving In," *Time,* January 4, 1993, 33.

45. Fred Barnes, "Cabinet Losers," *The New Republic*, February 28, 1994, 28–29.

46. Ibid., 23.

47. Fred I. Greenstein, "The Presidential Leadership Style of Bill Clinton: An Early Appraisal," *Political Science Quarterly*, volume 108, number 4, winter 1993/94, 596.

48. Michael Duffy, "The State of Bill Clinton," *Time,* February 7, 1994, 29.

49. Beth Donovan, "Calling Dr. Panetta," *Congressional Quarterly,* July 2, 1994, 1794.

50. For an overview of staff profiles in the Clinton administration, see Jeffrey Tramell and Gary P. Oscifchin, *The Clinton 500: The New Team Running America 1994* (Washington, D.C.: Almanac Publishing, Inc., 1994).

51. Douglas Jehl, "A New Lineup, But What Game?," *New York Times,* July 3, 1994, E4.

52. Elizabeth Drew, *On the Edge* (New York: Simon and Schuster, 1994), 52.

53. Burt Solomon, "A Debilitating Dose of Deja Vu," *National Journal,* September 17, 1994, 2168.

54. Ann Devroy, "President Struggling to Take out Strategy and Take Offensive," *Washington Post,* November 30, 1994, A4. See also Robert Rankin, "Clinton Challenges GOP to Join His Effort," *Philadelphia Inquirer,* December 7, 1994, A9.

55. Michael Frisby and Christopher Georges, "Clinton Weighs Dismantling of HUD, Energy, Transport Cuts Also Studied," *Wall Street Journal,* December 9, 1994, A2.

CHAPTER 9

1. Charles O. Jones, "Presidential Negotiator with Congress," *Both Ends of the Avenue,* Anthony King, ed. (Washington D.C.: American Enterprise Institute, 1983), 118.

2. Jimmy Carter, *Why Not Be the Best,* 161.

BIBLIOGRAPHY

GENERAL BOOKS ON THE PRESIDENCY AND RELATED SUBJECTS

Albertson, Dean, ed. *Eisenhower as President.* New York: Hill and Wang, 1963.

Allison, Graham T. *Essence of Decision, Explaining the Cuban Missile Crisis.* Boston: Little, Brown and Company, 1971.

Amlund, Curtis Arthur. *New Perspectives on the Presidency.* New York: Philosophical Library, 1969.

Ambrose, Stephen E. *Eisenhower, The President.* New York: Simon and Schuster, 1984.

Anderson, Martin. *Welfare: The Political Economy of Welfare Reform in the United States.* Stanford, California: Hoover Institution Press, 1978.

Anderson, Patrick. *The President's Men.* Garden City, New York: Doubleday and Company, 1969.

Bagehot, Walter. *The English Constitution,* rev. ed. Ithaca, New York: Cornell University Press, 1963.

Barber, James David. *The Presidential Character: Predicting Performance in the White House,* 4th ed. Englewood Cliffs, New Jersey: Prentice-Hall, Inc., 1992.

Berman, Larry. *The Office of Management and Budget and The Presidency, 1921–1979.* Princeton, New Jersey: Princeton University Press, 1979.

Binkley, Wilfred E. *President and Congress,* 3d rev. ed. New York: Vintage Books, 1962.

Brauer, Carl M. *Presidential Transitions: Eisenhower Through Reagan.* New York: Oxford University Press, 1986.

Brownell, Herbert, and Burke, John P. *Advising Ike: The Memoirs of Attorney General Herbert Brownell.* Lawrence, Kansas: University of Kansas Press, 1993.

Burke, John. *The Institutional Presidency.* Baltimore: Johns Hopkins University Press, 1992.

Burns, James MacGregor. *The Deadlock of Democracy.* Englewood Cliffs, New Jersey: Prentice-Hall, Inc., 1967.

————. *Presidential Government: The Crucible of Leadership.* Boston: Houghton Mifflin Company, 1965.

Califano, Joseph A., Jr. *A Presidential Nation.* New York: W.W. Norton Inc., 1975.

Channing, Edward. *A History of the United States.* Vol. 2. New York: MacMillan Company, 1938.

Cohen, Jeffrey. *The Politics of the U.S. Cabinet: Representation in the Executive Branch 1789–1984.* Pittsburgh: University of Pittsburgh Press, 1988.

Corwin, Edward S. *The President: Office and Powers 1787–1984*, 5th rev. ed. New York: New York University Press, 1984.

Crabb, Cecil V., Jr., and Holt, Pat M. *Invitation to Struggle: Congress, the President and Foreign Policy.* Washington, D.C.: Congressional Quarterly Press, 1980.

Cronin, Thomas E., editor. *Rethinking the Presidency.* Boston: Little, Brown and Company, 1982.

Cronin, Thomas E. *The State of the Presidency*, 2nd ed. Boston: Little, Brown and Company, 1980.

Cronin, Thomas E., and Greenberg, Sanford D., ed. *The Presidential Advisory System.* New York: Harper and Row, 1969.

Dahl, Robert A. *Democracy in the United States: Promise and Performance,* 2d ed. Chicago: Rand McNally and Company, 1972.

Davidson, Roger H., and Oleszek, Walter J. *Congress and its Members,* 2nd ed. Washington, D.C.: Congressional Quarterly Inc., 1985.

DiClerico, Robert E., ed. *Analyzing the Presidency.* Guilford, Connecticut: Dushkin Group, 1985.

————. *The American President,* 3d ed. Englewood Cliffs, New Jersey: Prentice-Hall, 1990.

Diamond, Robert A., ed. *Origins and Development of Congress,* 2d ed. Washington, D.C.: Congressional Quarterly Inc., 1982.

Dodd, Lawrence C., and Oppenheimer, Bruce I., ed. *Congress Reconsidered,* 2d ed. Washington, D.C.: Congressional Quarterly Inc., 1981.

Downs, Anthony. *Inside Bureaucracy.* Boston: Little, Brown and Company, 1967.

Edwards, George C., III. *Implementing Public Policy.* Washington, D.C.: Congressional Quarterly Press, 1980.

Edwards, George C., III, and Wayne, Stephen. *Presidential Leadership: Politics and Policymaking*, 2d ed. New York: St. Martin's Press, 1990.

Fenno, Richard F., Jr. *The President's Cabinet*. New York: Vintage Books, 1959.

Finer, Herman. *The Presidency: Crisis and Regeneration*. Chicago: University of Chicago Press, 1960.

Finletter, Thomas K. *Can Representative Government Do the Job?* New York: Reynal and Hitchcock, 1945.

Fisher, Louis. *The Politics of Shared Power — Congress and the Executive*, 2d ed. Washington, D.C.: Congressional Quarterly Press, 1987.

————. *President and Congress; Power and Policy*. New York: Free Press, 1972.

————. *Presidential Spending Power*. Princeton, New Jersey: Princeton University Press, 1975.

Franklin, Daniel P. *Extraordinary Measures: The Exercise of Prerogative Powers in the United States*. Pittsburgh: University of Pittsburgh Press, l991.

Frendreis, John P., and Tatalovich, Raymond. *The Modern Presidency and Economic Policy*. Itasca, Illinois: F.E. Peacock Publishers, Inc., 1994.

Gilmour, Robert S., and Alexis A. Halley. *Who Makes Public Policy? : The Struggle Between Congress and the Executive*. Chatham, New Jersey: Chatham House, 1994.

Greenstein, Fred I. *Leadership in the Modern Presidency*. Cambridge, Massachusetts: Harvard University Press, 1988.

————. *The Hidden-Hand Presidency*. New York: Basic Books, Inc., 1982.

Halperin, Morton H. *Bureaucratic Politics and Foreign Policy*. Washington, D.C.: Brookings Institution, 1974.

Hamilton, Alexander, Madison, James, and Jay, John. *The Federalist Papers*. New York: New American Library, 1961.

Hargrove, Erwin C. *The Power of the Modern Presidency*. New York: Alfred A. Knopf, Inc., 1974.

Hart, John. *The Presidential Branch: From Washington to Clinton*. Chatham, New Jersey: Chatham House, 1995.

Hazlitt, Henry. *A New Constitution Now*. New York: McGraw-Hill Book Company, 1942.

Heclo, Hugh. *A Government of Strangers: Executive Politics in Washington*. Washington, D.C.: Bookings Institution, 1977.

Heineman, Ben W., Jr., and Hessler, Curtis A. *Memorandum for the President*. New York: Random House, 1980.

Henderson, Philip. *Managing the Presidency*. Boulder, Colorado: Westview, 1988.

Herring, E. Pendleton. *Presidential Leadership.* Westport, Connecticut: Greenwood Press, 1972, originally published 1940.

Hess, Stephen. *Organizing the Presidency.* rev. ed. Washington, D.C.: Brookings Institution, 1988.

Hobbs, Edward H. *Behind the President.* Washington, D.C.: Public Affairs Press, 1954.

Hodgson, Godfrey. *All Things to All Men.* New York: Simon and Schuster, 1980.

Horn, Stephen. *The Cabinet and Congress.* New York: Columbia University Press, 1960.

Hoxie, R. Gordon, editor. *The Presidency of the 1970's.* New York: Center for the Study of the Presidency, 1973.

————, editor. *The White House: Organization and Operations.* New York: Center for the Study of the Presidency, 1971.

Hughes, Emmet John. *The Living Presidency.* New York: Coward, McCann, and Geoghegan, Inc., 1972.

————. *The Ordeal of Power.* New York: Atheneum, 1963.

Hummel, Ralph P. *The Bureaucratic Experience,* 2nd ed. New York: St. Martin's Press, 1982.

James, Dorothy Buckton. *The Contemporary Presidency,* 2nd ed. Indianapolis: Pegasus, 1974.

Johnson, Lyndon Baines. *The Vantage Point: Perspectives of the Presidency, 1963–1969.* New York: Holt, Rinehart, and Winston, 1971.

Judd, Dennis R. *The Politics of American Cities.* Boston: Little, Brown and Company, 1979.

Kaufman, Herbert. *The Administrative Behavior of Federal Bureau Chiefs.* Washington, D.C.: Brookings Institution, 1981.

Kearns, Doris. *Lyndon Johnson and the American Dream.* New York: New American Library, 1976.

Kellerman, Barbara. *The President As World Leader.* New York: St. Martin's Press, 1991.

Kerbel, Matthew Robert. *Beyond Persuasion: Organizational Efficiency and Presidential Power.* Albany, New York: State University of New York Press, 1991.

Kernell, Samuel. *Going Public: New Strategies of Presidential Leadership,* 2nd ed. Washington, D.C.: Congressional Quarterly, 1992.

Kessel, John H. *The Domestic Presidency: Decision-Making in the White House.*

North Scituate, Massachusetts: Duxbury Press, 1973.

King, Anthony, ed. *Both Ends of the Avenue.* Washington, D.C.: American Enterprise Institute, 1983.

———, ed. *The New American Political System.* Washington, D.C.: American Enterprise Institute, 1978.

Koenig, Louis. *The Chief Executive,* rev. ed. New York: Harcourt, Brace and World, Inc., 1968.

Kramer, Fred A. *Perspectives on Public Bureaucracy.* Cambridge, Massachusetts: Winthrop Publishers, 1973.

Laski, Harold J. *The American Presidency.* New York: Grosset and Dunlap, 1940, 1968.

Lawler, Thomas Bonaventure. *Essentials of American History,* rev. ed. Boston: Lothrop, Lee, and Shepard Co., 1910.

Learned, Henry Barrett. *The President's Cabinet: Studies in the Origin, Formation, and Structure of an American Institution.* New York: Burt Franklin, 1912, reprinted 1972.

Light, Paul C. *Still Artful Work: The Continuing Politics of Social Security Reform.* New York: McGraw Hill, 1995.

———. *The President's Agenda: Domestic Policy Choice From Kennedy to Carter.* Baltimore: Johns Hopkins University Press, 1982.

———. *Vice Presidential Power.* Baltimore: Johns Hopkins University Press, 1984.

Link, Arthur, ed. *The Papers of Woodrow Wilson.* Volume 2. Princeton, New Jersey: Princeton University Press, 1967.

Link, Arthur S. *Woodrow Wilson and the Progressive Era, 1910–1917.* New York: Harper and Row, 1954.

Livingston, William S., Dodd, Lawrence C., and Schott, Richard L., ed. *The Presidency and the Congress — A Shifting Balance of Power?* Austin: University of Texas, 1979.

Loewenstein, Karl. *British Cabinet Government.* New York: Oxford University Press, 1967.

McConnell, Grant. *The Modern Presidency.* New York: St. Martin's Press, 1967.

———. *Private Power and American Democracy.* New York: Vintage Books, 1966.

Macintosh, John P. *The British Cabinet,* 2d ed. London: Stevens and Sons, Limited, 1968.

MacKenzie, G. Calvin. *The Politics of Presidential Appointments.* New York: Free Press, 1981.

Malek, Frederic V. *Washington's Hidden Tragedy.* New York: Free Press, 1978.

Mansfield, Harvey C., Jr. *Taming the Prince: The Ambivalence of Modern Executive Power.* Baltimore: Johns Hopkins University Press, 1993.

Mayhew, David R. *Congress, The Electoral Connection.* New Haven, Connecticut: Yale University Press, 1974.

Meltsner, Arnold J., ed. *Politics in the Oval Office.* San Francisco: Institute for Contemporary Studies, 1981.

Merry, Henry J. *Five Branch Government.* Urbana: University of Illinois Press, 1980.

Milkis, Sidney, and Nelson, Michael. *The American Presidency Origins and Development,* 1776–1993, 2nd ed. Washington, D.C.: Congressional Quarterly, Inc., 1994.

Monsen, R. Joseph, Jr., and Cannon, Mark W. *The Makers of Public Policy: American Power Groups and Their Ideologies.* New York: McGraw-Hill Book Company, 1965.

Moynihan, Daniel Patrick. *The Politics of a Guaranteed Income.* New York: Vintage Books, 1973.

Moynihan, Daniel Patrick. *Maximum Feasible Misunderstanding.* New York: Free Press, 1970.

Nachmias, David, ed. *The Practice of Policy Evaluation.* New York: St. Martin's Press, 1980.

Nachmias, David, and Rosenbloom, David H. *Bureaucratic Government USA.* New York: St. Martin's Press, 1980.

Nakamura, Robert T., and Smallwood, Frank. *The Politics of Policy Implementation.* New York: St. Martin's Press, 1980.

Nash, Bradley D., ed. *Organizing and Staffing the Presidency.* New York: Center for the Study of the Presidency, 1980.

Nathan, Richard P. *The Administrative Presidency.* New York: John Wiley and Sons, 1983.

Nelson, Michael, ed. *The Presidency and the Political System,* 4th ed. Washington, D.C.: Congressional Quarterly Inc., 1995.

Neustadt, Richard E. *Presidential Power and the Modern Presidencies.* New York: Free Press, 1990.

———. *Presidential Power — The Politics of Leadership from FDR to Carter,* rev. ed. New York: John Wiley and Sons, Inc., 1980.

Owen, Henry, and Schultze, Charles L., ed. *Setting National Priorities: The Next Ten Years.* Washington, D.C.: Brookings Institution, 1976.

Patterson, Bradley. *The President's Cabinet.* Washington, D.C.: American Society for

Public Administration, 1976.

————. *The Ring of Power: The White House Staff and Its Expanding Role in Government.* New York: Basic Books, 1988.

Peabody, Robert L. *Leadership in Congress.* Boston: Little, Brown and Company, 1976.

Peterson, Mark A. Legislating Together: *The White House and Capitol Hill from Eisenhower to Reagan.* Cambridge, Massachusetts: Harvard University Press, 1990.

Pfiffner, James. *The Modern Presidency.* New York: St. Martin's Press, 1994.

————. *The Strategic Presidency.* Chicago: Dorsey Press, 1988.

Pious, Richard. *The American Presidency.* New York: Basic Books, Inc., 1979.

Polsby, Nelson, and Wildavsky, Aaron. *Presidential Elections,* 8th ed. New York: Free Press, 1991.

Porter, Roger B. *Presidential Decision-Making: The Economic Policy Board.* Cambridge, England: Cambridge University Press, 1980.

Price, Don K., and Siciliano, Rocco C. *A Presidency for the 1980's.* Washington, D.C.: National Academy for Public Administration, 1980.

Reedy, George. *The Twilight of the Presidency.* New York: World Publishing Co., 1970.

Relyea, Harold C. *The Presidency and Information Policy.* New York: Center for the Study of the Presidency, 1981.

Richardson, Elliot. *The Creative Balance.* New York: Holt, Rinehart and Winston, 1976.

Roberts, Charles, editor. *Has the President Too Much Power?* New York: Harpers Magazine Press, 1973.

Rockman, Bert A. *The Leadership Question: The Presidency and the Political System.* New York: Praeger, 1984.

Rose, Richard. *Managing Presidential Objectives.* New York: Free Press, 1976.

————. *The Postmodern President: George Bush Meets the World,* 2nd ed. Chatham, New Jersey: Chatham House Publishers, Inc., 1991.

Rossiter, Clinton. *The American Presidency,* 2nd ed. New York: Time, Inc., 1960.

Rourke, Francis E. *Bureaucracy, Politics, and Public Policy,* 3rd ed. Boston: Little, Brown and Company, 1984.

————. *Bureaucratic Power in National Politics,* 3rd ed. Boston: Little Brown and Company, 1978.

Sabine, George H. *A History of Political Theory,* 3rd ed. New York: Holt, Rinehart and Winston, 1961.

Schlesinger, Arthur M., Jr. *The Imperial Presidency.* Boston: Houghton Mifflin Company, 1973.

————. *A Thousand Days.* Greenwich, Connecticut: Fawcett Publications, Inc., 1965.

Seidman, Harold. *Politics, Position, and Power.* New York: Oxford University Press, 1970.

Seligman, Lester, and Covington, Cary, R. *The Coalitional Presidency.* Pacific Grove, California: Brooks/Cole, 1989.

Sheffer, Martin S. *Presidential Power: Case Studies in the Use of the Opinions of the Attorney General.* Lanham, Maryland: University Press of America, 1991.

Shull, Steven A., ed. *The Two Presidencies; A Quarter Century Assessment.* Chicago: Nelson-Hall Publishers, 1991.

Sorensen, Theodore C. *Decision-Making in the White House.* New York: Columbia University Press, 1963.

Stanley, David T., Mann, Dean E., and Doig, Jameson W. *Men Who Govern.* Washington, D.C.: Brookings Institution, 1967.

Stuckey, Mary E. *The President as Interpreter in Chief.* Chatham, New Jersey: Chatham House, 1991.

Sundquist, James L. *Politics and Policy: The Eisenhower, Kennedy and Johnson Years.* Washington, D.C.: Brookings Institution, 1968.

Szanton, Peter, ed. *Federal Reorganization.* Chatham, New Jersey: Chatham House, 1981.

Tourtellot, Arthur Bernon. *The Presidents on the Presidency.* Garden City, New York: Doubleday and Company, 1964.

Townsend, Malcolm. *Handbook of United States Political History,* rev. ed. Boston: Lothrop, Lee, and Shepard Co., 1910.

Travis, Walter Earl, ed. *Congress and the President.* New York: Teachers College Press, Columbia University, 1967.

Truman, David B. *The Governmental Process,* 2nd ed. New York: Alfred A. Knopf, 1971.

Truman, Margaret. *Harry S. Truman.* New York: Pocket Books, 1974.

Tugwell, Rexford, and Cronin, Thomas E., ed. *The Presidency Reappraised.* New York: Praeger Publishers, 1974.

Valenti, Jack. *A Very Human President.* New York: W.W. Norton and Company, Inc., 1975.

Warshaw, Shirley Anne, ed. *Reexamining the Eisenhower Presidency.* Westport, Ct.: Greenwood, 1994.

————, ed. *The Eisenhower Legacy.* Silver Spring, Md.: Bartleby Press, 1992.

Waterman, Richard W., ed. *The Presidency Reconsidered.* Itasca, Illinois: F.E. Peacock, 1993.

Watson, Robert Abernathy. *Presidential Vetoes and Public Policy.* Lawrence: University Press of Kansas, 1993.

Wayne, Stephen J. *The Legislative Presidency.* New York: Harper and Row, 1978.

Weiss, Carol H., and Barton, Allen H., editors. *Making Bureaucracies Work.* Beverly Hills, California: Sage Publications, 1979.

White, Theodore H. *America in Search of Itself.* New York: Harper and Row, 1982.

————. *The Making of the President 1960.* New York: Atheneum, 1961.

Wilson, Woodrow. *Congressional Government.* Baltimore: Johns Hopkins University Press, 1981, first published in 1885.

————. *George Washington.* New York: Schocken Books, 1969, first published in 1896.

Wise, Sidney, and Schier, Richard F. *The Presidential Office.* New York: Thomas Y. Crowell Company, 1968.

Witherspoon, Patricia Dennis. *Within These Walls: A Study of Communication Between Presidents and Their Senior Staffs.* New York: Praeger Publishers, 1991.

Woll, Peter. *American Bureaucracy.* 2nd edition. New York: W.W. Norton and Company, 1977.

RICHARD NIXON

Aitken, Jonathan. *Nixon—A Life.* Washington: Regnery Publishers. Lanham, Maryland: Distributed to the trade by National Book Network, 1993.

Ambrose, Stephen E. *Nixon.* New York: Simon and Schuster, 1987.

Arnold, James R. *Presidents Under Fire: Commanders-in-Chief in Victory and Defeat.* New York: Orion Books, 1994

Bernstein, Carl, and Woodward, Bob. *All the President's Men.* New York: Warner Paperback Edition, 1974.

Casper, Dale E. *Richard M. Nixon: A Bibliographic Exploration.* New York: Garland Publishers, 1988.

Dean, John. *Blind Ambition.* New York: Simon and Schuster, 1976.

Drury, Allen. *Courage and Hesitation.* New York: Doubleday and Company, Inc., 1971.

Ehrlichman, John. *Witness to Power: The Nixon Years.* New York: Simon and Schuster, 1982.

Evans, Rowland, Jr., and Novak, Robert D. *Nixon in the White House.* New York: Random House, 1971.

Genovese, Michael A. *The Nixon Presidency: Power and Politics in Turbulent Times.* New York: Greenwood Press, 1990.

Greene, John Robert. *The Limits of Power: The Nixon and Ford Administrations.* Bloomington: Indiana University Press, 1992.

Greenstein, Fred I. *The Hidden-Hand Presidency.* New York: Basic Books, Inc., 1982.

Haldeman, H.R. *Ends of Power.* New York: Dell Books, 1979.

————. *The Haldeman Diaries.* New York: G.P. Putnam's, 1994.

Hersh, Seymour M. *The Price of Power, Kissinger in the White House.* New York: Summit Books, 1983.

Hess, Stephen. *Organizing the Presidency.* Washington, D.C.: Brookings Institution, 1976.

Hickel, Walter J. *Who Owns America?* Englewood Cliffs, New Jersey: Prentice-Hall, Inc., 1971.

Hilleary, John T. *My Thousand Days at the President's House.* New York: Carlton Press, 1988.

Hoff-Wilson, Joan. *Nixon Reconsidered.* New York: Basic Books, 1994.

Jaworski, Leon. *The Right and the Power: The Prosecution of Watergate.* New York: Reader's Digest Press: distributed by Crowell, 1976.

Kissinger, Henry. *White House Years.* Boston: Little, Brown and Company, 1979.

Klein, Herbert. *Making It Perfectly Clear.* Garden City, New York: Doubleday and Company, 1980.

Landau, David. *Kissinger.* Boston: Houghton Mifflin Company, 1972.

McGinniss, Joe. *The Selling of the President 1968.* New York: Pocket Books, 1969.

Magruder, Jeb Stuart. *An American Life.* New York: Atheneum, 1974.

Malek, Frederic V. *Washington's Hidden Tragedy.* New York: Free Press, 1978.

Mazo, Earl. *Richard Nixon: A Political and Personal Portrait.* New York: Harper and Brothers, 1959.

Mazo, Earl, and Hess, Stephen. *Nixon: A Political Portrait.* New York: Harper and Row, 1967.

Medved, Michael. *The Shadow Presidents.* New York: Times Books, 1979.

Mollenhoff, Clark. *Game Plan for Disaster.* New York: W.W. Norton and Company, 1976.

Morris, Roger. *Richard Milhouse Nixon.* New York: Holt, 1990.

Nadel, Laurie. *The Great Stream of History: A Biography of Richard M. Nixon.* New York: Maxwell McMillan, 1991.

Nathan, Richard. *The Plot That Failed: Nixon and the Administrative Presidency.* New York: John Wiley and Sons., Inc., 1975.

Nixon, Richard M. *In the Arena: A Memoir of Victory, Defeat and Renewal.* New York: Simon & Schuster, 1990.

————. *Leaders.* New York: Simon & Schuster, 1990.

————. *RN, The Memoirs of Richard Nixon.* New York: Grosset and Dunlap, 1978.

————. *Six Crises.* New York: Warner Books, 1962 (revised 1979).

Osborne, John. *The Nixon Watch.* New York: Liveright, 1970.

————. *The First Two Years of the Nixon Watch.* New York: Liveright, 1971.

————. *The Second Year of the Nixon Watch.* New York: Liveright, 1971.

————. *The Third Year of the Nixon Watch.* New York: Liveright, 1972.

————. *The Fourth Year of the Nixon Watch.* New York: Liveright, 1973.

————. *The Fifth Year of the Nixon Watch.* New York: Liveright, 1974.

————. *The Last Nixon Watch.* Washington: Republic Books Co., 1975.

Parmet, Herbert S. *Richard Nixon and His America.* Boston: Little, Brown, 1990.

Price, Raymond. *With Nixon.* New York: Viking Press, 1977.

Rather, Dan, and Gates, Gary Paul. *The Palace Guard.* New York: Warner Paperback Library, 1975.

Reichley, James. *Conservatives in An Age of Change: The Nixon and Ford Administrations.* Washington, D.C.: Brookings Institution, 1981.

Richardson, Elliott. *The Creative Balance.* New York: Holt, Rinehart and Winston, 1976.

Safire, William. *Before the Fall.* Garden City, New York: Doubleday and Company, Inc., 1975.

Schlesinger, Arthur M., Jr. *The Imperial Presidency.* Boston: Houghton Mifflin Company, 1973.

Schoenebaum, Eleanora W. *Profiles of An Era: The Nixon/Ford Years.* New York: Harcourt Brace Jovanovich, 1979.

Sheehan, Neil. *The Pentagon Papers.* New York: Bantam Books, 1971.

Strober, Deborah Hart, and Gerald S. Strober. *Nixon as President: An Oral History.* New York: Harper Collins, 1994.

Thompson, Kenneth W., ed. *The Nixon Presidency: Twenty-Two Intimate Perspectives of Richard M. Nixon.* Lanham, Maryland: University Press of America, 1987.

White, Theodore H. *Breach of Faith.* New York: Dell Books, 1975.

————. *The Making of the President 1968.* New York: Atheneum, 1969.

Wills, Gary. *Nixon Agonistes.* New York: New American Library, Inc., 1969.

GERALD FORD

Cannon, James. *Time and Chance.* New York: Harper, Collins, 1994.

Casserly, John T. *The Ford White House.* Boulder, Colorado: Colorado Associated University Press, 1977.

A Discussion with Gerald R. Ford: The American Presidency: held on March 25, 1977, at the American Enterprise Institute for Public Policy Research, Washington, D.C. Washington: The Institute, 1977.

Firestone, Bernard J. *Gerald R. Ford and the Politics of Post-Watergate America.* Westport, Connecticut: Greenwood Press, 1993.

Ford, Betty. *The Times of My Life.* New York: Harper and Row, 1978.

Ford, Gerald R. *A Time to Heal.* New York: Harper & Row, 1979.

Greene, John Robert. *The Limits of Power: The Nixon and Ford Administrations.* Bloomington: Indiana University Press, 1992.

————. *The Presidency of Gerald R. Ford.* Lawrence: University Press of Kansas, 1995.

Hartmann, Robert. *Palace Politics, An Inside Account of the Ford Years.* New York: McGraw-Hill, 1980.

Nessen, Ron. *It Sure Looks Different from the Inside.* New York: Simon and Schuster, 1978.

Porter, Roger. *Presidential Decision Making: The Economic Policy Board.*

Cambridge, England: Cambridge University Press, 1980.

Reeves, Richard. *A Ford, Not a Lincoln.* New York: Harcourt Brace Jovanovich, 1975.

Reichley, A. James. *Conservatives in An Age of Change: The Nixon and Ford Administrations.* Washington, D.C.: Brookings Institution, 1981.

Schapsmeier, Edward L. *Gerald R. Ford's Date with Destiny: A Political Biography.* New York: P. Lang, 1989.

terHorst, Jerald F. *Gerald Ford and the Future of the Presidency.* New York: The Third Press, 1974.

Thompson, Kenneth W., editor. *The Ford Presidency: Twenty-Two Intimate Perspectives of Gerald Ford.* Lanham, Maryland: University Press of America, 1988.

Winter-Berger, Robert N. *The Gerald Ford Letters.* Seacaucus, New Jersey: L. Stuart, 1974

JIMMY CARTER

Abernathy, M. Glenn. *The Carter Years: The President and Policymaking.* New York: St. Martin's Press, 1984.

Adams, Bruce, and Kavanagh-Baran, Kathryn. *Promise and Performance.* New York: D.C. Heath and Company, 1979.

Bell, Griffin B. *Taking Care of the Law.* New York: William Morrow and Company, Inc., 1982.

Brauer, Carl. *Presidential Transitions: Eisenhower Through Reagan.* New York: Oxford University Press, 1986.

Brzezinski, Zbigniew. *Power and Principle.* New York: Farrar, Straus, Giroux, 1983.

Califano, Joseph, A., Jr. *Governing America.* New York: Simon and Schuster, 1981.

Carter, Jimmy. *A Government as Good as its People.* New York: Simon and Schuster, 1977.

———. *Keeping Faith.* New York: Bantam Books, 1982.

———. *Why Not the Best?* New York: Bantam Books, 1976.

Congressional Quarterly. *President Carter.* Washington: Congressional Quarterly Inc., 1977.

Derbyshire, Ian. *Politics in the United States: from Carter to Reagan.* Edinburgh: Chambers, 1987.

Dumbrell, John. *The Carter Presidency: A Re-Evaluation.* New York: St. Martin's Press, 1993.

Germond, Jack. *Blue Smoke and Mirrors: How Reagan Won and Why Carter Lost the Election of 1980.* New York: Viking, 1980.

Glad, Betty. *Jimmy Carter, In Search of the Great White House.* New York: W.W. Norton and Company, 1980.

Grover, William. *The President as Prisoner: A Structural Critique of the Carter and Reagan Years.* Albany: State University of New York Press, 1989.

Haas, Garland. *Jimmy Carter and the Politics of Frustration.* Jefferson, N.C.: McFarland and Co., 1992.

Hargrove, Erwin C. *Jimmy Carter as President: Leadership and the Politics of the Public Good.* Baton Rouge: Louisiana State University Press, 1988.

Johnson, Haynes. *In the Absence of Power.* New York: Viking Press, 1980.

Jones, Charles. *The Trusteeship Presidency: Jimmy Carter and the U.S. Congress.* Baton Rouge: Louisiana State University Press, 1988.

Jordan, Hamilton. *Crisis.* Berkeley: Berkeley Press, 1983.

Kaufman, Burton I. *The Presidency of James Earl Carter.* Lawrence: University of Kansas Press, 1993.

Kucharsky, David. *The Man From Plains.* New York: Harper and Row Publishers, 1976.

Lance, Bert. *The Truth of the Matter: My Life In and Out of Politics.* New York: Summit Books, 1991.

Lankevich, George J. *James E. Carter, 1924–: Chronology,* Documents, Bibliographical Aids. Dobbs Ferry, N.Y.: Oceana Publications, 1981.

Lasky, Victor. *Jimmy Carter: The Man and the Myth.* New York: Richard Marek Publishers, 1979.

Lynn, Lawrence E., Jr., and Whitman, David deF. *The President as Policymaker— Jimmy Carter and Welfare Reform.* Philadelphia: Temple University Press, 1981.

Mazlich, Bruce. *Jimmy Carter: A Character Portrait.* New York: Simon and Schuster, 1979.

Medved, Michael. *The Shadow Presidents.* New York: New York Times Book Co., Inc., 1979.

Mollenhoff, Clark. *The President Who Failed.* New York: MacMillan Publishing Company, Inc., 1980.

Orman, John. *Comparing Presidential Behavior: Carter, Reagan and the Macho Presidential Style.* New York: Greenwood Press, 1987.

Powell, Jody. *The Other Side of the Story.* New York: William Morrow and Company, 1984.

Rosenbaum, Herbert D. *The Presidency and Domestic Policies of Jimmy Carter.* Westport, Connecticut: Greenwood Press, 1994.

Sarkesian, Sam. *Defense Policy and the Presidency: Carter's First Years.* Boulder, Colorado: Westview Press, 1979.

Shogan, Robert. *Promises to Keep.* New York: Thomas Y. Crowell Company, 1977.

Stroup, Lawrence. *The Carter Presidency and Beyond.* Palo Alto, California: Ramparts Press, 1980.

Thompson, Kenneth. *The Carter Presidency: 14 Intimate Perspectives of Jimmy Carter.* Lanham, Maryland: University Press of America, 1990.

Vance Cyrus. *Hard Choices.* New York: Simon and Schuster, 1983.

Wheeler, Leslie. *Jimmy Who?* Woodbury, N.Y.: Barrons Publishing Company, 1976.

Witcover, Jules. *Marathon: The Pursuit of the Presidency, 1972–1976.* New York: Viking Press, 1977.

Wooten, James. *Dasher.* New York: Summit Books, 1978.

RONALD REAGAN

Anderson, Martin. *Revolution: The Reagan Legacy.* Stanford, California: Hoover Institution Press, 1988, updated 1990.

Bell, Terrel. *The Thirteenth Man: A Reagan Cabinet Memoir.* New York: Free Press, 1988.

Berman, Larry, ed. *Look Back on the Reagan Presidency.* Baltimore: Johns Hopkins University Press, 1990.

Boaz, David. *Assessing the Reagan Years.* Washington, D.C.: Cato Institute, 1988.

Brauer, Carl M. *Presidential Transitions: Eisenhower Through Reagan.* New York: Oxford University Press, 1986.

Butler, Stuart, Sanera, Michael, and Weinrod, W. Bruce. *Mandate for Leadership II.* Washington, D.C.: Heritage Foundation, 1984.

Campbell, Colin. *Managing the Presidency: Carter, Reagan, and the Search for Executive Harmony.* Pittsburgh: University of Pittsburgh Press, 1986.

Cannon, Lou. *President Reagan: The Role of a Lifetime.* New York: Simon and Schuster,   1991.

————. *Reagan.* New York: G.P. Putnam's Sons, 1982.

Carter, Hodding. *The Reagan Years.* New York: G. Braziller, 1988.

Combs, James E. *The Reagan Range: The Nostalgic Myth in American Politics.* Bowling Green, Ohio: Bowling Green State University, 1993.

Deaver, Michael K. *Behind the Scenes.* New York: William Morrow, 1987.

Derbyshire, Ian. *Politics in the United States: From Carter to Reagan.* Edinburgh: Chambers, 1988.

Dugger, Ronnie. *On Reagan: The Man and His Presidency.* New York: McGraw-Hill, 1983.

Durant, Robert F. *The Administrative Presidency Revisited: Public Lands, The BLM, and the Reagan Revolution.* Albany, New York: State University of New York Press, 1992.

Edel, Wilbur. *The Reagan Presidency: An Actor's Finest Performance.* New York: Hippocrene Books, 1992.

Fitch, Nancy Elizabeth. *The Management Style of Ronald Reagan, Chairman of the Board of the United States of America: An Annotated Bibliography.* Monticello, Illinois: Vance Bibliographies, 1982.

Grover, William F. *The President as Prisoner: A Structural Critique of the Carter and Reagan Years.* Albany, New York: State University of New York Press, 1989.

Haftendorn, Helga, and Jakob Schlissler, editors. *The Reagan Administration: A Reconstruction of American Strength?* Berlin and New York: W. de Gruyter, 1988.

Haig, Alexander. *Caveat.* New York: MacMillan Co., 1984.

Hall, David Locke. *The Reagan Wars: A Constitutional Perspective on War Powers and the Presidency.* Boulder, Colorado: Westview, 1991.

Hogan, Joseph. *The Reagan Years: The Record in Presidential Leadership.* Manchester and New York: Manchester University Press, 1990.

Inouye, Daniel K., and Hamilton, Lee H., ed. *Report of the Congressional Committees Investigating the Iran-Contra Affair.* New York: Times Books, 1988.

Johnson, Haynes. *Sleepwalking Through History.* New York: Doubleday Books, 1991.

Jones, Charles O., ed. *The Reagan Legacy.* Chatham, New Jersey: Chatham House Publishers, 1988.

Kymlicka, B.B., and Jean V. Matthews, ed. *The Reagan Revolution?* Chicago: Dorsey Press, 1988.

Langston, Thomas S. *Ideologues and Presidents: From the New Deal to the Reagan Revolution.* Baltimore: Johns Hopkins University Press, 1992.

Mackenzie, Calvin, ed. *The Insiders and Outsiders.* Baltimore: Johns Hopkins University Press, 1987.

McFarlane, Robert C. *Special Trust.* New York: Cadell and Davies, 1994.

Meese, Edwin, III. *With Reagan: The Inside Story.* Washington, D.C.: Regnery Gateway, 1992.

Mervin, David. *Ronald Reagan and the American Presidency.* London and New York: Longman, 1990.

Muir, William K. *The Bully Pulpit: The Presidential Leadership of Ronald Reagan.* San Francisco: Institute for Contemporary Studies, 1992.

Orman, John M. *Comparing Presidential Behavior: Carter, Reagan, and the Macho Presidential Style.* New York: Greenwood Press, 1987.

Reagan, Nancy. *My Turn: The Memoirs of Nancy Reagan.* New York: Random House, 1989.

Rector, Robert, and Sanara, Michael. *Steering the Elephant: How Washington Works.* New York: Universe Books, 1987.

Regan, Donald. *For the Record.* New York: Harcourt Brace Jovanovich, 1988.

Salaman, Lester M., and Lund, Michael L., ed. *The Reagan Presidency and the Governing of America.* Washington, D.C.: Urban Institute Press, 1986.

Schaller, Michael. *Reckoning with Reagan: America and Its President in the 1980s.* New York: Oxford University Press, 1992.

Shultz, George. *Turmoil and Triumph.* New York: MacMillan, 1993.

Speakes, Larry. *Speaking Out: The Reagan Presidency from Inside the White House.* New York: Scribner, 1988.

Stockman, David. *Triumph of Politics.* New York: Avon Books, 1986.

Thompson, Kenneth W. *Leadership in the Reagan Presidency: Seven Intimate Perspectives.* Lanham, Maryland: University Press of America, 1992.

Tower, John, Muskie, Edmund, and Scowcroft, Brent. *The Tower Commission Report: The Full Text of the President's Special Review Board.* New York: Random House, 1987.

Weinberger, Caspar W. *Fighting for Peace.* New York: Warner Books, 1990.

Wills, Garry. *Reagan's America.* New York: Penguin Books, 1988.

GEORGE BUSH

Bush, George. *Looking Forward: An Autobiography of George Bush.* Garden City, New York: Doubleday, 1987.

Campbell, Colin, S.J., and Bert A. Rockman, ed. *The Bush Presidency: First Appraisals.* Chatham, New Jersey: Chatham House, 1991.

Crabb, Cecil V., and Kevin V. Mulcahy. *American National Security.* Pacific Grove, California: Brooks/Cole, 1991.

Cramer, Richard Ben. *What It Takes.* New York: Random House, 1992.

Gimlin, Hoyt, ed. *President Bush—The Challenge Ahead.* Washington: Congressional Quarterly Inc., 1989.

Goodsel, Charles T. *The Case for Bureaucracy,* 3rd ed. Chatham, New Jersey: Chatham House, 1994.

Haas, Lawrence J. *Running on Empty: Bush, Congress, and the Politics of a Bankrupt Government.* Homewood, Illinois: Business One Irwin, 1990.

Harris, Fred R. *Deadlock or Decision.* New York: Oxford University Press, 1993.

Heatherly, Charles L., and Burton Yale Pines, ed. *Mandate for Leadership III: Policy Strategies for the 1990s.* Washington, D.C.: Heritage Foundation, 1989.

Hill, Dilys and Williams, Phil, ed. *The Bush Presidency: Triumphs and Adversities.* New York: St. Martin's Press, 1994.

Kolb, Charles. *The White House Dazed: The Unmaking of Domestic Policy in the Bush Years.* New York: Free Press, 1984.

"President Bush: The Challenge Ahead." Washington, D.C.: *Congressional Quarterly,* Inc., 1989.

Schick, Allen. *The Capacity to Budget.* Washington, D.C.: Urban Institute Press, 1990.

White, Joseph, and Aaron Wildavsky. *The Deficit and the Public Interest.* Berkeley and New York: University of California Press and Russell Sage Foundation, 1989.

Woodward, Bob. *The Commanders.* New York: Simon & Schuster, 1991.

BILL CLINTON

Drew, Elizabeth. *On the Edge.* New York: Simon and Schuster, 1994.

Lowi, Theodore J., and Benjamin Ginsberg. *Democrats Return to Power.* New York: W.W. Norton & Company, 1994.

Marshall, Will, and Martin Chram, ed. *Mandate for Change.* New York: Berkley Books, 1992.

Tramell, Jeffrey, and Gary P. Oscifchin. *The Clinton 500: The New Team Running America 1994.* Washington, D.C.: Almanac Publishing, Inc., 1994.

Renshon, Stanley A., ed. *The Clinton Presidency: Campaigning, Governing, and the Psychology of Leadership.* Boulder, Colorado: Westview, 1995.

Waldman, Steven. *The Bill.* New York: Viking, 1995.

Woodward, Bob. *The Agenda: Inside the Clinton White House.* New York: Simon and Schuster, 1994.

INDEX

G